MANDATE
FOR CHANGE

We at Berkley Books are pleased to be the publishers of this book. *Mandate for Change* presents us with a special and timely publishing opportunity. It is our hope that we have contributed to keeping readers informed in our changing times.

Most Berkley Books are available at special quantity discounts for bulk purchases for sales promotions, premiums, fund raising, or educational use. Special books or book excerpts can also be created to fit specific needs.

For details, write or telephone Special Markets, The Berkley Publishing Group, 200 Madison Avenue, New York, New York 10016; (212)951-8894.

MANDATE FOR CHANGE

Edited by

Will Marshall and Martin Schram

THE PROGRESSIVE POLICY INSTITUTE

BERKLEY BOOKS, NEW YORK

MANDATE FOR CHANGE

A Berkley Book / published by arrangement with
Progressive Policy Institute of the Democratic Leadership Council

PRINTING HISTORY
Berkley trade paperback edition / January 1993

ISBN: 0-425-13964-6

A BERKLEY BOOK ® ™ 757,375
Berkley Books are published by The Berkley Publishing Group,
200 Madison Avenue, New York, New York 10016.
The name "BERKLEY" and the "B" logo
are trademarks belonging to Berkley Publishing Corporation.

PRINTED IN THE UNITED STATES OF AMERICA

10 9 8 7 6 5 4 3 2

Acknowledgments

This book was a team effort. In addition to the chapter authors, we want to thank the team members for their ideas and the long hours they devoted to producing this book under intense deadline pressure. Book coordinator Nadine Thomas managed the logistics and production of this project with skill and diligence. Jeremy D. Rosner and Robert J. Shapiro made valuable contributions to many chapters. David Kurapka provided significant editorial support. Copy editor Ellen Jaffe offered intelligent insights and improvements to every chapter. Steven Nider, Ray LaRaja, and Jeff Blank tirelessly researched facts large and small. Deb Smulyan, Bette Phelan, Tovah Ravitz, Debbie Boylan, Leslie Harroun, and Theresa Sheh provided valuable support for this project in innumerable ways. Toby Phipps and Michael Riegel kept our information system up and running.

We also want to express our special thanks to co-editor Martin Schram, who brought the skills and insights of a veteran political journalist and author to bear on this project. In addition to his many substantive contributions, Marty's insistence on high editorial standards and good writing helped to make this book more accessible to general readers.

We are most grateful to attorney Ronald Goldfarb, who served as our agent on this book and helped make its publication a reality.

Finally, we wish to thank the many individuals who have supported the Democratic Leadership Council and Progressive Policy

Institute through the years, including our elected officials; PPI's Board of Trustees, including Chairman Michael Steinhardt, Jon Corzine, Richard Fisher, Charles S. Johnson, James M. Kiss, Robert P. Kogod, Lewis Manilow, Peter Mathias, W. G. Champion Mitchell, Linda Peek, William F. Podlich, David M. Roth, and Barrie Wigmore; DLC Chairman Senator John Breaux; our members and supporters; the staff and volunteers of the DLC and PPI, who have helped sustain this movement; and, not least, our families.

—Al From
President, Democratic Leadership Council
—Will Marshall
President, Progressive Policy Institute

In addition, the chapter authors wish to acknowledge the contributions of the following individuals:

Robert J. Shapiro: My chapters owe an intellectual debt to Senator Daniel Patrick Moynihan, Professors Mancur Olson, Michael Porter, Robert Reich and Rudiger Dornbusch. Research assistance by PPI's Jed Kolko and Jordan Rappaport and intern Carlos Sole was invaluable.

Doug Ross: My thanks to Professor Paul Courant of the University of Michigan Department of Economics for his ideas and good counsel and Jane Stolkey for her general assistance.

D. Holly Hammonds: My thanks to Claude Fontheim, Paula Stern, and Allan Wolff for their advice and assistance.

Jeremy D. Rosner: Thanks to all who provided ideas and reviewed drafts; several, but by no means all, are mentioned in the chapter. Particular thanks to David Kendall, Richard Smith and Steven Nider for their research and general assistance.

Ed Kilgore: Thanks to Joel Berg for his research assistance.

Elaine Ciulla Kamarck: Thanks to Dr. Margaret Beyers for her contributions on family policy, and Arnie Miller and Rick Hernandez for their advice on presidential transitions.

William A. Galston: My thanks to Isabel Sawhill, Douglas Besharov, and Barbara Whitehead for their contributions on family policy.

David Osborne: Thanks to Bob Stone, Bob Knisely, John Mercer, Buddy MacKay and Robert Atkinson.

Will Marshall: My thanks to Peter Cove, Gary Burtless, Larry Diamond, Gordon Adams, U.S. Representative Dave McCurdy, David Lyles, Michael Mandelbaum, and Samuel Huntington, Stanley Kober, Sandy Berger, Tony Lake and Bill Lynn.

Contents

Contributors

AL FROM is president and executive director of the Democratic Leadership Council (DLC), a policy group of elected Democrats from every state in the nation. As founder of the DLC and its think tank, the Progressive Policy Institute, From leads a dynamic movement that is challenging America's political orthodoxies and redefining the Democratic Party.

A veteran Capitol Hill and White House aide, From helped form the DLC in 1985 based on the belief that ideas drive politics. In seven years, the DLC has become the progressive voice of reform and a center of policy innovation.

The DLC is made up of over 750 elected Democrats from across the country, including some of the nation's most respected lawmakers. The DLC is chaired by Louisiana Senator John Breaux. Previous DLC chairmen include President-elect Bill Clinton, Georgia Sen. Sam Nunn, Virginia Sen. Charles S. Robb and House Majority Leader Richard Gephardt of Missouri.

From's work has appeared in the editorial pages of *The New York Times, The Los Angeles Times* and *The Philadelphia Inquirer* and has been the subject of articles in almost every major news publication in the country. Mr. From has recently been appointed to President-elect Clinton's staff in the area of domestic policy.

WILLIAM A. GALSTON is a professor at the School of Public Affairs, University of Chicago. He taught at the University of Texas at Austin for nearly a decade before moving to Washington, D.C., in 1973. Dr. Galston served as Issues Director in Walter Mondale's presidential campaign (1982–1984) and as an adviser to Senator Albert Gore, Jr., during the contest for the 1988 presidential nomination, as well as consultant to candidates for state and local office.

Dr. Galston is the author of four books and numerous articles on political philosophy, American politics and public policy. His most recent book, *Liberal Purposes,* was published in 1991.

THOMAS GRUMBLY is president of Clean Sites, Inc., in Alexandria, Virginia. Clean Sites is a nonprofit organization that was formed to accelerate the voluntary cleanup of hazardous waste sites.

Mr. Grumbly was executive assistant to the commissioner of the U.S. Food and Drug Administration from 1977 to 1979; deputy administrator of the Food Safety and Inspection Service, U.S. Department of Agriculture from 1979 to 1981; and staff director of the Subcommittee on Investigations and Oversight, House Committee on Science and Technology from 1981 to 1982. He spent three years as executive director of the Health Effects Institute. Grumbly has also served as a consultant to the U.S. Environmental Protection Agency in the area of risk assessment and has served on the National Research Council's Panel on Reform of the Federal Meat and Poultry System.

D. HOLLY HAMMONDS joined the Progressive Policy Institute in the summer of 1992 as a Senior Fellow working in the field of trade and international economics. Immediately before coming to the PPI she served as the lead Services Negotiator for the North American Free Trade Agreement and was on the staff of the United States Trade Representative from 1989 to July 1992.

Ms. Hammonds served as Assistant General Counsel to the Office of Management and Budget from 1988 to 1989. In March of 1992, Ms. Hammonds was named an International Affairs Fellow of the Council on Foreign Relations.

Ms. Hammonds holds a law degree from the Yale Law School and a master's degree in Public Policy Affairs from the Woodrow

Wilson School of Public and International Affairs at Princeton University.

DR. ELAINE CIULLA KAMARCK received her Ph.D. in political science from the University of California, Berkley, and her A.B. from Bryn Mawr College. She is a veteran of the Democratic National Committee and three Democratic presidential campaigns.

She is currently a Senior Fellow at the Progressive Policy Institute and a regular columnist for *Newsday* and *The Los Angeles Times.*

Dr. Kamarck is the author of *The Politics of Evasion,* with William A. Galston, and of numerous articles on American politics in the popular and academic presses.

ED KILGORE is Director of Intergovernmental Relations for Governor Zell Miller of Georgia. He served previously as an aide to Governors George Busbee and Joe Frank Harris; was a policy analyst for the Democratic Leadership Council; and the Communication Director and Legislative Counsel for Senator Sam Nunn. He coauthored a 1990 Progressive Policy Institute policy paper on Police Corp and Community Policing. He holds an A.B. from Emory University and a J.D. from the University of Georgia.

TED KOLDERIE has been involved in public affairs in Minnesota for his entire career. In the 1960s and '70s he was involved with the legislature's restructuring of local government and finance in the Twin Cities metropolitan areas. In the 1970s and '80s he played a role in the legislature's restructuring of public education.

Before joining the staff of the Center for Policy Studies, Mr. Kolderie was a Senior Fellow at the Hubert H. Humphrey Institute of Public Affairs at the University of Minnesota and, prior to that, executive director of the Citizens League, a policy studies group in the Twin Cities area.

ROBERT LERMAN is Chair of the Department of Economics at The American University. Dr. Lerman has written widely on poverty and welfare programs, youth employment programs and patterns, family formation of young people and most recently on "The Case for Youth Apprenticeship" in *The Public Interest.* Currently, Dr. Lerman is serving on a National Academy of Sciences panel examining the nation's post-secondary education and training system for the work place.

SEYMOUR MARTIN LIPSET, one of America's most distinguished political sociologists, is Caroline S. G. Munro Professor of Political Science, Professor of Sociology and Senior Fellow at the Hoover Institution, Stanford University. Before moving to Stanford in 1975, he was George D. Markham Professor of Government and Sociology at Harvard University. Coeditor of the *International Journal of Opinion Research,* Lipset is the author or coauthor of 19 books or monographs, editor of 20 books, and has published more than 300 articles in the fields of political sociology, social stratification, public opinion and the sociology of intellectual life. His newest book, *Continental Divide: The Institutions and Values of the United States and Canada,* was published in April 1990.

Lipset received the MacIver prize for his book *Political Man,* the Gunnar Myrdal Prize for his work *The Politics of Unreason,* and the Townsend Harris Medal. He has been judged the most frequently cited author in political science. A former president of the American Political Science Association, he has been elected to membership in the National Academy of Science and the American Academy of Arts and Sciences. He joined the Progressive Policy Institute as Senior Scholar in 1989.

WILL MARSHALL is president and a founder of the Progressive Policy Institute (PPI), a new center for policy innovation in Washington, D.C.

Marshall previously was policy director of the Democratic Leadership Council (DLC) from that organization's inception in 1985.

Marshall is the author of *War Powers in a New Security Era* (1990), *Defending America* (1986), and *Citizenship and National Service* (1988).

CHARLES MOSKOS is the author of many books including *The American Enlisted Man, The Military—More Than Just a Job?,*

The New Conscientious Objection, and *A Call to Civic Service.* A leading figure in military sociology, Dr. Moskos is chairman of the Inter-University Seminar on Armed Forces and Society. He is the architect of the Citizenship and National Service Act introduced in Congress in 1989. Dr. Moskos serves on the President's Commission of the Assignment of Women in the Military.

DAVID OSBORNE is a former editor at Pacific News Service in San Francisco, and a former staff writer at the *New Republic* in Washington, D.C. He graduated with honors from Stanford University, and he has taught at Yale University as a visiting lecturer. He is the author of *Laboratories of Democracy,* published in 1988, and coauthor of *Reinventing Government.* He is also the author of numerous articles in *Harpers, The Atlantic, New Republic, The New York Times,* and *The Washington Post.*

He serves as a Fellow of the Progressive Policy Institute, and associate of the Council of Governors Policy Advisers, and a member of the Board of Advisers of the Nebraska Research and Development Authority.

JEREMY D. ROSNER is vice president for domestic policy for the Progressive Policy Institute, where he directs policy studies on such issues as health care, crime, the environment, and housing. His previous positions in Washington include Policy Director for Sen. Bob Kerrey (D–NE) and research associate for Common Cause. From 1986 to 1990, he worked on community development and low-income housing with state and local government in New Haven and Boston.

Rosner holds a master's degree in Public Policy from the Kennedy School of Government at Harvard University (1983) and a B.A. in Politics from Brandeis University (1979).

DOUG ROSS is president of Michigan Future, Inc., and a senior consultant for the Corporation for Enterprise Development (CFED), a nonprofit economic development research, technical assistance, and consulting organization based in Washington, D.C. Before going to the CFED, Ross was director of the Michigan Department of Commerce for five years. His work gave rise to innovative human investment programs, including the Michigan Youth Corps, the Michigan Opportunity Card, the Neighborhood

Builders Alliance, and a welfare self-employment program. Based on that record, in August of 1988, the National Governors' Association honored Mr. Ross with its annual Award for Distinguished Service to State Government.

Mr. Ross is a graduate of the University of Michigan and the Woodrow Wilson School at Princeton. He completed further graduate study in economics at the London School of Economics.

MARTIN SCHRAM has been a Washington journalist, editor, and author for more than a quarter century. He is a nationally syndicated newspaper columnist and appears frequently as a commentator on Cable News Network.

Schram is the author of two books: *The Great American Video Game: Presidential Politics in the Television Age* and *Running for President 1976: The Carter Campaign.*

Schram has received a number of honors for his writing. In 1988 he received the Lowell Mellett Award from Pennsylvania State University for outstanding Media Criticism for his book *The Great American Video Game*. He has twice been a finalist for the Pulitzer Prize.

ROBERT J. SHAPIRO is the vice-president of the Progressive Policy Institute, where he directs economic studies, and a principal economic adviser to Governor Bill Clinton. Before joining the Institute, Dr. Shapiro served as the Deputy National Issues Director and economic adviser for the Dukakis-Bentsen presidential campaign. Before that, he was associate editor at *U.S. News & World Report*, where he wrote about macroeconomic policy. He also wrote the "Tomorrow" column on politics and policy. Dr. Shapiro also has served as Legislative Director and Economic Counsel to Senator Daniel Patrick Moynihan. Before that, he was Senator Moynihan's counsel on tax policy and the Senator's chief aide on budget policy.

ROBERT STAVINS is an Assistant Professor of Public Policy at the JFK School of Government at Harvard University, and a Senior Research Associate of its Center for Science and International Affairs. He is an economist with primary interest in environmental and natural resource policy, and subsidiary interest in applied econometrics and welfare economics. Professor Stavins has held positions as staff economist at the University of California and at the Environmental Defense Fund, both in Berkeley, California.

Preface

AL FROM AND WILL MARSHALL

Throughout the 1992 presidential campaign, Bill Clinton challenged Americans to have "the courage to change." In *Mandate for Change,* the Progressive Policy Institute (PPI) answers that challenge with an action plan for dramatically changing America's course in the 1990s.

Mandate for Change is a guide to the progressive ideas and themes that energized Bill Clinton's winning campaign. These innovative, non-bureaucratic approaches to governing are central to the new thinking that is changing the basic contours of American politics. The policy recommendations in this book are inspired by a new wave of progressive innovation sweeping the country. From public school choice in Minnesota to tenant management in Chicago's public housing to community policing in Houston, Americans are experimenting with new ways to solve their problems. They are inventing a new politics that transcends the exhausted Left-Right debate that has immobilized our nation for too long.

The themes and ideas in *Mandate for Change* cannot be easily categorized in conventional political terms. Some may assail them as too liberal, others as too conservative. This does not mean, however, that our proposals lie at some mythical midpoint on the political continuum. On the contrary, they call for a radical departure from the status quo. They are certain to upset the comfortable arrangements of politics as usual in Washington.

Mandate for Change is not a comprehensive, agency-by-agency guide for managing the federal government. Instead, it offers highly specific recommendations for tackling America's most pressing problems. *Mandate* calls for reinvigorating America's anemic economy by breaking the fiscal impasse in Washington; opening world markets and forging a new compact for economic security with U.S. workers; harnessing market forces to control health care costs and combat pollution; revolutionizing America's ailing education system; making Americans more secure in their homes and on their streets; bolstering families with children; reinventing government to make the public sector a catalyst for innovation rather than an obstacle to it; and shaping a new U.S. security policy for the post–Cold War era based on support for democracy and free markets. The book concludes with advice to the new President for managing the presidential transition to ensure that his administration gets off to a fast start in January 1993.

PPI was founded in 1989 as the policy arm of the Democratic Leadership Council. Bill Clinton, in his capacity as chairman of the DLC from 1990–1991, encouraged PPI's efforts to develop new policies that challenge both liberal and conservative orthodoxies. The publication of *Mandate for Change* is the culmination of seven years of work by DLC and PPI to renew America's tradition of progressive governance by crafting a new governing agenda that expands opportunity, rewards responsibility, and fosters community.

Taken together, the ideas presented in this book, and the principles that underlie them, constitute a new governing philosophy for a new era in American politics. Threading through the following chapters are five core themes that define the new progressive politics: opportunity, responsibility, community, democracy, and entrepreneurial government.

Opportunity. The new progressives emphasize economic growth generated in free markets as the prerequisite for opportunity for all. They define equality in terms of opportunity, not results. Hence, progressives reject the recent liberal emphasis on redistribution in favor of pro-growth policies that generate broad prosperity. They equally reject the Right's notion that wealthy investors drive the economy, believing that government's role is not to favor the privileged, but to set fair rules of market competition for everyone. At the center of their concern are ordinary working Americans. Progressive economic and social policies seek to unite the interests of Americans who are struggling to get into the middle class and those who are struggling to stay there.

Reciprocal responsibility. Progressives favor a new governing compact between citizens and government based on reciprocal obligation. Under such a compact, government's responsibility to stimulate growth, equal opportunity, and upward mobility must be matched by citizens' willingness to work, support their families, play by the rules, and give something back to their communities and country. The new politics of reciprocity is an alternative to the Right's politics of social neglect and the Left's politics of entitlement. The emblematic progressive idea is voluntary national service—a civilian GI bill that offers public aid for college in return for community service.

Community. Progressives believe that America's strength ultimately resides in our families and communities, where the character and values of our citizens are formed. Unwilling to frame every public question in terms of a choice between government provision and market competition, progressives place new emphasis on the voluntary associations and institutions of community—America's "third sector." Government's role is to empower families, voluntary organizations, and institutions to solve their own problems, not to try to replace them with public programs or institutions. Community also means taking care of citizens in need and affirming the common civic values that unite us as Americans.

Democracy. Now that the Cold War is over, America needs to organize its security policies around a new goal: protecting our national interests by promoting democracy and free markets. Progressives reject the false choice between a foreign policy based solely on power and one based solely on idealism. They embrace a realistic, tough-minded policy that keeps America strong while working patiently to encourage the spread of free political institutions and markets. Democracy and free enterprise are the best stabilizing forces because they offer nonviolent means of resolving political disputes and giving people the freedom to help themselves. Free institutions also act as a check on governments' conduct abroad. Progressives believe that strong U.S. global leadership can only be sustained if our foreign policy is grounded in the moral sentiments of the American people.

Entrepreneurial government. Progressives seek innovative, nonbureaucratic ways of governing. The old government model—centralized, top-down, offering standardized services delivered by public monopolies—worked well during the industrial era but no longer fits the needs of our increasingly diverse society in the information age. Progressives support introducing choice, competition and market incentives into the public sector through such innovations as managed competition, public school choice, social service vouchers, and market-based ways to combat pollution. Just as U.S. businesses have reorganized to meet the challenge of global competition, a radical revamping of America's public sector—schools, public housing, welfare, federal, state, and local agencies—is now required.

Bill Clinton's campaign call for a New Covenant between the American people and their government embraced these themes. Now, President Clinton must translate these commitments into new public policies for a nation profoundly disillusioned with politics and government.

However, change will not come easily. In Washington, President Clinton will encounter all the inertia of a massive federal bureaucracy, a risk-averse Congress, and deeply entrenched interests intent on protecting existing programs, subsidies, and regulations.

President Clinton will not succeed by accepting the existing rules of the political game, but by changing them. The American people have given President Clinton a mandate for change. Now he must make the most of it.

Foreword: Interpreting the 1992 Election

SEYMOUR MARTIN LIPSET AND MARTIN SCHRAM

Redefining elections occur only rarely in presidential politics—and the extraordinary campaign of 1992 produced one of them. Voters emphatically rejected the conventional political solutions of the Left and Right and demanded a new direction for America. They spurned the traditional liberalism that had fueled the Democratic Party for 60 years since Franklin Roosevelt's New Deal; and they overwhelmingly repudiated the conservative counterthrust of the Reagan Revolution. The voters were motivated, essentially, because our two major political philosophies and ideological orientations, liberalism and conservatism, failed to adapt to new realities. The public does not see viable answers coming from either.

With the economy mired in an unrelenting slowdown and weakened by massive federal debt, voters lost confidence in President Bush's ability to improve conditions at home. With the world suddenly safer after the collapse of Soviet communism, voters no longer rallied to the Republican Party's national security cry. Americans gave Democrat Bill Clinton a 43 percent plurality that translated into an electoral college landslide.

But perhaps the most significant change of all occurred in the primary election campaign that marked a political redefinition of the Democratic Party. For the first time since 1964, the battle for a Democratic presidential nomination was waged almost entirely on concerns reflected by the party's mainstream—indeed, America's mainstream. The debates in New Hampshire were about how to reinvigorate American business, make America competitive in a global economy, and protect the jobs and insure the health of a beleaguered working middle class.

There were no quarrels over the antiwar and social activist issues that had divided Democrats and driven away many middle-class voters ever since the bloodbath at the party's Chicago convention in 1968. In the generation that followed, newly empowered Democratic activists and constituency groups had plunged the party sharply leftward, out of the mainstream liberalism of FDR and JFK. The bond forged by FDR, a Democratic coalition of diversity—working-class whites, blacks, Hispanics, Protestants, Catholics, Jews—had remained basically intact until it was shattered by the bitter divisions of the Vietnam War. But, in 1992, all the Democratic presidential candidates were again addressing real security concerns of middle-class voters—people who had been led to believe they were secure in their jobs, health insurance, and pensions, but who now felt their futures were in jeopardy.

One early sign that 1992 was a year of political readjustment was that the Democratic presidential primaries quickly settled into a contest between two moderates with similar plans for helping businesses and workers: Governor Bill Clinton of Arkansas and former Senator Paul Tsongas of Massachusetts.

Meanwhile, other Americans were signaling that a significant rethinking was sweeping the entire electorate—that majority of people who do not vote in Democratic party primaries. In January, before the first primary votes were cast in New Hampshire, about two-thirds of the voters were telling pollsters they wanted someone other than the Republican incumbent, George Bush, to be their president for the next four years. Throughout the year, Bush could not crack 40 percent in the polls. It became his cellophane ceiling; he could gaze up through it, bump up against it, but could not break through it. On the first Tuesday of November, Americans gave Mr. Bush just 38 percent of their votes. In other words, 62 percent opted to put their trust and votes in someone other than their incumbent president.

Clinton carried latterday Republican strongholds in the South, industrial Midwest, Rocky Mountains and the West. Independent Ross Perot, the billionaire who ran as a populist and personally financed his entire campaign, received a sizable 19 percent of the popular vote. It was the largest share for an Independent since Theodore Roosevelt, a popular former president, ran as a Bull Moose Progressive. The exit polls indicated that without Ross

Perot in the race, Clinton would have received about 55 percent of the popular vote.

Importantly, Clinton was elected on the broad appeal of a Democratic Party that had rediscovered its traditional middle-class values, while promising to fulfill them in new, progressive ways. He campaigned on the promise that he was a "New Democrat," a "Different kind of Democrat." And he won largely because the "Reagan Democrats," who in 1988 became "Reagan-Bush Democrats," deserted the GOP in 1992. Some went to the Independent Perot, but many returned to the Democratic fold.

Clinton reclaimed important segments of the classic Democratic coalition. He won 44 percent of the Catholic vote, compared to Bush's 36—a plurality that was impressive considering that most Catholics had voted for Reagan twice and Bush once. He increased the Democratic majority among Jews, receiving 78 percent—14 percent more than the Jewish vote for Michael Dukakis in 1988. He retained the strong Democratic support among blacks and Hispanics. He gained among trade unionists. In short, Clinton won in every coalition category except white Protestants—and, even among that group, Clinton trailed his Republican opponent by just 13 percentage points—a margin far less than any recent Democrat's including that of Jimmy Carter who, in 1976, fell 17 percentage points short of Gerald Ford in the white Protestant vote, despite Carter's penchant for publicly affirming his born-again Christian beliefs.

In the last 12 years, the Democratic nominees for President carried only the lower-income voters. In 1992, Clinton captured all income classes except the upper-middle-class and the wealthy. Viewed by education level, Clinton won every category from high school dropout to post graduate, except one—Bush drew to a statistical tie (a one-percentage-point margin) among college graduates. Clinton also was the first Democrat since 1976 to lead among young first-time voters.

Clinton turned out to be the first Democratic presidential candidate since the Vietnam War years to win the battle of party loyalty. That is, Clinton secured a larger percentage of his own party's voters than Bush received of Republican voters. According to surveys of people who had just voted, Clinton received the votes of 77 percent of the registered Democrats, while Bush took the votes of only 73 percent of the registered Republicans—a sharp decline from his 91 percent of the Republican vote in 1988, which was about what Ronald Reagan and Gerald Ford had gotten.

For some time now, the electorate has been exhibiting discontent with the old two-party system. Consider the nonpresidential-year elections of 1990. Three states elected Independent candidates: Governors Walter Hickel in Alaska and Lowell Weicker in Connecticut and Congressman Bernard Sanders in Vermont. Two-fifths of Texans opted for "none of the above" for governor in a poll taken a week before the election. And the average vote for congressional incumbents of both parties fell off from the previous contest, the first time this had happened, at least since World War II.

Remember the talk-show political eruption of 1992: Ross Perot touched off a groundswell on February 20, when he first conceded, under the hot-pursuit questioning of CNN's Larry King, that if enough people in all 50 states wanted him to run for President, well, he just might do it. And before his withdrawal in June, Perot was supported by close to a third of the electorate—a showing that attested to the widespread public disquiet in 1992. Opinion surveys conducted all through the election year reported overwhelming majorities, between 75 and 90 percent, agreeing that "the country is on the wrong track." The opposition to traditional politics was also reflected in the considerable support given in many states to term limits for Congress—and on election day, term limits were approved in all 14 states where they were on the ballot.

The most electorally relevant development, the one that most accounts for much of the electoral shift between 1988 and 1992, is the long-term slowdown of the American economy, particularly the prolonged recession of 1991–1992. Of course, that is not the sole explanation, since the symptoms of economic stagnation, which were evident in 1990, preceded the Bush recession. Still, the electorate is deeply worried about our seeming inability to come to grips with the federal deficit and revive America's competitive prowess in world commerce. And voters blame Republican presidents and Democratic congresses alike.

The breakdown of communism in Eastern Europe and the Soviet Union—the fulfillment of our most utopian geopolitical dreams—has upset political moorings on the Left and the Right. Foreign policy and defense issues related to dealing with the Communist world deeply divided Americans from the early 1960s to the end of the 1980s. The Left had gained greatly from the alienation of the intelligentsia, of the intellectually creative and the professional strata, which began with the Vietnam War, and then continued through the debates over increased military strength and Star Wars. These divisions helped to deepen and institutionalize the cultural conflicts linked to the emergence of the 1960s "movements."

With the end of the Cold War, much of the passion has gone out of both the Left and Right. And there has been, in both camps, a new political ordering which has made adversaries of old partners. One-time foreign policy allies are now divided over defense policies and issues such as protectionism and free trade, the nature of American involvement in alliances like NATO, assistance policies to third-world and former-communist nations, and the extent of American responsibility for and willingness to help in severe crises abroad (Somalia, Yugoslavia). In short, the argument between isolationists and interventionists has returned, cutting across the liberalism-conservatism divide, just as it did before 1941.

Finally, Americans in 1992 registered their intense frustration with government itself. They believe that government, on the bureaucratic and political levels, appears to have become increasingly inept, unable to formulate decisions, and unresponsive to changing public needs.

A GENERATION OF LEFT-RIGHT CONFLICT

The ideological battles that were waged during the Reagan-Bush years began in the 1960s. On the Republican side, an intensely ideological New Right had emerged, stimulated by William Buckley and his magazine, the *National Review*. The conservative "movement" succeeded in nominating Barry Goldwater for president in 1964. Goldwater and the movement projected a consistent ideological position, backing laissez-faire, and denouncing state intervention and the welfare state.

Democrats under Kennedy, and even more under Johnson, took the opposite tack, seeking to expand and elaborate on the goals of the New Deal. These included an expansive role for government, support of the labor movement, programs that embraced both the poor and middle class, civil rights for minorities, and a liberal internationalism, that while it subsumed strong anti-communism, also supported aid for Latin America and other less developed areas.

The Democratic coalition foundered and broke down in the late 1960s over issues of race, war, and cultural alienation. The party split bitterly over military failure abroad, as a Democratic commander-in-chief tried to preside over a war that many in his party protested as unwise, unwinnable, and, in the minds of some, immoral. The Democrats were also pulled asunder due to government overreach at home; through well-intentioned antipoverty programs and expanded welfare efforts that unexpectedly undermined individual initiative and morale; through the unintended consequences of extending the civil rights crusade into support for affirmative action quotas (a move initially opposed by the National Association for the Advancement of Colored People—NAACP—and a majority of congressional Democrats, including Hubert Humphrey), and because of a perceived decline in morality.

From 1968 on (with the exception of 1976), successive Republican presidential candidates continued to run against a Democratic party that they tied to the activist Left, to black militants and feminist activists, to various social changes that seemingly were undermining traditional American values, a formula first successfully employed in 1966 by Ronald Reagan in California. Foreign affairs issues also helped the Republicans, since they ran as the strong anti-communist and nationalist party. The Cold War basically strengthened the GOP. The racial tensions that characterized this era also contributed to Republican support, since the evidence gathered by many pollsters and social scientists indicates that a sizable part of the white population, including many trade unionists, saw affirmative action quotas, "forced busing," and other forms of compulsory integration as attacks on their own interests.

While the Social Democrats in Europe were moving toward greater acceptance of market economics, Democrats in Congress and as presidential nominees, influenced by liberal activists in primaries, increasingly supported redistribution policies. This trend was documented statistically by the Americans for Democratic Action (ADA), which tracks the ideological behavior of members of Congress. The ADA data indicate a steady increase in liberal voting, notably favoring government expansion, among congressional Democrats from the 1970s to the end of the 1980s.

THE CONSERVATIVE COUNTERREVOLUTION

The past 12 years were the first in modern experience to be dominated on the presidential level by a popular conservative movement. The movement reached its crescendo with Reagan's election in 1980, which gave the rightists a chance to implement their ideology. They were able to do so most fully in the international arena with an intensified hard-line policy toward the Soviet Union. Ironically, Reagan's most important impact on the domestic front was the enormous growth of the federal deficit, basically the outcome of his securing a tax cut while drastically increasing military spending. Consequently, he did not live up to his promise to reduce the scope of government, although he cut back on regulations and weakened the labor movement. Beyond his appointment of conservative judges, Reagan's greatest contribution to the movement was symbolic; as President, he continued to give considerable support in his speeches and messages to right-wing social issues, such as banning abortion, crime, religious and family values, and opposition to affirmative action and busing. Bush continued in Reagan's footsteps, although with less emphasis on deregulation and tax cuts.

The recession of the 1990s helped to disrupt the Republican coalitions of the 1980s, particularly affecting the so-called Reagan Democrats—working-class people, and to some extent southern whites, who supported the GOP because of their response to defense and social issues. Social conservatism is associated with lower levels of education and, hence, also with lower socioeconomic status and income. The recession, however, made people in these categories sensitive to the renewed need for activist government policies to deal with the problems of the unemployed and the less privileged. They could be Republicans during periods of prosperity, but not during economic downswings.

Also, a number of liberal anti-Communist intellectuals—the so-called neoconservatives—who went over to Reagan because they agreed with his foreign policy, returned to support Clinton in 1992.

The Democratic reclamation of the middle class began with the start of the 1990s. The congressional Democrats in 1990 were the first in decades to score in the ADA records as less liberal ideologically than their predecessors. Then, in the 1992 presidential nominating process, a number of prominent liberal Democrats opted not to run. Clinton, a former chair of the Democratic Leadership Council, ran as a moderate with regard to economic and welfare policies and social issues. He built a new coalition, reaching out to all sectors of the party, including the large minority who voted Republican in the 1980s; a coalition that resembles the pre-1965 New Deal to Great Society alliances.

Importantly, the liberal intelligentsia and left ideologues, demoralized by the successive electoral defeats they had suffered in the 1980s—and perhaps aware themselves of the need to find new progressive solutions to America's domestic problems—appear to have accepted the change. Many of them, as well as leaders of the trade union movement and, to some extent, civil rights activists, came to understand what Barry Goldwater noted in a talk to the Republican convention of 1968: that under normal conditions ideologues cannot dominate a major party in the United States, that the parties have to be heterogeneous coalitions in which the center normally has more impact on policy than the extreme Left or Right. In a similar vein, many who have been involved in liberal movement politics now seem to recognize the need for more progressive approaches that are rooted in mainstream interests and values.

The 1990s offer a renewed opportunity for a progressive movement for change in the American polity. There have been four such developments in the twentieth century. At its start, Theodore Roosevelt spoke of the need for a Square Deal for all and pressed for greater economic equality and the reduction of the power of the special interests. The focus at that time was on antitrust policies, designed to eliminate monopolies and to encourage competitive independent businesses. Second, Woodrow Wilson introduced the concept of a New Freedom and successfully pressed for greater rights for labor, for women workers, and supported a progressive income tax.

Franklin Roosevelt's New Deal, reacting to the challenge of the Great Depression, was the most innovative. It brought government into the picture more strongly than ever before in efforts to deal with problems of the unemployed, depressed farm prices, and the rise of threats from abroad. The New Deal introduced the welfare state to America and helped to produce strong trade unions.

The first three movements, however, did not face up to the problem of racial division. That was to be the task of Lyndon Johnson's Great Society. It sought to equalize the racial disparities. As with the earlier movements, the solution was tied to more government, both through regulation and increased spending. And it must be noted that Jim Crow was effectively ended, that schools were integrated, and that a sizable black middle class emerged. But a large white and black underclass, subject to many social morbidities, remained. And a quarter of a century later, it was apparent that many of the earlier "solutions" had produced undesirable unanticipated consequences, such as welfare dependency. The increase in income inequality that was stimulated by the Reagan "revolution" only made matters worse.

This book appears immediately following a bitter campaign that produced a national consensus for change. It is important to recognize the 103rd Congress has more new members than any since the Watergate election of 1974. A number of the new Democratic senators and representatives are clearly more closely tied to the traditional liberal interests of the party than is the new President. It is a situation not without precedent; when Franklin Roosevelt arrived at the White House in 1933, Congress had a strong and highly active group of senators and representatives much more liberal than he. Roosevelt's task, however, proved to be the implementation of a recovery program that was much in tune with the views and inclinations of these members of Congress. Clinton, in contrast, faces a much more difficult task, if, as this book urges, he seeks to lead his party and the nation toward a series of progressive reforms that are not always akin to the traditional solutions long espoused by the most liberal special interests.

To implement a progressive program will require cooperation between the President and Congress. The American system of government was deliberately designed for a weak presidency, not an imperial one. The President has power in foreign relations; he has much less authority than heads of government in parliamentary systems for dealing with domestic policy. This is true even when the President and the majority of Congress belong to the same party. Jimmy Carter was unable to get his major legislation, such as his energy bill, enacted. Lyndon Johnson vetoed more bills passed by a Democratic Congress than Richard Nixon and Ronald Reagan did in a comparable period. Despite a landslide reelection, Franklin Roosevelt had trouble with Congress during his second term.

Great presidents have been great politicians. They have been able to influence Congress by reaching the people, by mobilizing the various potential parts of their coalitions. Franklin Roosevelt did this extremely well. He addressed the public through his fireside chats. He brought to the White House thousands of the leaders of groups who were seeking political change. Lyndon Johnson succeeded in his first years in office because he was a master tactician in dealing with the Congress. Ronald Reagan, like Roosevelt, reached out both to the public and to individual members of the Congress. Like their most able predecessors, presidents in the 1990s can achieve only if they are willing to take risks, to continue to campaign, to communicate with the public, to keep the pressure on the Congress.

President Clinton's task will not be easy. The approval ratings of heads of government everywhere in the democratic world have fallen far below those of George Bush in 1992. The only one reelected this year, British Prime Minister John Major, is in deep trouble with his own party. With increasing complexity in society, the capacity of politicians and governments to satisfy the often contradictory demands of constituencies and bureaucracies has declined greatly since Roosevelt's day. As various publics have been educated and have the technical organizational capability to demand more from their leaders, officeholders find it difficult to deal with them. Those at the apex are blamed for increasingly complex economic and social problems and, not surprisingly, their support in the polls has fallen precipitously. Ironically, the very growth of government makes leaders appear weak and ineffective.

Clinton's strongest asset as President will be not his political skills, nor his persuasive ways, but his mandate for change. Although he was elected by just a plurality, a large majority—almost two-thirds—of the voters, shaken by the prolonged recession and economic weakness, demanded new activist policies. Now, once again, it will be up to a Democratic president to set a new agenda—one that will provide security in the 1990s and beyond for those middle-class Americans who played by the rules only to discover their futures were in jeopardy.

Clinton proved he could bring the working middle-class back into a winning Democratic electoral coalition. And the American people have given him a chance to prove his party can govern and thereby establish an enduring Democratic majority. Only by charting a progressive course can President Clinton keep faith with those who voted for him, earn the support of those who voted the independent line—and answer the call of the real majority of 1992, the Americans who delivered their mandate for change.

1

Enterprise Economics: Rebuilding the American Economy

ROBERT J. SHAPIRO AND DOUG ROSS*

INTRODUCTION

The United States faces a genuine, long-term economic crisis. Whatever else the new President accomplishes, the American people will hold him directly accountable for providing a new strategy for rebuilding the American economy.

By nearly every basic measure, the U.S. economy's fundamental capacity to create wealth has been deteriorating. The presidential campaign focused on the protracted slowdown of the last four years, but the problem has been unfolding for a generation. Over the last 20 years, America's productivity gains, net investment rates, income gains, and overall growth all have lagged behind the records of both other advanced economies and our own past performance. The choice is clear: change, or face stalled living standards for the rest of this century and beyond.

To reverse these trends, the new President must leave behind the conventional economic prescriptions of both Right and Left. His strategy must go beyond the traditional conservative approach by

*The authors want to acknowledge the many valuable insights of D. Holly Hammonds concerning trade and competition that are incorporated in this chapter.

recognizing that, in a global economy, government must focus on more than the cost of capital and the tax burden on wealthy investors. He also must break with the conventional liberal program by recognizing that the globalization of capital and commerce limits the effectiveness of policies to pump up demand or micromanage resources among industries.

The President must chart a new progressive strategy for the 1990s that we call Enterprise Economics. As the name suggests, Enterprise Economics focuses on the pivotal forces in the economic life of a free people: the enterprise of all workers, and the enterprises where they produce the goods and services that comprise our national wealth. It concentrates on upgrading the human and capital resources common to all economic activities. It is committed to expanding world trade and world growth, and America's share of each. It regards the success of U.S. workers and firms in their head-to-head competition in the global economy as the most meaningful test of its policies. The strategy is built on five pillars:

1. **The first pillar of Enterprise Economics is a dramatic commitment to national investment.** Its purpose is to empower U.S. firms and workers with the resources to become more productive. This effort must focus on the factors common to all wealth-producing activities: the education and skills of every worker; the research and development of the technologies that can create new industries and greater efficiencies; the quality of the communications and transportation systems that connect our businesses and bind together our markets; the capacity of entrepreneurs to create new businesses; and the plant and equipment at the disposal of America's firms and workers. Public investment in the 1990s should not mean more tax and spending subsidies nor trade and regulatory protections for particular industries or wealthy investors. This strategy from the 1970s and 1980s left economic policy at the mercy of special-interest politics. In the 1990s, the President must steer his economic program with both eyes fixed on raising the rate of return on all economic activity.

2. **The second pillar of Enterprise Economics is a new regimen of fiscal and monetary discipline.** As the new President and Congress invest more in the nation's common economic resources, government also must restrain its consumption-related spending. The President must fundamentally reform

the budget process to ensure that total federal spending for all purposes except investment grows more slowly than the economy itself—lest government deny the economy the resources it needs to sustain private investment and growth. Enterprise Economics also stands for broad price stability as a concomitant of slower government spending and smaller deficits. The President must ensure that the government does not tolerate rising inflation that prices long-term capital out of the reach of American business.

3. **The third pillar of Enterprise Economics is a new strategy to enhance competition and liberate markets.** A new national government must peel away layer upon layer of subsidies and protections that encrust our economy and dampen the market competition that drives innovation and productivity growth. The new President also must phase out unproductive economic regulations that insulate one sector or another from competition and burden businesses. Meeting this challenge will require that the President break the gridlock in Washington and turn government away from the politics of powerful interests and unlimited entitlements and toward policies that liberate market forces.

4. **The fourth pillar of Enterprise Economics is a new compact with America's workers and firms.** The President should propose a new economic compact: As workers and firms accept the risks of competing in an open domestic and global economy, government must help workers improve their skills and help firms become more flexible and innovative. The federal government should guarantee every young person the opportunity to build market competency through apprenticeship tracks in high schools and provide college assistance for anyone willing to perform national service. The President should also propose an Employment Insurance System that ensures access to retraining for jobless people and for displaced and low-wage workers. Firms should be required to provide workers with yearly opportunities to upgrade their skills. Government should support basic research and development that generates technological advances, and should become a clearinghouse where firms can obtain information about new techniques and processes. Finally, firms should be allowed to collaborate in using this information and in developing new techniques and processes.

5. **The fifth pillar of Enterprise Economics is a new strategic commitment to open world trade.** The new President must

place America's economic success at the center of U.S. post–Cold War international relations. American productivity and innovation have suffered from the reactive, ad hoc trade and international economic policies of the 1980s and early 1990s. The President's goal must be open markets in a global trading system that promotes U.S. and world growth. To achieve this goal, he must systematically employ every means of economic, political, and diplomatic leverage at his disposal, and use aspects of national and even domestic policy to establish collaborative relationships with other advanced economies.

Enterprise Economics has a single goal: To enable America's workers and firms to secure high-paying jobs, rising living standards, and higher profits. It offers the new President a strategy for once again expanding economic opportunity and restoring sustainable economic growth.

THE SHORT-TERM PROBLEM: JUMP-STARTING GROWTH

In his first 100 days, the new President must take bold actions to spark growth and create jobs in 1993, as well as to rebuild the economy's long-term productive potential. This is the first task expected of him by most Americans.

In his response to the country's immediate economic doldrums, the President must make a critical decision about deficit stimulus. In theory, a further increase in the deficit could stimulate the economy in the near term. In practice, the results are less clear. First, the growing importance of international trade will, in all likelihood, substantially dampen the impact of additional deficit spending. Some measure of new purchasing power for U.S. consumers and firms will be spent on foreign goods, reducing the stimulus to America's economy.

A further increase in the deficit also could do harm. Financial markets today assume that any short-term spending increase will become permanent. The prospect of subsequent easy-money policies to help finance a larger federal deficit could push up long-term interest rates, undercutting the impact of the stimulus.

Serious harm could come if the new President, while seeking short-term stimulus, sacrifices the opportunity to address the long-term structural deficit in his first year in office. Once his honeymoon with Congress has passed, another opening might not arise again during his term; and his presidency could be dominated by the same struggles over marginal spending and tax changes that crippled his predecessor. Expanding the deficit could carry other significant costs for the new President, namely the chance to implement his new program of national investment and economic opportunity.

At the same time, the President must not weaken the fragile U.S. economy by large and immediate deficit reductions designed to balance the budget quickly.

The new President has a third choice: He can carefully target temporary stimulus to the job-creating forces in the economy and pay for it in the present, while tackling the structural deficit with long-range spending reforms. The long-term reforms are addressed in chapter 2. To get the economy moving in 1993, the President should initiate four steps:

1. **Spur job creation without falling back on the old economics of a public-jobs program.** For 12 months, firms should be eligible to receive a tax credit for a significant portion of the first $10,000 in wages paid to new employees. This tax credit should be capped for any one firm and limited to businesses that increase both their total work force and their total wage bill. Based on a similar strategy adopted by the federal government between July 1977 and December 1978, such a measure could create as many as 500,000 jobs. The net cost to the Treasury would be less than $3 billion for 1993 and 1994, taking into account tax revenues from new workers and savings in unemployment benefits. This remaining cost to the deficit could be offset by a number of measures that would make economic sense on their own, such as reforms to modestly restructure federal-debt financing, or to tighten Internal Revenue Service procedures for collecting taxes due on unearned income.[1]

2. **Spur business investment without falling back on subsidies for particular industries.** Firms that raise their rate of investment in productive plant and equipment should receive a permanent investment tax credit. However, the credit should be available at a higher rate through 1993. The cost to the Treasury and the deficit can be offset by promptly enforcing the tax liabilities of foreign corporations operating profitably in the U.S. but not currently paying taxes.

3. **Spur state and local capital investment.** Grants to cities and states, especially infrastructure and community development funds, should be temporarily accelerated, moving one-third of planned 1994 spending into 1993. Federal support would decline as state and local economies recovered, with a net cost of zero to the Treasury and the deficit.
4. **Spur U.S. exports.** The new President must recognize that America's short-term problem is not unique. Throughout Europe and Japan, most of the world's advanced economies face slow growth or recession in 1993. Should the U.S. economy begin to revive while Europe and Japan remain stalled, exports will not be a source of U.S. growth. The U.S. balance of payments could worsen, reigniting protectionist pressures. The new President should press for coordinated international steps to stimulate the world economy, especially through trade liberalization and interest-rate action.

These measures, taken together, could help stimulate growth and jobs in 1993 and 1994, leaving to Enterprise Economics the central challenge of restoring long-term growth and productivity.

THE COSTS OF FAILED LEADERSHIP IN A GLOBAL ECONOMY

While national economic policy has seemed paralyzed for a decade or more, change is the rule of economic life. The most critical factor driving economic change in the United States today—and for the last generation—is the eclipse of the economic rules that worked in the domestic economy of the 1950s and 1960s by the new forces and terms of global competition.

Today, U.S. firms and workers compete with foreign counterparts that draw on different, and often superior, stores of labor, technology, and infrastructure.[2] Successful firms must organize materials and processes from around the world in order to produce the particular goods and services demanded by countless market segments. In the new economy forged by the new terms of competition, the national government must support not simply our ability to produce standard goods and services, but our capacity to innovate efficiently.

The failure of American leadership to help our firms and workers meet the competition in a global economy has undermined American prosperity. Over the last 20 years, the country's basic capacity to create wealth has deteriorated. Through these years, the country's Gross Domestic Product (GDP), the economy's gains in productivity and net investment, and personal incomes all have grown at average annual rates of only one-half to two-thirds those of the generation before. The deterioration has been systemic, affecting the entire economy from business cycle to business cycle. The major tax and budget changes of the early 1980s had no discernable impact on this disappointing performance. In simple economic terms, the U.S. economy has settled into a substandard equilibrium.

The chief victims of the slow economy have been the frontline workers and average firms that form the core of the U.S. economy. Workers' real wages have declined, and firms' profits have narrowed. By contrast, those at or near the top have done well. The 10–15 percent of the work force with the education and skills to fill professional and managerial positions have prospered, as have the owners of capital who comprise the richest 2 percent. Our long-term challenge is to restore the productive, wealth-creating capacities of the great majority of workers and firms who have been left behind.

For the first time in a half-century, foreign economies outperform our own. Japan and Germany produce more wealth per person than we do; even France has closed the gap with America.[3] In productivity, measured as Gross Domestic Product per worker, Japan, Germany, France, and Italy all lead the U.S.[4] And our national savings rate and trade balance are the worst of any advanced nation.[5]

During the last four years, this long-term problem has become

Table 1. Economic Performance, U.S. versus Other Advanced Economies

	Wealth/Person, (Per-capita GDP)	Productivity, 1990 (Per-worker GDP)	Nat'l Savings Rate, 1990	Trade Balance 1990, % of GDP
U.S.	$21,449	$43,211	2.2%	−1.5%
Japan	$23,822	$46,098	20.5%	0.7%
Germany	$23,536	$49,891	12.7%	5.5%
France	$21,105	$49,764	8.5%	−0.1%
Italy	$18,921	$45,940	7.4%	0.1%

more critical. Since 1989, the U.S. economy has recorded the slowest growth, and the smallest gains in productivity and net investment since the Great Depression. For the first time since Herbert Hoover, personal incomes are falling and private-sector job creation has stopped. And the economy is mired in a business cycle shaped like none other in recent times. Recession has been followed not by upsurges in demand, investment, and growth, but by stagnation and periodic downward dips.

The Bush administration has tried to push and pull the standard macroeconomic levers of lower interest rates and higher deficits. Like its predecessors, it has offered more tax and spending subsidies for powerful constituencies frightened by the stalled economy. The results were predictable: spiraling spending and larger permanent deficits, fiscal gridlock and paralyzed government, sluggish growth and falling incomes. The danger is that without a sound long-term strategy, the U.S. economy's productive capacity will ratchet down again to an even more depressed equilibrium.

For Americans to prosper in the 1990s—or even to maintain their current living standards—the new President must set a new course in economic policy.

THE FAILURES OF CONSERVATIVE AND LIBERAL ECONOMIC POLICIES

In crafting a new economic strategy, the new President must recognize that the reigning economic approaches—both conservative and liberal—cannot do the job. In the new global economy, neither approach will be able to enhance growth and productivity for American workers and firms.

The conservatives' approach to the economy

Throughout the postwar years, conservative economic policy has depended on two insights: markets are the best way of distributing resources and producing rewards; and the government's chief role in the economy is to help firms invest in new plant and equipment by increasing the availability of capital.

This view produced a three-part strategy. First, that government should steer clear of most aspects of the economy—and especially stay out of the competition for capital by running balanced budgets. Second, that government should promote predictable business decisions by maintaining near-zero inflation. Third, that the only acceptable active role for government is to foster businesses' efforts to get the capital necessary to increase efficiency, regardless of the economic policies and trade practices of our foreign competitors. In the conservative world view, this single, active role for government can best be accomplished by lowering taxes on investors' profits and on the earnings of firms that invest in plant and equipment.

In the new global economy, this conservative strategy is doomed to fail. On its face, a hands-off approach loses its logical force when the rates of growth of the whole economy, and of productivity and investment, trend downward for 20 years. Conservatives are forced to insist that either the economy is in fine shape or, when it isn't, that nothing should be done about it.

The hands-off approach also has no place for international economic strategy. It sees no point in coordinating trade and economic decision-making, and perpetuates the Cold War practice of systematically subordinating national economic interests to geopolitical considerations. The result is often unilateral economic concessions, as when we opened our formerly regulated telecommunications market to foreign firms in the mid-1980s without seeking comparable access in foreign countries.

The second fundamental defect in the conservative analysis is its failure to appreciate that, in a global economy, the availability of domestic capital is not the preeminent factor in economic success. In global competition, capital is only one of a number of productive inputs that affect productivity. Moreover, the globalization of capital markets provides large businesses with access to the whole world's capital pool, from which they borrow freely at home and abroad. While many small and medium-sized firms today have less access to capital, this problem arises not from the size of the domestic capital pool but from institutional barriers to their borrowing. The answer to this problem is deregulation and new financial institutions, not another tax cut for the wealthy.

The conservatives' claim that government can increase investment by cutting taxes on investment profits is also not supported by facts. The foreign capital that provides much of the pool for U.S. investment today is unaffected by tax incentives for U.S. savings. That's one important reason why the vast majority of economists have concluded that the four cuts in capital-gains taxes between 1977 and 1985 did not raise our net investment. Rather, a lower capital-gains rate mainly shifts savings and investment from instruments denied it, such as money-market accounts, to those granted it, such as stocks.[6] And this was the conclusion reached in 1984 by Ronald Reagan's Treasury Department when it recommended the end of the capital-gains tax preference.

The record for more narrow capital incentives also does not support the conservative strategy. These tax cuts for special interests may affect some firms' decisions about what to do with their funds, but not in ways that increase the entire economy's capacity to create wealth.[7] To be sure, they can raise the rate of return for certain investors. But they do not increase net national investment.

The conservative tax agenda has one undisputed effect: It exacerbates existing inequalities of income and wealth. Lower capital-gains taxes favor those with the most capital gains to claim, and other investment incentives increase the incomes of those who invest the most. These are the same people—mainly the 2 percent richest among us, with annual incomes averaging more than $200,-000. According to the Joint Committee on Taxation, two-thirds of the tax benefits generated by cutting capital-gains taxes go to such high-income people.[8]

The failure of the conservative approach gave rise to a more radical, supply-side strategy in the 1980s, based on a claim that sharply lower marginal income-tax rates, especially for wealthy people, would spur growth. Once again, the record shows decisively that the deep tax cuts of the early 1980s did not catalyze productivity or growth. Comparing U.S. economic performance in the business cycle of 1976–1979, before the tax cuts, and the business cycle of 1983–1989, after the cuts—or through the entire 1970s and 1980s—reveals that the economy performed no better *after* the supply-side experiment than before.[9]

By only one measure—curbing inflation—did the 1980s outperform the 1970s. Controlling inflation, however, was the great achievement not of the supply-side tax program, but of tight monetary policies in the late 1970s and early 1980s.

The supply-side program did *not* cripple the economy, however. Rather, the country's substandard economic performance was unaffected by supply-side's deep, marginal tax cuts—much as high, marginal tax rates in the 1950s and 1960s coexisted with robust growth and strong income gains. As a macroeconomic event, the supply-side tax-cut program was trivial.

Capital still counts to the American economy. But in a global capital market, differences in the cost of capital among advanced economies don't reflect differences in tax rates. Rather, different costs of capital across nations reflect mainly two more basic factors: each nation's rate of expected inflation; and the close relationships in some countries between banks and businesses. In the 1990s

Table 2. U.S. Economic Performance
Before and After Supply-Side Policy Changes

Average Annual Rate of Growth	Pre-Supply-Side 1970s	1976-1979	Post-Supply-Side 1980s	1983-1989
Real G.N.P.	3.1%	4.1%	2.8%	3.9%
Civilian Jobs	2.7%	3.7%	1.9%	2.6%
Real Personal Income	3.0%	4.0%	3.1%	3.5%
Share of National Income	**Pre-Supply-Side** 1970s	1976-1979	**Post-Supply-Side** 1980s	1983-1989
Real Capital Spending	3.9%	2.6%	2.7%	2.3%
Personal Savings	6.7%	6.0%	4.1%	3.4%
Trade Balance	−0.04%	−0.4%	−3.0%	−4.0%

America's competitive advantage in capital will depend mostly on how tenaciously the President and his government avoid rising inflation, how dedicated they are to opening up access to capital for small and medium-sized firms, and how effectively firms make use of the capital they raise.

Moreover, the conservatives' dogged focus on capital, instead of on productivity and economic enterprise, has made America poorer in the following ways. First, the Reagan tax and monetary policies artificially raised the post-tax rate of return on capital. This, in turn, attracted more of our total national income to financial instruments and investment partnerships. But the Reagan and Bush programs also reduced the public investment that raises the pre-tax return on all economic activity and reduced competitive pressures on business to upgrade their productivity. As a result, they failed to raise the rate of return on the other source of national income, people's labor.

The end result is that more capital went to paper transactions with artificially high returns, instead of to productive economic uses—which helped underwrite the 1980s' consumption-spending spree by wealthy investors. Shunting capital to paper and consumption rather than to more productive uses also slowed the growth of national income. And with more of a slow-growing national income going to capital, the share left for labor became smaller still. That is precisely what has been happening through the 1980s and early 1990s: fast-growing incomes for wealthy investors and falling wages for most workers.

The liberals' approach to economic policy

While conservatives would have the new President rely on tax-preferred capital to drive U.S. competitiveness, many traditional liberals argue that deficit spending and low interest rates offer the best path to prosperity. Like conservative policy, the orthodox liberal approach will not succeed in a global economy.

The liberal strategy begins with the proposition that government can maintain healthy growth by manipulating the size of the budget deficit to affect overall economic demand. Whenever the economy slows, orthodox liberals prescribe greater government spending to place more buying power in the hands of consumers.

The problem for this approach in the 1990s is that the globalization of capital and commerce sharply limits how much stimulus you can get by increasing deficit spending. While a higher deficit may increase demand, in a global economy foreign producers will fill a sizable share of that new demand with imports. An American family with more spending power may decide to purchase a new Toyota or a Sony television, helping workers in Nagoya while doing little for workers in Detroit.

In short, in the 1990s some measure of new deficit stimulus at home ends up stimulating economies abroad by increasing U.S. imports. At the same time, demand for goods produced by U.S. workers and firms is vitally affected by the strength of demand in foreign countries that buy U.S. exports—beyond the reach of our deficit policies. Just as the role of foreign capital today dilutes the impact of domestic tax incentives for savings, so the rising importance of world trade dilutes the impact of domestic demand stimulus.[10]

In addition, the record shows that new, short-term spending almost always becomes permanent spending. A dose of stimulus, therefore, is likely to be seen as increasing the structural deficit, which in turn dampens its impact by raising long-term interest rates.

The good news is that when the economy begins to expand again, a large deficit will not shut down the economy by crowding out private investment at home. As the 1980s demonstrated, when the deficit absorbs the lion's share of private domestic savings, savings from abroad flow in to meet our demands for credit. But there's a catch. Over time, relying on foreign credit to finance our permanent deficit feeds back on itself and limits our growth. As foreign ownership of U.S. stocks and bonds, firms, and real estate has increased, our growth has been slowed by a rising outflow of U.S. profits, dividends, and rents. By one recent estimate, payments to foreign lenders and owners already costs us 1–2 percent of our annual national income.[11]

The record shows that more large, permanent deficits will not produce the vigorous economic growth that helps average workers and firms.[12] While the government was tripling the national debt in the 1980s, average wages fell and increasing numbers of Americans found themselves unable to afford home ownership, health-care insurance, or a college education for their children.[13]

Cutting the deficit is the right policy for *long-term* growth. But doing so will have little *short-term* positive effect on the economy. The capital released to the private sector will be absorbed through the global credit market, diluting the impact on U.S. interest rates.[14] In addition, the spending cuts and tax increases required to cut the deficit will dampen domestic demand.[15] On the other side of deficits, the traditional liberal tonic of expanding the deficit as the economy enters a downturn can help. But a strategy of maintaining demand through periodic stimulus, which worked credibly in a preglobal economy, is undermined today by the globalization of capital and commerce. It no longer packs the power to produce healthy, sustained growth.

Just as the failure of traditional conservative economics spawned a supply-side successor, failed demand-side economics produced an offshoot in industrial policy. Like their predecessors, industrial-policy advocates cast government in a central role in producing economic growth. But like its progenitor, industrial policy ultimately offers too little to enhance the productive capacities of American workers and firms—the key to long-term national prosperity.

Industrial policy in the 1980s and early 1990s has looked to targeted subsidies or trade protection for industries in trouble or those seen as especially promising. The first problem is that under nearly all circumstances, industry subsidies and protections make special-interest politics the driving force in economic policy. There are additional difficulties. The goal of these policies is to channel more resources to particular sectors, especially distressed industries threatened by cheap imports. But these resources have to come from other, more prosperous sectors, penalizing industries that improve their productivity on their own. And paradoxically, in a global economy this approach often harms those it intends to favor, because subsidies and protections reduce the pressures to innovate and become more productive.

Industrial policies to support specific emerging industries also cannot produce a strong economy in the 1990s. Once again, special-interest politics would play the decisive role in divvying up the subsidies. Once again, the help would reduce healthy, competitive pressures on firms to figure out how to efficiently produce new goods or services. And even if Washington could allocate subsidies free from political pressure and the lucky industries remained intent on innovation, government has no reliable way of distinguishing a genuine sunrise industry from an idea whose economic time has yet to come.

The real danger is not that industrial policy will become America's economic strategy. Rather, the danger is that some of its prescriptions will be adopted inadvertently, in less recognizable guises. Bad policy comes in many forms. Special spending subsidies for favored companies and industries have much the same effect as special tax breaks, special trade protection, or special regulatory advantages. In every form, the result is the same—less efficient allocation of resources driven by political influence, and weakened incentives to become more productive.

In short, neither the traditional conservative nor the traditional liberal economic program—nor their 1980s stepchildren, supply-side and industrial policies—offers the new President a sound strategy for restoring growth and broad-based prosperity.

THE LESSONS OF RIGHT AND LEFT

The sterile debate between the two traditional approaches has gridlocked policy innovation and obscured the imperatives of the new global economy. The result has been lagging U.S. productivity and growth. Yet both sides have something to contribute to a new Enterprise Economics.

The new President should draw three lessons from the conservatives. To begin, market competition *is* the best means we have for producing wealth—but every firm and worker must have the resources and opportunity to be productive in these markets. Conservatives are also right that capital counts—but tax changes are weak mechanisms for increasing its supply. What counts today is how much capital, both public and private, goes to productive investments, and how much discipline government exercises to ensure that consumption doesn't crowd out investment in the budget or drain private capital to finance large budget deficits. Finally, inflation matters, because expected inflation is a critical factor in the differences among nations in their costs of capital.

The supply siders also deserve their due. They are right that lower taxes are generally better for the economy than higher taxes—so long as they are high enough to finance the social and economic goals of the nation. And so long as they are not considered a magic bullet for transforming productivity.

The new President also can draw three insights from liberal economics. Today, markets alone are not producing healthy growth—but the correct response is to strengthen them through public investment in the nation's common economic resources, not to redistribute their results. Liberals are also correct when they argue that equity cannot be divorced from growth—but the correct conclusion is to expand average people's access to opportunity, not promise equal results. Finally, maintaining aggregate demand *can* help promote economic growth—but in a global economy this effort should be directed to aggregate *world* demand through greater economic-policy cooperation and convergence, especially among the advanced economies.

The advocates of industrial policy also have something to contribute. Public support for new ventures *can* yield benefits—but the assistance must be generic, not for specific industries, as in support for basic research and development or for entrepreneurs starting new businesses. They are also right that government can perform useful services for industry, principally by providing information about new business techniques, export opportunities, and other market matters. Last, certain sectors are affected adversely by cheap imports and open trade—but the correct response is to help them meet competition with other advanced economies, not to protect them from competition with less-advanced ones.

ENTERPRISE ECONOMICS: PROMOTING U.S. PRODUCTIVITY AND GROWTH IN A GLOBAL ECONOMY

Enterprise Economics is a policy strategy that places the insights of traditional conservative and liberal economics in the new context of international competition. Enterprise Economics goes beyond the conservatives' fixation on financial capital and many liberals' reliance on aggregate demand, and focuses policy on the common productive needs of U.S. firms and workers in a global economy.

Enterprise Economics can provide the new President with a five-part strategy for empowering every firm and every worker to be more productive and competitive within free markets.

1. The new President must revitalize public and private investment to ensure that U.S. workers and firms can draw on the best productive resources in the world. Without world-class work force skills, modern plant and equipment, advanced technology, and state-of-the-art infrastructure, the men and women who create our goods and services cannot compete in a global economy. In this way, the President can help enhance everyone's capacity to create wealth, raising the rate of return on all economic activity for workers and companies alike.

   This effort must begin with strong presidential leadership. The new President must offer us a candid explanation of our present difficulties and provide a positive vision of a successful future. American workers must have genuine access to the education and skills that are our ultimate source of economic security in an uncharted global economy. The President also must shift the focus of federal research-and-development funding from military to commercial uses, and provide new incentives for firms to expand their commitment to long-term technological development. He must help rededicate government to rebuilding our aging transportation, communications, and environmental networks, and investing in new, more efficient and innovative systems. And he must nourish the entrepreneurial spirit of American enterprise by using tax policy to support Americans who risk their savings to invest in new businesses.

2. The new President must restrain the government's claims on the private economy (as described in chapter 2). The budget should be divided into three parts: a Future (or investment) Budget covering the nation's commitments to rebuild our common economic resources; a Past (or obligations) Budget covering interest and savings and loan payments; and a Present (or consumption) Budget covering all other spending. As government invests more in creating opportunities for workers and firms to become more productive, it must also reduce public spending on consumption by even more. Public spending for all purposes except national economic investment and past obligations must increase more slowly than the economy.

To achieve this restraint, the President must lead Congress and the country in reforming Pentagon spending and entitlement programs, and in reviewing the entire catalog of noninvestment domestic spending. To facilitate this, the new Congress should amend every spending and tax program with a sunset provision, and grant the President a line-item veto.

3. The new President must strengthen the forces of economic competition by reviewing and reforming spending and tax subsidies, and trade and regulatory protections, for particular industries. Provisions that reduce the incentives for firms to become more productive should be phased out. In the 1990s, America's economic policy must not be shaped by the distribution of influence among interest groups. Here, as elsewhere, the new President's economic program must be dedicated to raising the rate of return on *all* economic activity.

Sector-specific subsidies and protection threaten U.S. competitiveness and innovation in three ways. They help drive the growth of government spending and claim scarce public resources that otherwise could go to investments in economic productivity. They produce an uneven playing field handicapping firms and industries that don't receive largesse. They also undermine the competitiveness of firms granted subsidies and protection by enabling them to maintain their return without taking steps to become more productive.

4. The new President should lay out a new compact between government and America's workers and firms (described in chapter 3). As government works to promote open markets in both the domestic and global economy, it should provide new resources and supports for firms and workers striving to become more efficient and flexible. Government should guarantee every American the opportunity to build marketable skills through apprenticeship tracks in high schools, college assistance for anyone willing to perform national service, and lifelong learning on the job. U.S. workers threatened by global competition should be able to secure retraining through a new Employment Insurance System. Businesses should be able to turn to government for support for basic research and development, and for information about new techniques and processes. Finally, firms should be permitted to collaborate in using this information, developing new technologies, providing ongoing training, and meeting new market demands.

5. The new President should embrace a strategic commitment to open foreign markets and expand world trade (described in chapter 4). In the 1990s, America's productivity will be vitally affected by our economic relationships with other nations. In world markets shaped by both free-form competition among global firms and a range of national barriers to open trade, traditional strategies for either laissez-faire or protectionism will not work. The President should prepare and implement a strategy using every policy means available. When negotiations fail he must be prepared to use sanctions in order to ensure fair access for American firms and workers. And he can overcome the trade politics of narrow interests by involving other advanced nations in cooperative efforts in many areas of economic policy.

These five pillars of Enterprise Economics provide a new economic strategy based on the terms and realities of competition in a global economy. This strategy is committed to promoting productivity and growth by investing in the capacity for enterprise of every worker, every firm, and the entire nation. It believes in promoting competition that provides both the opportunity and rewards for genuine enterprise. It offers the new President a framework for joining together the economics of growth and the economics of equity for the 1990s.

MANDATE FOR ACTION

In addition to offering the long-term program discussed above, the new President should implement this carefully targeted plan for spurring the U.S. economy in 1993:

1. **Spur job creation.** The new President should propose a temporary, limited tax credit for firms that increase both their employment and total wage costs, and the cost to the Treasury could be offset by reforms in federal-debt financing or in tax collection on unearned income.

2. **Spur business investment.** The new President should propose a permanent tax credit for firms that increase their net investment in productive plant and equipment, available at a higher rate through 1993. The cost

to the Treasury should be offset by stricter enforcement of corporate tax liabilities.
3. **Spur state and local capital investment.** The new
President should accelerate from 1994 into 1993 one-
third of total grants to cities and states for infrastructure
and community development funds.
4. **Spur U.S. exports.** The new President should engage
the world's other advanced economies in a collaborative effort to promote world growth, especially
through trade liberalization and coordinated interest-
rate actions.

2

Enterprise Economics and the Federal Budget

ROBERT J. SHAPIRO

PAYING FOR PROGRESS: A STRATEGY FOR PROGRESSIVE FISCAL DISCIPLINE

The new President's most urgent task for 1993 is to make the national budget once again an instrument of economic growth and fiscal discipline.

First and foremost, the new President must control the growth of spending while strengthening public and private investment in the resources that promote a productive economy. The major areas for renewed investment should be the skills of all workers, the equipment they use, and the plants where they work; the quality of the nation's communications and transportation systems; research and development into new technologies; and the ability of entrepreneurs to create new businesses and new ways of doing business.

The federal government, by its own spending priorities, bears major responsibility for the stagnating economy and fiscal impasse gripping the United States today. The past 12 years of economic underinvestment are a direct result of consumption-related spending, large tax and spending subsidies for narrow interests, and the deficits these policies produce. Most American households have paid the price. While the federal government quadrupled the national debt from 1980 to 1992, the average worker's real, weekly wage fell, and the distribution of both American incomes and wealth grew less equal. The share of U.S. households with access to college education, home ownership, and health-care coverage all declined. And as the business cycle deteriorated in 1990, the persistent and large federal deficit weakened government's ability to reignite growth.

National productivity cannot be rebuilt without channeling more public and private resources to support education and training, rebuild infrastructure, and fund research and development. Yet, today, more than $200 billion a year of scarce public resources is claimed to pay the interest on the growing national debt. The large, permanent deficit also forces the U.S. to borrow hundreds of billions of dollars from abroad, creating an outflow of interest, dividends, and rent payments to foreign lenders that depresses both private investment and living standards.[1] And these deficits have led inexorably to higher taxes—seven increases in payroll taxes in the 1980s, and higher taxes on both businesses and middle-class Americans in 1990.

If the new President continues to tolerate fast-rising public consumption spending and the large, permanent deficits that accompany it, this decision could preclude the long-term investment, both public and private, and lower tax burdens that underwrite a growing economy.

The President should make fiscal policy a force for national prosperity once again by undertaking basic budget reforms in four areas.

1. Reorder our spending priorities. The new President should reorder and reform our current spending priorities. Public investment in our common economic resources should increase by 50 percent over four years; and total federal spending should decline for all other purposes, from entitlement transfers to defense and the administration of the federal government.

2. Reform the budget process. To promote and enforce fiscal discipline while expanding public investment, the new President should press for four reforms in the budget process:

Step 1:   The President and Congress should divide the budget into three parts: a "Past Budget" covering interest and savings and loan payments; a "Present Budget" covering all consumption-related spending, from government operations and entitlement programs to defense and most other domestic programs; and a "Future Budget" covering economic investments in education, training, economic infrastructure, and research and development.

Step 2: The President and Congress should balance the Present Budget and Past Budget (except savings and loan payments). By 1996, annual revenues should cover all annual, noninvestment spending, and annual federal borrowing should be limited to no more than the year's Future Budget.

Step 3: The President and Congress should set a new legal limit on the annual growth of the Present Budget, so that noninvestment spending increases no faster than the economy generates resources to support it, or no faster than the average household's capacity to pay for it.[2]

Step 4: The President and Congress should require that every spending program and tax expenditure have a sunset provision requiring its reauthorization at least once every seven years. This process should incorporate a new standard for continued spending and tax expenditures: Does each program's achievements justify the tax burden required to maintain it? The President also should have the authority to enforce this standard through a line-item veto.

3. Restrain federal spending. To achieve fiscal discipline while expanding public investment, the new President should press for fundamental spending reforms in three major areas of the Present Budget.

Step 1: The new President and Congress should create an independent, nonpartisan commission, modeled on the Base Closing Commission, to review and evaluate all programs that provide federal subsidies for special interests. Special spending and tax breaks for particular industries and groups should be phased out if they subsidize unproductive activities or create uneconomic advantages. These reforms should be carried out over several years so that those affected can adjust to operating without continued support from the taxpayers.

Step 2: The new President should offer basic reforms for slowing the growth of entitlement programs. These reforms should strengthen the connection between individual contributions and benefits and end disproportionate benefits for high-income people.

Step 3: The new President should cut the costs of the federal establishment by raising productivity throughout the bureaucracy. Mission responsibilities should be consolidated. Unproductive boards and commissions should be terminated. Every federal office, agency, and department should be granted discretion to reorganize its operations, while their personnel should be trimmed and their administrative budgets should be reduced by 3 percent a year—the benchmark for annual productivity gains in a well-run business.

4. Reshape the tax burden. The new President should challenge Congress to create a progressive and pro-enterprise tax system that can both promote growth and finance the Present Budget. For business, the President should propose carefully targeted investment incentives in three areas where markets fail—the formation of new businesses, long-term research and development, and the purchase of new plant and equipment. The President and Congress also should ease the tax burden on middle-class people whose incomes have stagnated or fallen, and finance this relief through higher taxes on wealthy people whose incomes have risen sharply.

The new President can lead Congress and the country beyond the deadlocks that have gripped federal policy for more than a decade. The Enterprise Economics budget program outlined below would, over four years, expand by half the public investment in our common economic resources. It would restrain other federal spending sufficiently to cut the current deficit by nearly half over the same four years. At the end of four years, the remaining deficit would roughly equal government investment in the nation's economic future. These policies, therefore, will balance federal operating and consumption-related spending—the Past and Present Budgets—over the new President's term. (See table 8.)

This program requires basic changes in the ways that Congress and the President create a federal budget. It directs fiscal policy away from tax and spending subsidies for powerful interests and wealthy people, and toward a renewed commitment to broad economic opportunity for America's average workers and firms.

Even a popular new President will find that many of these choices are controversial. He must grasp the opportunities created by this controversy if he truly intends to change the course of fiscal policy. The challenge is great, but so are its rewards: a sound national budget and a healthy American economy for the 1990s.

WHAT'S BEHIND THE DEFICIT: SPENDING OR TAXES?

At the heart of our current low level of public investment and high deficit level lies basic spending decisions, not tax policies. In the normal course of events, Congress and presidents agree to spend more—typically to satisfy groups and interests that help elect them—and then ask how to get the money. Put another way, the federal government spends money because it chooses to, and can do so; and it raises taxes when it has to. This logic has produced steady growth in federal spending for 45 years, and large, chronic deficits for the past 15 years.[3]

What truly matters most for the economy, however, is not how fast federal spending grows, but how fast its burden on the economy increases. Real federal spending grew substantially *faster* in the 1950s and 1960s than in the 1970s and 1980s. Yet, in the past, the faster-growing spending included more public investment spending, coincided with rapid economic growth, and built on a smaller spending base. As a result, the burden on the economy from supporting fast-growing spending in the 1950s and 1960s was less than in the 1980s, when slower-growing spending focused on consumption, came on top of a larger government, and claimed more of a slower-growing economy. The bottom line for the economy was this: As a share of GNP, the rate of increase in federal spending was nearly twice as great in the 1980s as in the 1950s and 1960s.

It is too early to judge the 1990s; but in the decade's first years, the growth rate of government spending accelerated to 3.6 percent a year, and overall spending has claimed nearly 24 percent of GNP a year.

The new President should draw two lessons from the long record. First, that federal spending becomes a burden on the economy when spending decisions outpace the economy's capacity to provide the necessary resources. Second, that the right fiscal policy must respect and expand the economy's productive capacity through an effective alliance of public and private investment.

BUDGET PRIORITIES: INVEST IN OUR ECONOMIC FUTURE

The proper goal of national fiscal policy is not to achieve book-keeping balance, but to promote a prosperous and progressive

Table 1. The Growth and Burden of Federal Spending

Decade	Average Annual Growth Rate of Real Spending	Spending as a Share of GNP, Annual Average	Average Annual Increase in Share of GNP Claimed by Federal Spending
1950s	4.4%	18.0%	0.8%*
1960s	4.1%	19.0%	0.6%
1970s	3.2%	20.5%	0.7%
1980s	3.2%	23.1%	1.2%

*The base for calculating the rate of increase for the 1950s in the share of GNP claimed by federal spending is limited to the four postwar years of the 1940s.

Source: Calculations derived by the author and Jed Kolko from *Budget of the United States Government,* Fiscal Year 1991, "Historical Tables," table 1.3.

economy, and the new President should reorder the federal government's fiscal priorities to advance this goal.

The need for greater public investment is urgent, and its focus is clear. National resources should be targeted not to help one sector or another, but to rebuild the resources common to all economic activity—an educated and skilled work force, high-quality communications and transportation systems that connect businesses and bind markets together, and research and development in the new technologies that can create jobs, businesses, and growth. In this way, the national government can help raise the rate of return on all economic activity within the United States, which in turn will attract greater private investment.

Public investment in the United States has lagged for more than a decade. The share of GDP committed by the federal government to nonmilitary research and development fell by about half from the 1960s to the 1980s.[4] The share of federal spending going to investments in physical capital, such as roads, waterways, housing, and military purchases, dropped by nearly 60 percent from the 1950s to the 1980s.[5] In the 1980s, U.S. net investment in infrastructure consumed only 0.3 percent of GDP, as compared to 5.7 percent in Japan, 4.8 percent in Italy, 3.7 percent in Germany, and 2.7 percent in France.[6] The shares of America's GDP committed to elementary and secondary education and to job training have declined as well.

The goal of the investment part of the budget program should be to increase federal spending dedicated to public investment by 50 percent over four years. As outlined in this and subsequent chapters, the Future (or investment) Budget comprising spending on education, training, infrastructure, and civilian research and development should increase by $55 to $60 billion by 1996.

While increasing public-investment spending, the new President and Congress will have to restrain other spending sufficiently to both sharply reduce the deficit and finance the new administration's commitment to the economic factors that drive productivity. The success of the President's fiscal strategy, therefore, will depend equally on his resolve to increase public investment and on his discipline to reduce spending for other purposes.

THE BUDGET PROCESS: PROMOTE AND ENFORCE THE NEW FISCAL PRIORITIES

In order to make the federal budget an instrument of economic growth, the new President should reform the budget process so that the process itself will both encourage greater public investment and enforce limits on the growth of other spending.

Table 2. Current Investment Spending and a New Future Budget
($ billions)

Current Investments	1993	1994	1995	1996
Education	29.1	29.1	29.1	29.1
Training	5.7	5.7	5.7	5.7
Civilian R&D	36.0	36.0	36.0	36.0
Infrastructure	44.4	44.3	44.2	44.2
Total	115.2	115.1	115.0	115.0
New Investments				
Education	10.1	14.3	17.2	21.7
Training	3.5	6.0	8.0	9.0
Civilian R&D	5.0	5.0	5.0	5.0
Infrastructure	20.0	20.0	20.0	20.0
Total Investment Budget	153.8	160.4	165.3	170.7
Percent Increase	33.5%	39.3%	43.7%	48.4%

1. The President should propose a new budget divided into three parts: a Future (or capital) Budget covering investments in a more productive national economy; a Past (or obligations) Budget covering interest and savings and loan payments; and a Present (or consumption) Budget covering all other spending. This basic distinction between spending for the long term, spending to cover past obligations, and spending for current operations is standard procedure in corporations and in state and local governments—nearly everywhere except in the federal government.

2. The President and Congress should change the budget process so that public investment is financed differently than other federal spending. The Treasury should be allowed to borrow to fund the Future Budget, because its investments generate economic returns that provide the economic means to repay the loan. At the same time, government should raise the revenues every year to pay for all consumption-related spending, including the interest payments on the national debt (except during recessions, wartime, or other grave national emergencies).

By requiring that Washington collect the revenues every year to pay for the Present Budget and the Past Budget (except savings and loan payments), this reform would restrain Congress' tendency to cut taxes without cutting spending.[7] By limiting the annual deficit to no more than net investment spending, the approach will also deter Congress from increasing spending without raising revenues. And by permitting the Treasury to borrow only to finance the Future Budget, the reform will channel new spending pressures away from government operations and transfers, and toward the wealth-producing investments that increase the country's capacity to meet its obligations.

What is at stake is not whether any particular program should exist, but whether it should be paid for by current revenues or by borrowing. The heart of the distinction lies not in whether the spending promotes the country's well-being, but in whether it can generate economic returns that government or taxpayers can tap into to redeem the commitment.[8] Support for medical research and medical education would qualify for deficit financing, but support for most health benefits would not. Public investment would include infrastructure repair and construction, and certain business-loan supports, but not most new weapons procurement. Job training and support for engineering education would qualify as investment, while law enforcement and income-support transfers should be considered items in the Present Budget.

The new President will have to narrowly delimit the Future

Budget and resist strong pressures to classify more spending programs as "investment." However contentious these decisions prove to be, these divisions in the budget will represent important progress over the practice of drawing no distinctions at all, which has helped produce the worst of all worlds—rising public consumption and falling personal incomes, along with lagging public investment and huge deficits that reduce private investment.

3. The President should propose that the annual growth rate of total public noninvestment spending be limited by law. Economics alone cannot provide a model for determining precisely how much spending will promote the richest, the most civil, the most free, or the most equal society. Nonetheless, there are sound economic reasons for setting limits. Generally speaking, if government is not to claim resources that the economy needs to maintain its current levels of investment and growth, the share of the nation's income used for public consumption should increase no faster than the economy itself. The same idea from a taxpayer's vantage point can be stated as follows: So long as most of the federal budget is financed directly from the incomes of average Americans, federal spending should expand no faster than an average person's ability to pay for it.

This perspective provides another basic reform in the budget process: By law, the growth rate of Present Budget spending should not be allowed to exceed the growth rate of per capita personal income in the preceding year (except during recessions and wartime, or during other grave national emergencies).[9] Almost all spending would come under the aggregate limit—entitlements and discretionary spending, civilian and military expenditures, "on budget" and "off budget" programs. The only exceptions should be interest and savings and loan payments, which are beyond annual control, and the public investments in common economic resources.[10] In the end, annual spending would grow slowly when Americans make small income strides and more rapidly when they enjoy greater gains, modulating the growth of federal expenditures according to the rhythms of ordinary people's economic lives.

Year after year, modest reductions in spending growth based on per capita income growth will add up to a revolution in spending policy. Had Ronald Reagan adopted this rule in 1980, nominal, noninvestment spending would have grown at an average annual rate of 6.9 percent through the decade, as compared to the average of 7.6 percent a year actually recorded.[11] The difference would have been enough to all but eliminate the deficit by 1989—a shortfall of $10 billion instead of the actual $152 billion—and to reduce the publicly-held national debt of $2.2 trillion at the close of 1989 by more than $850 billion.[12] If George Bush had respected this limit, the 1993 deficit would have been cut by half.

The key is that, under normal conditions, revenues grow modestly faster than per capita income. Revenues are based on (net) national income, and however quickly national income grows, per capita income will grow more slowly when the population is increasing. As a result, spending will increase more slowly than revenues.[13]

Modulating spending increases according to an average person's ability to support them won't satisfy hard-line conservatives who want to turn back the clock to a time of small government; nor will it hearten others who want government to transfer more benefits to more groups. But it should appeal to the political mainstream that provides the support necessary to carry out hard decisions. For many Republicans, this strategy will force the Congress to offset new spending commitments with cuts elsewhere in the budget; and for Democrats, it can underwrite an active government capable of pursuing progressive reforms along with most current commitments.

4. The new President should propose that every current spending program be subject to a sunset provision requiring its reauthorization every seven years. Limiting federal spending to the level that average taxpayers can afford and paying for our current consumption will require, for the first time in a generation, that Congress make choices. A sunset program offers a systematic way of reexamining existing spending on a continuing basis, in order to make these choices.

The purpose of a sunset provision is to force Congress to face a series of questions. Does each particular program's achievements justify the attendant tax burden? Or could the same or better results be achieved by reforming the program or shifting its mission to the private sector or to state or local governments—where most policy innovation has occurred in the last 15 years. Often, the conditions that created a demand for new spending change over time, sometimes because the programs funded to deal with them have worked. Yet spending normally continues, because interests inside and outside government come to depend on it.

The new President should accompany his sunset proposal with another granting him a line-item veto for seven years, through the first sunset cycle. This authority is most vital during periods of divided government when the President and Congress are partisan adversaries. But as long as Congress combines all annual appropriations in 13 or fewer bills, and aggregates numerous items of legislative business in single bills, a line-item veto can be an important instrument of fiscal restraint and presidential leadership. In the end, a line-item veto backing up a rigorous sunset process could prove to be a powerful way for the new President to find resources to both expand public investment and reduce the structural deficit.

SPENDING RESTRAINT: REFORM OR END UNPRODUCTIVE SUBSIDIES

The new President should open his campaign for fiscal restraint by reforming or phasing out unproductive subsidies for powerful economic interests. In this way, he can, at once, restrain the growth of spending *and* help enhance economic productivity. This approach is a progressive alternative to cutting basic social services used by everyone, from law enforcement to national parks, and basic supports for low- and moderate-income people.

These subsidies take many forms. The current federal budget includes more than $30 billion in annual special spending benefits for one industry or another, from below-market timber sales from national forests to grants for airport expansion. The budget also includes some $35 billion in direct tax subsidies for selected economic interests, from a special tax preference for credit unions to the tax credit for rehabilitating older buildings. These estimates do *not* include more than $100 billion a year in tax preferences that go to individuals but ultimately benefit a particular industry—from tax deductions for mortgage interest and employer-provided health insurance, to the tax exclusion for employer-provided group-term life insurance.

By creating layer upon layer of special spending and tax subsidies, successive Congresses and presidents have built an economic policy shaped by the influence of interest groups. These sector-specific subsidies undermine the nation's economic productivity as well as put a strain on the budget. Industries that don't receive special treatment have to compete at a disadvantage, because those that do enjoy an artificially elevated rate of return that attracts private investment away from those left to operate on their own. The subsidies also can enable the favored sectors to avoid taking steps necessary to become more productive and, as a result, may ultimately end up harming those they are intended to help. Finally, they claim scarce resources that otherwise could go to public investment, deficit reduction, or tax relief.

The new President should propose that every industry-specific spending and tax subsidy be subject to a special sunset clause requiring its reauthorization within four years. To help shield these decisions from special-interest politics, the President and Congress could create a permanent, independent Board on Budget Subsidies, modeled on the Base Closing Commission, to evaluate each provision's economic merits. The board should begin by evaluating subsidies already identified by the Congressional Budget Office as potential sources of deficit reduction.[14] For example:

Reforms of Selected Spending or Spending-Related Subsidies (FY= Fiscal Year)

- Change market rates for timber sales from federal lands. Savings: FY 1993: $0.03 billion; FY 1993–96: $0.2 billion.
- Auction use of the electromagnetic spectrum. Savings: FY 1993: $1.7 billion; FY 1993–96: $3.5 billion.
- Auction off import quotas for textiles, apparel, and sugar. Savings: FY 1993: $2.5 billion; FY 1993–96: $11.1 billion.
- Reduce support for Tennessee Valley Authority activities. Savings: FY 1993: $0.2 billion; FY 1993–96: $0.6 billion.
- Phase out grants for airport expansion. Savings: FY 1993: $2.0 billion; FY 1993–96: $8.3 billion.
- Increase private financing for Superfund cleanups. Savings: FY 1993: $0.5 billion; FY 1993–96: $1.8 billion.
- Reduce overhead rate on federally sponsored university research. Savings: FY 1993: $0.7 billion; FY 1993–96: $3.1 billion.
- Cancel NASA's advanced-solid-rocket-motor project. Savings: FY 1993: $0.5 billion; FY 1993–96: $2.0 billion.
- Cancel NASA's space station project. Savings: FY 1993: $2.1 billion; FY 1993–96: $8.8 billion.
- Cancel NASA's space exploration initiative. Savings: FY 1993: $0.1 billion; FY 1993–96: $0.4 billion.
- Phase out grants for wastewater treatment plant construction. Savings: FY 1993: $2.5 billion; FY 1993–96: $10.4 billion.
- Reduce rural housing loan subsidies. Savings: FY 1993: $0.3 billion; FY 1993–96: $1.6 billion.
- Phase out postal subsidies for not-for-profit organizations. Savings: FY 1993: $0.4 billion; FY 1993–96: $1.5 billion.

- Reduce farm supports (as U.S. negotiates foreign-subsidy cuts). Lower target prices. Savings: FY 1993: $0.4 billion; FY 1993–96: $7.3 billion.
- Raise share of acreage ineligible for deficiency payments. Savings: FY 1993: $0.4 billion; FY 1993–96: $3.1 billion.
- End special subsidies for honey, wool, and mohair. Savings: FY 1993: $0.02 billion; FY 1993–96: $0.44 billion.
- Reduce dairy supports. Savings: FY 1993: $0.1 billion; FY 1993–96: $0.8 billion.

Without prejudging any particular measure, the new President could cut the deficit by $7 billion in the first year and $35 billion over four years by achieving savings equivalent to just *half* of those from this partial list.

The Congressional Budget Office also has identified many questionable tax expenditures for powerful interests. For example:

Reforms of Selected Tax Expenditures or Tax-Related Subsidies

- Phase out special expensing provision for extractive industries. Savings: FY 1993: $0.6 billion; FY 1993–96: $3.2 billion.
- Phase out special percentage depletion for extractive industries. Savings: FY 1993: $0.5 billion; FY 1993–96: $3.5 billion.
- Phase out the special tax credit for profits earned in U.S. possessions. Savings: FY 1993: $1.7 billion; FY 1993–96: $6.7 billion.
- Reduce accelerated depreciation on rental housing and other buildings. Savings: FY 1993: $1.0 billion; FY 1993–96: $12.0 billion.
- Reduce the deductibility of business expenses for meals and entertainment from 85 percent to 50 percent. Savings: FY 1993: $1.6 billion; FY 1993–96: $11.9 billion.
- Phase out the special tax preference for credit unions. Savings: FY 1993: $0.3 billion; FY 1993–96: $2.2 billion.
- Phase out the special tax preference for private-purpose revenue bonds. Savings: FY 1993: $0.2 billion; FY 1993–96: $3.1 billion.
- Reduce the special tax credit for rehabilitating older buildings. Savings: FY 1993: $0.1 billion; FY 1993–96: $0.4 billion.
- Amortize a portion of advertising costs. Savings: FY 1993: $3.3 billion; FY 1993–96: $16.5 billion.

Again, without prejudging specific proposals, the new President could cut the deficit by nearly $5 billion in the first year and by more than $27 billion over the next four years if he achieved savings equal to just *half* those from this partial list of reforms for tax subsidies.

These reforms should be phased in gradually and in ways that permit affected firms to adjust. For example, agricultural supports for commodities that compete in global markets with heavily subsidized foreign competition should be reduced as the U.S. negotiates reductions in foreign farm supports through the General Agreement on Tariffs and Trade (GATT).

Many responsible people have called for the reform or repeal of every spending and tax subsidy listed above; each one has been well defended by the industry benefiting from it. Nonetheless, the new President's choice is clear: He can sidestep the controversies and tolerate the spending and revenue drains from special-interest subsidies, or he can break the structural deficit. He cannot do both.

In a decade when government must spend more on public investment while maintaining basic social services—a time when everyone will be asked to work harder—the new President must spend real political capital to reduce the costly, special treatment long enjoyed by selected industries. If necessary, as each subsidy faces its sunset deadline, the President can use a line-item veto to eliminate those imprudently reauthorized by Congress. If he doesn't make the attempt in his first year in office, his presidency ultimately will be dominated by struggles over marginal cuts in popular programs, and the cause of expanding public investment could be lost.

SPENDING RESTRAINT: REFORM ENTITLEMENT PROGRAMS

The second part of the new President's strategy for restraining spending should involve reforms in major entitlement programs, which today account for nearly half of all federal spending. The President should focus this effort on the fast-growing health and retirement programs,[15] which together account for 90 percent of all entitlement spending and which, without serious reform, will *by themselves* claim half of the federal budget by 1997.[16] Without entitlement changes, the prospects for increasing public and private investment are slim—and without these investments, U.S. growth and productivity gains will continue to lag.

The difficulty can be stated simply: The rapid growth of these programs reflects their value to voters, which in turn has seemed to preclude reform. To get beyond this impasse, the new President has to establish a popular basis for serious changes. To mobilize this support, entitlement reforms must represent more than simply a way of cutting the deficit. In addition, the changes should be based on a genuine social covenant of mutual responsibility governing public transfers. Under this compact:

> All Americans should be entitled to health care and a decent retirement after working for a lifetime. In return, at least one able person in every household is obliged to work to provide a meaningful portion of these goods for the family—through job-based health coverage or by earning the means to buy it, and by saving for retirement and paying payroll taxes.
>
> All Americans should be entitled to a share of these benefits reflecting at least what they contribute to finance them. Those who can take care of their own health care and retirement are obliged not to claim a disproportionate share of the programs: High-income people should not receive a share of these federal benefits that exceeds their share of the population.

Individual work and retirement benefits

The first aspect of entitlement reform should focus on the basic relationship in federal retirement programs between working and receiving benefits. Social Security in particular contains a national commitment to help working people provide for their retirement by guaranteeing them public pensions if they pay a tax on the income they earn from working. This relationship is also evident in the size of the pension, which is related to how much income has been subject to the retirement tax on work.[17]

Another aspect of this relationship involves the number of years of working that fully qualifies a person for a taxpayer-financed pension—and the number of years an average retired person can expect to receive benefits. When Social Security was created in the 1930s, people fully qualified by working until age 65. At the time, someone retiring at age 65 could expect to collect a pension for an average of 11.9 years (men) to 13.4 years (women). Today, Americans reaching age 65 can expect to collect Social Security for considerably longer: 15 years for men and 18.8 years for women. In 1983, Congress passed a law to take account of the average American's longer productive work life and life span. The retirement age is scheduled to rise by two months a year starting in

2002, to reach age 66 in 2009; and start rising again in 2020, to reach age 67 in 2027.

The new President should appoint a special presidential commission to study the effects of accelerating these 1983 changes. Late-twentieth-century Americans clearly do live longer and can work longer, too. This approach to entitlement reform would spread the burden among all working Americans, in contrast to COLA cuts or caps on Social Security spending, which concentrate the costs on elderly people with few options for offsetting their losses. This strategy, therefore, could reduce Social Security spending while preserving its great achievement of effectively ending poverty among elderly Americans. This approach also would provide a very broad base for savings, and so could produce large, permanent deficit savings at limited, individual cost.

Some $60 billion could be saved over the next two decades, for example, by phasing in a retirement age of 66 by the year 2002 and 67 by 2008. After such a change, people's Social Security benefits would continue to substantially exceed the value of their lifetime Social Security tax payments, adjusted for inflation *and* an average rate of return on their payments (see table 3). Workers retiring at age 66 in 2002 after earning an average income all their lives would recoup the value of their payroll taxes by age 74. Yet the average retired man could expect to live and collect benefits until age 81, and the average woman would do likewise until age 84. Even high-income people who paid the maximum Social Security taxes would reach their break-even point at age 76.

Before pursuing such a strategy, the new President and the special commission have to address several important economic questions. What effects would a higher retirement age have on productivity and on the wages of younger workers? What should be the relationship between such reforms and Medicare eligibility? The conclusions should be part of a wide-ranging national debate over entitlement reform.

This debate must also face up to the genuine threat to Social Security posed by *not* addressing the growing, permanent budget deficit. In the 1980s, Congress and the President raised the payroll-tax rate seven times and used "surplus" revenues from these tax increases to finance some non-Social Security spending. If the new President does not address the deficit, including long-term pension spending, Americans eventually will face more payroll-tax hikes and, just possibly, an era of bitter, generational conflict.

Table 3. Age of Full Recovery of Social Security Taxes

Year Retired	Age of Retirement	Life Expectancy		Age of Full Recovery Earnings Level	
		Male	Female	Average	Maximum
1991	65	80	83	71	72
2002	65	81	84	73	75
2002	**66**	**81**	**84**	**74**	**76**
2010	66	81	84	75	77
2010	**67**	**81**	**84**	**76**	**78**
2020	66	81	85	75	78
2027	67	82	86	76	80

Sources: Author's calculations; Robert Myers and Bruce Schobel, "An Updated Money's-Worth Analysis of Social Security Benefits," *Transactions,* XLIV; *1989 Report of the Board of Trustees of the Federal Old Age and Survivors Insurance and Disability Insurance Trust Funds,* table 11.

Fairness and entitlement reform

A second aspect of entitlement reform should focus on fairness. The new President should propose reforms for federal retirement and health programs that will ensure that wealthy people receive no more than their fair share of these taxpayer-financed benefits.

This approach provides a new, progressive standard for federal health and retirement-related transfer programs financed by the taxpayers. This standard is based on a simple social imperative: A democratic government should not redistribute wealth, in the aggregate, from moderate- and average-income people to wealthy people. Otherwise, a progressive tax system has no significance. By applying this social imperative to transfer programs, the new President can also promote the current economic imperative of slowing the growth of spending and tax expenditures.

Applying this standard to entitlement spending in the aggregate—from Aid to Families with Dependent Children (AFDC) and student loans, to Medicare and Social Security—shows that middle-class households collect a modestly smaller portion of this total spending than their share of the population. Those more affluent and those less affluent than the average receive modestly greater relative shares.

The distribution of the benefits from entitlement spending programs, therefore, resembles a U-shaped curve.

- At the start of the curve, the 42 percent of all households living on taxable incomes of under $20,000 receive nearly 46 percent of all entitlement spending, reflecting mainly programs targeted to lower-income people, such as AFDC, food stamps, and Supplementary Security Income for elderly poor people.
- At the next income level, the curve plateaus. The 16 percent of households with taxable incomes of $20,000 to $30,000 receive 16 percent of all entitlement spending.
- From this point, the curve descends into a trough. Nearly 38 percent of all households have taxable incomes of $30,000 to $100,000; they receive less than 34 percent of all entitlement spending benefits.
- At this point, the curve moves up again, as the 4 percent of U.S. households with taxable incomes of more than $100,000 receive nearly 5 percent of all direct entitlement spending.

Table 4. Distribution of Direct Entitlement Spending

Taxable Income Amount	% of U.S.	Benefits (Billions)	Share of All Benefits
Below $10K	21.9%	$108.4	23.4%
10K-20K	20.4%	$103.7	22.3%
20K-30K	16.3%	$ 75.6	16.3%
30K-40K	12.1%	$ 52.8	11.4%
40K-50K	9.0%	$ 37.2	8.0%
50K-75K	12.2%	$ 48.5	10.5%
75K-100K	4.2%	$ 16.7	3.6%
100K-200K	2.8%	$ 14.3	3.1%
Over $200K	1.1%	$ 6.8	1.5%

Source: Calculations by Jed Kolko and Jordan Rappaport based on expenditure data from the Congressional Budget Office and tax-return data from the Joint Committee on Taxation.

Retirement spending and tax benefits

Nearly all of the spending and deficit pressures generated by entitlements come from retirement and health-care programs. In both cases, the data show that the spending favors affluent Americans. Moreover, the federal government's retirement and health-care programs consist not only of direct spending, but also of tax benefits. In the retirement area, the important tax benefits include the deductions for IRA and Keogh contributions, and the exemptions for half or all of Social Security income and for employer contributions to pensions. In health care, the relevant tax provisions include the tax deductibility and exclusion of employer-provided health insurance and the deduction for major medical expenses. The data show that the distribution of tax benefits for retirement and health care strongly favors well-to-do people.

Focusing first on retirement programs, the data show that fairness reforms should focus on upper-income people. Starting at the bottom, households with taxable incomes of less than $20,000 today receive a smaller share of federal pension spending than their share of the population, which reflects lifetimes of lower earnings subject to payroll taxes. In addition, their share of retirement-related tax benefits is insignificant. Next up the income ladder are the middle class, who collect shares of both pension spending and retirement-related tax benefits that reflect roughly their share of the American population.

At the top, the distributional data for upper-income people is nearly the reverse image of that for low-income people. The distribution of pension spending, especially the federal civilian and military retirement programs, clearly favors retirees with taxable incomes above $100,000. And retirement-related tax benefits strongly favor the same affluent income group, plus those earning $75,000 to $100,000 a year.

- The most affluent 3.9 percent of American households, with taxable incomes of $100,000 or more, collect more than 8 percent of all federal support for retirement, including almost 6 percent of federal pension spending, and nearly 17 percent of retirement-linked tax benefits. In dollars, in 1990 these very well-to-do Americans collected more than $16 billion in tax-payer-financed pension checks, plus another $14 billion in retirement-related tax benefits.
- At the preceding income level, the 4.2 percent of households

Table 5. Distribution of Federal Pension Spending and Tax Benefits

Taxable Income Amount	% U.S.	Spending Outlays	Share	Tax Benefits Benefits	Share	Total Value	Share
Below 10K	21.9%	$51.2	17.5%	$2.4	2.8%	$53.5	14.2%
10K-20K	20.4%	$64.5	22.1%	$9.8	11.5%	$74.3	19.7%
20K-30K	16.3%	$50.8	17.4%	$14.3	16.7%	$65.1	17.3%
30K-40K	12.1%	$36.4	12.5%	$12.9	15.1%	$49.4	13.1%
40K-50K	9.0%	$26.0	8.9%	$10.9	12.7%	$36.8	9.8%
50K-75K	12.2%	$34.6	11.8%	$14.9	17.5%	$49.5	13.1%
75K-100K	4.2%	$12.3	4.2%	$6.0	7.0%	$18.2	4.8%
100K-200K	2.8%	$11.0	3.8%	$7.5	8.8%	$18.5	4.9%
Over 200K	1.1%	$5.3	1.8%	$6.7	7.8%	$12.0	3.2%

Source: Calculations by Jordan Rappaport based on expenditure data from the Congressional Budget Office and tax-return data from Joint Committee on Taxation.

with incomes of $75,000 to $100,000 received 4.2 percent of all direct public-pension spending, but nearly twice their share of all retirement-related tax benefits.

On this basis, the new President should target fairness reforms in federal retirement programs to federal pension benefits for retired people with taxable incomes of $100,000 and more, and to retirement-related tax benefits for people with incomes of $75,000 and more. The President and Congress could promote fairness *and* reduce the deficit by $6–$7 billion a year, for example, by three reforms: (1) Tax 85 percent of the Social Security benefits collected by retirees with incomes of $100,000 and above; (2) reform federal civilian and military pensions to modestly limit the benefits of wealthy beneficiaries; and (3) modestly lower the cap on retirement-related tax benefits for well-to-do people.

Health-related spending and tax benefits

The distribution of federal health-care benefits presents a more complicated, and somewhat more equitable, picture than retirement benefits—until we reach high-income households.

At the bottom, lower-income Americans receive a larger share of direct federal health-care spending than their share of the population, reflecting the benefits that only they receive under the Medicaid program. But they also claim very small shares of the major health-related tax benefits—the tax exclusion for employer-provided health insurance and the deduction for major medical expenses.

At middle- and upper-middle-income levels, American households with taxable incomes of $30,000 to $200,000 receive a share of total health-care spending that is somewhat less than their share of the population. This reflects a fair share of Medicare spending, offset in part by their ineligibility for Medicaid. But they also collect more than their proportionate shares of the health-related tax benefits. And within this large group, those with incomes of more than $50,000 receive such large shares of the tax benefits that their share of all federal health-care benefits exceeds their share of the population.

Finally, at the very top of the income ladder, households with taxable incomes of more than $200,000 receive more than their fair share of both direct federal health spending and health-related tax benefits.

Fundamental reforms of the nation's entire health-care system ultimately will provide for a fair distribution of these spending and tax benefits (see chapter 5). Until these more basic reforms are phased in, the new President should target interim fairness reforms on federal health-care spending for wealthy retired people and on

Table 6. Distribution of Spending and Tax Benefits for Health Care

Taxable Income Amount	% U.S.	Spending Outlays	Share	Tax Benefits Benefits	Share	Total Value	Share
Below 10K	21.9%	$26.8	25.9%	$0.6	1.2%	$27.4	18.0%
10K-20K	20.4%	$25.3	24.4%	$5.4	11.1%	$30.7	20.1%
20K-30K	16.3%	$17.2	16.6%	$8.6	17.7%	$25.8	17.0%
30K-40K	12.1%	$11.2	10.8%	$7.6	15.6%	$18.8	12.3%
40K-50K	9.0%	$7.3	7.1%	$7.1	14.5%	$14.4	9.4%
50K-75K	12.2%	$9.1	8.8%	$11.2	22.9%	$20.3	13.3%
75K-100K	4.2%	$3.0	2.9%	$4.3	8.8%	$7.3	4.8%
100K-200K	2.8%	$2.5	2.4%	$2.2	4.3%	$4.6	3.0%
Over 200K	1.1%	$1.2	1.2%	$1.9	3.8%	$3.1	2.0%

Source: Calculations by Jordan Rappaport based on expenditure data from the Congressional Budget Office and tax-return data from the Joint Committee on Taxation.

health-related tax benefits for people with upper-middle-class incomes and above.

- The richest 1.1 percent of American households, with taxable incomes of more than $200,000, collect 1.2 percent of all Medicare spending, plus nearly 4 percent of all taxpayer-financed health-related tax benefits. In dollars, these wealthy Americans receive $1.2 billion in taxpayer-financed medical care, plus nearly $2 billion in retirement-related tax benefits.
- The 2.8 percent of all households with taxable incomes of $100,000 to $200,000 claim 3 percent of all federal support for health care—but retirees at this income level receive only 2.4 percent of all Medicare benefits, while the entire income group collects 4.3 percent of all health-related tax benefits. In dollars, these affluent people receive $2.5 billion in taxpayer-financed medical care, plus $2.2 billion in health-related tax benefits.

The President and Congress could promote fairness *and* reduce the deficit by $4–$6 billion a year by enacting interim fairness reforms. For example: (1) Count the insurance value of Medicare coverage as taxable income for retirees with incomes of more than $200,000; and (2) cap the tax exclusion or deductibility of employer-provided health insurance for employees paid $100,000 and more.

SPENDING RESTRAINT: REDUCE THE COST OF GOVERNMENT

The third major part of the new President's strategy to restrain spending in the Present Budget should focus on the administration of government itself. The federal establishment today spends more than $200 billion a year on personnel and administrative expenses, excluding the uniformed military, and these costs are rising steadily. In the 1990s, Washington should emulate successful businesses, which cut costs by routinely downsizing their work forces and reorganizing their operations to raise their productivity.

The President should begin with permanent operating reforms at the Pentagon, the nation's largest bureaucracy. The General Accounting Office has outlined a series of changes in the military-procurement system that could save nearly $6 billion, for example, and Congressman Bryan Dorgan's Task Force on Government Waste has analyzed new inventory procedures that could cut the

Defense Department's operating costs by $10 billion over four years.[18]

Next, the President could cut the cost of the savings and loan bailout by $16 billion over four years by adopting administrative reforms for the Reconstruction Trust Corporation. The President should cut other operating costs by consolidating program responsibilities that are now dispersed across numerous agencies, including border control, federal energy conservation, social service programs, agriculture field offices, and overseas broadcasting operations. Finally, scores of independent commissions and offices should be eliminated or folded into existing cabinet departments.[19]

The new President's major challenge, however, involves permanent productivity reforms for the routine operations of the national government. He should follow the lead of the national governments of Australia, Canada, Denmark, England, and Sweden, which have developed broad productivity programs for their own bureaucracies.[20] In the first stage, experts develop reliable measures for tracking and assessing the outputs of every government office, agency, and department. Next, each unit is granted broad discretion to develop its own strategy for producing the same outputs with fewer resources.[21] Third, the government enforces its commitment to raise productivity by cutting most units' budgets for personnel and administration.

The new President and his administration should follow this model, and enroll the federal bureaucracy in the growing movement to reinvent government. First, develop output measures for every federal agency, office, and department. Next, grant them authority to reorganize their operations. Finally, cut their operating budgets by 3 percent a year, a level corresponding to the average annual productivity gains of a well-run business. This strategy will generate permanent, baseline savings of more than $2 billion a year from each round of 3-percent cuts. It also should encourage federal managers and workers—the majority of whom are committed public servants working in a system years behind most other large organizations—to approach their missions and their jobs more creatively.

The new President also should reduce the current federal civilian work force of 2,972,000. Our government today employs 2.8 percent of the nation's work force—twice the share employed by the German or Japanese governments, and a 50 percent larger share than in the United Kingdom.[22] The President should begin by cutting 100,000 positions in the first two years, generating annual savings of more than $4 billion. If these reductions are absorbed successfully, another 100,000 positions should be cut, with comparable additional savings. These reductions can be achieved through attrition, since every year roughly 20 percent of all U.S. federal workers resign, retire, or lose their jobs.[23]

All told, a serious productivity program comprising these personnel cuts and the administrative reforms described above could produce deficit savings of more than $45 billion over four years.

FINANCING GOVERNMENT: PROGRESSIVE, PRO-ENTERPRISE TAX REFORM

The final fiscal-policy issue facing the new President involves tax reforms to promote economic growth and ease the tax burden on moderate-income and middle-class Americans.

The President can achieve these goals by straightforward measures. While reducing special-interest tax breaks for particular industries, the federal government can encourage economic enterprise generally by providing incentives in three selected areas of "market failure," where capital markets fail to direct a volume of credit that reflects their true economic potential.

First, the new President should promote new business formation—and new jobs created by new businesses—by proposing to exclude from taxation half of the profits earned by the people who provide initial capital for new companies, when the investors leave the capital in the company for five years or longer.[24] Second, the President should propose to make permanent the current temporary tax credits for business investments in long-term research and development. Third, the President should propose an "incremental investment tax credit" for firms that increase their rate of investment in productive plant and equipment. This reform is based on growing evidence that capital markets do not efficiently support rising business investment in plant and equipment that enhance labor productivity.[25]

Revenues to offset these carefully targeted investment incentives should come from revising the regulations governing the definitions of "taxable profits" earned by the American subsidiaries of foreign-owned corporations, and enforcing them. Nearly three-fourths of these companies pay no U.S. corporate income tax on their American profits. Our Treasury's current laissez-faire approach to this problem reflects a Cold War attitude that always placed diplomatic and military relations with our major allies above nearly any matter of economic interest. These noneconomic issues are now less pressing, and foreign-owned companies operating in the United States should face the same liability as our own firms.

In addition to these pro-enterprise tax revisions, the new President also should propose progressive reforms of the personal tax burden.

For most Americans, the large, permanent deficits of the 1980s and early 1990s have not brought lower taxes. As federal spending doubled and redoubled, the distribution of the federal tax burden shifted in three important ways. First, the share of federal spending covered by corporate taxes fell steadily. Second, the portion covered by payroll taxes increased dramatically. Third, excise and estate taxes moved from a major revenue role to a minor one. In addition, borrowing grew from an incidental factor to a fundamental one. The only relatively constant factor has been the share of spending covered by personal income taxes, which has trended down very gradually despite regular tax-rate cuts.[26]

These results show a persistent tendency by the federal government to both raise payroll taxes and tolerate a rising deficit in order to finance spending increases and cuts in corporate, excise, and estate taxes.[27]

The consequence for moderate-income and middle-class Americans is a higher tax burden—even as their incomes stagnate, the deficit increases, and the tax burden on well-to-do people falls.[28]

Table 7. Source of Funds for Federal Spending
(Average Annual Shares)

Decade	Personal Income Tax	Corporate Income Tax	Payroll Tax	Excise/ Estate	Borrowing
1950s	42.0%	26.9%	11.5%	17.2%	2.5%
1960s	42.0%	20.4%	18.4%	14.9%	4.4%
1970s	40.3%	13.3%	27.7%	11.3%	11.1%
1980s	38.0%	7.7%	29.2%	8.2%	17.7%
1990s	36.3%	7.4%	30.1%	7.1%	19.0%

Source: Calculations by the author and Jed Kolko based on *Budget of the United States Government,* Fiscal Year 1991, "Historical Tables," tables 1.1 and 2.2; *Budget,* Fiscal Year 1992, tables 3-X-1 and 4-A-1; *Budget,* Fiscal Year 1993, tables 22-1 and A 1-1.

The new President should propose three measures to redress this situation and restore a strong dose of progressivity to the tax burden. The first priority is to relieve the tax burden on moderate-income and middle-class people, whose incomes have stalled or declined while their taxes have increased. To begin, provide income-tax relief for nonaffluent Americans without children by cutting their 15 percent income-tax rate to 13.5 percent. Second, for nonaffluent families with children under age six, replace the current $2,300 tax exemption for dependents with an $800-per-child tax credit, phasing out this additional support as the child ages from six to ten (see chapter 7). In effect, this change would exempt about $5,300 a year from income tax, or the money an average-income family needs to raise a young child.

The new President should finance middle-class tax relief by raising the tax burden on high-income Americans. The necessary revenues could be raised by adding a fourth income-tax rate of 36 percent for taxable income above $150,000 for joint returns (roughly equivalent to Adjusted Gross Income of $200,000), plus a 10 percent surtax on income above $750,000, and by raising the Alternative Minimum Tax rate to 27 percent.[29]

Additional resources for deficit reduction should be secured by two other measures affecting wealthy Americans. The Internal Revenue Service estimates that underreporting or outright tax evasion by high-income taxpayers regarding their unearned income—principally capital gains, but also including interest, dividends, and rental income—costs the Treasury more than $17 billion a year.[30] Stricter reporting requirements and enforcement could easily raise $2 to $3 billion a year. It also is time to end the tax exemption for capital gains held when a person dies, which distorts our capital markets by providing an incentive—and a boon—for wealthy investors to hold on to their assets until they die. The Treasury could raise $4 to $5 billion a year by limiting this exemption.[31]

These progressivity reforms are matters of social policy, not part of the economic program. Despite the protests of supply siders, there is no evidence that modest increases in marginal tax rates for high-income people will adversely affect economic growth or productivity (see chapter 1). The top 39.6 percent marginal tax rate for millionaires would be 30 points lower than the 70 percent rate in the late 1970s, ten points below the 50 percent rate that supply siders hailed in 1981—and considerably lower than the tax rates and tax burdens on far less affluent Japanese or German taxpayers. These reforms would have only one certain effect: They would reverse the long-running trend of rising tax burdens on working Americans and declining tax burdens on wealthy people.

THE ENTERPRISE ECONOMICS BUDGET

If the new President and Congress adopt the fiscal-restraint strategy of Enterprise Economics, in four years they could both increase public investment by 50 percent and cut the deficit by nearly 50 percent. Moreover, the Enterprise Economics strategy produces a deficit in fiscal year 1996 of approximately $177 billion, roughly equal to the fiscal year 1996 Future Budget for federal investment in the nation's common economic resources. In short, this program will balance the federal operating and consumption budget over four years.

These projections include the investments in education, training, research and development, and infrastructure outlined above and in subsequent chapters. Also, on the outlay side of the federal ledger, the estimates include costs for additional proposals from Bill Clinton's economic program, *Putting People First,* including 100,000 new police officers, urban enterprise zones, and welfare reform. The spending cuts include those outlined in this chapter, plus the defense and intelligence reductions proposed in *Putting People First.* The estimates also assume four other spending cuts from Bill Clinton's program: proposals to reform foreign aid and debt financing, implement a line-item veto, and cut White House staff.

On the revenue side of this budget, the estimates include the tax changes and enforcement measures described in this chapter. The estimates also include four additional tax-reform proposals from *Putting People First:* limits on the deductibility of corporate compensation and lobbying expenses, higher taxes on corporate polluters, and repeal of tax benefits for moving business operations overseas. The revenue estimates also include an expansion of the Earned Income Tax Credit (EITC) for working poor families. Finally, the revenue forecast includes Bill Clinton's proposal to enforce a reasonable tax liability on American subsidiaries of foreign corporations, but the Enterprise Economics budget assumes revenue increases equal to two-thirds of those forecast in *Putting People First.*

Table 8. Enterprise Economics Budget
($ billions)

	1993	1994	1995	1996
OUTLAYS (Congressional Budget Office Baseline)	1493	1511	1567	1644
New Investments				
Education	10	14	17	22
Training	4	6	8	9
R&D	5	5	5	5
Infrastructure	20	20	20	20
Spending Reductions and Reforms				
Industry Subsidies	14	14	13	13
Entitlements	12	15	17	19
Defense	13	13	15	21
Government	12	19	26	28
Interest Savings	2	6	9	14
NEW OUTLAYS	1479	1490	1538	1605
REVENUES (CBO Baseline)	1162	1242	1323	1390
Revenue Increases				
High-Income Rates	18	21	22	23
Enforcement	2	2	2	2
Capital Gains at Death	0	3	4	5
Industry Subsidies	12	21	23	23
Foreign Corporations	6	7	8	9
Revenue Losses				
Business Incentives	6	7	9	10
Middle-Class Tax Relief	0	9	10	11
EITC	2	3	3	3
NEW REVENUES	1191	1277	1360	1428
DEFICITS				
CBO Baseline	331	268	244	254
Enterprise Economics	288	213	178	177
Future Budget	154	160	165	171

MANDATE FOR ACTION

1. **Reorder spending priorities to make the federal budget an instrument of economic growth.** The new President should expand public investment in our common economic resources, while reducing spending for other purposes, from entitlement transfers to defense and the administration of the federal establishment.

2. **Divide the federal budget into three separate parts reflecting the different economic impacts of different kinds of spending.** The new President should divide the budget into a Future Budget covering economic investments in education, training, infrastructure, and research and development; a Past Budget covering interest and savings and loan payments; and a Present Budget covering all consumption-related spending.

3. **Enforce annual fiscal discipline on all Present Budget and Past Budget spending.** The new President should propose that all Present Budget and Past Budget spending be funded by annual revenues, and that annual borrowing be limited to no more than the year's net Future Budget.

4. **Limit by law the growth rate of consumption-related public spending.** The new President should propose that Congress limit by law the annual growth rate of Present Budget spending, so it can increase no faster than the growth rate of the economy or of per capita income in the previous year.

5. **Introduce a comprehensive sunset procedure for all government programs and grant the President a line-item veto.** The new President should propose that Congress attach a sunset provision to every spending program and tax expenditure in the budget, requiring its reauthorization at least once every seven years, and grant the President authority to veto line items in spending and authorization bills.

6. **Reform or eliminate special-interest spending and tax subsidies.** The new President and Congress should create an independent, nonpartisan commission, modeled on the Base Closing Commission, to evaluate all spending and tax subsidies for particular industries or groups. Based on these evaluations, the commission should recommend appropriate reforms and repeals.

7. **Reform retirement and health-care entitlements and tax expenditures.** The new President and Congress should reform federal health and retirement spending programs and related tax expenditures to ensure that high-income people receive no more than their fair share. The new President also should appoint a presidential commission to evaluate the effects of accelerating scheduled increases in the retirement age for Social Security.

8. **Cut the administrative costs of the federal establishment.** The new President should cut the routine operating costs of government: consolidate program missions currently spread across numerous departments, reform the spending operations of the Pentagon and the Reconstruction Trust Corporation, and terminate unnecessary boards and commissions. He also should challenge every agency, office, and department to reorganize their operations while cutting their administrative budgets by 3 percent a year.

9. **Cut the federal work force.** The new President should reduce the federal work force by at least 100,000 positions.

10. **Make the tax code more pro-growth.** The new President should propose carefully targeted investment incentives for the formation of new businesses, long-term research and development, and the purchase of new plant and equipment. The revenue losses should be offset by reforming the taxation of U.S. subsidiaries of foreign corporations.

11. **Make the tax burden more progressive.** The new President should propose tax relief for moderate-income and middle-class Americans, especially those with young children, and offset the revenue loss by increasing the tax burden on wealthy people.

3

Enterprise Economics on the Front Lines: Empowering Firms and Workers to Win

DOUG ROSS

INTRODUCTION

Enterprise Economics is a new framework and set of investment priorities. Its heroes are the entrepreneurs and workers who are America's actual performers in the world economy. It is built on the belief that Americans cannot aspire to a rising standard of living unless we systematically and steadily increase the productive capabilities of the firms and people who produce our wealth. And it argues that opportunities and resources to enhance these capacities will work only if entrepreneurs and employees find them sensible and usable—grounds on which the current economic policies of the Left and Right fall short.

As its name implies, Enterprise Economics puts the ultimate focus on the place where America's economic energies meet the road—the enterprises where we struggle to increase the quality and efficiency of the goods and services we produce. Like our efforts to field winning Olympic teams in Barcelona, our commitment to support the development of the most productive workers and firms in the world requires thoughtful investment and extensive preparation. But, as in Barcelona, the real test of those investments and preparations in the new global economy is measured in the head-to-head competition between our enterprises and the best in the world.

The focus of Enterprise Economics on building the productive capacities of U.S. workers and firms is especially important today, *for it is only through steadily increasing productivity that we can achieve strong growth and a vigorously rising standard of living in the 1990s.*

During the 1980s, we were able to grow faster than our productivity (average GNP growth of 2.4 percent versus productivity growth of 1.2 percent).[1] But the sources of that growth are increasingly behind us. A rising number of women entering the work force helped America's output increase faster than our productivity. But with most women now working full time, fewer families can contribute additional work hours to the labor market. Foreign borrowing of nearly $1 trillion during the 1980s permitted consumption to grow in excess of production. However, America's new status as a debtor nation, and increased competition from Europe and elsewhere for investment funds, make more debt a dubious growth option in the 1990s.

In short, if Americans want to live better in the decade ahead, we will each have to produce more. To restore the upward mobility and growing middle class that have been at the heart of the American Dream, Enterprise Economics aims at an overriding goal: long-term growth in productivity with the rising real wages that come with it.

To empower U.S. workers and firms to boost their productivity and compete successfully, President Clinton must provide leadership and a set of initiatives as bold and dramatic as those put forth by Franklin Roosevelt 60 years ago. During the first 100 days of the new administration, the President should:

Lead the nation and its people into the new global competition. To do so, he must provide a positive vision of the future—a vivid picture of how the U.S. can win in the new world economy. He must offer candid explanations of the causes of our competitive difficulties. And he must establish national standards for quality firms and skilled workers that embody what is world-class, and against which we can measure our own performance.

Forge a new compact with American workers. Specific jobs can no longer be protected in an age of fierce foreign competition. If the men and women who make up America's work force are to embrace such a future, they must have new sources of economic opportunity and security to replace those dissolving under competitive pressures. President Clinton should therefore propose a new Employment Insurance System for U.S. workers. It would create a Career Opportunity Card that would give Americans direct control of the education and career development resources that are the principal new source of economic security. The President must also require private investment by firms to upgrade the skills of their existing employees. And he should encourage firms to reorganize their workplaces to allow for more participation and ownership by workers.

Supply U.S. firms with the best-trained work force in the world. Human brain power and skill have become the principal sources of sustainable national competitive advantage. Firms not only need broadly educated workers, but also increasingly require people with the specialized skills demanded for high performance in their particular industries. To increase the number of specially trained new workers, the new President must earmark federal vocational education funds exclusively to promote more apprenticeship programs operated jointly by high schools and industries.

Increase the availability of patient, productivity-building capital for U.S. firms. The macroeconomic policies of Enterprise Economics to increase private savings and reduce the federal deficit should lower the cost of capital in the U.S. But U.S. financial institutions will continue to operate more as speculators seeking short-term returns unless incentives and regulations favoring long-term investments are created. President Clinton can increase the amount of productivity-building capital by permitting banks to take equity positions in smaller, closely held companies and by moving to eliminate capital gains on equity investments in new businesses held for at least five years.

Strengthen America's position in critical technologies. The U.S. invests less in development of commercial technology and applications than its principal international rivals. President Clinton should work to correct this situation by shifting $10 billion annually out of the federal military budget and into civilian research and develop (R&D). The President should also move to make the present R&D tax credit permanent and invest in the creation of a network of industry-directed teaching factories to enable U.S. manufacturers to apply existing technology more effectively.

Build an entrepreneurial business climate. America's success increasingly depends on the success of the men and women who start and grow our businesses. To provide them with a more supportive business environment, President Clinton should amend the antitrust laws to encourage the formation of business networks in America—groups of small and midsized U.S. firms that pool efforts to learn new production processes and discover new markets as rapidly and efficiently as their foreign rivals. Also, President Clinton should move to replace bureaucratic regulations of business with more efficient market-based regulations whenever it can be done without compromising the public interest. And he should use regulatory changes to encourage private efforts to build a modern telecommunications infrastructure that will create boundless opportunities for U.S. entrepreneurs.

THE NEW RULES OF GLOBAL COMPETITION

Conventional liberal and conservative economics have long ignored considerations of the international quality and cost of productive factors available to U.S. firms and workers, because, for the first three decades following World War II, only America was capable of producing the products that required the most advanced technology, extensive plant and equipment, and skilled workers. American firms competing with one another drew on the same stock of productive resources; when foreign competition did exist, it was safe to assume that the challenge was based on cheap labor, not superior inputs.

The days of easy U.S. superiority are over. Our advanced competitors are investing in most of the critical productive factors at a more rapid rate than the U.S. Japan is investing three times more per employee in plant and equipment.[2] Both Germany and Japan commit 50 percent more of their GNP to civilian R&D.[3] The Germans spend three times more on the post-secondary education of their non-college-bound young people than we do.

U.S. machine tool manufacturers have seen their competitive capacities stunted by an inability to match the steady stream of highly trained designers and operators flowing into the German machining industry. Big Three auto and steel makers, trying to play catch-up in markets where they were losing share, confronted real interest rates in 1989 of 6 percent compared to real rates of 2.9 percent in Japan,[4] making the capital cost of a 20-year investment for plants and equipment for Ford or USX 32 percent greater than a comparable investment for Nissan or Nippon Steel.

Unless we assume our people and firms to be smarter than those of our competitors, we cannot tolerate such differing rates of investment in these key productive factors and expect to compete and maintain a world-class standard of living. Indeed, these lower rates of investment in the quality and quantity of our technology, plants and equipment, and work force undoubtedly contributed to our dismal productivity performance during the 1980s (an annual

U.S. productivity growth of 1.2 percent compared to the Japanese rate of 3.1 percent, and our own historical performance of nearly 3 percent).[5]

If American firms are expected to boost productivity in markets where value is increasingly determined by our foreign competitors' abilities and not just our own, U.S. firms must have access to human and physical resources at least comparable to those provided by other nations.

Meeting this challenge is a central objective of Enterprise Economics. As we shall see, the trick is not in recognizing the urgent need to upgrade the quality of productive resources in the U.S. It is rather in how to use limited federal resources to *leverage* large changes in private investment and firm and worker behaviors.

THE NEW ECONOMY

Enterprise Economics is designed to address changes that have occurred in three fundamental areas of our economic lives: the way we make things, the role of people in the new production processes, and the sources of individual economic security in the emerging American economy.

1. The basic way goods and services are produced in the advanced economies is changing. The mass production system that America contributed to the world 75 years ago is being superseded by a new production system as different from the mass production system as that system was from the craft system it rendered obsolete.

The importance and extent of this shift in the production process was highlighted several years ago in the international auto industry. Stunned by the success of Japanese automakers in winning over U.S. car owners , the Big Three auto companies and their workers braced themselves for the promised invasion of Korean automobiles. After all, the reasoning went, if the Japanese can beat us at our own game with wages that are nearly equal to ours, think what the Koreans will do with manufacturing wages of $2 to $3 an hour. Combining their lower costs with a legendary willingness to work longer and harder, everyone expected the Koreans to seize huge chunks of the U.S. car market from both the Big Three and the Japanese.

But they didn't. After some initial success, especially on the West Coast, the Korean invasion fizzled. Hyundai created the Excel to enter the U.S. market. Its strategy was to compete by underpricing the Japanese entry-level models with low wages and high volume. It was a time-tested formula that was supposed to work—our old Henry Ford-style mass production system with cheaper labor.

The quality of the Excel, however, was inferior (a comparable Japanese model had an average of 0.6 defects per car, compared to 3.1 for Hyundai). As American consumers caught on, Hyundai's U.S. sales plummeted 50 percent between 1988 and 1990.[6]

The Korean experience, along with the dismal failure of the Yugo in the U.S., highlighted what too many Americans had missed. The high volume, mass production system of producing goods and services was no longer competitive. A new way of making things had emerged in Japan and, more recently, in the United States. This new production system, sometimes called *lean* or *agile production,* provides higher quality and more customized products than the mass production system, and it does so at comparable costs.

The enormous competitive advantage of the new production system over mass production is its flexibility. Henry Ford's production line achieved its competitive advantage over the craft system from its ability to produce thousands or even millions of a particular product. Workers were taught (usually in several hours) to perform one routine task as part of the system. To capture the full-scale economies of the system, long runs of the product were necessary. Once the system was set in place for a particular product, defects built into the system were inspected out at the end for repair or rejection.

But a production system that could economically manage short runs of different products on the same line to meet varied and rapidly changing customer tastes offered an enormous advantage. Similarly, one that could eliminate defects in products would bestow a further competitive edge. These are precisely the advantages offered by the new production system.

New production workers are able to change the machines quickly to produce different products or customized versions of the standard product. Workers are taught to do so either by mechanically changing the machines or reprogramming them if they are computer controlled, which, of course, requires a lot of training.

Similarly, new production workers are taught to use this power to change the system to identify and correct for defects at the source—rather than the more expensive mass production process of inspecting them out at the end of the line. The result is much higher quality and lower cost.

With this new system of customized mass production, it is possible to manufacture a bicycle in one day built to a specific body size rather than a one-size-fits-all model; to make an affordable, laser-cut suit customized to an individual's measurements rather than one off the rack; and to have a car assembled specifically for the customer with all the features the customer wants rather than the best available model off the lot.

Nor is this new way of making things limited to manufacturing. Service and retail firms also are increasingly turning to more flexible, customized processes to meet customer demand. Examples include cable and pay-for-view television programming designed for specific market segments; the trend toward more specialized savings and investment plans from banks to meet different family requirements; and the growing use of retail sales people to maintain customer preference data bases and to operate as store buyers to make sure individual customer's needs are met.

It is already clear from the marketplace that consumers prefer these affordable, customized goods and services to their standardized mass production competition. Thus, U.S. firms and workers that wish to compete will be forced to learn these new ways of making things.

2. The emergence of new processes for producing goods and services that provide better quality and lower cost than mass production has transformed the nature of work. People perform a much more central role in the new production system. Democracy in the workplace—the flattening of firm hierarchies, production teams, gain-sharing plans, more worker participation in firm decision-making, and employee ownership—is rapidly being introduced as an economic imperative instead of a social ideal.

This change in the way work is organized is not always easy to see upon entering a modern factory employing the new production process. Autos and other durable goods travel on rapidly moving conveyers attended by dozens of dancing robots that stamp and weld them. People appear incidental, passing by briefly to check the process or make adjustments. The technology has reached the point where a new Nissan plant in Japan can shift from the production of sedans to minivans on the same line with hardly any downtime if customer demand changes.

Yet the heart of this process is not technology: It is a new set of social relations in the workplace. The competitive advantages of the new production system over mass production are its flexibility to create varied products and its ability to identify and correct defects. Therefore, people move to the center of the system. Only those who work directly with the production process can actually change the machines to produce new products, only they can identify defects at their source and correct the cause, and only they can implement on a daily basis the numerous tiny improvements in the system that cumulatively can keep their company ahead of the competition.

Executives sitting in an office 300 miles away or even two floors above simply cannot make these decisions. They lack both the real-time information of new production process workers and the capacity to act immediately.

New production workers are no longer required to simply provide the eye-hand coordination for the blind and clumsy machines tended by their mass production predecessors. These tasks are either being automated or shipped to low-wage workers in developing nations.

Workers in a new production system must supply the problem-solving ability and judgment to govern the system. They are the brains. They must have the power to stop and change the system to achieve the new goals for quality, customization, and productivity.

Empowered workers taught to think and act also employ the new information technology much better than mass production workers. General Motors learned this lesson at its Hamtramck, Michigan Cadillac plant when it equipped mass production workers with the latest technology and witnessed declines in productivity. The Japanese always work out the social relations first and then introduce the technology, with far better results.

So the key to the new production system is the empowered worker. Ralph Miller, former CEO of Modern Engineering, a 4,000-employee engineering and design firm doing work in the U.S., Japan, and Europe, put it succinctly: "Empowering workers and building teams to help them exercise that power on the factory floor and in the office is the only path to global competitiveness. Whether a corporate leader is autocratic or democratic is no longer an issue of personal style. Only workplace democracy is capable of providing international economic success."[7]

On one hand, the importance of workplace democracy to competitive firms represents good news: Economic efficiency and empowering employees to perform as adults with a voice in determining what they do at work have become complementary social goals, not choices (yet another reason for Marx to turn over in his grave). At the same time, implementing such democracy on the shop floor and in the office involves unprecedented shifts of power within businesses, which is demanding the wholesale reinvention of the American business organization. In short, moving from hierarchy and autocracy to decentralization and democracy is a tough road for both business leaders and employees.

Both of these seismic changes in the economic environment— the emergence of a new production system and the new roles for workers it creates—have combined to turn the global economic game upside down. They have elevated the capacity of a nation's people and the ability of its firms to organize them effectively as the principal contributors to growth in productivity.

A stern test of Enterprise Economics and the initiatives of the next president will be their ability to support the continuing capacity of American workers and firms to learn these new roles.

3. The third profound change in the economic game involves the source of economic security for most Americans. In the 1950s and 1960s, the formula for life-time employment, decent fringes, and a good pension was pretty well known: land a job with a Fortune 500 corporation like IBM or General Motors or AT&T. And if you were a wage earner, because salaried workers were seldom laid off, join a strong union to protect your job and your earnings. Not everyone could get these jobs, even during the peak of the postwar boom. But if you got one, it was generally agreed you had it made.

The new realities of global economics have shattered this ideal of economic security for millions of American workers. The Fortune 500 companies laid off 3.5 million men and women during the past decade alone.[8] Corporations, driven by lean competitors to increase productivity in stagnant or declining markets, have downsized dramatically.

The rate of change in most globally contested markets has enhanced the competitive advantage of innovation and flexibility, tipping the competitive balance in a growing number of markets like computers and biotechnology against large corporate bureaucracies and in favor of smaller, more entrepreneurial firms. These agile smaller companies have succeeded in creating enough new jobs in the aggregate to replace lost corporate jobs. But they do not offer the same security.

They are born and die at a dizzying rate. In their start-up phase, they pay lower wages and seldom offer fringe and pension benefits comparable to their corporate competitors. They are seldom unionized (fewer than 25 percent of the 11,000 new and small manufacturing firms that created jobs in heavily unionized Michigan in the 1980s were unionized).[9] And as aerospace workers in Los Angeles, autoworkers in Flint, and telephone workers in New Jersey sadly discovered, even a strong union cannot save your job if your company is in trouble. The traditional sources of economic security for most American workers have dissolved in the productivity pressures of the past 20 years.

This situation has left most Americans with but one manageable source of economic security for themselves and their families: the ability to get the knowledge and skills the market wants in a timely manner.

Though American politicians have been loathe to admit it, virtually no middle-class jobs are being created in the U.S. for unskilled or old-skilled workers. This new reality can be seen in the 12 percent drop in real earnings between 1973 and 1987 for those with only a high school diploma and the nearly 20 percent decline for dropouts. In contrast, a college degree that typically bestowed an income 40 percent greater than a high school degree in 1980, produced an income advantage of more than 70 percent that amount by 1989.[10] Indeed, the economic returns on education have been soaring throughout the developed world in recent years.

Beyond statistics, evidence of the new economic importance of skill and education can be recognized in a visit to any of the growing number of businesses implementing the new production system. Routine, repetitive jobs have nearly disappeared. The emphasis is on making decisions and solving problems based on continuous learning. Information technology is omnipresent, generating a constant pressure on all employees to measure quality and make immediate adjustments. Henry Ford's old line worker looks as out of place here as Madonna in the Mormon Tabernacle Choir. And the projected layoff of almost half the bank tellers in America as automatic teller machines take over the routine tasks of receiving and dispensing money reveals the beginnings of a similar revolution in the service sector.

The uncertainty of corporate fortunes and the volatility of the entrepreneurial companies beginning to dominate high-value-added markets increasingly are forcing men and women in the U.S. work force to regard themselves as independent contractors. With the almost certain prospect of having to change employers during their work lives, and probably career fields as well, workers increasingly are left to manage their own retirement benefits, health insurance, and, most important, the skills they have to sell in the labor market.

If Enterprise Economics is to restore to Americans some effective control over their economic lives, it must offer opportunities and resources for navigating in this new labor market. Each of us must be able to invest in new skills when we need them to take the next step in our careers. Enabling Americans to claim this remaining source of economic security in the face of the disappearance of more traditional sources is a central challenge for the new President and a further test of the relevance of Enterprise Economics.

NEW ROLES FOR GOVERNMENT

The new production system also demands changes in the way government works to spur the productivity and competitiveness of U.S. firms and workers. The past decade taught us much about the capabilities and limits of government actions to positively affect the world in which individual firms and people battle to survive and succeed.

Republican deficits and partisan gridlock have stymied national economic policy for more than a decade. But it has been a golden age for innovative economic policy at the state level. According to the National Association of State Development Agencies, the states spent more than $8 billion to revitalize their economies during the decade.

Battered by the national recession of the early 1980s and global challenges to their agricultural, energy, and industrial economies, the governors first turned to Washington for ideas about what to do. They found a raging ideological debate but few answers.

The Reagan administration counseled laissez-faire: "Get government out of the way and let the free market do its work." But from Pennsylvania to Mississippi, the market was doing its work. It was shifting unskilled jobs to developing nations and more advanced production to sophisticated competitors like Japan and Germany. When they looked to the national Democrats, state leaders found little more. Most liberal Democrats called for trade barriers to protect America's sunset industries and for subsidies to support sunrise industries. The former were outside the jurisdiction of the states, and the latter struck most governors as impractical.

After consulting with businesses struggling to survive in the new competitive climate in their states, the states pioneered a new direction in economic development. *They focused on developing and strengthening the local markets that supply firms and workers with the capital, technology, and skills they need to compete.*

The states' experience in pursuing this new market-strengthening strategy led them to discover some significant limitations in the use of government that apply at the federal level as well (see chapter 12.)

1. **Federal government cannot substitute the direct delivery of public services to firms and workers for services from private markets it views as underperforming.** U.S. Department of Commerce regional centers provide advice on exports. The SBA's small business counseling centers and the Hollings Centers serve as extension resources for small manufacturers, and all suffer from the same programmatic maladies: The scale is invariably too small to be transforming, reaching only a tiny fraction of the firms in the marketplace. Surveys indicate that most entrepreneurs reject government sources of assistance as worthless and never even sample them. And virtually none of these efforts can document any long-term impact on the economy. More than anything in the 1980s, the states proved that public agencies cannot successfully retail services to individual firms and workers.

2. **The federal government cannot directly replace serious shortfalls in private investment with public expenditures.** Public resources are simply too limited relative to the size of capital, technology, and training markets, especially given the state of the federal deficit for the foreseeable future. Even more limiting are the mistakes public bureaucrats are sure to make when they substitute their judgments for market decisions in the allocation of public funds for industries' or firms' specific uses. The exploding complexity of markets filled with foreign players, rapidly changing technology, and waves of entrepreneurial star fighters stealing product and customer niches from corporate starships should have moved that temptation beyond even the most self-confident bureaucrat.

3. **The federal government cannot boost long-term productivity through subsidies or trade protection for specific industries or firms viewed as either critically ill or especially promising.** As a quick review of the troubled loan portfolios of state development agencies during the 1980s reveals, government workers have a hard time looking beyond broad trends to assess the prospect of a particular firm or industry sector (or

resisting political pressures to adjust their views). Further-more, such subsidies and protections paradoxically tend to undermine the prospects for survival of their recipients, since they tend to shield firms from competition, the principal spur to the innovation that is the source of gains in productivity.

Fortunately, the states also identified some promising avenues of action at the federal level. Presidential leadership, the leverage of public funds in private markets, the promotion of new learning environments for firms and workers, changes in the business climate, and the judicious provision of public goods such as education and modern transportation systems all possess the power to stimulate substantial change.

President Clinton should create new federal policies intended to strengthen and create the markets that supply these world-class production inputs and learning opportunities to entrepreneurs and workers. Rather than direct federal services and large-scale subsidies to particular industries and firms, the tools of Enterprise Economics are leadership, leverage of private resources, investments in new learning relationships, and public goods delivered in effective market-driven ways unavailable to private markets.

The role of government is neither as minimal as the supply siders posit nor as central as industrial policy supporters presume. It is, in Michael Porter's word, "partial." For no matter how competent, government cannot directly perform the critical task of combining human and physical capital in more valuable ways. Only the organizations of men and women who make up the enterprises on the economic frontlines can upgrade productivity by increasing quality and efficiency.

At the same time, in a global economy the quality and cost of a competitor's productive inputs, opportunities to learn, and business environment can be the difference between winning and losing. So while necessarily "partial," the competence with which government does its job can be the competitive edge in the head-to-head competition between industries and firms from different nations.

EMPOWERING WORKERS AND FIRMS: NEXT STEPS

When it moves to action, Enterprise Economics takes sides. Recognizing that rising productivity is the key to vigorous national economic growth and a steadily increasing standard of living, Enterprise Economics stands behind the entrepreneurs and workers on the frontlines of the global economy.

If they succeed, our country will restore the reality of the American Dream for millions of Americans, for whom it has begun to fade. If they fail, our society will be forced to accept a second-rate standard of living and all of the political and social conflicts that accompany frustrated national and personal expectations.

What follows are six proposed initiatives for the new President. If implemented effectively, they possess the power to help steer the American economy onto a higher-growth, higher-wage track by boosting productivity. They seek to focus on the new production and competitive realities confronting U.S. workers and firms. And they respect the lessons learned over the past decade concerning the limits and opportunities for using government effectively in an information age.

1. Mobilizing Americans to compete.

President Clinton must begin with a call to arms. We are in a global race to a new economic frontier—a race that most impartial observers believe we are not winning. We need a candid description of why we are in competitive trouble. We need a hopeful direction for the future—a path to national and individual prosperity we can understand and pursue. And we need a place at the federal level that will implement this leadership task for the new President.

Doing so calls for several separate but related steps:

President Clinton must begin by offering the American people a vivid picture of the U.S. succeeding in the new world economy. To exert power, a positive vision of the future must be constructed of pictures we can carry around in our heads. We must see what the new work looks like, in both manufacturing and service settings, which is the source of future middle-class jobs. We must be able to picture the new learning necessary to prepare us and our children to perform the new high-skill, decision-rich work better than our foreign rivals; we must grasp at a glance that old-style mass education with its industrial rows, fixed 40-minute classes, and passive learning approaches is out of step with the flexible, participatory, and creative demands of the new workplace. We must have access to a new set of pictures of effective parenting for preparing our children to enter and flourish in this new economy.

A vision of competitive success must also be accompanied by

standards. Firms must know what constitutes world-class quality, and workers must understand what level of skills will make them the most productive workers in the world. Only when U.S. firms and workers use such performance standards as benchmarks can "Made in America" again become a mark of unparalleled international excellence.

The President should support current efforts by the National Center for Manufacturing Science and a number of leading American corporations to establish a unified quality standard for U.S. firms. Establishment of such a standard is especially critical to the growing number of smaller firms entering the international market that simply cannot afford the costs of complying with the myriad of standards for quality.

President Clinton must also move quickly to work with educators and business leaders to establish national performance standards for American students. As parents, teachers, and pupils, we need to know what constitutes world-class educational attainment at any given time and be able to measure our own performance against this standard. Indeed, without spelling out what American students must know if they are to be part of a high-productivity economy, educators have no guideposts for their efforts, and parents have no way to determine whether their children are progressing satisfactorily. For these performance standards to substantially affect students' behavior, it is critical that the President convince a majority of American high-wage firms to use these standards as central hiring criteria.

Another priority of the President's leadership initiative must be to create a place within the federal government to provide this ongoing economic direction. That place should be a sweeping overhaul of the U.S. Department of Commerce, including its incorporation into a new Department of Trade and Technology (see chapter 4.)

Such a new department should focus the energies of a vastly reduced Commerce staff on communicating the visions and quality standards that are among the new President's most important economic policy tools. Rather than direct services, its products should be benchmarking studies comparing key U.S. industries with their foreign counterparts; research and conferences identifying new trends in products and processes in different industries around the world; encouragement for business networks to penetrate new markets and manage internal resources like training and access to capital; and recognition for firms, industries, and communities meeting world performance standards and achieving the vision. It should provide the visioning, information, and convening role of MITI without the Japanese agency's capital-controlling and industry-coercion powers.

To finance the leadership efforts of the new President, we should eliminate a set of federal programs that primarily deliver subsidies to individual firms. The Small Business Administration's business loan and counseling programs, the Economic Development Administration's business loan guarantees, and the Community Development Block Grant program of loans and grants to businesses serve only a tiny fraction of America's entrepreneurs. Their impact on overall U.S. productivity is marginal at best. The growing importance of entrepreneurs and smaller businesses demands the focus of mainstream national economic policies, not their relegation to minor federal agencies.

2. Forging a new compact with U.S. workers.

President Clinton should forge a compact with American workers that offers a new source of economic opportunity and security for those willing to brave the challenges of the global economy.

In the new economy, most of us can expect to hold as many as seven or eight jobs over our work lives and change careers once or twice to boot. Individual opportunity and job security today depend on our ability to get the career skills we want when we need them. President Clinton must move immediately to give every American worker direct access to this personal source of security.

This is what Bill Clinton's call for "putting people first" is about. A particular job can no longer be guaranteed in an economy marked by tough foreign competition, constant technological change, and the birth and death of thousands of firms each year. But a worker's job security can and must be protected by guaranteeing every man and woman in the labor force the learning resources they require to get their next job. The new President should launch three initiatives aimed at forging this new compact with American workers:

First, President Clinton should call for the establishment of a federal Employment Insurance System to supplement our unemployment insurance system. The latter provides a temporary living stipend for unemployed workers. The former would supply the resources to purchase career education and skills to enable such workers to find well-paying jobs to replace the ones they lost.

When unemployment insurance was established during the Great Depression, it was assumed that most laid-off workers would be called back to their jobs when the economy picked up. Unemployment was seen largely as a problem of the business cycle. Workers needed temporary income to tide them over until rising consumer demand allowed their former employers to rehire them.

But today, growing numbers of laid-off workers are never called back to their former jobs. They are the victims of competition and the restructuring of the marketplace. When their unemployment benefits run out, they usually are no better positioned to find a good job than the day they were let go.

At the heart of a new Employment Insurance System would be a Career Opportunity Card—a voucher or wallet card much like the health insurance cards many Americans carry. In case of a threat to a person's economic security, such as being laid off, being able to find only part-time work, or working full time at less than 150 percent of the poverty wage, this card would entitle a person to purchase up to $1,200 in education or training—the approximate cost of one year of community college training. Workers will have five years during which to expend this $1,200. The actual operation of the system could be contracted out to companies with credit or debit card experience, avoiding the need for a new federal bureaucracy.

Like the GI Bill, workers could use their career opportunity cards to purchase career learning from public or private sources of their choice. To be eligible to receive such funds, an education or training institute would have to participate in a performance information system operated by each state. In this way, workers would have access to *Consumer Reports*-type information regarding the completion rates, placement rates, and starting wage rates of those who had purchased training from the various vendors.

Initial funding for a federal Career Opportunity Card would come from the elimination of the Job Training Partnership Act, the training provisions of the Trade Adjustment Act, and other federal job training programs. With every unemployed and underemployed worker having individual access to career learning resources, the institutional middlemen set up by these programs become redundant.

Redirecting existing adult training funds into such a voucher system would finance a substantial amount of worker-controlled career development education. Federal appropriations for adult training totaled just over 4 billion for the past fiscal year.[11] Offering states incentives to fold in their adult education funds would add another $600 million to the pot.[12] This total of $4.6 billion constructed entirely from existing federal and state adult training funds would permit learning investments in as many as 7.6 million unemployed and underemployed Americans each year (assuming an average card user expended the equivalent of a half-year of full-time career education, or $600).

Additional funding could be raised from a modest co-payment to increase the worker's stake in the careful use of this public resource. And, to underscore our nation's determination to ensure that U.S. workers will not be losers in the global competition for well-paying jobs, the new President should urge Congress to commit up to $5 billion in additional federal spending for the Employment Insurance System.

Putting such an opportunity resource directly under the control of workers themselves is critical to a new compact in which Americans accept the risks and dislocations inherent in a world of freer trade and enhanced competition. It is not reasonable to ask Americans to reject protection in favor of new tariff-free trading zones— even if such trade promises long-term U.S. economic growth and a rising standard of living—if individual workers do not possess the means to manage their own economic well-being in a global economy marked by rapid change.

Second, President Clinton should propose a substantial increase in the level of private investment in worker skill-training in the U.S. The private sector also has a role to play in increasing the number of American workers with specialized training and the economic security that comes from having marketable workplace skills. Too many U.S. firms do not provide such training and those firms that do are frequently penalized when competing with firms that don't train, and use part of the savings to lure away skilled workers trained by others. When such practices are common, firms lose much of their incentive to invest in training, as they cannot count on retaining employees long enough to earn a reasonable return.

President Clinton should require that all U.S. firms, save the very smallest, invest the equivalent of at least 1.5 percent of their payroll in upgrading the skills of their employees. Firms would be required to allocate this training investment among front-line and management employees in rough proportion to the size of each group within their particular company (current spending by U.S. firms is heavily weighted in favor of training for top management). Firms falling short of this 1.5 percent minimum would distribute the shortfall to individual workers on a per capita basis in the form of training vouchers that could be redeemed with public and private training vendors.

Current overall training by private employers in the U.S. averages approximately 1.5 percent of payroll.[13] Insisting that every firm contribute its fair share to the enhancement of the work force's skills, however, will both increase the amount of such training in the U.S. and provide workers with another important source of lifetime learning and the increased economic security that comes with it.

Third, President Clinton also should strengthen the economic security of U.S. workers through support for the democratic workplace that is at the heart of the new production processes. Moving workers to the center of the battle to upgrade U.S. productivity requires radically different behaviors from both labor and management. The President could help promote a rapid American transition from obsolete autocracy in the workplace to competitive democratic capitalism in several ways.

To begin with, the President must explain this dramatic shift in the rules of the economic game to the American people. Too many employers and employees still cling to the outdated belief that confrontational labor-management relations organized around constrictive work rules remain the best way to organize a workplace. The full weight of the White House must be applied to altering this view.

The President also should support changes in tax laws that reinforce business practices that strengthen workplace democracy, such as profit-sharing, pay-for-performance plans, and employee stock ownership.

3. Preparing a trained work force for U.S. firms.

President Clinton must move to ensure that U.S. firms have access to the best-trained work force in the world. America does a brilliant job of preparing the top 20 to 25 percent of our work force, the people we rely on to invent new products and organize better processes for producing them. But when it comes to the next 75 percent of our men and women, who do not graduate from universities, and upon whose skills America's ability to produce high-productivity goods and services depends, we have fallen behind the competition. Like an army without trained troops, U.S. firms cannot be expected to become productivity leaders in their industries without the frontline workers to operate the new production system with its increasingly advanced technology.

Of course, higher levels of general education for all working Americans are important (chapter 6 suggests ways to improve U.S.

efforts in this critical area). But to be leaders in high-productivity, high-wage industries, U.S. firms need workers with specialized training to meet technical and skill requirements specific to those industries.

To increase the number of American workers with specialized training, the new President should earmark federal vocational education funds exclusively for learning programs that are jointly operated by education institutions and local industries. Such earmarking should be phased in over no more than a three-year period.

Currently, the content and format of most career education carried out by secondary schools are under the control of the local K-12 system. While many systems have forged "school-business partnerships," most are pro forma. Business partners might be consulted on course offerings but seldom possess real decision-making power or a role in the teaching and learning process. The result is that few high-productivity firms look to high school vocational education programs to fill shortfalls of skilled workers; 60 percent of young people educated in such programs do not find their way into the occupations for which they were trained.[14]

Requiring all such programs using federal dollars to create joint school-industry operating boards would improve the chances that the resultant training would meet the current and anticipated needs of industries and firms in the region. To be of real economic value to both participating students and firms, such programs would likely cover the last two years of high school as well as a year or two of post secondary study. By also insisting that federal dollars be limited to those career-preparation programs that provide at least 15 to 20 percent of all learning in actual workplaces, the result would begin to resemble the apprenticeship programs the U.S. has lacked to prepare its non-college-bound youth. In this way, federal funds would trigger greater interest and investment in the school-to-work apprenticeship path outlined in chapter 6. They would leverage far greater private investments by businesses in valuable, on-the-job training for young Americans, particularly those not bound for college.

Recent allocations of federal vocational education monies for Tech Prep programs in which high schools and community colleges organize coherent three- and four-year courses of occupational study are a step in the right direction. Community colleges, the part of the public education system that has the most direct experience with the private sector, should be included in vocational training consortia whenever possible. But unless the industries that expect to employ the young people coming out of these programs are forced to jointly operate them, the chances are minimal that their graduates will enter the labor market with both the basic learning skills and specialized training demanded by high-productivity firms.

Many models of American-style apprenticeship, jointly operated by schools and businesses, are popping up across the country. Eligibility for federal funds should depend only on the creation of a school-business operating consortium for vocational education, not on the specific form of local efforts. Indeed, broad experimentation at the state and local levels should be encouraged.

Vocational education funds out of Washington account for less than 10 percent of total school spending on such training.[15] If past changes in federal guidelines are any indication, however, the requirement that federal dollars be reserved for joint school-business training where a portion of the learning occurs in the workplace should help refocus the estimated $15 billion in state and local vocational education funds on meeting the real needs of U.S. firms.

4. Increasing productivity-building capital.

The new President must increase the availability of patient, productivity-building capital for U.S. firms. The fiscal and budget reforms presented in the previous chapter should reduce the real cost of capital for U.S. firms. However, the amount and cost of available capital are not the only important factors. The ways in which we allocate capital also have a significant impact on productivity.

In the high-productivity, high-growth U.S. economy we seek, firms are expected to make long-term investments to upgrade their productive capacities and those of their workers—investments in new plant and equipment, the latest technologies, employee skills, and in learning the new production processes and ways of organizing work. But the current U.S. system for allocating capital contains strong biases against such long-term productivity-building investments, especially in intangible assets as training and R&D.

Public policies regulating the behavior of financial institutions often force them to operate more as speculators seeking to maximize short-term returns than as owners with long-term interests. U.S. banks are prohibited by law from holding equity in firms to which they provide debt. Pension and mutual funds, which hold 60 to 70 percent of the shares of most publicly listed companies, are limited to owning only a small fraction of the stock in any one company.[16] They also are prohibited from sitting on boards of directors or having access to inside information about the operation of firms. In short, American law treats the principal institutional sources of capital in our society as outsiders to be kept at arm's length from the ownership and management decisions capital commands in the rest of the industrial world.

Larger, publicly held corporations at least have the option of searching for investors with longer-time horizons in the international capital markets. Smaller, closely held firms and start-up businesses lack this option; they are forced to look closer to home for patient capital, especially for the equity investments necessary to take advantage of the debt financing more available from local banks.

The new President should take two actions that would substantially increase the amount of patient capital of smaller, closely held firms and new businesses need to modernize and grow:

First, President Clinton should seek amendment of the Glass-Steagall Act of 1933 to permit banks to take and exercise long-term ownership positions in smaller, closely held U.S. firms. Providers of debt that also contribute equity are likely to become more informed about the firm's activities and more interested in long-term prospects. Allowing American banks to operate as merchant banks, as is currently the cases with their Japanese and German counterparts, will provide an important new source of longer-term capital for smaller companies that are not publicly held. By restricting banks' new merchant role to smaller, closely held firms, we can test this important reform in the capital market on a limited scale without subjecting federally insured deposits to the volatility of the stock market. If this partial amendment of Glass-Steagall is successful over the next few years, broader exemptions should be considered.

Second, President Clinton should exempt all capital gains taxes on equity investments in new businesses held for at least five years. Under current law, budding businesses do not attract the investment capital appropriate to their returns because it costs investors and banks more to gather the information they need to make a lending or investment decision about a new business than it does for existing companies. Therefore, a new incentive to encourage investment in new businesses is needed to offset this market failure.

5. *Regaining technology leadership.*

President Clinton must move to help American firms establish a leadership position in the development and use of critical technologies. The marketplace in which America invents new technologies and puts them to commercial use resembles the U.S. capital market described earlier. We are investing less than Japan and our leading rivals in Europe, and we are allocating what we do invest with less emphasis on long-run growth in productivity.

The U.S. currently invests only 1.9 percent of its GNP in civilian R&D, compared to 2.8 percent by Germany and 3 percent by Japan.[17] Domestic industrial R&D spending in the U.S. slowed from an annual growth rate of 7.5 percent during 1980–85 to only 0.4 percent during 1985–91.[18]

United States R&D expenditures are nearly equal to those of the other leading technology nations. But 29 percent of American R&D is directed to military purposes, while our civilian R&D spending lags badly. When the federal contribution to R&D is subtracted and only private R&D spending is considered, the U.S. ranks twentieth out of 23 industrial countries.[19]

America also allocates much of its R&D spending in ways that are less likely to produce productivity gains than those of our rivals. Military research, in which the U.S. is a leader, no longer is the rich source of civilian spin-offs that it was in the 1940s, 1950s, and 1960s; in fact, more and more cutting-edge military technology is originating on the civilian side. In an era when those who can manufacture a product better and cheaper can pirate it away from its inventors (VCRs and color TVs, for example) the U.S. puts two-thirds of its industrial R&D into product technology rather than process technology.[20] In Japan, the reverse is true. The federal government has failed to establish an investment priority for those technologies that are critical to the competitiveness of a range of domestic industries—technologies involving new manufacturing processes, advanced materials, and information systems.

Allocation of R&D resources in the U.S., especially by the federal government, also has failed to generate enough commercial value. A 1991 survey by the World Economic Forum ranks the U.S. fourth in the world in the effectiveness of our basic research in meeting long-term economic needs.[21]

Traditionally, civilian technology development in the U.S. has been driven from basic research activities toward some vaguely suspected application. The idea has been to finance thinking and experimentation by smart people in the hope that something of commercial value will eventually result.

Increasingly, our competitors in Japan and Europe are organizing technology development from the opposite end of the research-commercialization continuum with promising results. This different technology strategy looks to customer, marketplace, and business requirements to "pull" needed research and experimentation efforts from both basic and applied sources of technology development. The U.S. must rethink its strategy of "pushing" technology from the basic research side, given the growing success of our competitors.

President Clinton should begin this process by taking four steps:

1. *Close the civilian R&D gap between the U.S. and its chief foreign rivals by shifting at least $10 billion annually out of the general military budget and into the federal civilian R&D budget.* The amount of federal civilian R&D behind each U.S. worker must rise over time to at least match that in Japan and Germany. Currently, 60 percent of the government's $76 billion R&D budget is devoted to defense programs. Some shift in the budget mix over a four-year period from military to civilian research would appear manageable for a nation with a substantial competitive advantage in the military arena and a slipping one in the world economy. If this approach proves imprudent from a defense perspective, however, resources from other parts of the Pentagon's budget resulting from force reductions should be used. As the budget deficit declines, additional federal resources for civilian R&D could be necessary to finish closing this investment gap with our competitors.

2. *Create a civilian counterpart to DARPA* (Defense Advance Research Project Agency), *the federal agency credited with providing coherence to the government's military R&D efforts.* This new agency must focus our limited federal commercial R&D resources on technologies that will translate into better processes and products for American firms. The best way to accomplish it is by investing in industry-led consortia and joint firm-university research projects focused on specific technology problems. Such consortia should be required to put up at least half the money for such projects.

In this way, federal resources follow perceived market needs, they encourage important learning relations among firms in the same or complementary industries, and they leverage private R&D spending through industry-match requirements. This intimate interaction with industry should also help this new agency identify generic technologies of critical importance to both existing and emerging industries for investment priority.

The key to investments in learning relationships, whether for technology or training, is that they not be targeted to specific industries or firms. Any industries or groups of firms willing to invest in their own learning capacities should be eligible for public support. The market leads and the government follows. The idea is to invest in marketplace partnerships, not government predictions.

3. *Propose making the present R&D tax credit permanent.* Private levels of R&D in most of America's major industries are below both prior U.S. levels as well as those of their principal Asian and European competitors.[22] Making the tax credit permanent is the best available federal signal in a tight budget context to communicate the nation's commitment to world technology leadership in the 21st century.

4. *Support the establishment of as many as 150 "teaching factories" across the U.S. over the next four years.* Many of the nation's 360,000 manufacturers with 500 or fewer employees are under intense pressure to learn how to apply new technologies to their production processes. Studies reveal a growing gap between the ability of such firms to introduce more flexible processes and the equipment to implement them and the much faster rates of process innovation in larger U.S. firms. Most smaller manufacturers are having great difficulty keeping up with the pace of technological change on their own.

During the 1980s, a number of states experimented with the establishment of government- or university-operated manufacturing extension services as a response to this challenge. But their performance has been disappointing. Like other government retail service efforts, these extension services have reached too few firms, and most manufacturers regard them as unlikely sources of practical expertise.

The teaching factory would overcome many of these extension service shortcomings by operating as an industry-owned and -operated learning center. It would offer groups of firms within a particular industry a place to put new processes into operation and experiment with new technical applications. Its relevance to real factory-floor problems would be reinforced by a requirement that firms provide at least half the operating costs of the facility. The rest would be supplied by the federal government as a way to accelerate such productivity-related learning by smaller firms.

6. Building an entrepreneurial business climate.

President Clinton must provide the nation's entrepreneurs with a more supportive business climate. The entrepreneurial spirit is America's most powerful competitive edge. Combining our Yankee roots with an endless stream of immigrant merchant experience, we are the premier business builders in the world today. We have the lowest fear of failure. We start more businesses than any other advanced nation.

But, we are failing as a nation to develop this advantage to its fullest potential. Our business climate—the rules of the economic games set by our public tax and regulatory policies—still reflects the demands of the disappearing Industrial Age. Instead of fashioning an environment designed to support and enhance entrepreneurial success, we inadvertently stifle such success with policies aimed at "countervailing" corporate oligopolies from the past that themselves are struggling to survive.

To begin with, many federal rules and regulations are designed by government bureaucracies for compliance by corporate bureaucracies. The costs of learning the rules, filling out the forms, and implementing the standardized measures for compliance are disproportionately heavy for smaller, entrepreneurial firms; they are even becoming too expensive for larger corporations seeking to shed their bureaucratic skins for leaner, more responsive organizational structures.

Federal antitrust policy is impeding the growth of business groups in the U.S. The advent of new production processes, changing work organizations, and the accelerated pace of innovation and market response instigated by global competition have placed a new premium on learning as a source of firm and worker competitive advantage. And while smallness is an increasing asset when it comes to agility, it can be a serious liability in purchasing the information and experimentation central to learning. Large corporations can spread these learning costs over a much larger volume of products and customers. Smaller firms cannot capture these learning scale economies internally.

The American entrepreneur as Lone Ranger is becoming obsolete. If small and midsized firms entering the international economy are to master the new production processes and discover new markets as efficiently as larger corporations, they must be free to pursue such learning with other firms. The day when most smaller firms could do this on their own is over.

Also, changes in the relationship between final producers of goods and their suppliers are forcing more firms to collaborate as the only way to compete and survive. One example is the movement by many large manufacturers to dramatically reduce their number of suppliers. Instead of letting large numbers of contracts for individual parts, with many smaller firms participating, they are offering contracts for the manufacture of complex modules to a smaller number of suppliers. If small firms wish to keep these large corporate customers, they will have to form production networks to be able to competitively bid on work that none of them could do alone but that becomes possible collaboratively.

President Clinton should concentrate on two ways to improve the business climate:

1. He should initiate an overhaul of federal antitrust law to send a clear message encouraging the formation of business groups that do not threaten price monopolies.

Prodded by the demands of global competition, business networks are beginning to form at an accelerating pace. For example, ten auto suppliers in Michigan have organized the Auto Body Consortium to develop ways to assemble auto bodies with more accuracy than their Japanese competitors. Heat treaters in Ohio united together to solve common training problems, as have a group of machine shops in northwest Indiana. Florida aerospace suppliers have formed a network to seek new business in the face of declining defense contracts.

However, until the antitrust laws are revised as part of an explicit campaign to encourage the formation of business networks, movement to create these new entrepreneurial learning organizations in the U.S. will be tentative. It is impossible to attend one of the meetings of these multifirm groups without encountering the uneasiness of the participants in not knowing exactly where the legal lines fall. Clearly redrawing the antitrust lines to encourage and exclude all such joint learning and even production behavior, except that which threatens the establishment of local price or market monopoly, would be one of the most powerful steps the new President could take to enhance the productive capacities of U.S. firms. The goal is not to reduce local competition that is the key to innovation and higher productivity. Rather, the objective of such business groups is to promote the degree of cooperation that makes real global competition possible.

2. He should impanel a Regulatory Sunset Commission (see

chapter 12). One of its charges should be to review existing federal rules and regulations affecting entrepreneurs and, where possible, recommend the replacement of bureaucratically controlled policies with market-based policies at least as effective but less costly.

Entrepreneurs have long argued that command-style federal regulations are inefficient. They have contended that "one-size-fits-all" compliance requirements rob them of the chance to find less costly ways of achieving a particular environmental, health, or consumer objective.

Previous federal efforts to lighten the regulatory burden on entrepreneurs, such as Vice President Dan Quayle's Competitiveness Council, have faltered by posing private efficiency and public protection as zero-sum choices. Issues like fuel efficiency standards were framed exclusively as a trade-off between cleaner air and lost auto jobs.

The new President must urge a different approach that concentrates on the search for "win-win" regulatory strategies. It takes no great genius to increase public environmental or consumer protections at a direct cost to business nor is it difficult to devise ways to reduce business costs at public expense. What most Americans want are reasonable public protections in the context of a competitive economy. Fortunately, we are beginning to discover market-based regulatory approaches as replacements for traditional command and control strategies that enhance both public interest and private efficiency.

The 1990 amendments to the federal Clean Air Act, and the tradable permit system they created, offer an example of harnessing market forces to combat acid rain. Chapter 4 provides a range of new ways that the new administration could put this market-based approach to work.

Another market-based idea to create a more entrepreneurial business climate involves telecommunications. It is estimated that we could boost U.S. productivity and increase our national output by over $300 billion by 2010 if we replaced copper wires with new fiber optic cables capable of vastly increasing the amount of information transmitted into businesses and homes.[23] Such a network could mix video, voice, text, and data transmissions, turning the family television set into an interactive "telecomputer." For example, doctors could perform "fiber-optic house calls" without leaving their offices, or "distance learning" programs could help teach students in remote areas. A new communications infrastructure built upon fiber optics would unleash a new wave of entrepreneurial energy and job creation.

The challenge is how to get such an information superhighway built quickly. Some argue that the government should build it, but the price tag—$100 to $400 billion—is daunting and government usually moves at a glacial pace. Instead, the new President should press for regulatory changes that encourage electric utilities to become investors in this new system, along with the local phone companies and perhaps cable television companies. New federal legislation could provide guidelines for state utility commissions (which already regulate both phone and electric utilities) to allow and encourage such joint ventures. Without a penny of public spending, we could speed the completion of a network that might do as much for our economy in the 21st century as the interstate highway system did after World War II.[24]

MANDATE FOR ACTION

1. **Explain the new terms of economic competition and set standards for world-class performance.** President Clinton must use the persuasive powers of the bully pulpit to provide Americans with a compelling vision of how we can succeed in global competition. Through a new Department of Trade and Technology, the President must also set standards of world-class quality for firms and educational attainment for students.

2. **Create an *Employment Insurance System* as part of a new compact with U.S. workers for economic opportunity and security.** President Clinton should propose a Career Opportunity Card for all workers, which will give them direct control over the learning and career development resources that are the only reliable source of economic security in the new economy. Such a measure should also require private firms to increase their investment in the skills of their employees and offer strong support for participation and ownership by workers.

3. **Use federal vocational funds to create joint school-business youth apprenticeship programs for job training.** President Clinton should propose that schools be required to share control over vocational education funds with local businesses willing to hire and train students.

4. **Create new sources of productivity-building capital for U.S. firms.** President Clinton should propose that banks be permitted to take equity positions in smaller,

closely held companies and eliminate capital gains taxes on equity investments in new businesses that are held for a minimum of five years.

5. **Increase the technology resources available to U.S. firms.** President Clinton should shift $10 billion annually out of the military budget into federal commercial R&D, establish a civilian DARPA to invest these funds in industry-led consortia, make the present R&D tax credit permanent, and invest in 150 teaching factories to increase the technical competence of America's smaller manufacturers.

6. **Build an entrepreneurial business climate.** President Clinton should overhaul federal antitrust laws to encourage the formation of business networks and establish a regulatory sunset commission charged with replacing bureaucratically-controlled regulatory policies that affect entrepreneurs with market-based policies that are at least as effective but less costly. He should also press for regulatory changes to encourage electric utilities, telephone and cable television companies to build a new fiber-optic system linking U.S. homes and businesses.

4

Strategic Success in the Global Economy

D. HOLLY HAMMONDS

INTRODUCTION

This year's election brought the global economy straight into voters' homes. The campaign focused national attention on many previously obscure trade rules and initiatives, particularly the North American Free Trade Agreement (NAFTA). The presidential candidates' speeches and proposals challenged voters to ask themselves: Is freer trade good or bad for my job? Does the U.S. win or lose as trade increases? What should our government do to make trade work more for the U.S.?

Trade concerns prompted some of the campaign's strongest language and exposed deep divisions among the candidates. During the primaries, Jerry Brown urged autoworkers to "keep Michigan jobs in Michigan." Pat Buchanan derided President Bush's 1988 pledge to create 30 million jobs: "What he didn't say was that they were in Guangdong Province, Yokohama, and Mexico." During the general election, after negotiators agreed on a NAFTA text, President Bush argued it would help the U.S. economy. Governor Clinton agreed it would help—if some of its provisions were improved. Ross Perot said it would hurt the U.S. and trigger "a giant sucking sound of jobs being pulled out of this country" to Mexico.

The attention to trade policy in this campaign may have been new, but it was firmly grounded in the growing importance of global commerce to the U.S. economy. Imports and exports now account for nearly a quarter of our Gross Domestic Product.[1] Vast numbers of American jobs are now dependent on global trade. American firms from Motorola to McDonald's, and from General Electric to General Mills, have increased their business through foreign trade, investment, and franchising. And greater opportunities should abound in a global economy four times the size of the U.S. market.

While trade competition raises emotional concerns for many Americans—from anxiety about job security in a dynamic world economy, to concerns about environmental degradation, to general feelings of unease about foreigners—it has undeniably become a crucial source of American jobs, business opportunities, and economic growth.[2] In short, trade and global commerce can work to the advantage of American firms and workers, as exposure to global competition makes our economy more dynamic and successful, not less.

A philosophical commitment to free trade must address at least two realities. One is that trade and global commerce, despite their aggregate benefits, can cause painful displacements for specific workers, firms, industries, and communities. Since 1970, for example, the U.S. textile and apparel industries have lost over 700,000 jobs. Steel and automobiles have lost almost 500,000.[3] Increased global competition has been a central cause of these job losses, and is seen by many as *the* cause. The AFL-CIO Task Force on Trade points out: "During the 1980s, American-made products steadily lost ground in terms of world market share, but by transferring production overseas, American corporations maintained or increased their percentage of the world's exports."[4]

The second reality is that too often the world's trading system is not open and growing. Japan systematically limits imports and outside investment through a host of laws, regulations, and culturally ingrained practices. Mexico imposes high import tariffs. U.S. inventions are routinely pirated in other nations that pay little regard to a meaningful system of patents and copyrights. As a result of these and other barriers, and aggressive and sometimes hostile foreign government economic and technology policies, U.S. firms and workers can be placed at a disadvantage, at home and abroad, as they compete with their foreign counterparts. Stagnant economies in the developing world and a recession in the industrialized world further inhibit American global opportunities—exports cannot be a source of U.S. job growth if other world economies are stalled.

A NEW APPROACH

A commitment to open trade and commerce cannot be sustained, analytically or politically, unless it is coupled with an activist commitment to improve the world's trading rules and expand export opportunities and to help Americans succeed in, and adjust to, the increasingly competitive global economy.

A winning trade policy starts with steps to build our economic resources and empower firms and workers to be more productive: improvements in education and skills for the entire work force, through such measures as worker training; government assistance for those hurt in the process of adjustment to the world's competitive forces;[5] improvements in the nation's transportation and communications infrastructure, through public and private investment; corporate reforms to expand employee participation; coordinated policies to facilitate the development and commercialization of critical technologies; new macroeconomic policies that promote savings and investment and a long-term plan to reduce the federal budget deficit.[6]

But policies to make our firms and workers more competitive are not enough. If we are to move beyond the controversy that surrounds trade, it must be clear to the American people that foreign markets are not hostile to our products, our jobs, our values, or our strategic interests. Our competitiveness policy must include an aggressive strategy to improve our international economic policies; eliminate foreign barriers to trade; promote U.S. export opportunities in growing world markets; and generally improve the rules under which we and our trading partners compete.

In brief, this chapter argues that the Clinton administration should:

- Elevate trade as part of foreign policy.
- Take steps to complete the General Agreement on Tariffs and Trade (GATT) Uruguay Round so effort can shift to even broader multilateral efforts to promote global economic expansion.
- Expand on GATT rules through bilateral market-opening

initiatives, especially with the E.C. and Japan, and by implementing the NAFTA.

- Seize opportunities to promote economic growth in tandem with noneconomic values, such as human rights, environmental protection, and promotion of democracy.
- Reorganize the government to reflect and carry out our new trade and economic priorities.

THE OLD APPROACHES

Rather than focusing on these challenges, past trade policies too often have wavered between strategies of "hands-off" laissez-faire and "hands-all-over" protectionism.

The laissez-faire model correctly celebrates how freer markets can expand opportunity, spur innovation, and raise productivity. But the model has no place for a competitiveness strategy. This makes no sense in the face of aggressive competition from countries that actively promote their industries and target ours, and in the face of the tremendous opportunity to foster global growth and opportunities for Americans by actively collaborating with our trading partners to align trade and economic decision-making and avert protectionism.[7]

Although the Reagan and Bush years did not hew tightly to the laissez-faire model, and although we obtained during those years—under Congressional and private-sector pressure—a range of market-opening accords that have benefitted the economy, the conservative approach minimized both the need for domestic action to enable U.S. firms and workers to succeed in the global economy and the need for an active, coordinated international commercial strategy.

The past two administrations' rhetorical devotion to free markets often seemed to be overwhelmed by their philosophical opposition to government activism. They neglected to help American workers and firms meet the challenge of global competition in open markets. They failed to promote public and private investment in education, training and retraining, and in research and development. Like other administrations before them, they failed to act promptly and effectively when other countries targeted our own industries, from autos to semiconductors.[8] They failed to offer dependable financing, promotional or informational support—at home or on the ground in foreign markets—for many U.S. firms as they sought to export and flourish abroad.[9] They failed to recognize how steps to open our domestic markets to more competition could be used to promote open markets abroad. For example, in the 1980s we deregulated long-distance telecommunications, unleashing competition to American Telephone and Telegraph from both U.S. and foreign firms, without insisting on commensurate access to the telecommunications markets of Europe and Asia.

This seeming indifference to trade dislocations, coupled with a willingness at times to put laissez-faire ideology aside when the interests of a major contributor were threatened, made GOP trade policies appear ad hoc, and made the mantra of free trade all the more suspect to many Americans. Moreover, the approach of the past decade tended to divorce trade policy from values about which many Americans care deeply. The Bush administration's refusal to take prompt action against evidence of Chinese imports produced by prison labor, for example, further fueled public alienation.[10]

In response, liberals have correctly underscored that trade policy ultimately must respond to and benefit a broader range of U.S. firms and workers, and must not undermine American values such as the protection of human rights and the environment. But many on the political left (and to be sure some notable spokesmen on the right) have channeled popular resentment toward foreign competition down the path of protectionism. Rather than emphasizing trade's benefits and urging improvement in its rules, these voices too often have focused disproportionately on how trade can eliminate jobs and cripple communities. Some have even fanned a mood of economic nationalism and have described trade as virtually a zero-sum game, in which foreign economic gains can only come at a cost to our workers and our environment.

But trade is not a zero-sum game. All countries that invest in the productivity of their own workers and firms can benefit from open and expanding markets. The healthy world growth of the 1960s, 1970s, and even the 1980s was fostered by the progress in opening markets under the GATT.

By contrast, protectionism, in both theory and practice, is a failed strategy. A country can increase jobs in a protected industry as a larger share of domestic demand for the industry's goods or services is satisfied by domestic companies. But the unavoidable consequence is less efficiency, smaller incomes, and slower growth for the entire economy. The resources vital to economic productivity and growth, from capital to labor, will flow away from more efficient sectors to the protected one. The artificial support for the protected sector will enable its firms to sustain themselves without taking steps to become more productive. Domestic prices for protected goods and services will be higher than without protection, harming consumers and, if the protected product is an economic input such as steel, other industries that depend on the input.[11] And when the economy finds itself at or near full employment, the extra demand channeled to the protected sector will fuel inflation, which in turn will lead to higher interest rates that depress the entire economy.

Some critics of traditional protectionism recently have advanced a new variant called "managed trade." Managed-trade theory arises in part from the important insight that an economy can reap special benefits by protecting its competitive positions, especially those of its high-technology industries. Industries such as semiconductors or biotechnology can stimulate innovation and productivity throughout an economy, leading countries such as Japan to both protect these sectors at home and target them abroad.[12]

Managed-trade advocates argue that rather than, or in addition to, pursuing policies of classical protection, the U.S. should undertake special market-sharing agreements with other countries, allocating a certain share of each country's market in a particular sector or product to foreign competitors. In practice such a policy often won't work effectively. Special-interest politics may step into the breach, channeling managed-trade supports to those sectors with the most political influence. Moreover, because capital is mobile, managed-trade agreements encourage firms to close down and open up operations according to the allocation of market shares. Foreign high-tech firms may set up shop in the U.S. and displace American firms in order to take advantage of the protected U.S. market; U.S. firms may set up shops abroad in order to participate in the protected foreign markets, costing U.S. workers jobs.[13]

A misleading polarization between laissez-faire and protectionism has left U.S. policy relatively rudderless in its economic diplomacy. The nation's international economic policy has even seemed to lurch from side to side within a single administration. The same President Bush who advocated a hands-off approach to trade went, hat in hand, to Japan in January 1992 to seek increased purchases of U.S. auto products.

Our trading partners appear similarly adrift. The past few years have seen a good deal of economic disarray, including gridlock in the GATT talks to open trade, and disharmony over issues as diverse as the environment and monetary alignment. Such disarray and disharmony can damage U.S. workers and firms by creating a climate where economic nationalism and regionalism can flourish, lead to closed markets and trade hostilities, and threaten U.S. export opportunities. It also can mean that important non-economic goals are short-changed. In the end, the lack of cooperative vision, especially in the face of a worldwide recession that further damages U.S. export growth, makes the need for U.S. engagement and leadership in the global economy pressing.

The end of the Cold War has created a new and important opportunity for such leadership. There are even fewer instances in which we (or our trading partners) need to make commercial concerns subservient to military imperatives. Scores of newly independent nations view the U.S. as a model and want to participate in the international trading system. And many lesser-developed nations continue to view expanded trade as their best hope to escape crushing debt burdens and raise their standards of living. President Clinton can use this moment to set a clearer and better course.

THE NEW COMMERCIAL DIPLOMACY

It is time for a change in our foreign policy priorities as fundamental as the changes that have swept the globe over the past four years. The most radical change must be this: Trade and economic success must now be considered a foreign policy priority every bit as important as geopolitical success. No one but the President can effect this kind of revolution in our priorities.

It is clear that, too often, competitiveness has not been at the top of our international agenda over the past 12 years. Perhaps most critically, we delayed action on important competitiveness problems, such as subsidized sales by the European Community (E.C.) government Airbus consortium, because they either weren't detected early or because they were implicitly or explicitly considered less important than maintaining friendly relations for overall geopolitical advantage. The same can be said for inaction or lack of effective action on consumer electronics and other issues with Japan. We simply have not understood or appreciated the importance to our national interest of prompt action to ensure competitive success. Moreover, our embassies and diplomatic missions abroad have failed to consider foreign trade and economic issues front-burner issues—with rare exceptions, ambassadorial and high-level staff attention on a day-to-day basis has been elsewhere.

There are three related steps the Clinton administration should take in order to elevate trade and competitiveness considerations as part of its foreign policy and to implement a muscular free-trade policy. First, it must focus on the cumulative effect of its policies that affect trade, and try to coordinate their impact in a way that improves the commercial success of American firms and workers. In substantial part, this means the administration must consider the impact on trade of its policy decisions in other areas, such as its macroeconomic stabilization, antitrust, investment, technology, and training policies.[14] We must avoid "unilaterally disarming"—taking steps that open our markets to foreign products and services without insisting on liberalization abroad. It also means that programs directly related to trade, such as export promotion and non-humanitarian foreign aid, do not work on an ad hoc basis. The Clinton administration should ensure that the resources spent under such programs flow from an overall competitiveness plan, and not just ad hoc political considerations; and that they benefit smaller exporters, and not just firms that are large or politically well connected.

Second, the Clinton administration should act more strategically. The policies of recent administrations ignored many early signs of American technological vulnerability, or anticompetitive practices by foreign governments or firms. This often led to reliance on cumbersome and adversarial remedies, such as antidumping suits, after the harm to U.S. competitiveness from those practices had been incurred.[15] These remedies often harm not only foreign governments and firms, but also other U.S. firms. For example, in a recent and controversial antidumping case involving laptop computer display screens imported from Japan,[16] duties were levied in spite of opposition from consumers—specifically the U.S. computer industry that depended on the foreign imports. Earlier intervention as part of a comprehensive trade and technology policy would have been preferable for both the industry and its customers.[17] U.S. foreign policy and intelligence agencies are ever alert to minute changes in other major nations' weapons production capacities, troop deployments, and governing coalitions, and to U.S. readiness. Now those agencies must develop a better capacity to detect and confront subtle changes in the competitiveness policies of our trading partners, and in the U.S. competitive position. By confronting such strategic concerns in their early stages, we will enhance our competitive position, and may often be able to address through pro-competitive domestic policies or quiet diplomacy what later might require angry negotiations, sanctions, or litigation.

Third, the Clinton administration must insist on results. It must be willing to use the strongest measures available to produce more open markets, and then to keep them open and growing. Moreover, U.S. trade and economic policies should be as well coordinated toward a "bottom line" of competitiveness as our military, industrial, and diplomatic efforts are toward victory in wartime.[18] As part of a strategy that uses all sources of economic and political leverage, we should use such tools as Section 301[19] to press for trade and investment agreements that spur global growth and gain reductions in foreign barriers,[20] and we should be willing to use sanctions where less confrontational strategies have failed to produce timely results. Credible threats are usually politically difficult, but they are essential: Most of the major market openings achieved in recent years, such as those in telecommunications, supercomputers, and satellites, have been under threat of sanctions. The administration should be ready to inform unfair traders as early as possible that specific sanctions will be imposed at a specific time unless the offending practices end. As such threats become credible, they will reduce the likelihood that sanctions will actually need to be imposed, and give U.S. firms hurt by such sanctions more time to anticipate and adjust to such measures.

These three steps should be applied with all trading partners and across all sectors of the U.S. economy. Taken together, they form the foundations of a new commercial diplomacy.

MULTILATERAL AGREEMENTS: COMPLETING THE GATT URUGUAY ROUND AND MOVING BEYOND IT

The best way to liberalize global trade and foster global economic growth is through global rules. The GATT, to which 105 nations currently belong, represents a steadily evolving set of global rules and standards for international trade. It has so far gone through eight "rounds" of negotiations, including the current Uruguay Round (the Round). Past GATT rounds have made significant contributions to global economic expansion. Moreover, the existence of the GATT process has reduced the tendency of the major trading powers to resort to hostile economic practices and to erect exclusive and discriminatory bilateral or regional trading blocs.

The current Uruguay Round of GATT negotiations is especially important. Its agenda has gone beyond the traditional terrain of tariffs and non-tariff barriers, to previously uncharted territory. The negotiations cover sectors of the world economy, such as services and investment, not previously subject to trade rules but likely to produce the fastest growth in global opportunities for American firms and workers; conceptually difficult issues, such as intellectual property rights; and, economic sectors, such as agriculture, that in most major trading nations are politically powerful and long accustomed to government subsidies. Successful resolution of such issues on a global basis would be an important step toward making world trade both more free and more fair.

But the Uruguay Round has languished. It has dragged on for nearly two years past its initial December 1990 deadline. The Round's potentially great gains have remained quite potential. Its never-ending nature has undermined popular faith in global rules for free trade and the will of individual nations to act globally and collaboratively rather than bilaterally or alone. The elusiveness of its agreements has bolstered the arguments of those who view the pursuit of broad, global rules for freer commerce as a waste of time and resources.[21] In the U.S., in particular, the inability to bring the Round's negotiations to a close has required pro-trade forces to expend political capital on periodic renewal of "fast track" negotiating authority.[22]

The particular stubbornness of the Uruguay Round thus has collided with the general attractions of multilateral trade agreements. It is time to complete this GATT Round. Very soon after taking office, President Clinton should take stock of the negotiations, and seek to close quickly on a realistic package. Its goal should be to take what gains we can, and to provide a framework for further expansion of trade rules—in later rounds and through other negotiating forums—in the areas where agreements cannot be concluded.[23] In particular, the administration should take three steps to close out the Uruguay Round:

1. **Don't let the perfect become the enemy of the good.** The U.S. should not hold out for an ideal agreement if we can achieve satisfactory results. In particular, we should move to conclude the Uruguay Round if the overall package is balanced, and if it secures some immediate market opening and establishes frameworks for further liberalization in key areas. These areas include services[24] and investment, intellectual property rights,[25] textiles,[26] agriculture,[27] subsidies, and dispute settlement. Pragmatism on these points is especially warranted since trade liberalization can never be fully comprehensive; there will always be new barriers to ad-

dress, particularly in the dynamic sectors of the economy that are at the heart of the Uruguay Round.

2. **Retain full rights to take further action outside the GATT.** The U.S. should not agree to provisions that would undermine our authority to take any necessary actions under U.S. laws in order to address issues that this Round fails to address satisfactorily. Nations must be able to work for further liberalization—bilaterally, regionally, or multilaterally.

3. **Engage Japan and the E.C. to help close the Round.** The Round can end quickly as soon as Japan and the E.C., in addition to the U.S., decide it is in their respective self-interests to conclude it. Therefore, the Clinton administration should make clear to both parties that it is prepared to take bilateral steps in the key sectors at issue in the Round, and to use other types of diplomatic pressure including appropriate geopolitical leverage, if they do not work with us for the best and quickest possible resolution of the Round.

The tough U.S. position to impose retaliatory duties against E.C. soybean and other oilseed subsidies, in the absence of an E.C. commitment to cut these subsidies, is entirely consistent with aggressive efforts to close the Round on reasonable and balanced terms. This policy is essential both to show U.S. resolve in the face of repeated denial by the E.C. of access to its oilseeds market, and to preserve the credibility of the current GATT system, which has ruled that the soybean program impairs U.S. rights under current GATT law. At this writing, the E.C. has not complied with the GATT ruling. The U.S. position underscores our commitment to take tough action to enforce our trading rights and shows how high the stakes are if we don't come to closure in the Round soon. The U.S. tried less confrontational approaches for six years, and delayed retaliation for 30 days to give the E.C. a chance to avert sanctions, and close on a fair deal. That was more than enough time to wait.[28]

Even before the Uruguay Round has concluded, the Clinton administration should start developing its strategy for the multilateral efforts that will succeed it. The scope of the world's trade negotiations and multilateral economic coordination will have to expand radically if global rules and collaboration are to keep up with the global economy. The Uruguay Round broke new ground in tackling internal policies toward such matters as copyrights and patents that can affect the terms of global trade, and in recognizing that they should conform to some global standards. This recognition opens the door to examining scores of other issues that have been largely outside the realm of trade negotiations or have been otherwise poorly or inconsistently coordinated globally. Consider the public policies that can affect the prices of any nation's goods and services: a nation's fiscal policy and tax structure; its health care system; environmental regulations; labor laws; technology strategies; its infrastructure plans. These all can have a critical impact on the terms of global trade,[29] but all were long considered to be overwhelmingly domestic matters—international coordination and joint action have been ad hoc at best.

The expansion of trade negotiations and international collaboration in these areas may become the most challenging aspect of international economic policy in coming decades. Global standards in these areas will edge the world's trading nations toward economic convergence—that is, toward increasingly consistent policies on the topics negotiated. Such convergence, as long as it does not compromise legitimate aspects of each nation's sovereignty, should help create a more open and sustainable global trading system, increase global prosperity, and expand global market opportunities for U.S. firms and workers.

The U.S. should support the prompt development of recommendations by the G7 nations[30] on the agenda for a new global trade and economic round or series of rounds to address such issues, to further liberalize in sectors affected by Uruguay Round rules, and to develop new common guidelines for bilateral and regional agreements across trade and trade-related issues. The recommendations must take into account the need to promote global cooperation on related foreign policy issues, such as environmental protection,[31] and the need for new common guidelines on the use of economic sanctions in response to such matters as weapons proliferation, human rights abuses, and foreign corrupt practices.[32] Adequately addressing this new slate of global challenges likely will require changes in the institutions that grew out of the Bretton Woods agreements of 1944—the GATT, the International Monetary Fund, and the World Bank.

OPPORTUNITIES FOR BILATERAL PROGRESS

Bilateral initiatives, such as those between the United States and the European Community, or the U.S., the E.C., and Japan, must play a key role in the Clinton administration's overall competitiveness strategy. The U.S., E.C., and Japan all should have strong incentives to work cooperatively to achieve global agreement on promoting economic growth, by facing up to the complex issues confronting us in the GATT and beyond. None has disproportionate economic strength, and all rely heavily on global trade and investment flows. Trade wars of any magnitude would hurt each and all of us.

The Clinton administration's bilateral trade agenda should take advantage of this interdependence to press for E.C. and Japanese cooperation to achieve mutually beneficial global economic expansion, reductions in barriers, and harmonization of policies.[33] In the near term, the U.S. must work with the E.C. and Japan to improve macroeconomic coordination, especially through interest rate action, to stimulate recovery in the advanced economies. The administration also should apply bilateral pressure, with regard to both Japan and the E.C., in order to complete the Uruguay Round.[34]

In addition, because achieving global agreement on many of the new trade and economic issues that lie at the heart of convergence may be quite difficult in the near term, forays into such issues will continue to take place within smaller, bilateral trade talks.[35] Bilateral and regional talks will also be crucial because such forums often offer the quickest means to address the most salient trade concerns of average Americans: the concern of the midwestern farmer over European crop exports that enjoy government subsidies; the concern of the autoworker over imports of Japanese cars; the concern of the Texan over environmental conditions along the Mexican border. Thus, political pressure is likely to drive the Clinton administration to focus on its bilateral efforts, specifically with regard to the E.C., Japan, and our trading partners in North America:[36]

1. **The European Community**. The U.S.–E.C. commercial relationship recently has been marked by conflict on many issues, such as commercial aircraft, a range of agricultural disputes (from oilseeds to the use of hormones in beef), government purchasing of telecommunications and heavy electric equipment,[37] and sales of U.S. films and other "cultural products."[38] Those tensions have been underscored by the impasse in the Uruguay Round over agricultural subsidies. The Clinton administration must recognize the paramount importance of cooperation with this economic region that will soon be the world's largest trading bloc, accounting for twelve nations and 300 million people. But it must also insist that the E.C.'s markets become as open to our firms as our markets are to European firms.

The U.S. should pursue regular consultations with the E.C. on

global and bilateral economic policies, coordinated by a high-level
E.C. Working Group. This Working Group should seek to address
many of the new aspects of convergence discussed above, and
should push for the most liberalizing rules possible as the E.C.
continues to harmonize economic rules among its own members.[39]

Where disputes with the E.C. exist, the Clinton administration
should refrain from moralizing about the E.C.'s failures, but
should still insist on a full resolution and comparable opportunities
for U.S. firms. In addition to oilseeds, a good example is Airbus,
the commercial aircraft produced by a consortium of four E.C.
members. E.C. governments have contributed an estimated $26
billion in subsidies to the development of Airbus, and have offered
subsidized financing terms for Airbus customers as well.[40] While
the U.S. and the E.C. recently reached an agreement putting limits
on Airbus subsidies, it is critical that it be tightly enforced in the
future and that its subsidy restrictions on aircraft be broadened
and extended globally.[41] E.C. support for this should be ensured
through dialogue and monitoring, and backed up by the threat of
fully countervailing U.S. measures in the event that broader disci-
plines cannot be achieved within a reasonable time.[42]

2. **Japan**. The U.S. trade relationship with Japan, the world's
second largest economy, has been in many ways our most challenging bilateral relationship. President Clinton should attempt to
work closely with Japan to expand global trade. He should also
pursue an aggressive, pro-competition strategy to open up and
improve access to the Japanese market and to redress a trade
imbalance that has become a serious economic and political problem for our countries.[43]

This bilateral relationship, in particular, demands frank and
personal diplomacy from the President himself. This does not
mean he should involve himself in the details of sectoral disputes;
nor does it mean he should lead favor-seeking trade missions, as
President Bush's trip to Japan in 1991 appeared to be. But the
President should meet with the Japanese prime minister early in
the new administration to underscore his commitment to economic security as a priority in his foreign policy, and to emphasize
his particular dedication to comprehensive economic collaboration with Japan. He should seek Japan's cooperation in a long-
term process of global economic coordination,[44] and he should
encourage Japan to adopt expansionary policies to reduce its $100-
billion trade surplus.

The Clinton administration should also establish a U.S.–Japan
Trade Forum, in order to institutionalize high-level negotiations

with Japan on the elimination of trade barriers affecting many different sectors of both economies, and on economic convergence. The trade forum would be staffed in the U.S. by a Japan Working Group, parallel to that established for talks with the E.C. The Structural Impediments Initiative, begun under President Bush, began to focus on many key issues contributing to our bilateral trade deficit with Japan. But it lacked the long-range follow-through needed to effect fundamental change. The new U.S.– Japan Trade Forum can create a framework for long-term, regular negotiations to: curb global dumping;[45] ensure antitrust enforcement;[46] ensure procurement reform;[47] and make investment more open to foreigners.[48]

There is cause for optimism about the prospects for better long-term coordination and convergence with Japan, especially because there appears to be greater support emerging within that country for such efforts.[49] U.S. pressure should reinforce that internal support. The administration can give this process "teeth," and ensure that timely progress is made, by insisting on results and using creative tactics—including some Japan has used in the past—to get them. For example, the U.S. could make it clear that export financing assistance and other types of U.S. federal and state assistance would not be available to U.S.-based Japanese firms unless the offending practices end.[50] The administration should also be willing to use political leverage—such as linking support for Japan's joining the United Nations Security Council to sustained responsible behavior by the Japanese government on both opening Japan's market and engaging actively to promote global growth, including through broader global trade rules.

The Clinton administration can supplement presidential diplomacy and institutionalized negotiations with Japan over structural trade barriers with the use of Section 301 in certain strategically important areas. Such targeted action may be essential both economically and politically to achieve change in the short term, and to secure Japan's active engagement in longer-term efforts to improve multilateral trade and economic rules. Sectors and technologies should be chosen for action on the basis of their importance to U.S. competitiveness and their relevance to the widest range of products and services. The Clinton administration's negotiators should focus on securing competitive purchasing opportunities from both the Japanese government and private Japanese firms, from design through delivery, and should back up these efforts with credible sanctions.

3. **The North American Free Trade Agreement.** While the politi-

cal importance of the NAFTA in the recent campaign was probably disproportionate to its practical importance as a trade agreement, it nonetheless is a milestone agreement and one that is beneficial to the U.S. As part of an overall strategy to expand foreign markets, the Clinton administration should move quickly to enact legislation to implement the NAFTA, and to ensure that it works well.[51]

The NAFTA, as initialled by the U.S., Mexico, and Canada, covers a broader range of subjects than the Uruguay Round and can serve as a model, on many points, for how to move ahead on multilateral negotiations.[52] At the same time, it safeguards strategic interests in our own hemisphere. Over time, the NAFTA should produce a net gain of jobs for the U.S. It also should help improve working conditions in Mexico, which can help stem the flow of illegal immigrants from Mexico into the U.S.

The basic commercial terms of the agreement take important steps toward expanding trade and investment opportunities among the three nations. With regard to traded goods, all tariff barriers between the U.S. and Mexico will be phased out over 15 years. As a result, the share of U.S. industrial exports to Mexico subject to tariffs—and such tariffs now average 10 percent—will fall from 81 percent to zero. In services, including investment, the NAFTA is the most comprehensive agreement among major trading partners ever negotiated. In telecommunications, the agreement locks in important new rights and enables all U.S. firms to operate state-of-the-art communications systems in Mexico. In intellectual property, the NAFTA provides for higher standards of protection for U.S. patents, copyrights, trade secrets, and trademarks; these provisions will benefit a range of U.S. firms, including those in pharmaceutical, biotechnology, computer, and other high-technology fields.

Despite these important gains, there are still certain issues that the Clinton administration should address as part of its efforts to implement the NAFTA. First, it should improve the agreement's environmental safeguards. The agreement already includes some important new provisions on the environment.[53] But the Bush administration left several holes in essential environmental provisions. For example, the agreement establishes few, if any, joint commitments concerning benchmarks for measuring improvements in air and water quality, or management of hazardous wastes. It also creates no specific enforcement mechanism. These gaps are particularly troubling given the environmentally distressed condition of the border region, which has been characterized as a "cesspool" by the American Medical Association. At a minimum, binding commitments on improving those border conditions, and on Mexican environmental enforcement, should be in place before the overall agreement takes effect.[54]

The Clinton administration should also address the NAFTA's impact on jobs and labor standards. As part of a new and comprehensive jobs program, the Clinton administration should ensure that assistance and retraining are available and easily accessible for all those who suffer job dislocation as a result of the NAFTA. The administration should also develop additional bilateral understandings regarding labor standards and their enforcement, including provisions for periodic review and updating; and these should go into effect before, or at the same time as, the NAFTA.

PROMOTING U.S. VALUES IN TRADE

Western, and often American, technologies and products have become central images in many of the world's geopolitical dramas of recent years. A McDonald's gained customers in Moscow as the former Soviet Union shed republics. Fax machines became the communications link among pro-democracy protesters in China. Restrictions on western trade with South Africa helped Nelson Mandela walk from imprisonment to liberty. The lack of such restrictions apparently helped build Saddam Hussein's weapons of mass destruction in Iraq. These images suggest that the impact of global trade often goes far beyond economics.

Certainly, our commercial interests will sometimes conflict with our security and diplomatic interests. Because of this, many economists and trade experts, both liberal and conservative, argue that the U.S. should formulate its competitiveness policies largely without regard to other national policies, and without attempting to promote American values. However, with the Cold War over, with democracy on the march worldwide, and with new global sensitivity to such considerations as the environment and human rights, the Clinton administration has an unprecedented opportunity to advance our noneconomic values. In addition, it is increasingly the case that trade policies that reflect concerns over the environment, fair labor practices, and democracy will also be in the long-term commercial interest of both the U.S. and the specific firms involved.

The Clinton administration therefore should place an explicit emphasis on seeking out and exploiting mutually beneficial policies that promote both values and competitiveness objectives. Moreover, where trade tools will be effective in curbing foreign policies that offend American values, we should be willing to use them. For example, the administration should insist that the government evaluate applications for U.S. export assistance, in part, on their impact on such factors as the environment and foreign labor practices.[55] Some foreign nations can be expected to object, as they often have in the past, that raising such issues interferes with their sovereignty. That objection must be seriously considered, but ultimately balanced against our own strategic interests—for example, our interest in a healthy and habitable planet.

While the U.S. government will sometimes have to take unilateral action to pursue noneconomic objectives through its trade policies, such action will be far more effective and be more equitable to U.S. firms and workers when it is multilateral. There are always other supply sources and other markets if the U.S. acts on its own. The Clinton administration should therefore place a high priority on developing more extensive multilateral guidelines on the use of trade and economic tools to promote common values, and must coordinate such efforts with our trading partners. Such coordination has an additional benefit on such value-laden issues as human rights and democracy. When the U.S. acts alone to pursue such values through its trade policy, the target nation may dismiss the action as narrow moralizing. Multilateral action is much harder to dismiss, since it implicitly expresses standards that are more universally shared.

The Clinton administration should incorporate four noneconomic concerns, in particular, into its trade and competitiveness strategy:

1. **The environment**. In the long run, economic growth and environmental health are mutually dependent.[56] Wealthier nations invest more in environmental protection; nations that have not suffered environmental degradation can grow more crops, attract more business, and have healthier workers. This relationship provides a clear basis for incorporating environmental concerns into our trade strategies. There is a short-run justification as well. The absence of rules requiring environmental protection in many instances can be thought of as a government subsidy to a particular industry. For example, a nation that imposes no clear-cutting restrictions or reforestation requirements on its loggers essentially enables them to operate at an artificial cost advantage relative to loggers in nations that have such rules. It is therefore in the interest of the U.S., which has relatively strict environmental rules, to

insist that its competitors pursue comparable policies. This lends further support for strong environmental provisions in the NAFTA.

One of the priorities for the new administration, therefore, should be to develop with our trading partners new guidelines on environmental safeguards that should be incorporated into trade agreements (the NAFTA provisions are a first step), and guidelines on the use of trade sanctions as part of environmental agreements (such sanctions should be tied closely to offending practices, and not be disguised restrictions on international trade).

Ultimately, incorporating environmental concerns into U.S. trade policy should create more opportunities than restraints. The annual global market in environmental products and services is already approaching $300 billion.[57] Major environmental projects planned in the former Soviet bloc, Taiwan, and Europe, as well as tighter and better enforced worldwide environmental laws, will only expand this market. The U.S., which pioneered many aspects of environmental protection, should be well suited to capitalize on the market for environmental technology and services, yet it has lost significant market share to Japanese and European firms. The Clinton administration therefore should view this area as especially conducive to the pursuit of economic and noneconomic goals simultaneously.

2. **Human and labor rights**. While it is clear that freer markets have created some pressures for freer political institutions in many nations, from China to Latin America, it is equally clear that capitalism by itself does not ensure either the advent of democracy or respect for human rights. The Clinton administration should be prepared to make strategic use of trade tools, combined with other diplomatic initiatives, where such actions offer a real opportunity to achieve critical human rights objectives. One example, of course, was the set of multilateral sanctions imposed against South Africa's apartheid regime.

The most important application of this principle may be the People's Republic of China (PRC). It is always difficult to target trade sanctions in a way that only damages those at fault; some U.S. importers and progressive Chinese entrepreneurs may well suffer from any restrictions. But as suggested in chapter 13, China's use of prison labor to produce goods sold in the U.S., as well as its brutal and continuing suppression of the pro-democracy movement, justifies further action, carefully targeted at the central government, to improve China's performance on human and labor rights. Our economic leverage with the PRC is powerful—we are the PRC's largest foreign market, and total bilateral trade has grown from $2.3 billion in 1979 to over $25 billion in 1991. And that leverage will be even more powerful if we act in concert with our other trading partners and multilateral banks.

3. **Arms control**. The Persian Gulf War highlighted some of the problems with pursuing trade in a world where weapons proliferation is a growing concern. Much of Iraq's arsenal was constructed with western weapons, or purchased from countries with whom the West actively trades. Yet the fight against weapons proliferation may be one of the most difficult noneconomic objectives to pursue through our trade policies, especially if we attempt to act unilaterally. Unilateral reliance on export restrictions on U.S. high-technology products (not primarily designed for military use) has damaged U.S. competitiveness in several key products and technologies—such as advanced materials, commercial aircraft and jet engines and computers—too often without succeeding in curbing the offending practices.[58] In many cases, U.S. export controls do not substantially impact the availability of proscribed materials on the world market, while costing billions of dollars a year in lost trade.[59] The use of economic leverage to address weapons proliferation is simply not likely to be effective unless it is very substantial and fully coordinated with other major trading nations. It should therefore be a last resort. While successful nonproliferation policies will require some export controls on "dual use" technologies—sophisticated equipment that can be used for both civilian and military purposes—these must be fully coordinated with our trading partners.

4. **Promoting democracy**. As we argue elsewhere in this book, the expansion of democracy abroad is likely to advance U.S. strategic interests enormously over the coming decades, and active support for this democratic tide should become one of the central organizing principles of the new administration's foreign policy. The success of many of the new democracies will depend, in part, on their success in improving the standard of living for their people. While the U.S. cannot guarantee the success of these new governments, we can increase the probability that democracy will take root by expanding our trade and economic ties with such nations.

In many cases we should seek expanded economic relationships with these nations simply because of the future markets they represent. But in some of these cases the Clinton administration should support expanded trade relationships, including export financing and other assistance, to nations struggling to foster free markets and societies, even where such efforts might not be fully justified by their immediate economic benefits to U.S. firms and workers. Examples include some of the new democracies of Eastern Europe and Latin America.[60]

ORGANIZING TO WIN

New priorities require new institutional arrangements. If the Clinton administration is going to elevate trade and competitiveness within its foreign policy priorities; if it is going to expand the scope, pace, and impact of multilateral and bilateral trade talks; if it is going to coordinate the pursuit of trade and noneconomic goals—then it will need to reorganize the system the government uses to pursue its trade and competitiveness objectives.

Right now myriad different agencies assert some jurisdiction over trade matters. Both the Office of the United States Trade Representative (USTR) and the Department of Commerce (DOC) have some trade negotiating and analytic functions. Moreover, State, Treasury, Labor, Agriculture, Transportation, Defense, and other agencies are represented on a regular basis in the development of trade decisions. Many of these agencies have trade sections that devote a great deal of time to analyzing the same trade issues, or even monitoring what USTR is doing (thus expending resources watching other agencies instead of monitoring trading partners and industry needs). Still other agencies are involved in export assistance and financing. The federal loans, loan guarantees, and insurance programs involved in these efforts have not been well coordinated.[61]

Although a range of interagency perspectives can be and often are useful, today trade policy formulation too often is fragmented and cumbersome. There is a great deal of redundancy that results more in inefficiency and bureaucratic infighting than in better policy. Telecommunications provides an excellent example of overlapping functions. In this area, four different agencies (Commerce, State, USTR, and the Federal Communications Commission) often have duplicative jurisdiction. Moreover, most of these agencies also have competing intra-agency jurisdiction (the National Telecommunications and Information Agency and the International Trade Administration at Commerce; Economic and Business Affairs and Communications and Information Policy at State; Services and Industry at USTR).

Only a fraction of the National Security Council (NSC) staff work on trade and competitiveness concerns, and the Council's role in many cases has been to ensure that trade does not interfere with smooth diplomatic relations—rather than to ensure that diplomatic relations promote trade and economic objectives. Economic and business activities at the State Department—both in Washington and in the field—very frequently are secondary to other activities, and in general the "fast track" jobs are not there.

This situation may have been tolerable when trade and competitiveness were second-order policy concerns. It is no longer tolerable given the rise of a global economy and the end of the Cold War. Bureaucratic reorganization alone will not solve the problem; President Clinton himself must elevate the importance of trade and competitiveness. But if that personal commitment exists, then reorganization will also be necessary to ensure that our new commercial diplomacy is coherent, coordinated, strategic, results-oriented, and incorporated into the highest levels of the government's decision-making. The administration should take two general steps:

1. **Reorganize the White House's National Security Council.** In an age when national security increasingly depends on economic security, the staffing of the President's National Security Council (NSC) should be reorganized to give much greater weight to economic concerns. The NSC staff should be given a mandate to advise the President on aspects of our competitiveness strategy such as: how to open key trading markets; how to balance key trade-offs in bilateral and multilateral trade talks; how to coordinate G7 macroeconomic policies to promote global growth; what the potential impact of proposed regulatory and deregulatory actions are on U.S. competitiveness; whether there is a national interest in preserving key manufacturing capacities; whether government should fund development of certain technologies; whether or not particular foreign policies take proper account of trade concerns; or whether and how to use trade policy to further noneconomic goals such as human rights and the promotion of democracy.

It makes sense to incorporate such economic concerns into a single NSC, which will force the President's staff to prioritize economic and military concerns in tandem. The total size of the new NSC staff should be small; it should act as an elite think tank for the President. However, the assistant to the President for national security affairs should have two deputies—one for trade and economic issues, and one for military issues. And the assistant to the President for national security affairs should have a substantial background in trade and commercial issues.

2. **Consolidate existing trade agencies into a Department of Trade and Technology.** The Clinton administration should take steps to create a Department of Trade and Technology that can eliminate much of the overlap and disarray in our current trade and competitiveness policies.[62] The new department would combine the functions of USTR and the international trade functions of the Department of Commerce.[63] Both agencies would be eliminated in their current form. (As noted in other chapters, non-redundant DOC functions should be reassigned.) The new department should have primary responsibility across all goods and services sectors for negotiating and implementing trade agreements,[64] for operational and analytic support, for technology policy, for many import and export controls, for export promotion, and for liaison to industry, labor, and environmental groups.

To improve export promotion,[65] the Clinton administration should coordinate federal export financing programs from the new department.[66] Special emphasis must be placed on financing for all qualified firms in key emerging markets where private-sector help is limited, on financing and investment guarantees for smaller businesses seeking to break into foreign markets, and on start-up financing to develop and bring to market new products and services.[67] Non-humanitarian foreign-aid projects should be targeted to stimulate growth in the recipient country and open up new markets for exports of U.S. products and services. The department should also work with the states to provide critical information on foreign markets (as well as new technologies and manufacturing techniques) to local firms. Although states and the private sector must take the lead in providing customized export assistance services to local firms,[68] the federal government is in the best position to obtain and analyze foreign market intelligence.

A new program of training in trade and industrial issues for the career trade service (as well as for those serving in critical economic positions in the State Department[69]) should be created that would be as extensive as that now given to foreign service officers. In addition, the Clinton administration should develop new mechanisms to permit improved consultation with a wide range of private companies, labor, and independent experts. In a constantly changing global and technological environment, useful analysis of trade and technology policy is not possible without systematic interaction with a broad range of private parties.[70]

MANDATE FOR ACTION

1. **Elevate trade and other economic concerns in U.S. foreign policy through a new commercial diplomacy.** President Clinton should use his ample authority to ensure that U.S. trade policies are *well coordinated,* so that we consider the impact of all economic and regulatory policies on the competitiveness of U.S. firms and workers; *strategic,* so that we empower firms and workers and open markets in advance of trade crises; and *results-oriented,* so that common rules of trade genuinely lead to success for competitive U.S. firms.

2. **Complete the GATT Uruguay Round and move beyond it.** The President should move swiftly to conclude the Round on balanced terms, in order to take advantage of the consensus on broad liberalization already reached and to avoid further undermining popular faith in the importance of global free trade rules. He should use U.S. trade and other diplomatic leverage to encourage Japan and the European Community to help us close the Round. In addition to removing market barriers, promoting global growth requires that the U.S. harmonize fiscal, monetary, and environmental policies with our main trading partners.

3. **Expand upon GATT rules through bilateral market-opening initiatives.** President Clinton should engage in personal diplomacy and create high-level working groups to reach, and then monitor the long-term success of, market-opening agreements with Japan and the European Community. These groups should focus on issues that affect the terms of trade in many sectors, such as subsidies and industrial targeting and antitrust policy. To ensure results, the President should make it clear that he is prepared to use U.S. trade laws, such as Section 301, and other forms of leverage.

4. **Press Congress to implement the North American Free Trade Agreement and seek new understandings on labor and environmental standards.** The NAFTA will be a net plus for the U.S. on jobs and economic growth, as well as a model for global agreements in many areas. In addition, the Clinton administration must take further steps to ensure enforcement of environmental and labor standards, and provide assistance for displaced U.S. workers.

5. **Advance America's trade goals in tandem with such noneconomic goals as promoting human rights and environmental protection.** Promoting American values, including human rights, labor rights, arms control, environmental protection, and democracy, should be a central element of the new commercial diplomacy. For example, we should impose stronger, targeted sanctions against the People's Republic of China because of their human rights abuses and suppression of pro-democracy activists. In shaping these policies, the following principles should apply: Action should be multilateral wherever possible, not unilateral; and both economic and noneconomic values should be advanced in tandem wherever possible.

6. **Reorganize the National Security Council staff to ensure that trade and economics become coequal with geopolitical concerns.** To institutionalize the new emphasis on competitiveness in the White House, the President should appoint two deputies to the assistant to the President for national security, one for military concerns and one for economic concerns.

7. **Consolidate federal trade-related functions in a new Department of Trade and Technology.** The Clinton administration should press for congressional cooperation to abolish USTR and the Commerce Department, moving their trade functions, and many similar functions in other departments, into a streamlined Department of Trade and Technology. The new department should have responsibility, in all goods and services sectors, for negotiating and implementing trade agreements, for operational and analytical support, for technology policy, for export financing, for many import and export controls, and for liaison to industry. By replacing many of the duplicative and fragmented divisions and agencies involved in trade today, such a department would provide better coordination and leadership on these critical issues.

5

A Progressive Plan for Affordable, Universal Health Care

JEREMY D. ROSNER

INTRODUCTION

In 1970, U.S. public and private spending on health care roughly equaled our public and private spending on education. In 1992, we will spend more on health care than on all of education—*plus all our nation's spending on defense, prisons, farm subsidies, food stamps, and foreign aid.* [1] Health care costs, climbing at twice the rate of inflation since 1981, have become the fastest growing major expense for the federal government, most state governments, many businesses, and millions of American families. [2]

Health care spending increased from 7 percent of our national output in 1970 to about 14 percent today, but few Americans believe the value of that care has doubled. [3] Ninety percent of all Americans are dissatisfied with the health system, the highest level of dissatisfaction among developed nations. [4] More than 60 million Americans periodically lack health coverage and 35 million lack any insurance whatsoever. [5] Insured families increasingly find their coverage at risk due to job loss, small businesses' difficulties in affording coverage, or benefit cutbacks for corporate employees and retirees. Despite the high quality and degree of choice within parts of U.S. health care, the cost of our medical system has outstripped its value.

Reforming that system may well be the largest domestic initiative for the next administration and Congress. Their new policies to control health spending and expand coverage will not only touch the health and security of most American households, but will also affect some nine million workers in an $800-billion economic sector, a figure that approaches the entire economy of Great Britain.

Most Americans agree our health care system should deliver high quality care, reasonable prices, broad access, and consumer choice. Yet the debate over reform is deeply divided. The most widely reported division is over how to finance expanded access to health insurance: whether to adopt a government-financed single-payer approach, an employer-based pay-or-play scheme, or a system of tax credit vouchers. This, however, is *not* the most important choice. Far more fundamental is the choice of how to restrain our health system's runaway costs. Many on the political right, including the Bush administration, suggest "the market," without fundamental reform, can cure the health care system's ills. Some on the left suggest that "the market" does not apply to health care, and so government must step in to set limits on health care prices, and perhaps to become the sole health insurer as well.

This is a false choice. The proper role for government, on health care and elsewhere, is neither to let broken markets run amok, nor to replace the market with bureaucratic mechanisms that set prices and allocate resources. Rather, government's primary role should be to improve the market's ground rules in order to decentralize decision making, spur innovation, reward efficiency, and respect personal choice.

The new administration's goal should be to achieve comprehensive health care reform and universal coverage without imposing public price controls and bureaucratic budgeting mechanisms on the U.S. health care system. We offer a comprehensive, market-based proposal built on the concept of "managed competition," which would result in universal coverage, restrained costs, incentives for efficiency and high-quality care, more equitable government subsidies, state innovation, and consumer choice. This approach offers the next administration a distinctly American model of reform—one that could leapfrog the performance of systems in other nations by building on the best of American medicine, capitalism, and federalism.

THE PROBLEM: FLAWED MARKETS

While the U.S. boasts many of the world's premier medical facilities, research institutions, and scientific breakthroughs, there is broad consensus that the health system requires fundamental change. Its problems are legion: soaring costs; declining insurance coverage; workers unable to change jobs due to uninsurable medical conditions; burdensome bureaucracy; rising billing fraud; little access to care for rural and inner-city residents; too many specialists and too few primary-care providers; inadequate prevention efforts; overuse of expensive technology; few affordable options for long-term care; doctors practicing "defensive medicine" to avoid malpractice suits; tragic numbers of low-birthweight babies; and high rates of unhealthy behaviors such as poor diet, smoking, alcohol and drug abuse, teen pregnancy, and firearms violence.

Yet many of these diverse problems trace back to one root cause: bad incentives. "Fee for service" insurance plans leave patients and physicians with little incentive to economize in demanding or prescribing tests and procedures. Insurance regulations, which allow premiums to be pegged to health status, give insurers an incentive to "risk skim"—to enroll healthier firms and reject firms with older or sicker employees. Most workers lack incentives or opportunity to seek more efficient health plans, since they receive an open-ended federal tax subsidy on their benefits, since most have little meaningful choice among plans, and since there is little information available on the relative performance of health plans. The list of skewed incentives goes on.

These adverse incentives add up to broken, inefficient, "cost unconscious" health markets. In well-structured markets, producers and consumers, pursuing their self-interest, can discover the best values—goods that meet a need at the lowest cost, sales that reap the highest profit—and their competition to find these values yields innovation and opportunity for society at large. But when consumers, providers, and others pursue their self-interest under our health markets' flawed rules, their efforts rarely single out the best values and often lead to socially harmful outcomes, such as inflated costs, unnecessary procedures, shrinking coverage, and discrimination against those with past illnesses. The first order of business should be a thorough reform of the ground rules in our health markets, particularly insurance, which is the funnel for most personal health spending.

But the idea of market-based reform has bogged down in polarized philosophies and rhetoric. On the right, President Bush introduced a health care reform proposal claiming it relied on the market to solve the system's ills.[6] That claim was untrue. Although the Bush administration's plan used market-based vouchers to provide somewhat greater access to insurance, it failed to remedy the worst incentives in the current health market. It did not reform the tax treatment of health benefits. It would not have led to universal insurance coverage. It did not create new insurance rules and institutions sufficient to end the risk skimming that has all but destroyed the private insurance market for small employers. As one commentator notes of the Bush plan, "ineffective proposals for market reform risk discrediting the whole idea."[7]

While the Bush administration's plan fell short, many Democrats in Congress have proposed single-payer or pay-or-play plans, most of which would significantly expand government's role as a direct insurer, and would rely on payroll taxes that could slow job creation and penalize low-wage workers. More troubling, however, most leading single-payer and pay-or-play plans call for national health care budgets and price setting, on the implicit grounds that market principles simply do not apply to health care.[8] This is demonstrably wrong. Certainly, there are many market failures inherent in health care,[9] and market forces cannot cure all of the health care system's ills. In particular, there are severe limits on how well market forces can work for direct consumer purchases of basic medical services; for example, no one could be expected to compare hospital rates at the moment they are struck with a heart attack. Yet most of American health care is provided through the private sector, and there is ample evidence that consumer choice and market forces can function effectively—under the right rules—in health insurance.

Democratic leaders in Congress deserve credit for drawing attention to the soaring health costs, benefit cutbacks, and gaps in insurance that have beset the nation's working families. But the bureaucratic models of reform that many of them have proposed would fall short of their authors' progressive goals. There is an opportunity now to move beyond the false choices that characterize the current health care debate—to recognize that market-based reform need not be callous or incremental; that universal coverage and restrained costs do not require public price setting; and that competitive markets can be consumers' and progressives' ultimate weapon.

We propose a Progressive Plan for health care that would comprehensively reform the health markets' ground rules, achieve universal coverage, enable consumers to shop for better value health plans, and focus providers on the highest value ways of delivering health care. The Progressive Plan builds on an approach to reform known as managed competition. Its core idea is this: The best means to hold down health costs is a market competition among private health plans that publicly report on their outcomes; and that competition must be managed by intermediaries to ensure the plans compete on the basis of value rather than risk.[10] As explained below, this concept is already working successfully in the health plans for public employees in California, Minnesota, and the federal government.

At the close of the last Congress, a path-breaking bill based on this approach, the Managed Competition Act, was introduced by Representatives Mike Andrews, Jim Cooper, Dan Glickman, Dave McCurdy, and Charles Stenholm, and by Senators John Breaux and David Boren. It represents an important change in the terms of the health care debate, for it proves that reform can be comprehensive *and* market based. That concept appears to hold bipartisan appeal; both Governor Clinton and President Bush invoked "managed competition" during the recent campaign. The test will be whether the market-based aspects of this approach can survive those in Congress and elsewhere who seek to expand public price setting, and whether the comprehensive aspects of the approach can survive the many vested interests who would prefer not to reform our health system much at all.

THE CURE: A PROGRESSIVE PLAN FOR HEALTH CARE REFORM

The Progressive Plan for health care reform calls for a state-based, market-driven, pluralistic approach to achieve universal coverage and restore the link between health spending and health value.[11] While it differs in some respects from the managed competition plans already proposed, what is noteworthy are the central ideas it shares with them: reliance on consumer choice in well-structured markets rather than on publicly-regulated prices to control costs; reliance on private health coverage rather than on expanded public programs (such as Medicaid) to achieve universal access to care; tax reform to make government subsidies more progressive and less inflationary; and better incentives and information to help providers focus on the highest-value forms of health care. The Progressive Plan would work as follows:

1. **Consumer choice**. The best way for the U.S. to weed out

low-value health care spending is for individual consumers to exercise choice among health plans—to vote with their own dollars on which health plans strike the best trade-off between economizing resources and delivering high-quality health care. To ensure that happens, the Plan requires every American to have the opportunity and obligation to choose among at least two private-sector health plans. This goal is effected through the tax code and other provisions, as explained below. To the extent consumers choose a higher-cost plan rather than a cheaper one, they must pay the full difference out of their own money without tax subsidies.

2. Universal coverage. The Progressive Plan would require health care coverage for all Americans. Universal coverage is fully justified on the grounds of equity, humanitarianism, and individual opportunity. But it is particularly important, on grounds of efficiency, in a market-based system. Without universal coverage, health providers in a newly competitive environment would minimize their uncompensated care for the uninsured in order to gain a price edge. Even more than under the existing system, the uninsured would be driven to delay needed care, which can result in more severe and costly health problems later, and to obtain care in less cost-effective sites, such as emergency rooms. The only effective way to prevent such discrimination against the uninsured with its resulting human toll and cost shifting is through universal coverage. This argument suggests a strong reason for those concerned about market efficiency to call for universal coverage, and it highlights a major economic shortcoming of supposedly market-based reforms, such as the one proposed by President Bush, which do not achieve universal coverage.[12]

3. Managed competition. For health plans to compete on the basis of value rather than risk skimming, the competition must be managed under some new rules. It must revolve around a standardized package of benefits, to be set by a new national board.[13] It also must be managed by an intermediary (health insurance purchasing cooperatives, or HIPCs) that can weed out practices that discriminate on the basis of health risks, aggregate the purchasing power of many thousands of consumers, and give small firms and the self-employed the administrative economies now enjoyed by large firms.

How it would work: *Federal legislation would define minimum requirements (size, governance, solvency, etc.) for HIPCs, through which most consumers would purchase their basic insurance coverage (the standardized benefits package).*

HIPCs could be quasi-public agencies, nonprofits, and potentially could take other forms as well, but in any case could not also be in the business of offering health plans.[14] Each year, the HIPCs would contract with a range of competing health plans and present this full range of plans to their customers. Consumers would select a health plan for one year, but then be free to change plans during an annual "open season." The HIPCs would provide their customers with materials that describe the plans and their performance, and act as the sole point of direct marketing allowed between insurers and consumers—another provision essential to prevent plans from risk skimming. To enable the creation of HIPCs and other parts of this plan, state laws restricting managed care would be preempted and the existing federal preemption of state regulation of employers' own health plans would be repealed.[15]

4. Informed consumers and providers. In order to create better information for both consumers and health providers, the federal government would define a set of reporting requirements for health plans, on such data as their use of resources, health outcomes, and patient satisfaction. This data would not only help consumers make informed choices among health plans, it would also become a critical body of data in helping providers determine what procedures and technologies work best.

How it would work*: Plans that agreed to report such information regularly (and that met other federal guidelines) would be certified as "accountable health plans." HIPCs could only market standardized benefit packages offered by accountable health plans, and consumers could only receive the tax credit described below if they subscribed to such a plan.[16] Accountable health plans would report the required information on a periodic basis to a new federal agency, just as competitors on our stock exchanges are required to report on their performance to the Securities and Exchange Commission. The new agency would develop procedures to protect patient confidentiality. A private-sector panel would set reporting standards, just as one now sets accounting standards to ensure that corporate reports flowing to the SEC are comparable.*

5. Tax reform. The Plan would end the practice of excluding employer-provided health benefits from taxation, and provide instead a tax credit against consumers' health costs. By doing so, the

Plan would eliminate one of the most regressive and inflationary sets of incentives in the current health care system.

> **How it would work:** *The Progressive Plan would only let firms deduct health benefits costs if they offered their employees a choice among at least two accountable health plans; and if they contributed a fixed dollar amount for each employee's basic health coverage, regardless of which plan was chosen, with the amount not to exceed 100 percent of the lowest cost accountable plan in the region. This provision ensures that consumers bear the full extra cost, or pocket the full savings, of choosing a costlier or cheaper plan, and would steer employer contributions toward accountable plans. In addition, the Plan would make any employer contributions to an employee's health benefits (directly, or through a HIPC) taxable as income. (Workers' W-2 forms would report both cash income plus any contribution the employer made toward health premiums.) Today's exclusion of these contributions from taxation would be replaced by a refundable fixed-amount tax credit for all households, up to some maximum income level, who subscribed to an accountable health plan through a HIPC.[17] To help achieve universal coverage, all taxpayers would be required to enclose a certificate as part of their federal income tax return proving they had obtained coverage.[18]*

6. Insurance reform. Federal law would set mandatory standards for state health insurance regulation, barring discriminatory practices among other things, and requiring all health plans to make coverage available and renewable without regard to preexisting conditions.

> **How it would work:** *The new law would ban health plans and insurers from charging different rates to different individuals, except to reflect certain actuarial factors or differences among contracts negotiated by different HIPCs.[19] When consumers bought basic coverage through a HIPC, they would be presented with a choice of plans, each with a schedule of rates for all members of that HIPC. Insurers marketing supplemental insurance also could not set rates based on the health experience of individuals or firms ("experience rating"). States and HIPCs would be encouraged to experiment with various forms of privately funded reinsurance and risk adjustment—systems*

to compensate health plans for an undue distribution of high-cost patients. Both HIPCs and the new federal SEC-like health agency would be empowered to investigate and discipline insurer practices by health plans that were found to be aimed at screening out high-risk, high-cost customers, such as only locating offices in wealthy neighborhoods.

7. State innovation. The Plan would make states the primary engine of reform, to spur responsiveness and innovation. The Plan would remove the barriers that effectively prevent states from pursuing comprehensive reforms, and then require that all states achieve universal coverage by some established date. The federal government would provide new resources to help them achieve this goal. Each plan would likely craft a unique approach, but the resulting plans would essentially be employer-based (like the Jackson Hole Group's plan), single-payer systems with competing private insurers (like the Garamendi proposal), or tax credit systems with little or no link to employers (as under the Heritage Foundation's approach).[20]

How it would work: *States would be required to enact a market-based model of reform that would achieve universal coverage for the standardized benefit package within a specified period (say, four years).[21] This transition period would enable states to phase in such provisions as new financial obligations for small businesses. The acute care portion of Medicaid (everything but long-term care for the elderly and disabled) would be abolished. States would continue to receive federal Medicaid funds in order to equalize their funding capacities, with some revisions in Medicaid's allocation formula to ensure that states' resources match their needs. States would be required to meet the acute care needs of their poor and disabled populations by subsidizing their purchase of private coverage through HIPCs. Federal waiver policies for both Medicare and the long-term care portion of Medicaid would be amended, to create more presumption toward innovation. Ultimately, Medicaid and Medicare could be fully integrated into the HIPC-based system. Federal provisions would ensure interstate portability of benefits. To promote public scrutiny of each state's choice of system, the federal government would collect and publish annual data on per capita health costs and outcomes by state.[22]*

8. Other. The Progressive Plan would also include:

- Medical malpractice reform, including both limits on awards and creation of alternative dispute-resolution methods.
- Federal leadership in cooperation with insurance plans to accelerate development of standardized and electronic billing and medical records.
- Federal and state efforts to expand the supply of health professionals and facilities in rural and inner-city areas, where their scarcity creates medical hardship and hampers the creation of effective health markets.
- Initiatives to address health-related behaviors and habits, among both patients and providers, which lead to poor outcomes or higher costs, including: expanded support for community-based efforts to improve outcomes; changes in federal policies regarding alcohol and tobacco; and possible changes in medical education curriculums and federal funding for medical research.

HOW THE PROGRESSIVE PLAN WOULD WORK FOR AN AVERAGE FAMILY

In many ways, consumers will obtain their health care much as they do now. They will still obtain health care through a range of private health plans, from health maintenance organizations (HMOs) to "preferred provider" physician networks to systems that virtually run on a fee-for-service basis. Each will have different rules about how enrollees choose their personal physician, how to see a specialist, and which hospital to use, and some may have very few rules on these issues (this will be one of the key aspects of the choice consumers will make among plans).

But in other ways, consumers will encounter a very different health care market. The biggest change will be that consumers, not their employers or the government, will make the decision of which health plan to join; and consumers, not their employers or the government, will pocket the savings that flow from making wise choices.

Consider Mr. Smith, an employee of a firm with 50 employees. He and his family currently have no choice among health plans; his firm offers one insurance plan, and pays half his premium. He has a heart condition, and knows that he would have trouble obtaining insurance if he changed jobs. Under the Progressive

Plan, by contrast, Mr. Smith can choose among a half dozen private health plans through a local health insurance purchasing cooperative (HIPC), and none of the plans can refuse to cover him for any reason. Once a year, during open enrollment, the HIPC sends the Smith family a booklet that describes the health plans with which the HIPC has negotiated contracts for the year. The booklet describes each plan, its resources, and its past performance, as measured by newly collected data on health outcomes, patient satisfaction, and the like. All the plans offer identical standardized benefits packages (although some also sell supplemental plans, to cover additional services). The data on outcomes, collected from all plans and regularly disseminated, helps Mr. Smith's health plan deliver his health care in the most cost-effective way.

During the first year of the Progressive Plan, Mr. Smith chooses the lowest price plan. Two years later, however, he decides this plan has been too restrictive in letting his family see specialists. That year, he switches to a plan that offers more freedom in selecting and seeing specialists. This plan costs somewhat more, and Mr. Smith himself pays the full difference.

The money Mr. Smith's employer was previously spending on health benefits, prior to enactment of the Progressive Plan, is now paid to the HIPC, and stays the same regardless of which health plan Mr. Smith chooses. That contribution shows up as taxable income on Mr. Smith's W-2 form; but he receives a federal tax credit that roughly offsets the additional taxes that result from this new "income" (as long as he attaches a certificate when he files his taxes proving that he is covered by an accountable health plan).

The reforms in each state may vary somewhat. But all states must ensure that the poor (as well as the unemployed, self-employed, etc.) can afford and obtain private coverage through a HIPC. All states will receive federal help in reaching that goal, since all of their low-income residents will receive a sizable, refundable tax credit. But each state may adopt different ways of providing the last margin of financing for their uninsured population, and may adopt different methods (such as mandates on employers or individuals) to help ensure that coverage is universal.

CONSUMER CHOICE IN ACTION: THREE PUBLIC EMPLOYEE HEALTH PLANS

There is already practical evidence that managed competition works. The health plan for federal workers and the ones for public employees in California and Minnesota already incorporate many of the features described above, and the results are impressive.

The Federal Employees Health Benefits Plan (FEHBP) covers some nine million Americans under a system that gives them a market-based choice among a wide range of competing private plans. This competition, managed by the federal Office of Personnel Management (OPM), helped hold FEHBP cost increases to an annual rate of 12 percent from 1980 to 1988, compared to 14 percent for private sector premiums over the same period.[23]

Minnesota also runs a multiple choice health plan system for its public employees, with about 120,000 persons covered. In the mid-1980s, the state changed the system in ways that made it more market-based and similar to managed competition. The state saw a dramatic slowdown in cost increases soon after. While the system's average premiums grew at double digits throughout the 1980s, their average annual growth rate for 1990–1993 has been 6.8 percent.[24]

The California Public Employees Retirement System (CALPERS), which covers some 800,000 people, has also proved the ability of a large health insurance purchasing cooperative to spread risk, cut administrative costs, and provide consumer choice. Like Minnesota, it recently changed its structure in ways that make it more market driven. Partly as a result, after seeing average premium increases of 16.9 percent and 11.3 percent in the two previous years, CALPERS's average premium increase was only 6.2 percent for 1992–1993, the first year premiums were negotiated since the rule changes.[25]

These systems, along with various studies, demonstrate that managed competition can dramatically control health costs, and that in well-structured health markets consumers can make informed choices based on the relative value of competing options.[26] The question arises: If millions of public employees already benefit from such a system, why shouldn't all Americans have the same opportunity?

ADVANTAGE ONE: MARKETS CONTROL HEALTH COSTS BETTER THAN PRICE SETTING

The Progressive Plan and other managed competition plans have many advantages over the other major health reforms. The most important is that they control the nation's runaway health care costs, not by having the public sector set universal health budgets and prices, but by using consumer choice and decentralized market forces to weed out the low-value parts of our excessive health spending.[27] While managed competition relies on regulation of the health market in certain ways, it focuses on regulating the ground rules of the competition, *not* the prices or volume of specific medical procedures. Price controls—public regulation of the price and volume of most medical procedures, as practiced under Medicare—appear to promise speed, certainty, and accountability in restraining health costs. But their proponents ignore the limitations of Medicare price setting and, more generally, the dismal record of price controls and central planning, from U.S. gas lines in the late 1970s to the worldwide fall of command economies in the past four years.[28] Specifically:

Markets are more likely to hold down health costs. While some have charged that all-inclusive national health budgets would lead to rationing, it may be more likely such budgets simply would not be met. Since most budgeted plans do not change the system's inflationary incentives, their effect would be like putting a lid on a boiling pot without first turning down the heat. At some point, the lid blows off. Medicare's price controls and existing state health budgeting efforts have an escape valve: Providers can make up any money lost due to the price controls by raising rates on nonregulated services or customers. Comprehensive budgets could make such cost shifting impossible, but then public budget-setters would win far fewer battles with providers. Exceptions and waivers would proliferate. Consider the Gramm-Rudman law: Congress exceeded every one of its supposedly binding annual budget limits—in the law's fifth year, by over $265 billion.

The Progressive Plan and other managed competition proposals, by contrast, simply turn down the heat, and provide a more comprehensive and sensible way to temper both consumer demands for services and provider demands for compensation. Public officials are not well suited to resist consumer and provider pressures; their political survival depends on saying yes. Health plan managers and personnel are ideally suited to balance those pressures; their economic survival depends on focusing both patients and providers on the most prudent and effective forms of care.

Markets are more effective at reducing low-value spending. Price controls, which have little means to reward high-quality medicine, would lock in or exacerbate the inefficiencies of our current health system. They would tend to cap prices for good and bad providers in equal measure. There is little question that Canada, Germany, and other nations with budgeted health prices have held their spending below American levels. But neither their experience nor our own suggests that public budgeting in the U.S. would help us weed out low value health care spending.[29] State rate setting (especially for hospitals) has had mixed results.[30] Medicare's system for pricing hospital services has restrained public spending in part by shifting costs onto private payers.[31] Public efforts here and abroad to limit physicians' fees have often resulted in physicians compensating for those limits by increasing their volume of procedures.[32] Medicare's new effort to control total physician costs, with across-the-board cuts in physician rates if necessary, may result in doctors performing a higher volume of services than needed, and not necessarily focusing on the procedures of greatest value to the patient.[33]

Under managed competition proposals, such as the Progressive Plan, the driving force for cost control would be neither a politically determined budget ceiling nor bureaucratic judgments about what constitutes a wise expenditure of health resources. Rather, it would be a consumer-driven competition among health care plans to provide the highest quality care at the lowest cost. Plans that cut costs without sacrificing quality could lower premiums and attract more customers. This competition would spur health plans to negotiate more aggressively with medical providers over prices. It would drive hospitals and clinics, in turn, to make hard choices about which acquisitions of expensive technologies they prudently can delay. It would leave health plans and physicians free to innovate on higher-value ways to deliver care while giving them better information for determining what procedures and delivery systems produce value. With this focus on value, the U.S. could actually leapfrog the health care systems in other developed countries—going from the most costly and arguably least efficient system in the developed world, to the only universal health care system organized around the principles of value and efficiency.

Faster, less bureaucratic, and more innovative. While budgets sound like a quick way to control health costs, public price setting is notoriously bureaucratic and slow. It would take years to develop the studies, regulations, and enforcement mechanisms needed to budget all of U.S. health care. Consider what it takes just to run Medicare, which accounts for less than a fifth of U.S. health spending. The Health Care Financing Agency (HCFA), which administers Medicare, must work with insurance carriers in each state to oversee more than 400 million bills from 7000 hospitals and 500,000 physicians, using 475 hospital price codes, and 7000 codes for physician payment.[34] Changes in this system proceed slowly. It took Congress and HCFA some five years to develop Medicare's new rate-setting system for physicians, which will phase in over an additional four years. That system's adjustments to physician rates each year will rely on 15-month-old data, and the system's methodology is required to be updated only every five years.[35] Medicare's regulations often lag years behind clinical innovations and provider scams. In the interim, existing regulations may discourage the use of newer and more cost-effective procedures, or overpay for an obsolete or low-value procedure. While Medicare has yielded its recipients many benefits, it would be a mistake to extend its cost-control techniques to the rest of the health care economy.

Market-based systems need some degree of regulation and public bureaucracy to set and enforce ground rules to ensure that specific health plans do not suffer from an undue concentration of high-cost patients, and to administer certain subsidies. But specific negotiations over prices and measurements of output and quality are left to private, decentralized negotiations, which tend to be quicker, more flexible, and less politicized. In FEHBP, for example, each of the participating health plans is free to negotiate rates with physicians and hospitals at will, and is instantly rewarded for cost-saving innovations. As the table on the next page suggests, this approach, relative to Medicare's centralized public price setting, leads to fewer public sector employees and fewer pages of statute and regulation per person insured. Certainly this is partly because HCFA carries out more of the insurance process for Medicare than OPM does for FEHBP. But that begs the question of what functions *need* to be carried out by the public sector, and the table suggests that FEHBP has produced an answer that relies far less on government. Nor is the issue administrative simplicity; Medicare boasts much lower administrative costs than the current private insurance market, probably including carriers that participate in FEHBP. The point, rather, is that private health plans in a competitive environment are more dynamic: they can and will exert stronger, quicker, and more fine-tuned cost controls internally than public regulators can impose from the outside. While private health plans have their own bureaucracies (including their own budgets and, often, price schedules), compared to public agencies each is far smaller and unencumbered with congressional second-guessing, multiagency sign-off procedures for new regulations, civil service rules, and other public constraints.

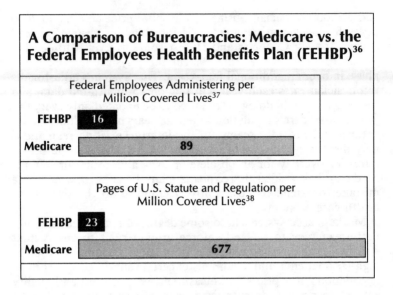

A Comparison of Bureaucracies: Medicare vs. the Federal Employees Health Benefits Plan (FEHBP)[36]

Federal Employees Administering per Million Covered Lives[37]

FEHBP 16
Medicare 89

Pages of U.S. Statute and Regulation per Million Covered Lives[38]

FEHBP 23
Medicare 677

More accountable and less politicized. Supporters of all-inclusive national health budgets claim that approach ensures political accountability. But the accountability is more to organized interests than the public. The history of Medicare is replete with cases of organized groups acting through Congress to add coverage for specific illnesses or procedures, or to affect changes in specific prices. If all of American health care functioned under a public budgeting system, health care firms and professions would have even more reason than they do today to make campaign contributions and exert political pressure on the health experts setting prices and the elected officials approving them (particularly members of key congressional committees). Populous states could be expected to use their political clout in Congress to press for favorable formulas in determining how the national budget was to be apportioned among the 50 states.

By contrast, the Progressive Plan and managed competition would be more accountable to *the public.* The key pressure point would be consumers' individual decisions about which plans to choose, not the decisions of a few public officials. Smart health plans would invest less on influencing public price-setting processes, and more on finding ways to cut costs without losing customers in each year's open enrollment.

Markets make government accountable in the right way. In a sense, health budgets make government *over-accountable*. They make every problem into a political problem, even on matters best resolved by the private sector. Every provider who feels his rate inadequately reflects some local variation; every patient who suffers waiting for use of a scarce technology; every hospital forced to effect layoffs—each of these individually wrenching problems is laid at the feet of the local member of Congress, and, ultimately, the party and the president responsible for creating and enforcing the public budget. And each effort to address such crises begets more detailed regulation.

Under managed competition, there is still accountability. A disgruntled patient can switch plans; an unhappy doctor can sign on with a different health plan. But, unlike in a budgeted system, neither is likely to focus as much resentment on public officials. The purpose of such an arrangement is not to abdicate public accountability, but rather to limit public accountability to the kinds of decisions the public sector is best suited to make. The public sector is the right place to make decisions about subsidy levels, methods of raising revenue, and the ground rules for health markets. It is the wrong place to make judgments about the relative values of procedures, providers, and systems for organizing and delivering care.

Mixing budgets and markets. Over the past year, the center of gravity in this debate between public budgeting and market competition fortunately has shifted toward markets. Unfortunately, many health reformers who have begun recognizing the value of competitive health markets still maintain we should expand public price controls and budgeting, either as a short-term solution, or as a complement to private competition.[39] New endorsements for national rate setting from prominent physician groups make this kind of mixed strategy seem politically possible.[40]

Some degree of public budgeting will need to occur under managed competition—if only to budget Medicare and public subsidies for lower income consumers. But, generally, a mixed strategy is a bad prescription. It repeats the key mistake of U.S. health care policy over the past 30 years: adopting fragmented policies for different parts of health care rather than one cohesive strategy. One leading argument for a mixed strategy—that tight budgets on fee-for-service medicine, with exemptions for HMOs, could push more providers into HMOs—ignores history and politics. There are few if any examples of regulators intentionally driving their subjects (even inefficient ones) out of business; more often, those who cannot survive in the market find a way to survive in the legislature. Thus, such budgets might simply perpetuate a safe haven for inefficient delivery systems. Moreover, the mammoth effort to create and enforce an all-inclusive national health budget would drain political and intellectual energy from the effort to create well-structured markets. Any ambitious health economist, politician, or lobbyist would want to be in the middle of the decisions over the budget and its price controls. Efforts to create a fundamentally new set of market rules would likely be placed on the back burner, where, in American politics, nothing ever boils.

A better strategy is to give a comprehensive market-based approach a chance to work. Later, if policy makers felt the need to do more to limit costs, they would be better able to do so. At that point, the system's incentives would work *with* budgets rather than against them—the heat would have been turned down under the pot. The information systems set up under this Plan would be producing more of the data needed to pursue budgets.[41] The fact that public budgeting remains an option may well prompt cooperation from some in the provider community who understand that their enlightened self-interest lies with better markets, not more regulation of prices and volume.

ADVANTAGE TWO: MORE EQUITABLE GOVERNMENT SUBSIDIES

One of many anomalies in the health care debate is the lack of attention to the inequities of the current tax treatment of health benefits. While reformers justify universal coverage in the name of equity, many of them ignore the distributional implications of the health provisions in our tax code, which are unfair not only to the poor and unemployed, but also to working middle-class Americans.

The fact is, the treatment of health benefits is one of the most pernicious elements of our tax code. These provisions are a prime culprit in rendering consumers and health providers cost unconscious and thus fueling health inflation. The current tax provisions are also enormously costly; in 1991 they lost over $66 billion in tax revenue, including federal income and payroll taxes, and about $88 billion including state taxes.[42] Those billions are distributed regressively, giving far more subsidy to upper-income households than those with lower or middle incomes. Because the current personal exclusion regarding health benefits is open ended, those with the most generous health plans, who tend to be better paid, receive a larger tax subsidy. Because the subsidy takes the form of an exclusion, its value is higher for taxpayers in higher marginal tax brackets. According to one analysis, these tax provisions provide 30 times more benefit to households earning more than $100,000, on average, than to those earning under $10,000—and they provide no benefit at all to those who lack private health insurance.[43]

The Progressive Plan would end this inflationary, expensive, and regressive tax policy. The exclusion of health benefits from taxable income would be replaced with a fixed tax credit, which would have the same dollar value for all who receive it (apart from low-income households, who would receive larger credits), and which would give consumers no tax benefit for buying a more costly plan. In addition, since both corporate and individual tax benefits would be linked to competition and would favor accountable health plans, the tax code would become an instrument of efficiency rather than inflation. While other managed competition proposals reform the existing tax exclusion somewhat differently, *some* reform of these tax provisions is essential to make managed competition work well.

The Progressive Plan would improve equity in other ways as well. One is that it would derive the bulk of the funding for expanding coverage from the progressive federal income tax, rather than from payroll taxes, which can be regressive and can slow job creation. A second is that it would end the acute care portion of Medicaid. While Medicaid's creation in the 1960s created health care access for millions, the program is today a deeply flawed way to meet the health needs of the poor. And while many states have been creative in their efforts to make the system work, its basic design has led to problems that have succeeded in angering taxpayers, governors, doctors, hospitals, and recipients alike. One of the worst aspects of most pay-or-play strategies is that they propose to expand Medicaid. There are many reasons government should ensure that all Americans can obtain health coverage, but few reasons government itself should be in the health insurance business, and fewer still to expand a program that has fared so poorly. The Progressive Plan, and other market-based approaches, would enable government to provide for the acute care needs of the disadvantaged in a far more efficient and equitable manner.

ADVANTAGE THREE: STATE-BASED REFORM IS MORE RESPONSIVE AND INNOVATIVE

Most of the leading comprehensive health reform proposals would create one financing system for the entire country. Some leave a role for state administration and an opportunity for state waivers. But very few start with the notion, which seems justified in a federalized nation, that states should fashion their own reforms and financing systems.[44] To the extent reformers justify a uniform plan, they tend to cite two reasons. The first is that current federal laws make it difficult for states to innovate effectively on health care reform. The key federal law regarding pensions blocks states from regulating self-insured employers, the federal tax code makes it impossible for states to change bad tax incentives, Medicare and Medicaid put hundreds of billions of health dollars beyond the states' effective control, and tax competition among states discourages states from moving to universal coverage unilaterally.[45] The second argument for national uniformity is that health care should be thought of as social insurance, and social insurance programs (like Social Security) are best run as national efforts.[46]

These two arguments are both right and wrong. Current federal laws do block effective state innovation in reform. But the right response is to amend the offending federal laws, not to preempt state reform. And while national health care reform is aimed at creating some level of social insurance, which requires some degree of federal action, it is also aimed at improving efficiency, which almost always benefits from decentralization. As one study concludes, "states are the logical unit through which to organize health care in a country as large as the United States."[47]

In fact, there are abundant reasons to give the states the opportunity and obligation to choose their own paths toward universal coverage and reform. First, there is tremendous variability among the states, their health care needs, their institutional capacities, and their civic cultures. Such key variables as per capita health costs, concentration of physicians, and enrollment in HMOs vary by more than 100 percent among states.[48] Their experience in health reform also varies widely. Some states, such as New York and Massachusetts, have extensively regulated health care over the years. Some have already adopted sweeping reforms; Hawaii, for example, has already attained nearly universal health care coverage. Others, such as Oregon and Georgia, have conducted extensive public debates over health care reform and have built great support for particular types of reforms.

Moreover, experimentation among the states will yield needed data about the relative merits of differing approaches to reform. Such data are particularly important, both substantively and politically, in the context of market-based reforms. Notwithstanding years of experience under FEHBP and other similar systems, as discussed above, critics of market-based reforms often complain that such approaches are "almost pure theory," unsupported by empirical evidence.[49] A system that resulted in 50 different variations on market-based reform with universal coverage would certainly cure this alleged empirical vacuum. The states would become prolific laboratories for testing how well different financing, regulatory, and delivery systems work in restraining health costs and rewarding high-value care.

CONCLUSION

Many of the challenges facing the new President, from making our streets safer to making our products more competitive, are so complex, deep-rooted, and increasingly global that the limited levers of federal policy are likely to produce only incremental improvement. Health care is an exception. Our health care system's problems of high cost and shrinking coverage are problems the new President can do something about. Without question, any effort to enact comprehensive health care reform will be a pitched battle, and reforms once enacted will take several years to work fully. But unlike so many other problems, the new President can have confidence that a legislative victory will actually result in far-reaching, near-term change.

If the new President does make health care reform a personal priority, the nature of that reform will likely be one of the hallmarks of his tenure. The model of reform proposed here would not only end America's lack of universal coverage and its spiral of health inflation, but also transform the American health care system in ways that reflect this book's signature ideas: consumer choice; political decentralization; progressive taxation; less public bureaucracy; the use of market forces to achieve public goals; encouragement of innovation; and a renewed emphasis on individual responsibility.

This course of reform is achievable. Many of this Plan's central ideas have already attracted support from progressive Republicans, moderate Democrats, liberal health reformers, and enlightened private-sector leaders who might be less supportive of reforms that rely on a greater level of government intervention. The public is clearly ready to support comprehensive change. The opportunity is real.

MANDATE FOR ACTION

1. **Create a new system of managed competition for health care.** All consumers would choose among private health plans within a system that ensures the plans compete on the basis of value rather than risk skimming. A well-managed market competition is a far better way to restrain wasteful health spending than imposing public price controls and budgets across the U.S. health care system.
2. **Better information for consumers and providers.** Create a new system to collect comparable information from health plans on their financial and clinical performance, to be used both by consumers choosing their health plan, and by providers deciding on the best course of treatment. This information is essential to help consumers comparison shop, and to focus providers on the most effective and efficient ways to deliver care.
3. **Reform the tax code's treatment of health care benefits.** Replace the existing subsidies with a fixed tax credit for households that choose qualifying health plans. The existing tax treatment of health benefits is regressive and inflationary, and must be changed for reform to work well.
4. **Make the states the primary engine of reform.** The system should be state based in order to spur responsiveness and innovation. Once certain federal laws are changed, states can and should develop their own market-based, universal coverage models of reform.

6

Educating America: A New Compact for Opportunity and Citizenship

TED KOLDERIE, ROBERT LERMAN, AND
CHARLES MOSKOS

INTRODUCTION

More than ever before, America's prosperity hinges on how well we educate and train our people. Yet our public schools are failing to meet new standards of performance being set by our global competitors. Our secondary schools are not producing graduates whose academic skills match those of their counterparts in other advanced countries. We are not doing as good a job as those of our economic competitors in preparing young people for work, a failure that strikes hardest at the "forgotten half" of America's youth who do not attend college.

For those who wish to attend college, the problem is not quality but access. Soaring costs, which rose 51 percent in the last decade for private colleges and 31 percent for public colleges (adjusted for inflation), are putting college beyond the reach of average working families.[1]

These two problems—the inferior quality of our secondary schools and lack of access to America's excellent system of higher learning—stand as obstacles both to individual opportunity for aspiring Americans and to the revival of our nation's ability to win in the world economy. The new President, therefore, must make revitalizing U.S. education an urgent priority of his administration. He should marshal public support for a radical redesign of

U.S. education: to improve the quality of our public schools dramatically while preserving their civic mission; create a more rigorous system for training young people in the skills needed for competing in the global economy; guarantee financial assistance for college for anyone willing to earn it through national service; and thereby underscore the responsibilities as well as the rights of citizenship.

This chapter offers three initiatives that, taken together, provide the basis for a new educational compact for work and citizenship. Under this compact, parents would be able to choose the schools their children attend; non-college youth would be offered opportunities to work as they learn; businesses would be assured a larger supply of skilled and mature workers; and federal support for college education would be made available to young people willing to serve their communities. Specifically, this chapter recommends that the new administration:

Promote charter schools and other experiments in public school choice. The new President should use both the power of the bully pulpit and the leverage of federal education aid to encourage the states to inject more choice and competition into public schools. The charter school movement, which began in Minnesota and has spread to California, allows enterprising teachers and others to start new public schools under contract, or charter, to a public agency. Its purpose is to invent a new kind of public school: innovative, flexible, and responsive to the special needs of students and their families.

Institute a nationwide system of school-based youth apprenticeship. For the half of our youth who do not attend college, America needs a comprehensive system for building the skills necessary to prosper in a new economy that is based on flexible, knowledge-intensive industries and services. Youth apprenticeships would allow high school students to combine classroom instruction and on-the-job training with a local business. Upon completion of a rigorous, three-year program of academic and vocational learning, students would earn valuable credentials certifying competence in their chosen occupation. Most of the costs of apprenticeship would be borne by businesses, which would also reap the benefits of a larger supply of well-trained and experienced workers.

Create a civilian GI bill. The new President should expand federal aid for college through a new "civilian GI bill" that offers young Americans generous scholarships in return for community service. Eventually, voluntary national service should replace economic need as the basis on which the federal government delivers assistance to students. Under this approach, young people would perform a year or two of work in exchange for vouchers they could use for a college education, vocational training, or a down payment on a first home. National service would thus mobilize hundreds of thousands of volunteers to address America's pressing social needs, including illiteracy and other educational deficiencies.

I. CHARTER SCHOOLS: INNOVATION THROUGH CHOICE

At the heart of the school reform debate is a central question: Are our schools failing because we spend too little on them, or because of the way they are organized? In general, liberals have been inclined to the view that our schools suffer from a lack of resources, while conservatives tend to see their problems as rooted in the political control of public education.

During the last decade, as the debate raged over school reform, the U.S. increased per-student funding in public schools by 36 percent (adjusted for inflation).[2] However, we have little to show for this surge in spending. Scholastic Aptitude Test (SAT) scores rose a little in the mid-1980s but have declined ever since—and they remain below the level reached in the early 1960s.[3] Scores from the National Assessment for Educational Progress, a more accurate indicator of student progress, also show little or no improvement.[4]

Crucial to our competitive ability, U.S. students rank in the bottom half of international tests for math and science.[5] In only one category do they lead the world: the number of hours of television watched.[6]

More resources are part of the answer, particularly in troubled inner-city school districts from Newark to Chicago.[7] But the disappointing record of the last decade strongly suggests the need to shift the focus of the debate about improving our schools from spending to structure—to the way the enterprise of public education is organized.

Our public school districts display in classic form the overcentralization and bureaucratic rigidity that afflicts government in general. Their inability to adapt to new circumstances and to the public demand for improvement is rooted in the monopoly character of the system; in the assumption that public education can be offered only in the schools of the district. Parents have little choice over which schools their children attend. Many cannot afford to move or to pay tuition on top of the local property taxes. Schooling, anyway, is much the same everywhere. The reform in vogue today—decentralizing management authority from district to school—looks in the right direction, but is often more rhetoric than reality. Change and improvement will not really begin until the state withdraws the districts' "exclusive" and affirms that it is okay for more than one organization to offer public education in the community.

Yet if conservatives have been right to focus on public bureaucracies that exercise monopoly control over education, they have picked the wrong solution: privatizing public education. For example, the Bush administration proposed offering vouchers to parents who want to enroll their children in private schools. While they may be justified as a necessary prod to public school improvement, vouchers in fact encourage parents to abandon the public schools. We cannot afford to leave education entirely to the vagaries of consumer sovereignty; that will only produce an educational marketplace stratified by class and race.

Universal public education is one of the great achievements of American democracy. Our public schools have been the principal catalyst for equal opportunity as well as a crucible for our common civic culture. They have been a great leveler of economic, social, and, lately, racial distinctions, as well as a conduit to economic opportunity and American citizenship for immigrants from the mid-nineteenth century to today.

We must save, not abandon, America's public schools. At the same time, however, a reflexive defense of the existing system can only play into the hands of those who want to privatize America's schools. There is another choice: harnessing the power of parental choice, competition and innovation to radically restructure our schools, while retaining their essentially public character.

The promise of choice lies in its ability to make public education a *self*-improving system. Government and blue-ribbon commissions may be able to identify systemic problems within our schools, but such outside groups cannot make a principal more entrepreneurial, a teacher more focused on achievement, or parents more involved in their childrens' school. It will not work to hook up public education to an external life-support system of outside money and mandates. *What is needed is a change of structure and incentives that will push public schools to improve on the basis of their own initiative, in their own interest and from their own resources.*

An early and compelling prototype for public school choice was in one of America's poorest communities: New York's East Harlem. In the early 1970s, in a radical move, New York had taken away the central office's control over the elementary and middle schools. In 1974, the new Community District 4 in East Harlem ranked 32nd out of 32 such districts in the city. Only 15 percent of its pupils were reading at or above grade level. It then began letting educators create new, small, alternative schools which parents could choose. The results were dramatic: by 1982, District 4's ranking had climbed to 15, with nearly 60 percent of its pupils reading at or above grade level. Math scores rose, as did daily attendance and the number of pupils going on to college. More than 1,000 students come from outside the district.

Seymour Fliegel, an architect of the successful District 4 experiment, explains: "A school is not a building. Students, teachers, ideas and learning are what make a school. And it is not uncommon in District 4 to have three schools in one building. In 1974, we started three alternative schools. By 1982, we had 26 alternative schools and 20 traditional schools in a total of 20 buildings."[8]

Most significant: In the last year or two this movement to create new and more diverse schools has spread all across New York City, involving both other community districts and the "New Vision" schools created at the initiative of the central office.

The Charter School Movement

The leading edge of public school choice experiments today is the charter schools movement. As pioneered in Minnesota, charter schools are intended to speed the rate of change by making it possible for somebody other than the local school board to try out different and better forms of public education which students could choose, available where they live.

Charter schools seek to foster healthy competition within the public school system by enabling administrators, teachers, and even other groups or individuals to create new schools, chartered by the state, which compete for students and the public funds that flow with them. Charter schools follow the principles of public education. They may not have a religious character, or charge tuition; cannot pick and choose their students, or discriminate. Their charter is contingent on a set of publicly established outcomes. Thus, they are accountable both to the public—for meeting defined student outcomes—and to parents, who are free to remove their children if they are not satisfied with the results. In return for agreeing to be judged on their performance, charter schools are allowed to design their programs free of the regulations and rules that pass for accountability today. The state pays directly to the charter school an average per-pupil amount.

Since the idea first appeared in policy discussions in 1988, charter school laws have been enacted in Minnesota (1991) and in California (1992). In 1993 they are likely to be under discussion again in the legislatures of Colorado, Wisconsin, Tennessee, New Jersey, Massachusetts, and Pennsylvania.

Charter schools offer an alternative form of public education. They are not intended to replace the schools we have today. Their likely effect is to stimulate the existing system in ways that will cause districts to improve. They offer some reward for taking risks. The new schools will be small, so that mistakes, which will occur, will be small. They let parents and teachers volunteer for change. Most important: They let an innovation appear without having to secure the prior approval of those who will be threatened if it succeeds.

The districts will not like this pressure. As when any business loses its exclusive they will not want others offering public education within their borders. They will try to discourage this competition, saying "We can do this now."

But without some real stimulus they don't and won't. The central problem with public schools was put perfectly by Albert Shanker, the president of the American Federation of Teachers (AFT), at a meeting in Minnesota in 1988: "This is a system that can take its customers for granted."[9] That's true. Children attend where they live. Within each district only one organization is allowed to offer public education. Together, these "givens" guarantee the district its success—its customers, its revenues, its jobs, its security, its existence—whether or not the district changes and improves and whether or not the students learn.

"We have an organization without consequences for failure," the new superintendent in Milwaukee, Howard Fuller, told the board at a retreat in August 1991, "where everyone is protected except the children."[10]

It is this guarantee of success that destroys the incentive to change. Practically nothing depends on whether the students learn. So, with what one close observer of public education describes gently as "weak incentives for the introduction of innovations that would cause internal stress," the cards are, as another says, "stacked against innovation."

Pushing for change upsets people. It might cause a strike, cost an election, or end a career. Unfortunately, there is nothing that requires kids' interests to be put first. Principals who want to change their schools, but are blocked, have nowhere else to go; parents and students have nowhere else to go; nor do teachers. Unless something quite unusual happens the students and the revenues will be there anyway. The system guarantees the districts their success and so invites adults to put their own interests first.

For a country that claims to be serious about improving its public schools this is an absurd arrangement. How can we expect teachers and administrators to make exceptional effort if we assure them their success whether they do or not?

This arrangement is unfair to those in education. It is wrong to give people incentives that are not aligned with the mission they have been given to perform. As Theodore Sizer says in *Horace's Compromise,* "The people are better than the system."[11] The present system has the structure of reward backward.

Changing the incentives in public schools cannot be done by federal legislation. Congress can add money and regulations. But, as we've seen in the last decade, when per-student spending has increased and performance has declined, that won't work. The problem is in the structure of public education. It is in state law. It can be changed only by changing state law. Correcting the reward system is the obligation of the state. It's the key to educational reform.

However, the new President has an opportunity to take the lead in activating the process of state law making. Nothing in the Constitution requires him to make proposals only to Congress, or prohibits him from making proposals to the states. A progressive agenda for reinventing government may in fact depend on connecting the power of national leadership to the power of the state legislatures over the organization of major domestic and urban systems, including, but not limited to, public education.

In addition to the bully pulpit, the new President can use the leverage of federal education aid to promote public school choice. He should support a proposal by Senators David Durenberger (R-MN) and Joe Lieberman (D-CT), which would permit the states to use federal education grants to set up charter schools.

Charter Schools vs. Vouchers

The purpose of choice is to create a new form of public education, not to finance private schools or to transform public education into private education. For too long, advocates of public and private schools, and the ideological arguments on the Left and

Right, have assumed the country had to choose between sending checks to superintendents or sending vouchers to parents. Not so: There is a third way. It is possible to introduce the dynamics necessary for change and improvement into the public education system while still retaining its essential principles, and the values of opportunity, diversity, and community that are so important to this democracy. Private education should remain and will remain; but as private education, privately financed. Our concern is with *public* education.

The charter schools do not drain funds from public education. They do reallocate dollars within the community, between existing schools and the new schools. This reallocation is essential to produce the new programs people want. In Minnesota deaf children in the Twin Cities area will have a new option: a day school in the area using American sign language; an alternative both to the state residential school for the deaf miles away and to schools where they cannot talk to their classmates.

Sometimes the new schools do not become charter schools. In one district in Minnesota parents had been pressing for a district Montessori option. The administration said it couldn't find space, couldn't find teachers, couldn't see how to handle the transportation. "Give us a charter and we'll solve those problems," the parents said. Quickly the administration decided it could answer those questions after all. "Fine," the parents said, "that's all we were after." The new Montessori school opened this fall.

Opponents of choice also argue that it can only yield results *after* we equalize resources among our public schools—that a choice between two underfunded schools is no choice at all. While it is true that many of America's schools are underfunded and physically run down, the experience with District 4 in New York suggests that choice can bring about radical improvement in precisely these schools. And it may well be that as these schools improve their performance under a charter school approach, they will have more success in making the political case for additional funding.

The charter idea, therefore, can deliver the benefits of choice without bankrupting the public schools, as a voucher system could. Perhaps that is why polls show support for public school choice at two to one. Significantly, support is highest in the big cities, among people of color, among younger people, among people who have only high school educations and families of average income.[12]

Teachers would also benefit greatly from charter schools. They are hurt as much as the kids by the obstacles to change. They know there are other and better ways for students to learn. Some will be willing to take the risk involved.

Schools organized on the public charter model could change the reward system for teachers dramatically. Such schools could be provided with a fixed sum of money, given the freedom to run their own instructional program, and allowed to keep whatever they do not need to spend. At the same time, they would be held accountable for results. This would provide a powerful incentive to adopt more economical and effective ways of learning. The teachers' success would be connected to the students' success.

In a real sense, of course, every state has a "choice" plan in law today. Nobody has to send their kids to the schools where they presently live. They can pay tuition to private (or to public) school. Or they can move and pay no tuition. Lots of people do this. All it takes is money. Choice exists—for those who can afford it. This deeply inequitable arrangement has turned public education in our big metropolitan areas into a system stratified by income and race. Those with little income have no choice. We should and can design a better plan, using public resources to offset the private inequalities and to enhance diversity.

The problem has been that—until recently—proposals to modify choice have been designed to provide funds for students to use in private schools. Governor Rudy Perpich's effort in Minnesota in 1985 changed that, opening up choice among public districts only. But this implied and required travel, since the other district is always in some other place. And—except for the option that lets tenth and eleventh-graders in Minneapolis (for example) finish high school at the University of Minnesota—it did not provide the dynamics that come from new choices in children's own communities.

The charter idea resolves this problem: New schools, free to try new forms of learning, operated on the principles of public education, located where the children live.

II. YOUTH APPRENTICESHIP: LINKING SCHOOL AND WORK

In the global economy, the collective skills and capacities of a nation's workers are its chief source of comparative advantage. Yet

America has no system for ensuring that the non-college half of our youth population receives the skills and training necessary to secure a decent living.

America thus faces a fundamental domestic challenge in the 1990s: reversing the stark and growing disparity between the fates of college educated and non-college educated youths in our society. The gap is growing between the skills possessed by youth who enter the work force after high school and those skills required by the knowledge-intensive manufacturing and service industries that are ascendant in the global economy.

Young workers who leave school with only a high school education face worsening job prospects today. Between 1973 and 1988, male high school graduates with ten years of work experience saw their wages fall by 40 percent relative to the wages of college graduates.[13] The erosion in jobs for high school dropouts was equally dramatic; their unemployment rates rose by 24 percent, while unemployment among college graduates declined.[14]

The high school graduate's deteriorating position in the job market is weakening the commitment of many young men to the economic mainstream and to family life.[15] Already, the country is losing a tragically large number of young black men to crime and drugs. In addition to these and related social problems, the country suffers from low productivity growth when it cannot take full advantage of a major part of its labor force.

Some of the income and employment losses for non-college workers stem from declining employment in traditional manufacturing industries, which often paid high wages to even semiskilled workers. But the main explanation is the rising demand for highly skilled workers in *all* manufacturing and service industries.[16] While the resulting wage inequality is bad news, the willingness of employers to pay an increased premium for skills represents an opportunity. If the nation can produce more well-trained workers with relevant skills, the market will be ready to absorb them (after the overall economy improves) and pay a good return on their investment.

The skills gap inevitably calls attention to U.S. public schools and their poorly designed system for preparing non-college youth for meaningful careers. Typically, high schools have close connections with colleges, but weak links with employers. After leaving high school, new workers usually rely on informal contacts to obtain a full-time position. Many test the labor market by bouncing from one employer to another before settling into a long-term job. This creates a vicious cycle: The frequent movement of young workers discourages employers from providing training, while the absence of training limits the incentive of young people to remain with and work hard at a given firm.

Non-college youth also have weak incentives to stay and do well in high school because they see little if any relationship between what they learn in school and future careers. Few employers request transcripts or otherwise check on the quality of the entry worker's school performance.[17] Those students who concentrated on vocational subjects experience similar problems. Over half end up in jobs that have nothing to do with the training they received in high school.[18]

These realities create particularly serious problems for disadvantaged youth. While most non-college youth see little gain from performing well in high school, they tend to stay anyway, if only because of social and family constraints. Inner-city minority youth, however, are more likely to fall prey to pressures from the street, including peers encouraging them to leave school altogether.[19] After finishing high school, these youth have the worst job market outlook, partly because formal connections between employers and schools are too limited. As noted before, most young workers turn to informal linkages to find jobs, and inner-city minority youth face a special disadvantage because so few of them have the relatives and friends who can provide the credible references required to obtain good jobs.[20]

Public policies have reinforced the growing tendency for academic skills to determine career success. Governments spend enormous amounts on grants and loans for low-income students to attend college. These help the most academically capable, but do nothing for the vast majority of low-income youth. Far less is spent on vocational education or other effective post-secondary training.

The natural impulse of policymakers has been to develop highly targeted programs for poor and minority youth. Yet such a strategy can easily backfire. When programs deal only with the most disadvantaged and least educated, their participants easily become stigmatized. Many employers are unwilling to take a chance on the graduates of these programs, and the youths themselves see such training as a weak substitute for existing jobs in the regular or underground economy. Funding is often unstable and difficult to sustain. At best, these programs provide only a marginal addition to the existing systems of education, training, and career placement. Evidence from recent, rigorous evaluation of the Job Training Partnership Act (JTPA) shows highly disappointing results for young workers. A year or more after the program, young men assigned to JTPA earned about $200 less per quarter (around 10 percent) than a control group not assigned to JTPA.[21]

An alternative strategy is at hand—a youth-apprenticeship option that combines classroom instruction with on-the-job training at a local business, starting in the late high school years. Similar apprenticeship systems have been operating effectively throughout Germany, Switzerland, and Austria for decades. Yet, until recently, educators and employment policymakers in the United States have ignored the lessons from this European experience.

The German system cannot be transplanted in American soil. However, the new administration should press for full-scale testing of American-style approaches to youth apprenticeship that likewise link school and work. To build a school-based apprenticeship system requires the following steps:

1. Change school curricula to expose students in the seventh through tenth grades to information about various occupations, including visits to and short internships at work sites.
2. Offer tenth-grade students a choice between pursuing a job apprenticeship or remaining on a purely academic track. Those choosing the former option would sign formal contracts with specific employers.
3. Create a range of three-year apprenticeships that begin in the eleventh grade. Students could earn skill certifications and academic credit as they combine workplace training with school courses.
4. Give apprentices a comprehensive test at the end of the twelfth grade to ensure educational and job proficiency.
5. Develop a combined work-based and school-based curriculum that involves spending increasing amounts of time at the work site. Their third year (thirteenth grade) would involve material advanced enough to permit the apprentices to earn one year of credit toward an Associate's degree.

GOALS FOR YOUTH APPRENTICESHIP

Does the promise of youth apprenticeships warrant such a dramatic restructuring of our school and job training systems? Combining job-based education with other school reforms can affect the nation's domestic problems in the following ways.

First, offering serious training and entry-level jobs to large numbers of non-college youth will increase the supply of skilled workers. The opportunity to acquire marketable skills will be particularly important to minorities and women, who will make up a disproportionately large part of new entrants to the work force. Since employers will be providing and paying for most of the training, they have every incentive to impart the specific skills they expect to need. This will raise worker productivity and help firms introduce new technologies more efficiently. In fact, quality and relevant training will do more to raise productivity than increased physical capital. However, it will take time before the apprentices trained through the new system make up a large share of the nation's labor force.

Second, as the productivity of non-college youth increases, an increase in their wages will follow. Rising earnings will reduce the income gap between non-college and college-educated workers. We can expect employers to build on the capacities of apprentices by developing new job ladders and providing additional career training. These steps, in turn, should create more professionalized careers for non-college workers and thus raise their social status.

Third, word of promising new career options and the chance to begin job training by eleventh grade will filter down to high school and junior high school students. This could well achieve more improvement in academic skills than most school reforms currently under discussion because of the new incentives to learn, especially among those students not planning to attend college. Raising the proportion of non-college youth who take their studies and mainstream career options seriously could change the atmosphere in troubled urban schools, so that peer pressure no longer discourages good students from succeeding academically.

Fourth, the enhanced education, training, and careers of non-college youth will revive hope among youth who today are harming themselves through drugs and early parenthood. Over the last century, sexual activity has been occurring at younger ages while entry into responsible jobs has been taking place at older ages. These changes have no doubt contributed to the decline in marriage rates and to the tragic rise in single-parent families. Within the black community, the situation is so serious that the absence of fathers has become the primary cause of child poverty.

If apprenticeships draw large numbers of young people, especially disadvantaged minority youth, into serious job training as early as eleventh grade, early parenting will become less attractive and marriage more attractive. Making appealing careers a realistic option will be one factor, but perhaps as important will be the mentoring and acculturation that takes place in an adult work environment.

Ultimately, the hope is that these effects will cumulate and penetrate the urban underclass. It is conceivable that a large, effective youth-apprenticeship program can provide inner-city youths the formal contacts they need to the world of work. Large impacts could take place quickly, since the program will primarily benefit non-college youth, the group that accounts for most neighborhood crime and a large part of the drug problem. However, only a strategy aimed at a broad spectrum of young people can make a significant difference. Both young people and potential employers will view programs geared only toward the poor as providing second-rate jobs and inferior workers.

This suggests a final and crucial advantage of the youth-apprenticeship strategy—its natural appeal to a broad public. Unlike programs targeted narrowly on the poor, this job-based education strategy is inclusive, not exclusive; it is productivity-enhancing, not simply redistributive; and it promotes the incentives to learn and earn instead of discouraging work. Apprenticeship could become affirmative action of the best kind, helping young minority workers, in a way that neither stigmatizes them nor gives them unfair advantages over other workers.

NEXT STEPS

Youth apprenticeship is just getting underway in the United States. Still, enthusiasm runs high in those few places where apprenticeship projects are already operating. Young people in Pennsylvania's machine-tool youth-apprenticeship system report they are learning more in school and have broadened their horizons because of their participation in the program.[22] The states of Wisconsin and Maine are planning to implement state-wide programs.

At this embryonic stage, federal leadership is critical. The new President should endorse the legislation proposed by Senators Sam Nunn and John Breaux that would provide federal grants for major youth-apprenticeship demonstration projects. He should triple the $50 million that bill earmarks for grants. Under the Nunn-Breaux proposal communities would compete for the federal funds on the basis of strong partnerships among local employers, schools, and labor. The proposal also calls for a National Youth Apprenticeship Institute, which would specify the academic and work skills necessary to become qualified as an appren-

ticeship in a specific occupation, develop ways to certify apprentices and their business trainers, and monitor the quality of on-the-
job training. According to Senator Nunn, apprenticeship should
require, "certifiable skills, involve employers as direct participants
with a stake in the individual students; academic and skills training
achievement and be an integral part of the school curriculum,
available to all students, not an add-on or adjunct program, and
[should carry] prestige in school and community."[23]

The new President can also use federal vocational education
funds to leverage movement toward youth apprenticeship. The
joint school business operating boards who take charge of federal
training moneys (as proposed in chapter 3) should promote programs to train workplace trainers of young apprentices and develop monitoring and technical assistance systems to assure that
workplaces deliver quality apprenticeship training. Such boards
could also convene groups of employers, school officials and labor
representatives to gain agreement on the competencies required for
specific apprenticeships.

The President should also push the expansion of apprenticeship
opportunities in federal employment and in large federally funded
programs. A solid apprenticeship training program for future federal employees in the secretarial and administrative assistant occupations could become a model for the private sector.

III. A CIVILIAN GI BILL: BALANCING
RIGHTS AND RESPONSIBILITIES

Although America has the finest system of higher education in
the world, skyrocketing tuitions in the last decade have made
college a distant dream for too many families, and an enormous
financial burden for all but the wealthiest Americans. Our current
student-aid system is failing to assure universal access to higher
education. Federal grants have not kept pace with soaring tuition
costs, forcing low- and middle-income families to borrow heavily.
Not surprisingly, student loan defaults have reached record highs.

The Clinton admininistration should begin the process of replacing the federal student aid programs with a civilian GI bill,
which would allow young Americans to earn college aid through
national service. Like its namesake, the new GI bill would guarantee access to college or post-secondary training for all Americans
willing to serve their country. Only instead of limiting GI education benefits to military veterans, it would mobilize a new "Citi-

zens Corps" of civilian volunteers to tackle America's most stubborn domestic and social problems.

As we reduce our Cold War military forces—foreclosing a traditional avenue to opportunity for Americans of modest means—national service also can be an important component of a defense transition strategy. Hundreds of thousands of young Americans who formerly looked to the military for training and upward mobility could be put to work on filling our nation's enormous backlog of social needs. Like the military, the Citizens Corps would both impart job skills and instill the values of discipline, responsibility and civic obligation.

National service is more than a government program. It is a new form of civic activism that relies on private volunteers rather than public employees to solve urgent social problems. Senator Barbara Mikulski has aptly described national service as the latest example of a venerable American tradition of "social inventions." Like settlement houses and night school, which helped successive waves of immigrants become part of American society, national service can open new paths to opportunity and upward mobility for young Americans and for the people they serve. And, like the GI bill, national service should be seen as a long-term investment in the education, skills, and ingenuity of our people.

National service is a civic compact that creates new opportunities for citizens to help themselves by helping others. In addition to providing educational benefits and new social services, it seeks to revive a spirit of civic obligation that has languished over the past 12 years. While conservatives have neglected the nation's public responsibilities, many liberals have encouraged Americans to demand more from government without giving anything in return. Rarely have our leaders challenged Americans to sacrifice for some public purpose—to give something back to their communities and country.

Consider the continuing fiscal paralysis in Washington. Big deficits persist because too many of us have come to expect government to provide more services and entitlements than we are willing to pay taxes for. Before he can break the fiscal deadlock that stymies progressive governance, President Clinton must confront the civic insolvency that underlies that impasse. To strike a better balance between citizen rights and responsibilities, he should call for a new generation of public policies based on reciprocity rather than one-way rights and entitlements. Besides national service, such policies should include a Police Corps, welfare reforms that stress reciprocal obligations, and a new emphasis on corporate responsibility.

The Citizens Corps

In 1989, Senators Sam Nunn, Charles Robb and Barbara Mikulski, and Congressman David McCurdy, introduced a bill calling for a large-scale (800,000 member) "Citizens Corps" that would offer young volunteers public benefits in return for community service.[24] While that bill met powerful opposition from education lobbyists and the Bush administration, in 1990 Congress approved $22 million for small national service demonstration projects, which are just now being organized.

In fashioning the Citizens Corps, national service advocates drew on many models, including Franklin Roosevelt's Civilian Conservation Corps (CCC), John Kennedy's Peace Corps and Lyndon Johnson's Volunteers In Service to America (VISTA). However, the prototype for national service is the World War II-era GI Bill of Rights. That measure transformed millions of returning World War II veterans into the best educated generation in American history. The GI Bill was a national investment on an unprecedented scale: In 1949, its peak year, the U.S. spent one percent of its gross national product on educational benefits for veterans—approximately $55 billion in today's dollars.[25]

The Citizens Corps would work like this: In return for one or two years' full-time work at low wages in some form of community service, Citizens Corps members would earn national service vouchers for college, job training, or housing. Originally valued at $10,000, vouchers should be adjusted periodically to keep them in line with changes in college costs.

Unlike the Peace Corps and VISTA, which recruit college graduates, the Citizens Corps would target high school graduates who need financial help for college or skills training. The labor-intensive tasks envisioned for volunteers do not require a college degree. Moreover, the costs of national service could be far lower if volunteers mostly lived at home, as would most likely be the case with high school graduates. In addition, some prominent educators believe that many such graduates would benefit from the maturity and self-reliance fostered by full-time work tackling community problems. For example, Joseph Duffy, president of American University in Washington, D.C., estimated that as many as a quarter of entering freshmen are emotionally or psychologically unprepared to take full advantage of college.

Unlike the CCC, the Citizens Corps is not intended to be a public jobs program. While labor unions fret that national-service volunteers might displace public employees, the Citizens Corps focuses on tasks that remain undone because there is no profit in it for the private sector, and because it is too costly for the public sector. As AFT President Albert Shanker says, "If national service volunteers do work that wouldn't be done anyway, unions should accept them."[26] The standard is simple: If national service cannot provide services more effectively or more cheaply than private enterprise or employees of public agencies, then there is no basis for it.

America's social needs are legion. For example, national service volunteers could be put to work combating illiteracy and serving as tutors and teachers' aids in public schools; working in hospitals, hospices, outpatient facilities, clinics and mental health centers; providing in-home care to the ill and elderly; expanding day care opportunities for working parents; repairing run-down housing; staffing shelters for the homeless; assisting in public safety; and more. A 1986 Ford Foundation study concluded that nearly 3.5 million positions could be usefully filled by volunteers, mainly in the areas of education, health, child care, libraries and museums, and environmental protection.[27]

To win broad public backing, voluntary national service must put the needs of society first. After all, the U.S. has a military to meet a pressing national need, not to mature young men or women. The same standard must be applied to civilian service. To focus on the server invites negative stereotypes on the character of the server. To focus on the service delivered is to invoke civic sentiments. Only when national service is cast in terms of meeting a real need can its positive, but necessarily derivative, benefits for the server be achieved.

To avoid a highly centralized and bureaucratic administrative structure, the Nunn-McCurdy bill provided for creation of local councils that would recruit and place volunteers. We envision some 200,000 youth servers within a year of enactment of the requisite legislation. National service would rely heavily on the nation's 100,000 private, nonprofit community groups to serve as potential sponsors and supervisors of Citizens Corp volunteers. Additionally, some 800 campuses already have organized college volunteer efforts. To discourage "make-work," such groups would be asked to pay a fee—perhaps $1,000 per year—for each volunteer they sponsor.

Boston's private City Year project and the City Volunteer Corps in New York are leading models for a comprehensive system of voluntary national service. City Year, for example, has had great success in attracting diverse volunteers from across race and class lines; performing work of genuine value to the community, not busy work; and operating with a minimum of overhead. Administrative costs are only about 20 percent of the total budget, including the salaries of 12 full-time and six part-time employees.[28]

National Service and Student Aid

In order to assure equal access to higher education, the U.S. must expand federal aid to students. However, it should do so, not on the basis of existing, means-tested loans and grants, but on the basis of service. Over time, as the Citizens Corps demonstrates its ability to deliver needed community services, and acquires the capacity to absorb large numbers of young Americans, we should phase out federal subsidies to students.

Existing federal aid programs are inadequate, unfair, and help too few needy students. For example, the size of the average Pell grant has lagged far behind the soaring growth in college costs—putting college out of reach for many and forcing others to borrow heavily. There are inequities in the formulas for determining eligibility for grants and loans. Despite recent action by Congress to expand eligibility for grants, given recent patterns of appropriation most middle income families do not receive Pell grants or receive minimal assistance.[29] It seems unlikely that the middle class will support dramatic increases in existing student aid programs from which they derive little or no benefit.

In contrast, national service would provide an opportunity for students from middle class families, who are currently not eligible for student aid, to afford post-secondary education without taking on large debts. During the late 1980s, student indebtedness rose sharply. Loan default rates have skyrocketed. Washington now spends $5 billion a year to guarantee $12 billion worth of student loans. About $3 billion is earmarked for past defaults, another $1 billion is set aside for expected future defaults, and $1 billion goes to banks to subsidize loans.[30]

National service vouchers would offer significantly more aid—$10,000 per year of service, compared to an average annual Pell grant award of $2,400. That, in turn, would reduce students' need to borrow to make up the difference between their grants and actual college costs.

Eventually, participation in the Citizens Corps should become a prerequisite for receiving federal student aid, replacing Pell and other federal grants. However, exemptions should be made for older students who are more likely to have jobs or families, as well as others, such as single mothers, for whom national service would pose a special hardship. They should also have the option of volunteering for part-time service, for commensurately smaller rewards.

National service should be a civic experience available to all young Americans, not just those who need college aid. Hence, the Citizens Corps was designed to appeal as well to what the William T. Grant Foundation has called the "forgotten half" of young Americans who do not go on to college.[31] These Corps members should be able to use their vouchers for other purposes: paying for vocational education or job training, or for a down payment on a first home.

A comprehensive system of national service could also play a key supporting role in a new work-based social policy that ends permanent welfare in America (see chapter 10). Under this approach, eligibility for welfare would be limited to two years. Welfare recipients who fail to find private jobs before their eligibility ends should be offered community service work at the minimum wage. This will allow them to help their communities in return for society's help, and to gain experience and contacts that will be helpful as they make the transition from welfare to work. Moreover, mixing former welfare recipients with youths from all social backgrounds will avoid the stigma that usually attaches to public jobs programs intended exclusively for the poor.

National Service: Pros and Cons

Predictably, conservative critics describe national service as a costly boondoggle that will spawn new layers of government bureaucracy. However, a true cost accounting must reckon not only the public costs but also the value of the services delivered by volunteers. These include potentially enormous savings from cutting illiteracy rates, giving elderly people an alternative to nursing homes, and reducing welfare payments, as well as the higher earnings—and tax payments—of people who finance college or job training through national service. Conversely, we must also consider the costs to society of not tackling our social dilemmas.

Overhead costs for the Citizens Corps can be minimized by relying extensively on voluntary associations as the principal sponsors of youth service. This not only reduces costs but makes for more effective grass roots delivery of services. Germany, for example, manages 130,000 civilian servers with a federal staff of only 400 people.[32]

Although it is difficult to estimate the value of the services delivered by volunteers, numerous studies of existing programs have shown they provide a greater benefit than cost. A study of the California Conservation Corps showed that it yielded benefits of $1.60 for every dollar spent, for example.[33] Additional savings will also come from eventually eliminating the current system of student loans and grants.

Some liberals and education lobbyists maintain that linking student aid to a service obligation discriminates against poor and minority Americans, who have no alternative means of paying for college. This argument, however, overlooks several realities. With median incomes stagnant since the early 1970s, and college tuitions rising faster than inflation, many middle-class families also need financial help to educate their children. Moreover, most students already must work to make up the difference between the federal aid they receive and college costs. Even more to the point, national service would open avenues that don't exist now for noncollege bound youth—a group that includes 78 percent of blacks and 82 percent of Hispanics aged 18–24.[34] Finally, the services rendered by Citizens Corps volunteers would primarily benefit poor and minority communities.

The idea of national service has intrigued Americans since William James first proposed it in his famous 1910 essay, "The Moral Equivalent of War."[35] James saw national service as an alternative to the military that would impart the same heroic and noble qualities in civilian service that he associated with warfare. But, by opposing civilian with military service, James set up a contradiction that handicapped the advancement of national service. The virtue of military service rests not in its martial values, but in its character as one of the deepest forms of citizenship obligation and sacrifice for the good of our democratic commonwealth. This quality is true of civilian service as well. Today, the need to engage young people in that kind of civic enterprise is greater than ever.

Finally, national service can be a democratizing and integrating force for an increasingly balkanized nation. The Citizen Corps would be a common civic endeavor for youths of all backgrounds, who meet in national service on terms of strict civic equality. And by linking government benefits to public service, national service could awaken a new spirit of civic enterprise and responsibility in America.

NEXT STEPS

In 1990, Congress passed the National and Community Service Act, which earmarked $22 million to support up to eight demonstration projects for a large-scale program of voluntary national service. That bill also established a National and Community Service Commission to administer these and other grants for youth service.

The new administration should propose an additional $2 billion to expand federal aid to post-secondary education. The money should be used to enlarge the eight demonstration projects and create others, and to raise the value of the vouchers volunteers earn from a year of service. The 1990 act set the value of vouchers too low; at $5,000, or roughly the average cost of just one year at a public university. By doubling that amount, volunteers could earn nearly enough from two years of service to pay for undergraduate studies at a public university. An immediate goal is to support legislation to expand student loan cancellation programs for those who serve as full-time, low-paid employees in community service. The National and Community Service Commission should be charged with assessing how well the demonstration projects meet the twin goals of national service: expanding student aid and mobilizing volunteers to tackle community problems.

In modern times both conservatives and liberals of a libertarian bent have de-emphasized the role of citizen duties in favor of highly individualistic ethic. Whether advocating an activist state handing out benefits, as liberals do, or favoring a state that needs to be curbed, as conservatives do, the view of citizenship remains undeveloped; individuals are bound by no meaningful obligations. The Nunn-McCurdy bill points to a more balanced and nuanced formulation of citizenship duties and rights. To the degree practical, recipients of taxpayers' money should earn their money, especially when it is being used to increase the lifetime earnings of its recipients. The linchpin of the Nunn-McCurdy bill was to extend the principle of the GI Bill—an education or job training or a home down payment as a reward for military duty—to civilian service.

MANDATE FOR ACTION

1. **Promote charter schools and other state efforts to harness choice and competition to improve our public schools.** President Clinton should put the resources of his Education Department behind state efforts to design and enact public school choice laws. He should further encourage the states by proposing that they be allowed to use a significant portion of federal education aid to set up innovative public schools. Presidential leadership also is essential for setting broad, national standards of performance for all public schools, including charter schools.

2. **Use federal grants to leverage school-business partnerships for youth apprenticeship.** The Clinton administration should propose $150 million for youth-apprenticeship demonstration projects that combine classroom instruction with on-the-job training with a local business. It should also set up a National Youth Apprenticeship Institute to set national standards for training and certifying apprentices. The President should also ask Congress to require that programs using federal vocational funds be required to set up joint, school-business boards that would oversee training and apprenticeship programs.

3. **Enact a new "civilian GI bill" to ensure equal access to higher education and job training for all Americans.** The President should ask Congress to authorize $2 billion to create large-scale national service demonstration projects around the country. Building upon the modest efforts already underway, a new GI bill should aim at the creation of a nationwide "Citizens Corps" mobilizing hundreds of thousands of young Americans to tackle our country's most stubborn social problems. If it works, national service should eventually replace existing grant and loan programs as the primary means of delivering federal student aid to young people.

7

A Progressive Family Policy for the 1990s

ELAINE CIULLA KAMARCK AND
WILLIAM A. GALSTON

THE WELL-BEING OF AMERICA'S CHILDREN AND FAMILIES

During the past generation, discussions about children and families have been mired in the fruitless dialogue that has led so many Americans to believe that politics can't help solve our country's problems. Many liberals have focused on family economics while overlooking family structure. Meanwhile, many conservatives have emphasized family structure while neglecting economics—witness this summer's farcical Murphy Brown brouhaha.

This debate represents a classic false choice. The reality, we believe, is this: America's children are in trouble, and their troubles are rooted in both economic stress and family disintegration. Hard-pressed parents are increasingly short of time, financial resources, and community support needed to raise their children properly. At the same time, epidemics of divorce, out-of-wedlock births, and family dysfunction have deprived too many children of vital relationships with adults. A progressive family policy must address these problems simultaneously, with programs that both increase the resources available to parents and improve the chances that children will grow up in stable, intact families. That is the agenda we propose in this chapter:

- a cultural agenda—focused on government, schools, and the media—that reinforces the values of parental responsibility and child development;
- a tax code that significantly eases the burdens of middle-class parents with minor children and other dependents;
- a dramatic expansion of the Earned Income Tax Credit, keyed to family size;
- legal reforms to strengthen child-support enforcement and to discourage unnecessary divorce;
- a range of measures to reinforce parental responsibility;
- a family-friendly workplace that seeks to ease tensions between work and parenthood;
- a new approach to public intervention that emphasizes family preservation rather than foster care for those families under severe stress.

This chapter begins by discussing the most recent evidence and best research available concerning the condition of America's families and children. This evidence documents the declining well-being of our children along many dimensions, as well as the critical role played in this decline by the economic dislocations too many of our families have experienced. It also documents the independent causal role of changing family structure.

Here as elsewhere we must be careful and precise. While a large body of evidence supports the conclusion that, in the aggregate, the intact two-parent family is best suited to the task of bringing up children, this does not mean that all single-parent families are bad or dysfunctional. Nor does it mean that preservation of a two-parent family is always the best option. There are obviously situations—such as those involving abuse—in which the two-parent family does not serve the best interests of the children. Clearly, there are millions of single parents who are struggling successfully against the odds to provide good homes for their children. Nevertheless, at the level of statistical aggregates, significant differences emerge between one-parent and two-parent families. We should not be afraid to talk about these differences, nor should we be afraid to talk about their effects on children—they can, and should, shape our understanding of social policy.

FAMILY ECONOMICS

For some years, liberals have been arguing that families with children are being squeezed by declining wages for young workers. This argument is supported by recent analyses. For example, economist Frank Levy has shown that between the early 1970s and late 1980s the mean annual earnings of young high-school-educated men working full-time declined by 16 percent. (Among those with less than a high school education, the decline was almost twice as steep.) Levy suggests that coupled with declining unionization, increased international competition since 1973 reduced the availability of low-skill, high-wage jobs (especially in the manufacturing sector) and forced many poorly educated younger men to accept lower paying jobs in the service sector. Income inequality widened, not because wages for college-educated men increased (they actually declined a bit), but because wages for high school graduates and dropouts declined so much faster.

For women, on the other hand, wages increased across the board regardless of age and education between the early 1970s and late 1980s. Gains were greatest for younger, higher-educated workers, but they were significant in every category.

As male earnings declined, young men became less able to sustain their families at a middle-class standard of living as sole breadwinners. In 1973, median annual earnings for young high-school-educated men amounted to about 90 percent of median family incomes. By 1986, their earnings were only 72 percent of median family incomes. Meanwhile, women became increasingly able to translate their skills into income.[1] Taken together, these facts go a long way toward explaining the surge of women, especially younger women, into the work force during the past two decades. Setting to one side (for the moment) questions of personal satisfaction, women's income earned outside the home became more significant in securing a middle-class way of life for their families.

It is sometimes argued that the economic rationale for the two-parent family has eroded during the past generation. The truth is just the reverse: Economically, the two-parent family is more, rather than less, necessary because more and more families need two incomes to sustain even a modest middle-class existence. This truth cuts both ways, however. Not only do husbands need wives more, but wives need husbands more. With the exception of the Murphy Browns of this country (who constitute an exceedingly small proportion of the single mothers in America), the thesis that increased economic opportunity for women makes it more possible for mothers with minor children to go it alone is not supported by the evidence.

THE DECLINING WELL-BEING OF AMERICA'S CHILDREN

By some measures, the well-being of America's children has actually improved during the past generation.[2] Nevertheless, most of the major trends have been headed in the wrong direction (table 1).

The breakdown of aggregate child poverty into subcategories helps pinpoint the areas of greatest distress. While among all children 18 years and younger, one in five is poor; among children younger than six, the figure is almost one in four; among children in families headed by adults younger than 30, the figure is one in three; among black children, the figure is almost one in two.

The surge in child poverty has occurred in the face of counter-

Table 1. Child Well-Being: Indices of Decline

	1960	1970	1980	Most recent
SAT scores (verbal)	477	460	424	424 (1991)
SAT scores (math)	498	488	466	474 (1991)
Suicide rate (ages 15-19, per 100,000)	3.6	5.9	8.5	11.3 (1988)
Homicide rate (ages 15-19, per 100,000)	4.0	8.1	10.6	11.7 (1988)
Juvenile crime rate (ages 15-19, per 100,000)	20.0	32.0	38.3	44.3 (1986)
Children in poverty (%)	26.9	18.3	20.6	20.6 (1990)

As this table indicates, one of the most worrisome economic trends is the sharp rise in the percentage of American children living in poverty—up by more than one third during the past 20 years. Today, more than one American child in five is poor.
Source: Isabel V. Sawhill, "Young Children and Families, Setting Domestic Priorities: What Can Government Do?" Eds. Henry J. Aaron and Charles L. Schultze (Washington, D.C.: Brookings Institution, 1992), 148-49.

vailing trends. In the U.S. population as a whole, poverty is no higher today than it was 20 years ago, and some groups have even experienced very significant declines. While fully one-quarter of those aged 65 or older had incomes below the poverty line in 1970, less than one-eighth of the elderly are poor today. For most of our history, elderly Americans were on average far worse off than children. It was not until 1974, in fact, that the two lines crossed. The current situation, in which Americans under 18 are almost twice as likely to be poor as those over 65, is unprecedented in the modern era.[3] It is also extraordinary by international standards. The U.S. poverty rate for the elderly is about average for advanced industrialized nations. By contrast, our poverty rate for children is the highest of any of the comparable countries.[4]

While incomes of families with children have declined in the aggregate during recent years, benefits and burdens have been unequally distributed among income groups. In fact, the best-off families have enjoyed significant improvements while the worst-off have endured major reductions (table 2).

FAMILY STRUCTURE: ECONOMIC EFFECTS

The dramatic rise in child poverty is fueled in part by declining wages for working parents, particularly those with limited education and skills. But we cannot overlook the independent impact of changing family structure. Indeed, the clearest consequence of raising children in one-parent homes is economic.

It is no exaggeration to say that a stable, two-parent family is an American child's best protection against poverty. As welfare expert David T. Ellwood has observed, "The vast majority of children who are raised entirely in a two-parent home will never be poor during childhood. By contrast, the vast majority of children who spend time in a single-parent home will experience poverty."[5] At the root of the problems faced by single-parent families is the simple fact that "single parents must balance the dual roles of nurturer and provider. Doing both well can seem almost impossible."[6] Family structure turns out to be such a powerful correlate of childhood poverty that changes in family structure over the past three decades provide the most dramatic explanation for the concomitant large increases in childhood poverty.

Not only have recent decades seen an increase in one-parent families as the result of rising out-of-wedlock births and rising divorce rates, they have also seen an increase in the poverty of

Table 2. Percentage Change in Median Income of Families with Children 1979–1990

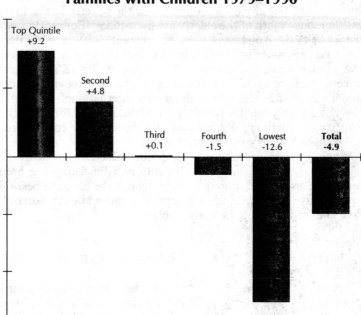

These adverse developments for the least well-off families are not the artifact of an arbitrarily selected time period. A glance further back reveals that inflation-adjusted family income in the bottom fifth of the population was 11 percent lower in 1987 than in 1973. Single mothers with children fared the worst: the two lowest quintiles had income 21 and 15 percent lower than their counterparts 14 years earlier.

To be sure, the situation is not quite as bad as these figures would seem to indicate. Family income statistics do not reveal, or correct for, the significant decline in the average number of children per family. By several measures, average income per child has actually gone up. In addition, the snapshot of poverty for any given year obscures the fact that many families will quickly move out of poverty. Still about 10 percent of all children will experience persistent as opposed to temporary, poverty, and the figure for African-American children is almost four times as high.

Source: Annie Casey Foundation, Kids Count Data Book (Washington, D.C.: Center for the Study of Social Policy, 1992).

those families. In 1949, children in single-parent families were almost twice as likely to be poor as children in the general population; by 1979, children in these families were three-and-a-half times as likely to be poor as the general population.[7] In a large statistical study using census data from the 1960s on, two Penn State sociologists, David Eggebeen and Daniel T. Lichter, conclude that "child poverty rates would have been one-third less in 1988 if family structure had not changed since 1960." Furthermore, "changing family structure accounted for nearly 50 percent of the increase in child poverty rates since 1980." Finally, they conclude that "child poverty and racial inequality cannot be separated from the issue of changing family structure in America."[8]

The conclusion that the best antipoverty program for children is a stable, intact family holds even for families with modest levels of educational attainment. For married high school graduates with children, the 1991 poverty rate was 7 percent, versus more than 41 percent for families headed by female high school graduates. For married high school dropouts with children, the poverty rate was 25 percent, versus more than 62 percent for families headed by female high school dropouts.[9]

Divergences in family structure between whites and African-Americans, already notable a generation ago, have continued to widen (table 3).

Equally notable, but far less discussed, is the impact of family structure on family income differences between blacks and whites. The gap in child poverty rates between black and white married couples has shrunk dramatically over the past 30 years, while the

Table 3. Family Structure: Key Indicators

	Black (1988)	White (1988)
Married-couple families as a percentage of all households	51	83
Female-headed family households (%)	43	9
Children not living with two parents (%)	61	21
Children born to unmarried mothers (%)	60	15
Children in poverty (%)	46	15

Source: U.S. Bureau of the Census, Census of Population: 1990 (Washington, D.C., 1990), and U.S. Bureau of the Census, Current Population Reports, series P-20 (Washington, D.C., 1990).

corresponding gap between black and white female-headed families has barely budged. During this same period, the poverty gap between black married couples and black female-headed couples has more than doubled and now stands at an astounding 50 percentage points (table 4).

Overall, Frank Furstenberg, Jr., and Andrew Cherlin conclude in their authoritative study *Divided Families*, the differences in family structure go "a long way toward accounting for the enormous racial disparity in poverty rates. Within family types, black families are still poorer than white families, but the racial gap in poverty shrinks considerably when the marital status of the household head is taken into account."[10]

To be sure, the causal arrow could point in the opposite direction: Differences in family structure might be thought to reflect differences in economic status. William Julius Wilson offered an influential statement on this counterthesis in *The Truly Disadvantaged*: Lower black marriage rates reflect dramatically higher rates of black male unemployment, which reduced the "male marriageable pool—under the assumption that 'to be marriageable a man needs to be employed.' "[11] But the most recent research offers only modest support for this hypothesis. Robert Mare and Christopher Winship find that changes in employment rates among young black males account for only 20 percent of the decline in their marriage rates since 1960; they speculate that the various family disruptions of the past three decades may be self-reinforcing.[12]

Table 4. Child Poverty and Family Structure

		1960	1970	1980	1988
	White	20.2	11.1	11.1	15.4
	Black	66.2	44.1	37.1	45.6
Percentage of children in poverty	Married-couple families	21.9	10.4	9.1	10.1
	white	17.6	8.0	7.3	9.0
	black	61.2	31.8	18.1	17.0
	Female-headed families	66.7	51.5	46.2	54.1
	white	58.2	42.3	36.2	45.8
	black	84.8	66.9	59.1	67.6

Source: David J. Eggebeen and Daniel T. Lichter, "Race, Family Structure and Changing Poverty Among American Children," American Sociological Review 56 (Dec. 1991): 801-17.

Though Wilson continues to defend the validity of his thesis for the hardest-hit central cities of the Northeast and Midwest, he is now willing to say that "the decline in marriage among inner-city blacks is not simply a function of the proportion of jobless men. ... It is reasonable to consider [as well] the effects of weaker social strictures against out-of-wedlock births."[13]

While much attention has been focused on the impact of family non-formation and out-of-wedlock births (especially to teenage mothers), the breakup of previously intact families is another potent source of poverty and declining well-being among children. According to a Census Bureau study headed by Suzanne Bianchi that identified and tracked 20,000 households, it turns out that after parents separate or divorce, children are almost twice as likely to be living in poverty as they were before the split.[14] The gross income of the children and their custodial parent (usually the mother) dropped by 37 percent immediately after the family breakup (26 percent after adjustment for the decline in family size) and recovered only slightly after 16 months. These findings support the arguments of scholars who have long contended that divorce under current law spells economic hardship for most custodial parents and their minor children.

FAMILY STRUCTURE: NONECONOMIC EFFECTS

The attempt to sort out the relationship between the poverty of single-parent families and the other problems that their children encounter in greater than average numbers brings us to the extraordinarily difficult problem of what social scientists call "covariance"—the problem of sorting out causal relations among factors that tend to occur together. There are many problems that occur frequently among the children of single-parent families which may result, in complex ways, from the greater poverty and lower educational levels of the mothers in many of these families.[15]

Nevertheless, a substantial body of research suggests that family structure is an independent factor influencing the well-being of children. Even after correcting for variables such as family income, parental education, and prior family history, children from single-parent families tend on average to fare less well economically, educationally, and emotionally, and to encounter more difficulties on the road to becoming self-sustaining adults. Regardless of the academic discussion about the direction of causality, an honest accounting of these problems is critical.

The economic consequences of a parent's absence (almost always the father's) are often accompanied by psychological consequences, which include higher than average levels of youth suicide, low intellectual and educational performance, and higher than average rates of mental illness, violence, and drug use.[16] The data also suggest that the daughters of teenage mothers are more likely to become teenage mothers themselves and are at higher risk of long-term welfare dependency.[17] Equally suggestive is the anecdotal evidence of the difficulties many young single mothers experience in raising their sons.[18] The absence of fathers as models and codisciplinarians is thought to contribute to the low self-esteem, anger, violence, and peer-bonding through gang membership of many fatherless boys.

Nowhere is this more evident than in the long-standing and strong relationship between crime and one-parent families. In a recent study Douglas Smith and G. Roger Jarjoura found that "neighborhoods with larger percentages of youth (those aged 12 to 20) and areas with higher percentages of single-parent households also have higher rates of violent crime." The relationship is so strong that controlling for family configuration erases the relationship between race and crime and between low income and crime. This conclusion shows up time and time again in the literature; poverty is far from the sole determinant of crime.[19]

But family structure is not an issue for the poor alone. A 1981 study by John Guidubaldi of children, half from intact families and half from divorced families, showed that the psychological consequences of divorce were significant regardless of income differences.[20] Likewise, the psychologist Judith Wallerstein studied 60 middle-class divorced families and found significant and long-lasting emotional and psychological effects on the children. "The effects of divorce," writes Wallerstein, "are long-lasting. . . . Divorce is almost always more devastating for children than for their parents."[21]

For most children, divorce comes as an unwelcome shock, even when the parents are openly quarreling. In the short-term, boys seem to have a harder time coping than girls, in part because of an "escalating cycle of misbehavior and harsh response between mothers and sons." Girls more typically respond not with outward anger but with heightened levels of anxiety, withdrawal, inability to form lasting relationships, and depression that may become apparent only years later.[22]

These differences reflect the fact that divorce almost always means disrupted relations with the father. Even in the period relatively soon after divorce, only one-sixth of all children will see their fathers as often as once a week, and close to one-half will not see them at all. After ten years, almost two-thirds will have no contact at all.[23]

The problems produced by divorce extend well beyond vanishing male role models. Children need authoritative rules, stable schedules, and ample contact time, which harried single parents often find hard to supply. Along with economic pressures, family disintegration and non-formation are key sources of the decline in time parents spend with their children.

Teachers and school administrators have known for some time that the disintegration of the American family is a major cause of America's declining educational achievement. During the 1980s per-pupil spending in the United States increased dramatically and yet, at the end of the decade, test scores registered virtually no gains.[24] John Ourth, principal of Oak Terrace High School in Highwood, Illinois, writes that "a child who is in crisis cannot learn until school personnel recognize the crisis and take steps to ameliorate its effects. . . . Any major change in a child's family (and separation and divorce are among the most major) can spell crisis."[25]

As we have acknowledged, untangling just what it is about family structure that makes for high or low educational achievement is a difficult task. Clearly, economics has to do with achievement; children from poor families consistently do less well than do children from non-poor or well-to-do families. Nevertheless, income is not the whole story. When studies control for income, significant differences in educational achievement still appear. In a study of 14,493 students conducted by the National Association of Elementary School Principals and the Institute for Development of Educational Activities, family structure had an important and significant effect on educational achievement above and beyond income level—especially for boys. Lower-income girls with two parents, for instance, score higher on achievement tests than do higher-income boys with one parent. At the very bottom of the achievement scale are lower-income boys with one parent.[26]

Government can help to cope with the consequences of family disintegration, but it cannot fully compensate for the absence of supportive families. To enhance the well-being—economic, emotional, and educational—of America's children, the new administration cannot overlook the need to foster and reinforce stable families.

A PROGRESSIVE FAMILY POLICY

The principles that should guide this new policy are straightforward: Public programs cannot fully substitute for healthy families; community responsibility can supplement, but cannot replace, parental responsibility. With the exception of those children and families in severe crises, the goal of government should be to reinforce and stabilize families while enhancing their child-rearing capacity. In so doing, government will have to provide additional resources. But, at the same time, it must minimize bureaucratic cost, complexity, and intrusion, working instead to broaden individual choice and opportunity. The purpose of family policy, in short, should be to support and compensate families as they carry out their critical social role—providing for the economic and moral well-being of children.[27]

The progressive family policy outlined below emphasizes the goal of family preservation through measures targeted to the needs of diverse families in different situations. Because the combination of early motherhood and the absence of two parents contributes to the most severe problems of well-being among children in America today, it begins with the need to use the entire ability of our society to persuade young people to avoid out-of-wedlock pregnancies. For middle-class families, the government can provide a package of tax cuts that includes a substantial increase in the personal exemption for young children and elderly parents. For the working poor, it can offer an increase in the Earned Income Tax Credit. For the poorest of the poor, the government must offer early family preservation strategies. And for all families, it must provide for the reform of divorce laws, the reinforcement of parental responsibility, the creation of "family-friendly" workplaces, and a cultural climate more hospitable to sound child rearing.

A NATIONAL COMMITMENT TO STABLE FAMILIES

The President should use the full force of his office to wage an all-out campaign against teenage pregnancy. School-based campaigns against smoking that combine factual information, personal testimony, and sophisticated use of media have been quite successful. Is it not time for a comparably intense campaign against teenage pregnancy and out-of-wedlock birth and in favor of marriage? There are scores of state and local programs already in existence, using a wide variety of carrots and sticks, which are designed to prevent teenage pregnancy. It is time to evaluate the collective experience of these programs and bring together government, academia, the private sector, and the talents of sports and entertainment figures in a nationwide campaign against teenage pregnancy. (Perhaps Murphy Brown would like to help.) This national campaign could underscore the long-term adverse consequences of short-sighted behavior for teens themselves and for their children, drive home the personal effort and moral responsibility that parenthood entails, and reinforce the practical and emotional benefits of stable marriages.

No doubt objections would be raised and fears expressed; it would be necessary to craft the message in close cooperation with parents, religious groups, and civil libertarians. Still, there seems little to lose in testing the efficacy of persuasion through the community's moral voice.

Senator Daniel Patrick Moynihan draws an interesting parallel between family policy today and economic policy after World War II. The Employment Act of 1946 did little more than create the Council of Economic Advisors, yet it had a far greater impact than any jobs bill. The reason, Moynihan notes, is that the act declared a national policy and marked the acceptance of a previously disputed social responsibility. Similarly, Moynihan suggests, it would be a significant step forward "for a national family policy to declare that the American government sought to promote the stability and well-being of the American family; that the social programs of the federal government would be formulated and administered with this object in mind; and finally, that the President, or some person designated by him, would report to the Congress on the condition of the American family."[28] While Moynihan does not identify a specific agency, it would seem appropriate for the commissioner for children, youth, and families, located within the Department of Health and Human Services, to take the lead in such an endeavor. This kind of declaratory policy could carry great weight.

TAX RELIEF FOR FAMILIES WITH DEPENDENTS

America is the only country among 18 rich democracies in the world that does not have a family allowance or some other sort of explicit government child subsidy.[29] We used to have a form of family allowance; we just did not call it that. In 1948, when the median family income was only $3,187, the personal exemption was $600.[30] This meant that a family of four at median income paid a minuscule 0.3 percent of its income in federal income taxes compared to today's 9.1 percent.[31]

Since 1945, the real value of the dependent exemption has been allowed to erode by three-quarters. The result over time has been, in economist Gene Steuerle's words, that "tax-exempt levels for households without dependents have been moving closer and closer to tax-exempt levels for households with dependents."[32] The idea of giving tax relief to families with children has gained popularity in recent Congresses. Senator Al Gore and Congressman Tom Downey proposed an $800 tax credit per child for all children up to age 18. Senator Joe Lieberman has proposed making the personal exemption progressive by enlarging it for the lower tax brackets, but he has targeted it to preschool-aged children—a precedent established in the recent expansion of the Earned Income Tax Credit, which gives some extra money to families with children under the age of one.[33]

To reverse decades of neglect we need a children's tax credit of $800 per child for all preschool children. It would be gradually phased out so that by the time a child is 11 the tax relief that a family receives per child would be equal to the current dependent exemption. An $800 tax credit is the equivalent of an expanded dependent's exemption of $5330 for an average income family. (A tax credit is automatically progressive, although the dependent's exemption could be made progressive as it has been in Senator Lieberman's proposal.)

The more critical point is the necessity of targeting tax relief to families according to the age of the children. This is important for two reasons: The first is that it is cheaper, and thus more politically feasible, given the tough budget deficits the new President will face; and second, it gives the most tax relief to the families who need it most—young families with children. A children's tax credit extended to all dependents would be an extraordinarily expensive proposition. Had a $5330 personal exemption been in effect for all dependents in 1990 it would have cost the government approximately $38.2 billion dollars. Thus, to be affordable as well as effective, the increase in the personal exemption must be crafted and targeted carefully. Limiting the personal exemption of $5330 to children under age four significantly reduces its cost, to just under $10 billion. Alternatively, the Joint Committee on Taxation estimated that a personal exemption of $4,000 for children under age five, phased down to the ordinary level by age eight, would cost the federal government $2.8 billion in 1991, $5.7 billion in 1992, and a total of $27.1 billion in the years 1991–1995.[34]

The second reason, in addition to cost, for targeting tax relief to families with young children, is that families often face the most stress when their children are very young and both parents are forced to work. Very few American mothers in the 1990s see themselves spending the rest of their lives out of the paid work force, but many American mothers (and some fathers too) would like the option of staying at home when their children are young. Significant tax relief, limited to young children, would allow the federal government to do away with all day-care expenditures and tax credits that are not targeted specifically to poor children or to children with special needs (such as the handicapped or the mentally retarded).

These steps will aid not only two-parent families, for whom the extra money might make it more feasible for one parent to stay home full time with small children or help pay for day care, but also single parents who must work and who need help with the costs of day care. In addition, there is another piece of tax law that must be changed to aid single parents. The tax code currently provides three filing statuses: single, married, and head of household. The latter is designed for single parents and is taxed at a rate which, as the economist Larry Lindsey points out, is "roughly midway between those applied to single filers (which are higher) and those applied to married couples (which are lower)." This makes no sense for, as Lindsey argues, "Single-parent families have nothing in common with single people and everything in common with other families."[35] Single-parent families should have the same tax rate as married-couple families.

Taken together, these steps would move us toward the goal of giving parents greater choice. The mother who is forced by economic necessity to work more hours than she wants to outside the home is as much a prisoner as the mother of an earlier era who was forced to stay at home for reasons of social pressure. Working mothers will have more money under this plan to pay for the kind of day care that every parent wants. For mothers or fathers who want to take some time off to be at home, this package of tax changes may help lighten the economic burden, especially when there are two or more young children at home.

And finally, nurturing has value to society not only at the beginning of life but at the end of life. In the last three decades our society has made enormous strides in the care of our elderly citizens. In fact, our elderly now have the lowest poverty rate of any age group in society. But this has come at an economic cost which—via Medicare—threatens to throw the federal government even deeper into debt, and at a social cost: loneliness and isolation for millions of elderly Americans.

For those Americans, primarily women, who are responsible for the care of their elderly parents, the government provides no support for what is a very costly proposition. Two years ago the cover of *Newsweek* trumpeted the "Daughter Track," the fact that American women will spend an average of 17 years raising children and an average of 18 years caring for elderly parents. The American Association of Retired Persons found that in recent years about 14 percent of care-givers to the elderly have switched from full-time to part-time jobs and 12 percent have left the workplace altogether.[36]

The same principle that governs the beginning of life applies to the end: Most families nurture better than government ever can. Although nurturing comes at an economic cost to the family, home care is cheaper than institutional alternatives, which can run to over $30,000 per year.

For these reasons we should explore the possibility that an increased personal exemption be made available to families who care for an elderly person over the age of 70 in their homes. This would involve one more change in the tax law. At present it is very difficult for families to claim elderly persons as dependents. The Treasury Department is currently exploring changing this in order to make it economically feasible for more families to care for their elderly parents. Once again, these changes will cost the government a significant amount of money, but these costs must be measured against the astronomical costs of institutionalization, hospitalization, and professional home nursing care.

An increased "elderly exemption" is entirely consistent with the thesis behind an increased "children's exemption": families are a proven and well-tested institution for nurturance and care. Rather than trying to reinvent the family via government programs, we should simply give the family the wherewithal to function properly.

EXPANDING THE EARNED INCOME TAX CREDIT

Ordinary tax relief will not help working-poor families, in whose ranks can be found more than half of all poor children. In 1988 there were more than 2.9 million poor American families with children under age 18 that were headed by someone who was working.

As with the middle class, government help for these families should vary with the number of dependents. In 1989, the Progressive Policy Institute published an analysis arguing for an expanded version of the current Earned Income Tax Credit. The Earned Income Tax Credit (EITC) wage supplement, once tied to family size, would be the most efficient way of helping working-poor families.

A significant increase in the EITC could help more than half of the nation's poor children. Moreover, it would be relatively simple and straightforward to redesign the EITC in order to guarantee that any parent working full-time, year-round, would be able to support his or her family above the poverty line. This would be a vastly more efficient way of moving families out of poverty than would another increase in the minimum wage, since 85 percent of minimum-wage workers live in non-poor households—and half of all poor workers hold jobs not covered by the minimum wage.[37]

Converting the current EITC program into a guaranteed "working wage" for poor families would require that the wage supplement be set at the level required to fill the gap between full-time, year-round minimum wage earnings and the poverty line, given the size of the family. Therefore, the benefit would grow with the number of hours worked and the number of children being supported. It would also require reducing the amount of complexity now associated with using the EITC.

In fiscal year 1991 Congress passed a $12.4 billion expansion of the EITC to take effect over five years. This legislation took important first steps by tying the benefits to family size and by including a special subsidy for children under the age of one year. Building on this foundation, the PPI proposal would help realize a basic principle of our social covenant, that full-time work should suffice to lift families out of poverty.

DIVORCE LAW REFORM

Given the enormously important social role that families raising children fill, it is appropriate for society to establish distinctions in its treatment of families with and without children. One prime candidate for this strategy of differentiation is the law of divorce. First, the child-support system should be federalized in order to ensure that payments are actually made. Second, the bases for awarding payments should be reformed to take into account the cost of motherhood to women's earning capacity and the existence of children in a household. And finally, we propose looking at braking mechanisms in the divorce law for parents considering divorce (but not for childless couples).

Twenty years ago the state of California enacted the much heralded "no-fault" divorce. It was supposed to end the use of the courtroom as a battleground and to make obsolete some of the more humiliating grounds for divorce as well as their widespread manipulation. Other states rapidly followed. No-fault divorce was and is a sensible and important reform for married couples without children. But for families with children it has been a driving force behind the feminization of poverty.

Even after the limited federal and state reforms of the 1980s, the child support system is a mess. More than one-third of all absent fathers simply ignore their legal obligation to support their children, and many others pay only a fraction of what they owe. The average annual payment for those who do pay is only $2,300, and many use delays or arbitrary reductions in support payments to achieve other bargaining objectives vis-à-vis the custodial parent. If a reasonable level of collections and payments were achieved, absent fathers could contribute $25 billion more each year than they do today.[38] And if the system were made less discretionary and more uniform, a major source of uncertainty, conflict, and distress for custodial parents would be removed.

Parental responsibility for children does not cease simply because of divorce, separation, or out-of-wedlock birth. And, as David Ellwood argues, to enforce this basic moral proposition we ought to take a page from the tax system and create a far more uniform and straightforward method of child support. The new administration should seek passage of measures along the lines of the Downey-Hyde proposal currently being formulated in Congress.[39] Among other things it would make the IRS the central collection agency for child-support payments. The major steps toward reform that should also guide the administration are as follows:

- Society should commit itself to identifying every child's father and mother. In the future, the Social Security numbers of both parents should appear on each child's birth certificate. All absent parents should be expected to contribute a portion of their income, and the portion should vary with the number of children they fathered or bore.
- Payments should be collected by employers, just like Social Security taxes, and remitted to the federal government, which should then send this money directly to the custodial parent. All absent parents should be included, not just delinquent ones. Failure to pay should be an offense comparable to tax evasion.[40]

By itself, rigorous enforcement of child-support decrees will not be enough. Realistic assessments of what happens to women's earnings once they become mothers are important in determining an adequate level of support for the child. Women enter marriages earning less than men for a whole host of reasons including sex discrimination and employment in low-paying "female" fields. But, if in the course of their marriage they have become mothers, they leave marriages earning substantially less than men. As divorce expert Lenore Weitzman points out, "marriage—and then divorce—impose a differential disadvantage on women's employment prospects, and this is especially severe for women who have custody of minor children. The responsibility for children inevitably restricts the mother's job opportunities by limiting her work schedule and location, her availability for overtime, and her freedom to take advantage of special training, travel assignments, and other opportunities for career advancement."[41]

Thus, divorce law reform must recognize that in the courts' new concern for parental "equality," children may suffer. A principle of equality is obviously appropriate in those divorces where the woman is childless. But in those cases where children are present, reform must take into account the impact of motherhood on a woman's earning capacity, as well as the per capita expenses of the household with women and children.

As Mary Ann Glendon, a leading American student of the law of divorce, has observed:

> When almost three-fifths of all divorces in the United States involve couples with minor children, it is astonishing that our spousal support law and marital property law treat that situation as an exception to the general rule.

> A "children first" principle should govern all such divorces. . . . The judges' main task would be to piece together, from property and income and in-kind personal care, the best possible package to meet the needs of the children and their physical guardian. Until the welfare of the children had been adequately secured in this way, there would be no question or debate about "marital property." All property, no matter when or how acquired, would be subject to the duty to provide for the children.[42]

Finally, a thorough reform of divorce law must go beyond even questions of economic support. Because of the shattering emotional and developmental effects of divorce on children, it would be reasonable to introduce "braking" mechanisms that require parents contemplating divorce to pause for reflection. There is transatlantic precedent for such procedures. A report from Britain's Law Commission has recommended that such couples "notify the courts of their intention and then spend at least nine months resolving crucial details of the divorce. Their first obligation would be to decide the future of their children before settling questions of property and maintenance. Only then could couples return to court for a divorce." As one account notes, "By encouraging parents to look at the consequences of a family breakup rather than at the alleged cause or excuse for it, the commission hopes couples will improve their prospects of saving the marriage."[43]

There are some efforts underway in the United States to emphasize the importance of the children's well-being in the postdivorce family. An experimental program in the Atlanta court system requires counseling sessions for parents considering divorce.[44] In Washington State a statute enacted in 1987 requires parents getting a divorce to submit a permanent parenting plan, the objectives of which are to provide for the child's physical and emotional care and to minimize the child's exposure to harmful parental conflict.[45]

ENCOURAGING PARENTAL RESPONSIBILITY

The government has limited ability to make adults into good parents. Nevertheless, there are measures in addition to economic support that can be taken to reinforce the parental role: The President can exercise substantial leadership using the bully pulpit of the presidency, and federal agencies can evaluate and promulgate successful state and local initiatives of the sort described below.

Sometimes parents may have to be held responsible in civil law for the criminal actions of their children. California's Street Terrorism Enforcement and Protection (STEP) Act makes it a misdemeanor for parents to knowingly permit their children to be involved in gang activities. In other instances, parents may be fined for failing to provide the minimum standard of parental authority with regard to a child's education. In Arkansas, for example, new laws were enacted providing for civil penalties against parents whose children have excessive school absences or parents who fail to attend school conferences at which a plan to help their child master basic skills is presented.[46]

Nowhere, however, is the issue of parental responsibility more acute than with the thousands of mothers who use drugs during pregnancy, with disastrous consequences for their offspring and society. States and localities must reverse the practice whereby most drug rehabilitation centers now refuse to take pregnant women.[47] In fact, the opposite must take place: Pregnant women must be given priority in treatment centers and, when they do not seek treatment on their own, the state must be empowered to force them into treatment. Mandatory treatment on the front end, during pregnancy, is far preferable to prosecution and separation after the child is born. This strategy could significantly improve the health of these children and the parenting skills of the mothers. Waiting until the child is born and then taking the child from the mother into the limbo of the foster-care system is a policy that is, at its heart, anti-family. Programs that go into neighborhoods, parks, and shopping areas looking for pregnant women at risk, such as the Maternity Outreach Mobile (MOM) Project in the District of Columbia, offer one promising avenue for reaching this population before it is too late.

THE FAMILY-FRIENDLY WORKPLACE

The private sector cannot be left out of any discussion of family policy. Slowly but surely, businesses are learning that they are dependent on female employees, and that dependence will only grow as the composition of the labor force continues to change in the 1990s. Several studies have now confirmed what employers have known for some time: A large number of personnel problems are related to child-care problems that affect parents. These problems mean real dollar costs to industries and businesses all over the United States.[48]

In response to the growing awareness that the labor force has a fundamentally different set of concerns from that of years past, employers are:

- developing family leave policies;
- making available flex-time arrangements;
- offering dependent-care plans either through on-site day care or through area day-care providers which they subsidize;
- offering sick-child care;
- offering time off to attend teacher conferences;
- making home-based employment possible for those employees whose jobs lend themselves to such arrangements.

This last suggestion (telecommuting) has great potential, especially in those businesses that employ hundreds of employees, the majority of whom are women, in repetitive data-processing tasks. The federal government, which as one of the nation's largest employers led the way in the use of flex-time schedules, should begin to offer telecommuting options to qualified interested employees. In addition to the parenting advantages that telecommuting provides for families with small children, it offers economic and environmental advantages for society by reducing the number of commuters.[49]

And finally, as more and more women enter the work force and become indispensable contributors to the economy, the provision of family-friendly workplaces becomes a business necessity justified at the bottom line by the desire to recruit new employees and to keep old and valued ones.[50] The opposition of the business lobby and of President Bush to the very modest proposal in the Family and Medical Leave Act of 1992 is incomprehensible—especially in view of a 1989 Government Accounting Office (GAO) report on the bill that states: "We believe there will be little measurable net cost to employers associated with replacing workers or maintaining output while workers are on unpaid leave."[51] The President should sign this bill as a minimum signal to business of what it should begin to do to create a family-friendly workplace.

Consistent with our policy orientation in favor of government aid directly to families with children we would add, as a caveat, that there is no need to provide government tax credits or other inducements to businesses in order to encourage them to adopt family-friendly measures that in fact serve their own interests. The government should promote the use of such measures in the federal work force and through the dissemination of information.

FAMILY PRESERVATION POLICIES[52]

The role of government vis-à-vis the vast majority of American families ought to be one of nonintrusive support. But the government has no choice but to become deeply involved with the lives and choices of those families who live under the severe stresses associated with extreme poverty, such as crime, drug and alcohol abuse, and violence. Here there are frequently no good options; often the children of these families are subject to abuse and/or neglect. Usually the state becomes involved with these families only at the point at which the child needs to be removed from the home for his or her own safety. The child then goes from one set of bad circumstances to another, as he or she enters the confusing and ultimately damaging world of foster care.

In the 1980s the foster-care system, stretched by the plague of crack cocaine and increases in poverty at the bottom of the socio-economic ladder, began to break down. The number of children in foster care in the United States increased from 262,000 in 1980 to 429,000 in 1991.[53] The damage done to children by multiple placements in a severely stretched system turned out to be immense. While foster-care placements were rising so were the number of children admitted to psychiatric hospitals, from 17,324 in 1982 to 23,484 in 1989.[54] During the decade of the 1980s class-action law suits against the child-welfare system were initiated and won in several states.

There is now widespread agreement that the child-welfare system is in need of a massive overhaul from the top down. This reform movement should revolve around the notion of family preservation when at all possible, and family stability when it is not. Simple programs, like the delivery of home-based services to families at risk of ending up in the child-welfare system, are much less costly in the long run than is the severe damage inflicted on children by the instability that results from moving in and out of the foster-care system. A GAO report looked at home visiting programs and concluded: "Compared to families who were not given these services, home-visited clients had fewer low birth-weight babies and reported cases of child abuse and neglect, higher rates of child immunizations and more age-appropriate child development."[55]

Additional evidence suggests the value of home-based services. The Edna McConnel Clark Foundation has sponsored a number of innovative programs including Citizens for Missouri's Children. This foundation group is in the forefront of emergency family intervention programs being experimented with around the country that may turn out to be alternatives to the disruptions now prevalent in the foster-care system. Another program, Home Builders, also funded by the Clark Foundation and some local governments, brings social workers into the homes of families on the verge of dissolution to work with them three to four hours per day. So far these "last-ditch" efforts to save families have worked in 80 percent of the cases and have proved to be less than half the cost ($4,000 to $5,000 per family) of foster care.[56]

By freeing up federal funds to focus on family preservation, state governments would have the flexibility to use monies for the kinds of creative and promising programs that now exist in a haphazard fashion and as the result of policy entrepreneurship. This is the purpose of the Family Preservation Act of 1991 sponsored by Congressmen Tom Downey and George Miller. The bill provides flexibility to states in designing their child-welfare programs and would mandate that some portion of funds be devoted to the support and preservation of vulnerable families. In a similar spirit, the new administration should advocate the widest possible experimentation in the welfare system, through the generous granting of waivers to the AFDC rules, in an effort to discover which methods are most effective for reconstructing the family in poor urban areas.

CONTEMPORARY CULTURE

Finally, a progressive, pro-family policy should examine the impact of the mass media on contemporary culture. Today, nearly every household has a television set, and the average child spends as much time watching television as with parents, and twice as much time as in school. While much research on the impact of television yields murky results, it is fairly well established that educational programming accelerates early learning and that televised violence exacerbates aggressive behavior.

It is difficult to believe that the accumulated impact of such stimuli on marriage and families is insignificant. Average citizens certainly don't think so. In a 1991 survey, for example, only 2 percent of respondents thought that television should have the greatest influence on children's values, but fully 56 percent believe that it does in fact have the greatest influence—more than parents, teachers, and religious leaders combined.[57] In the Institute for American Values researcher Barbara Whitehead's community-level interviews, television emerges in the eyes of parents as a prime vehicle for intensifying hard-to-control consumer and sexual desires among children.[58]

As the Urban Institute's Isabel Sawhill has recently observed, the 1980s witnessed a general effort to deregulate the broadcast industry as antigovernment conservatives seized control of the Federal Communications Commission.[59] In 1984, for example, virtually all restrictions on advertising and guidelines for children's programming were eliminated. More recently, however, the pendulum has begun to swing back. In 1990, Congress enacted the Children's Television Education Act, which "establishes the principle that the broadcast industry has a social responsibility in this area, limits the amount of advertising during children's programs, allows broadcasters to cooperate in limiting violence, and establishes a National Endowment for Children's Television."

The early returns have been disappointing. Rather than improving their offerings, broadcasters have responded to the act by relabeling them. Republicans who once presided over the recategorization of catsup as a vegetable have supinely accepted the reclassification of the GI Joe cartoon series as an educational program. As he implements the 1990 act, the new President should initiate a broad national discussion concerning the responsibilities of publicly licensed media in a free society.[60]

The dangers of excessive concentrations of government power cannot be ignored. But it is equally dangerous (and false) to argue that no alternative lies between moral laissez-faire and tyrannical censorship. For more than 60 years we have accepted the proposition that the allocation and conduct of licensed media present issues affecting the general public interest, not just the rights of individuals. It is time to apply this principle to the new problems of family disintegration, for which the media cannot escape its share of responsibility, and to craft new approaches appropriate to changed circumstances.

CONCLUSION

Once we understand that stable families are the bedrock of stable communities, we can begin to look at social policy with an eye toward strengthening and preserving families. In spite of their great diversity, all American families are both economic units and moral units. When they are functioning well they take care of the next generation's psychological and moral well-being as well as their physical well-being. Some families need economic assistance from the government; others merely need the government to be on their side when it comes to helping them work and raise children. Still other families need large and substantial help, from social workers and therapists, just to function at all. The new President needs to recognize these differences as he works toward a progressive family policy for the 1990s.

MANDATE FOR ACTION

1. **Wage an intense media campaign against teen pregnancy and out-of-wedlock births.** Our leaders should also encourage social responsibility in the area of children's broadcasting.
2. **Pass an $800-per-child tax credit for all preschool children.** The credit should be phased out between the ages of 6 and 10.
3. **Expand the Earned Income Tax Credit for all working poor families.** The benefits should be tied to family size.
4. **Establish a federal system of child-support payments.** Also, paternity must be established for all children whether or not their parents have been married.
5. **Establish model state codes for divorce law.** Such codes should stress the primacy of the children's well-being in divorce proceedings.
6. **Encourage parental responsibility.** This should be done through the bully pulpit of the presidency and through the promulgation and evaluation of state initiatives that seek to reinforce parental responsibility.
7. **Pass the Family Leave Bill and promote family-friendly workplaces.** The federal government should also become a pioneer in telecommuting.
8. **Help families under acute stress to stay together.** The new administration should establish early intervention programs and home-based social service delivery for troubled families.

8

Safer Streets and Neighborhoods

ED KILGORE

TAKING CRIME SERIOUSLY

The most fundamental right any government owes its citizens is personal safety—the right to live, work, and move about peaceably, secure in one's person and property. America's abhorrently high crime rates, especially the grim statistics of violent crimes, document a fundamental failure of domestic government.

By any measure, crime is at shocking levels. In 1991, nearly 15 million crimes were reported—more than four times the number in 1960.[1] Violent crimes rose 14 percent between 1980 and 1988,[2] and then 23 percent between 1988 and 1991.[3] During the last four years, reported murders have jumped 23 percent, rapes 17 percent, robberies 33 percent, and aggravated assaults 28 percent. Yet, it is estimated that 52 percent of violent crimes are not even reported.[4]

Most dramatically, it is estimated that eight out of every ten Americans can expect to be victimized by violent crime at some point in their lives.[5] Technicians look at our crime statistics and lock into an irrelevant debate: Has more frequent reporting spurred recent increases?[6] But whether our violent crime rate is skyrocketing or leveling off at a barbarous plateau, it remains the industrial world's worst. Our homicide rate is more than five times

179

that of Europe, and four times that of Canada, Australia, or New Zealand. Our rate of rapes is nearly nine times that of Europe.[7]

The fear of crime, moreover, dissolves the social fabric that binds Americans together into a community of common experience. It turns strangers into enemies, unfamiliar ground into dangerous turf, and random social contact into risky business. When crime afflicts a neighborhood, those who can avoid it, stay away; those who cannot, suffer alone. The former become isolated, the latter abandoned.

Crime and its consequences sharpen every racial and economic division of our nation, and blunt every popular impulse toward faith in government and willingness to undertake shared sacrifice. More than any other national problem, the failure to ensure domestic security undermines equally the basic values of opportunity, responsibility, community, and national security. Any progressive agenda for America that does not make this issue a top priority cannot pass a threshold test of credibility.

The new administration has a particular responsibility to take crime seriously. The last two Republican administrations waged a harsh inflammatory rhetorical war on crime, a war of words that masked a record of indifference to the measures that might have actually decreased crime and increased domestic security. The new President must have the courage to wage a real war on crime and make the necessary commitment to produce results. The new Democrats must be willing to commit themselves to "put people first" with strong actions that defend people's right to be safe from crime.

Taking crime seriously means *directly* addressing crime and its immediate breeding grounds—reclaiming public places, so that people no longer fear to walk the streets, patronize commercial areas, ride the buses and subways, or send their children to school. To help communities accomplish this, the new President should:

- Establish a national Police Corps—an initiative that can put 100,000 new cops on the streets. Under this plan, the federal government would pay for the college educations of students who, in turn, would commit to serve four years as police officers.
- Encourage community-policing deployment strategies and make them a condition to various federal law enforcement financial assistance programs.
- Promote community self-defense efforts to reclaim public

places, public housing, and public schools from the unsafe conditions that breed crime.

- Support police officers by proposing tough, long-overdue gun laws—a ban on Rambo-style assault weapons, a bill to make all crimes committed with guns federal offenses—and demand Congress finally enact the Brady Bill, a national waiting period for gun buyers. These laws would protect our police and civilians without infringing upon the right to bear arms for self-protection, hunting, or sports.
- Reduce the demand for drugs by increased funding for treatment and education. A million untreated addicts on the street are a constant contributor to crime and unsafe conditions.

Most of all, taking crime seriously means understanding the terrible human cost of crime, and moving beyond the equally empty rhetoric of many on the Right and the rationalizations of many on the Left.

A WAR OF WORDS AND RATIONALIZATIONS

Since Ronald Reagan's election in 1980, national crime policy has been bound up in a rhetorical war of words increasingly remote from the day-to-day struggle against crime. According to popular conservative mythology, we should blame our crime problems on permissive judges, guilt-ridden parole officers and parole boards, subversive civil liberties attorneys, and weak-kneed liberal lawmakers who have managed over the years to riddle the criminal justice system with "loopholes" and vitiate the deterrent power of apprehension and incarceration. They are the reason, say conservative mythmakers, why criminals are often "sprung" on "technicalities," given sentences too soft and too short to inspire fear, or paroled after serving just a fraction of their sentences.

But in their 12 years in power, the conservatives wound up subordinating real-life crime fighting and settling for mere symbolic measures. While the Reagan officials were giving ringing speeches calling for drastic action against crime, they were steadily reducing federal assistance to state and local law enforcement agencies, which employ 93 percent of all law enforcement personnel and spend 87 percent of all crime-fighting funds.[8] Then the Bush administration teamed with congressional Republicans to block action on sweeping anticrime legislation—on grounds that the Democratic bill did not impose the death penalty for a tiny class of federal felonies.[9]

In 1988 and again in 1992, the Bush campaign blamed lenient sentencing and parole policies for crime. Yet the number of inmates in U.S. prisons doubled during the last decade. America has by far the highest incarceration rate in the world: more than ten times Japan's, four times China's, and 46 percent higher than our nearest rival, South Africa.[10]

The disjunction between conservative anticrime rhetoric and real anticrime measures reached an all-time high in 1989, when President Bush called a press conference to announce his own package of crime legislation. It largely neglected assistance to state and local law enforcement agencies, and instead focused on federal prison construction, the death penalty for a few new federal offenses, and restrictions on use of habeas corpus petitions by criminal defendants.[11] Bush called this package "Take Back the Streets," which must have amused the vast majority of street criminals who manage to avoid federal offenses as they commit their crimes.

Finally, in 1992, President Bush made his chief anticrime promise of the presidential campaign—to make carjacking a federal offense—in response to an egregious crime that happened to occur within the Washington media market.[12]

But the failure of the Right's paper-tiger crime rhetoric does not mandate a return to the habit of many on the Left who instinctively respond to public demands for fighting crime by rationalizing crime as primarily a symptom of social injustice.

While poverty, lack of job opportunities, discrimination, inadequate housing, poor schools, and disintegrating families are all "root causes" that contribute to crime, they do not excuse it. Nor do they excuse reluctance to tackle crime directly as well as indirectly.

Crime is a cause, as well as an effect, of poverty and social discrimination; and the victims of social injustice tend also to become the preeminent victims of crime. Consider: Nearly half of all homicide victims are blacks—murder has now become the leading cause of death among young black urban males.[13]

Those who would deflect concern about crime into concern about social injustice must also consider that crime profoundly erodes the sense of community and mutual obligation that must serve as the foundation for any broad-based progress toward justice and equality. On a more practical level, the fear of crime, especially in urban settings, has led those citizens who have a choice, to exercise it—to avoid living, working, or shopping in high-crime neighborhoods or public facilities. By doing this they lose most, if not all, immediate experience of the worst of the root-cause social conditions. To cite the most obvious example, middle-class suburbanites, whose experience of the homeless population is often limited to a few fearful experiences of intimidation or psychotic behavior, are unlikely to explore, much less support, options for creating affordable housing.

As Professor Alexander Bickel of Yale said during the civil disorders of the 1960s: "No society will long remain open and attached to peaceable politics and the decent and controlled use of public force if fear for personal safety is the ordinary experience of large numbers."[14] Just because conservative "get tough" rhetoric has failed is no reason to conclude that crime should be tolerated as the inevitable if deplorable result of social pathology. Indeed, one reason the public has continued to support the Right's prescriptions despite evidence of their failure is the corresponding failure of the Left to generate a credible alternative approach that takes crime seriously. Also, the Right has won public support through its willingness to emphasize moral accountability in the fight against crime—an accountability too many on the Left felt uncomfortable in publicly espousing. It is simply this: Those who commit crimes deserve to be punished and those who are victims of crimes deserve to be protected. Regrettably, after the strife-torn struggles of the civil rights and antiwar eras, and the abuses of power committed in the name of law enforcement, it simply became unfashionable to be a self-declared law-and-order liberal.

IDEOLOGICAL CO-DEPENDENCY

In the final analysis, conservatives and liberals have unwittingly cooperated to make crime a symbolic issue, rather than a serious challenge. A deadly example of this ideological co-dependency was supplied by the Rodney King case and the resulting riots.

A habitual offender was caught after leading Los Angeles police on a high-speed chase, risking the lives of officers and bystanders. The police were caught on videotape using unconscionable excessive force in subduing him. A suburban jury, clearly more concerned with the symbolism of the case than the facts, acquitted the police of criminal charges.

Riots broke out, and an understaffed, out-of-touch police department led by a get-tough conservative icon, failed to gain control. Opportunists joined the disorders, which turned into the most destructive civil violence since the mid-1960s, spreading to several other cities.

The news media highlighted incidents of violence against innocent, and usually white, bystanders, drawing explicit parallels with the King beating. And too many politicians focused on the symbols that fit their ideology. Liberal politicians hastened to blame American society generally, and the Reagan and Bush administrations specifically, for not tending to the root causes of the violence. Conservative politicians rushed to react to the most extreme liberal rhetoric. The result: ethnic tensions were exacerbated in Los Angeles and many other cities, the police were demoralized, and crime remained as large a problem as before.

Ideological ax grinding is not only an impediment to anticrime efforts, but an actual inducement to crime. Those who would justify riots to vindicate Rodney King, and those who would justify a vigilante jury's vindication of his tormentors, are equally to blame for the resulting collapse in law and order.

Since tough talk is not deterring crime, and crime itself undermines progress on its root causes, the search for an approach that can produce results must begin by looking squarely at crime as it actually occurs. This means looking to the streets—where police officers can deter crime through creating increased risk of apprehension; where the most immediate causes of crime can be isolated and reduced; and where the community support critical to any anticrime initiative can be mustered and mobilized.

TOO MUCH CRIME—TOO FEW COPS

For all the tough anticrime rhetoric heard in recent years, governments at all levels have failed to supply the most basic crime-fighting resource available in the quantities necessary to keep pace with, much less overcome, rising crime: police officers.

In 1951, cities with populations over 50,000 employed more than three police officers for every violent crime. By 1988, the ratio was reversed, with three violent crimes occurring for every police officer.[15]

In practical terms, this means our effective strength in police per violent crime has been reduced by about 87 percent since 1951, despite ever-increasing public concern and repeated official pledges to wage war on crime.

This true reduction-in-force is all the more remarkable because it has coincided with steady increases in other areas of public employment, especially at the state and local levels where most law enforcement officers work. From 1975 until 1988, a period of soaring state and local employment, police manpower actually dropped as a percentage of population.[16]

Even within the criminal justice system, cops have gotten the short end of the fiscal stick. From 1979 to 1990, total per capita spending by all levels of government on justice system activities rose 35 percent, with a 31 percent increase for courts, 55 percent for prosecutors, and 99 percent for corrections. But spending on police rose just 6 percent.[17]

Not surprisingly, a 1985 survey of police chiefs showed that 70 percent indicated serious manpower shortages, many of critical dimensions.[18] In addition to shortcomings in the quantity of police officers, there are serious concerns about the quality of their preparation and the degree to which they adequately represent the population they must protect.

Most police recruits still have only a high school education, even though average starting salaries nearly doubled between 1978 and 1988.[19] And despite widespread use of advanced technology in police work, average training hours have barely increased since 1967.[20]

Most big-city police forces have adopted some sort of affirmative action program to recruit more officers familiar with minority communities. Still, most cannot remotely meet their minority recruitment targets. Currently, New York City's police force is only 11 percent black, about the same proportion as in 1983, though the black population of the city is now nearly 29 percent.[21]

THE POLICE CORPS

Given the fiscal constraints facing state and local governments in the 1990s, some national effort is in order to help reverse the unequal struggle between police and criminals on our streets. Fortunately, there is one well-defined approach that would simultaneously increase both the quantity and quality of police officers, while promoting minority recruitment and opening a new "upward mobility" track whereby high school graduates could earn the means to go to college.

The Police Corps Act, introduced in the Senate in 1989 by Democrat Jim Sasser and Republican Arlen Spector, and in the House by the remarkable duo of Democrat Barney Frank and

Republican Bob Dornan, aims at increasing state and local police forces by 100,000 college-educated officers within four years.[22] The Police Corps concept has been spearheaded since 1982 by Adam Walinsky, a New York attorney and former chief legislative assistant to Senator Robert F. Kennedy.

The Police Corps would offer prospective college students up to $10,000 per year in college assistance in exchange for a four-year commitment to serve as police officers. Participating state and local police departments would pay the recruits the normal entry-level salary, but would realize a 40 percent reduction in personnel cost per recruit by avoiding pension obligations and other costs associated with career officers. Police Corps members would also receive 16 weeks of federally operated preassignment training.[23]

The first-year cost to the federal government, based on an enrollment of 25,000 Police Corps members, would be roughly $1.7 billion, significantly less than the law enforcement expenditures in the last omnibus drug legislation.[24] It would raise the total federal contribution to crime efforts to no more than 10 percent of national expenditures, but would increase total force levels by over 20 percent, total patrol units by 40 percent, and the percentage of college-educated officers by as much as 50 percent in many cities— the largest step toward reversing the unequal struggle between cops and criminals in a generation.

There is clear evidence that the Police Corps could meet its recruitment goals while attracting a much higher percentage of minority officers. A survey of Boston-area students found that 40 percent of all college attendees would "very likely" or "fairly likely" make the four-year commitment the Police Corps requires. The positive reaction rose to more than 50 percent among minority students.[25] This showing of disproportionate interest in the Police Corps among the best-educated segment of minority Americans is an especially promising sign.

Aside from its law enforcement benefits, the Police Corps would quite obviously have a major impact on the ability of young people to obtain college educations at a time of rising tuitions and inadequate student financial assistance. By allowing them to earn cash benefits through a commitment to serve the community in a vital capacity, it incorporates the principle of the GI Bill, offering the means to upward mobility and reinforcing the ethic of mutual obligation.

In addition, the Police Corps could help reduce the dependence of college students on loans. The federal government is currently spending about $1.6 billion per year to cover defaulted student loans, about half of all annual student loan expenditures, and roughly equivalent to the annual cost of a full-fledged Police Corps program.[26]

A demonstration Police Corps program was included in the Senate's version of omnibus crime legislation—but it was stalled throughout the last Congress due to wrangling between congressional Democrats and President Bush over details of the package's death penalty provisions.

We recommend a full-scale commitment to the Police Corps. Rarely has this country had an opportunity to accomplish so many vital objectives with one breakthrough initiative, and the new administration should pursue this opportunity immediately. One element of the Police Corps Act strongly promotes the next recommendation this chapter makes: redeploying police officers to prevent crime through community policing.

911: THE SLOW DEMISE OF RAPID RESPONSE

Despite rising evidence of its futility, most local police forces in America today remain addicted to a deployment strategy that treats communities as enemy territory. A 1988 Justice Department report summarized recent police tactics as concentrating on motorized patrol forces, rapid response to calls for service—usually through 911 telephone systems—and retrospective investigation of crimes.[27]

This "rapid response" strategy became standard procedure for most police departments during the 1980s. Given the limited resources available to police forces, its popularity was understandable: It placed a premium on the use of telecommunications technology as opposed to manpower; it allowed fewer officers to cover greater territory; and most of all, it supplied an apparently objective measurement of police effectiveness: number of calls responded to, and speed of response.

This strategy is also, of course, inherently reactive, and tends to become a circular exercise. Once police deployments and department budgets are organized to reflect the rapid-response approach, then any and all negative evidence of its effectiveness simply becomes a justification for more motorized units and more rapid response times.

As James Q. Wilson and George Kelling observed: If each call is treated as a separate incident with neither a history nor a future, then each incident will be handled by police officers anxious to pacify the complainants and get back on patrol as quickly as possible.[28]

More succinctly, Boston Police Commissioner Mickey Roache admitted: "I hate to say this, but in Boston we run from one call to another. We don't accomplish anything. We're just running all over the place. It's insane."[29]

A 1988 Justice Department study surveyed the available evidence on the effectiveness of rapid-response as "uniformly negative."[30] Most striking was an experiment in Kansas City where doubling the number of patrol cars had no significant effect on crime. In fact, the Kansas City study concluded that the speed with which police arrived on the scene in response to a 911 call had no real effect on the probability of making an arrest.[31]

Aside from its apparent ineffectiveness, the rapid-response strategy has levied a high cost in police-community relations and the overall understanding police departments have of the crime problem and its most immediate causes.

Like the French and American armed forces deployed in Southeast Asia from the 1950s until the 1970s, motorized rapid response forces have surrendered control of the territory to the enemy. Stationed in garrisons remote from the population, our police use the best available technology to arrive on the scene in response to unconfirmed reports of enemy activity. After surveying the scene and filing the necessary paperwork, they return to "base," with no better understanding of the conditions that produced the particular incident. As Commissioner Roache said, it is indeed "insane."

AN ALTERNATIVE TO 911 JUSTICE—
COMMUNITY POLICING

As the deficiencies of rapid-response became more apparent during the 1980s, a number of police forces around the country experimented with an alternative approach, generally known as "community policing" or "problem-solving policing." The key to community policing is to think in terms of patterns of crime, not individual 911 calls; to deploy police visibly and continuously in specific neighborhoods, not occasionally when incidents have occurred; and to work actively with citizens to identify crimes-in-the-making and conditions likely to produce crime.[32]

Whether it is implemented through foot patrols in an urban setting, or through a highly organized neighborhood watch in the suburbs, community policing makes long-term progress against crime the objective, rather than number of calls received and average response times.

Most of all, there is strong evidence community policing works. Foot patrol experiments in Newark, New Jersey, and Flint, Michigan, were very popular with residents, reduced fear of crime, and improved police morale. In Flint, the crime rate dropped significantly, along with emergency calls for service.[33] In New York City, a broader commitment to community policing was made, and may have had something to do with the first across-the-board decrease in every major crime category in 36 years.[34]

New York's community policing effort includes one innovation that should vitally contribute to long-term cooperation between citizens and police: community advisory boards that supply police with feedback on deployment decisions and an early warning of conditions likely to generate crime.[35]

Given the dismal record of rapid-response, there is absolutely no reason to further delay a national commitment to this alternative approach, which clearly improves police-community relations, creates a framework for a more sustained assault on crime, and seems to work.

One of the most attractive features of the Police Corps Act is that it requires police departments to deploy most corps members through community policing methods. As a result, the overall percentage of police officers working in communities will rise significantly, with a corresponding drop in the high percentage of officers currently assigned to both administrative positions and motorized rapid-response.

We strongly recommend other administration efforts to encourage community policing, including Justice Department assistance, more widely disseminated research, and vigorous use of the bully pulpit of the White House. Indeed, until community policing has at least been tried in every American city, we recommend that any and all federal law enforcement assistance be made contingent upon an agreement to experiment with the community policing strategy.

One encouraging recent development in law enforcement was the partial conversion of the Bush administration to community policing during 1992. The administration-supported "weed and seed" initiative aimed at low-income urban neighborhoods incorporated both community policing strategies and an attack on the immediate conditions leading to crime—both unprecedented experiments, given the administration's previous exclusive commitment to high-tech law enforcement and postapprehension punishment as crime-fighting measures.[36]

The new administration should capitalize on this emerging consensus, and use every opportunity to promote community policing.

Dealing with the immediate causes of crime. One aspect of the crime problem that community policing is especially suited to address is the variety of neighborhood-specific factors that directly breed crime.

While root-cause explanations of crime tend to become justifications for doing nothing directly about crime, addressing these more immediate causes can become an important part of a community-based assault on crime.

Community self-defense. A community's first line of defense against crime is often right on the surface, in its appearance.

In their highly influential 1982 article "Broken Windows," James Q. Wilson and George Kelling argued that "signals" of disorder, including neglected buildings, trash-littered vacant lots, and instances of intimidating behavior, "both create fear in citizens and attract predators." Intimidated citizens gradually abandon the territory to the arriving predators, and before long, what began as noncriminal disorder can develop into a steep rise in actual crime.[37]

Where the territory affected by disorder is a public facility or a widely used commercial or retail area, the chain of intimidation and abandonment can have serious consequences for an entire city or metropolitan area.

A good recent example of this pathology and efforts to reverse it has occurred in the New York subway system's Operation Enforcement. In recent years, subway cars and stations in New York became heavily populated with the homeless, many of them substance abusers or mentally ill, who refused requests to move to available shelter space. Gradually, the disorderly behavior of the homeless and other transients began to affect subway ridership, and at the same time, violent crime in the system was rising steadily. The "Broken Windows" chain of events was fully underway, in a city uniquely dependent on public transportation.[38]

Operation Enforcement is based on a simple premise: no one, homeless or otherwise, will be barred from the subway system, but basic rules of orderly behavior will be insisted upon. The program is gradually having a positive effect, but has been opposed vociferously in the courts and in public forums by civil liberties groups and homeless advocates, who believe the presence of the homeless population in so visible a public facility will help generate support for better services.[39]

If the new administration is to make community policing successful, it will need to take a firm stand in favor of efforts to maintain order in public places without compromising anyone's constitutional rights. The way to maintain our communities and fight crime is to insist that Americans accept a mutual obligation to allow each other use of common areas without intimidation or fear of crime.

Special attention should be paid to reducing disorder in public facilities especially vulnerable to crime, such as schools and public housing projects. Students and public housing tenants can never be "empowered" so long as they cannot insist on being treated decently and with basic civility in their daily lives.

Chicago's Operation Clean Sweep is an especially instructive example of both the dramatic effect on crime that can be produced by a concentrated effort to enforce rules in public housing projects, and of the misguided resistance of the traditional Left to initiatives that empower low-income citizens.[40]

In Operation Clean Sweep, public housing officials, assisted by police, targeted high-crime projects and moved in to simultaneously take care of repair needs and identify unregistered tenants, guns, and drugs. At one project where the violent crime rate was 13 times the national average, crime dropped 32 percent. An interesting byproduct of the effort was a marriage boom, as unregistered tenants who were living in violation of housing authority rules against overnight visits chose to establish two-parent families rather than face eviction.[41]

Local civil liberties lawyers fought Operation Clean Sweep on grounds that it violated the constitutional protection against unreasonable search and seizure. But all opposition ceased following a highly publicized incident in which a child living in the Cabrini-Greene project was gunned down while walking hand-in-hand with his mother.[42]

Both Operation Enforcement in New York and Operation Clean Sweep in Chicago show that we can reclaim public places lost to crime—if we listen to the people most affected, rather than defer to their self-appointed advocates.

The new President should personally take the initiative to encourage community self-defense against crime. At the earliest possible occasion, he should say to all Americans: If you have the courage to reclaim your communities from crime, I'll be with you, with every resource available to the federal government.

GUNS

Perhaps the greatest dereliction of duty in today's much-promised war on crime has been government's unwillingness to heed the pleas of our nation's police officers who have testified they are being out-gunned on our streets by gangs armed with military-style, semiautomatic assault weapons. Gangs have been able to purchase with ease weapons made only for the mass-murder of people, not for hunting or sports shooting; weapons that can be equipped with magazines loaded with 20 rounds of ammunition and often many more, and with Rambo-style, spray-from-the-hip gunstocks, and flash-suppressors and silencers. Yet the official policy of the Bush administration was to look the other way.

In 1989, after the nation was shocked by horrifying pictures from a schoolyard in Stockton, California, where a deranged man killed five children and wounded 30 more by firing 100 rounds in two minutes, the Treasury Department's Bureau of Alcohol, Tobacco and Firearms identified a list of assault weapons manufactured overseas—such as China's AK-47—that they said were made only for combat use and not for hunting or sports. President Bush banned the importation of these foreign-made weapons—but, yielding to the lobbyists of the National Rifle Association and the gun industry, he refused to ban sales of identical weapons that are made in the U.S.

There is no justification for the past administration's failure to respond to the urgent calls for help by leading law enforcement officials who feel their cops are in daily danger from these most dangerous weapons. After two Los Angeles police officers were killed by assault weapons, Police Chief Daryl Gates pleaded before Congress for a federal ban on the sales and import of assault weapons. "I do not want any more officers to be spray-gunned to death by street punks armed with high-tech killing machines," said Gates, who had also been Bush's 1988 campaign adviser on crime issues.

No president or political party can pose as a friend of police officers so long as it tolerates the sale and distribution of cop-killing weapons in the name of individual rights. The Bush administration's bizarre "buy American" policy on assault weapons, which opposes their importation but not their domestic manufacture, is an especially egregious example of official hypocrisy on guns and crime. And even Bush's political allies know that.

Consider the views of former Senator Barry Goldwater of Arizona. Not only was this 1964 Republican presidential standard bearer the original "conscience of the conservatives," but he has also posed with his favorite hunting rifle in the NRA's national magazine advertisements that proclaim: "I am the NRA." He champions the right of every American to own firearms—"I've been a member of the NRA," Goldwater has said. "I collect, make and shoot guns." But he has no fear of taking direct aim at his NRA friends when he knows they are wrong. So, in 1989, he was quoted by the *Washington Post*'s Chuck Conconi as saying: "I'm completely opposed to selling automatic rifles. I don't see any reason why they ever made semiautomatics. . . . I've never used an automatic or semiautomatic for hunting. There's no need to. They have no place in anybody's arsenal. If any SOB can't hit a deer with one shot, then he ought to quit shooting."

Today, the urgent need to rid our streets of uncontrolled firearms, including military assault weapons, is recognized by an overwhelming majority of Americans—even an overwhelming majority of the gun owners. In a poll for *Time* magazine, a national waiting period for gun purchasers was backed by 87 percent of America's gun owners—law-abiding citizens whose main concern was to keep guns out of the hands of felons. But President Bush, bowing to the lobbyists of the NRA, vowed to veto the Brady Bill, the measure passed by both the House and Senate that would order a modest five-working-day national waiting period for a background check on gun purchasers.

At a minimum, the new President should insist on a national waiting period for gun purchases, and a ban on military assault weapons. Neither step could even conceivably limit the legitimate purchase of firearms for use in hunting, collecting, or self-protection.

This is one area of criminal justice where tougher laws and courts might help. We suggest making the commission of a serious felony with a firearm a federal offense punishable by long mandatory sentences.

DRUGS

The effect of drug abuse on crime rates is universally accepted, but again, our attack on drugs has been heavy on rhetoric but light on systematic efforts to reduce demand as well as supply for drugs.

During the Bush administration roughly 70 percent of federal antidrug spending was channeled into reduction of drug supplies—mainly through interdiction of drug shipments by law enforcement officials. Only 30 percent of the federal funding was aimed at reduction of demand, this nation's voracious appetite for drugs—an appetite that is fed and financed by addicts who commit crimes to pay for their drugs.[43] The new President should give treatment and education—the demand-side drug efforts—equal priority and equal funding with law enforcement and other interdiction efforts.

Despite recent claims that the Bush administration's supply-side attack on drugs is working, the evidence is at best mixed. A just-completed national survey of schools found drug use among high school students rising during the last school year in seven of ten drug categories. More alarmingly, drug use rose in all categories for junior high school students. At every age level, increased drug use was pronounced among African-American students, with use of uppers, downers, and hallucinogens among the black high school population rising more than 25 percent in just one year.[44]

Most antidrug experts agree that a much higher emphasis on treatment and education is in order. An immediate problem is the lack of treatment facilities. There are currently about one million treatable hard-core drug addicts in America who do not receive treatment, often because it is not available.[45] For example, every day the Fulton County Treatment Center in Atlanta places an average of 20 new addicts requesting treatment on a waiting list with 2,000 already in line.[46]

We should make sure that addicts seeking treatment are immediately helped. Otherwise, they often return to, or resort to, crime to support their habits. In particular, we should insist that inmates in our prison system with drug problems—nearly half according to one estimate—receive drug treatment and education.[47] A current federal Bureau of Prisons effort to treat inmates before they are released back on the streets should be extended to state correctional facilities.[48] Making funds available for that purpose is one crime-fighting investment the federal government should undertake immediately.

CONCLUSION

We can make progress on crime in this new administration, and the federal government can make a valuable contribution to this effort. We need only abandon yesterday's empty rhetoric and rationalizations about crime, and quickly embrace tactics and strategies that not only work against crime and the conditions that breed it, but that restitch the fabric that holds our communities together.

MANDATE FOR ACTION

1. **Establish a national Police Corps.** This initiative can put 100,000 new cops on the streets while raising the educational level and representative character of police departments and supplying a new "upward mobility track" for young people willing to serve their communities in exchange for help in going to college.
2. **Promote community policing through every available avenue.** Require police departments receiving federal law enforcement assistance to adopt community policing methods.
3. **Order federal agencies to use all available resources to support community self-defense against crime.** In particular, public places, public housing, and public schools should be reclaimed from the unsafe conditions that breed crime.
4. **Enact the Brady Bill, ban assault weapons, and make the commission of crimes with guns a federal offense.** We can protect our police and our citizens from gun-toting criminals without abridging the right to bear arms for self-protection, hunting, or sports.
5. **Give drug treatment and education efforts equal funding with law enforcement efforts.** All addicts should have access to treatment, beginning with those already in prison.

9

The Greening of the Market: Making the Polluter Pay

ROBERT STAVINS AND THOMAS GRUMBLY

INTRODUCTION

The environmental movement is poised to enter a second generation. For two decades it has prompted significant improvements in the quality of our air, water, land, and natural resources, primarily through "command-and-control" regulations that essentially have told firms which pollution control technologies to use and how much pollution they could emit. Now, in an era of new environmental challenges and heightened sensitivity to regulatory compliance burdens, market forces can offer in many circumstances a more powerful, far-reaching, efficient, and democratic tool than centralized regulations for protecting the environment.

The progressive challenge for environmentalists in the 1990s is to harness the power of markets, which can be more effective and far-reaching than centralized regulations. Command-and-control regulations were powerful in the early battles against environmental degradation, but they have begun to reveal many of the same limitations that led to the collapse of command-and-control *economies* around the globe. They can be inefficient; they hamper innovation in pollution control methods; and they ignore important differences among individuals, firms, and regions. And command-and-control regulations tend to make the environmental debate a closed, technical discussion among bureaucrats and vested interest groups rather than an accessible public dialogue.

Market-based policies start with the notion that the best way to protect the environment is to give firms and individuals a direct and daily self-interest in doing so. They aim to strengthen environmental protection not with more centralized rule making, but through decentralization—by changing the financial incentives that face millions of firms and individuals in their private decisions about what to consume, how to produce, and where to dispose of their wastes. As a result, market-based policies, which include "green taxes," tradable permit systems, and a range of other approaches, offer many important advantages:

- They enable environmental protection to be pursued at a lower cost of compliance to private industry, and thereby at a lower cost to consumers.
- They give firms a constant incentive to find new and better technologies for combating pollution rather than locking one kind of pollution-control technology into place.
- They can move environmental rules out of the exclusive domain of scientists, economists, lawyers, and lobbyists, and open the process to the public.
- They make the incremental costs of environmental protection more visible, and thus can focus public debate on the most efficient ways to protect the environment, rather than simply on the evils of pollution.
- Because some market-based approaches such as pollution charges raise substantial revenues, they enable government to reduce "distortionary" taxes—ones that reduce market efficiency by taxing *desirable* activities, such as investment and labor—and replace them with levies that discourage socially *undesirable* behavior, such as pollution and degradation of natural resources.

Despite these benefits of market-based approaches, their use has been widely resisted by environmentalists who view the market as the problem rather than the solution; by environmental bureaucrats who resist change from an old regulatory system that emphasizes highly technical specifications about pollution control devices and standards; by lobbyists on both sides of the debate whose role in the process could be endangered by this new approach to environmental protection; by elected officials who resist new ideas in general or who worry that the public will view these market-based approaches as new taxes; and, of course, by those who oppose environmental protection altogether.

Market-based approaches to environmental protection have also become entangled in partisan politics. The Bush administration highlighted its promotion of market-based policies, such as the tradable permits system in the new Clean Air Act, as evidence of its environmental advocacy. But the Bush administration's failure to meet many of the deadlines in that law for implementing specific rules, together with the fact that many of its market-based programs are strictly voluntary, called into question the strength and sincerity of the administration's commitment.[1] Unfortunately, as a result of this record, many Democrats and environmental advocates have reflexively come to view market-based approaches as an evasive tactic or a capitulation to business interests.

Now, however, a confluence of forces has heightened interest in market-based approaches and raised the likelihood that the nation can move beyond the polarized environmental debate of the past decade. Sluggish economic growth, high public sector deficits, and concerns over international competitiveness have focused new attention on the private and public costs of environmental regulation. Changes of attitude within the environmental movement and bureaucracy also seem to herald a new openness to using market forces to regulate the market itself. And the emergence of new threats to the environment has combined with the stubbornness of old threats to spur the search for better ways to control pollution. These forces are likely to focus even more attention on market-based environmental policies, if not as a replacement for current regulatory approaches, then at least as a valuable new set of tools for pursuing environmental quality. The new administration should capitalize on these changes and seek to apply market-based approaches to a variety of environmental challenges, including municipal solid waste, recycling, hazardous waste disposal, air and water pollution, and international environmental threats such as global warming and the loss of biodiversity. If it does so, the new administration can move beyond the old questions of whether simply to spend more or less on environmental protection or on whether simply to raise or lower existing standards. It can focus the nation, instead, on how to set and reach our environmental goals in ways that are smarter, cheaper, and better for economic growth.

BEYOND COMMAND-AND-CONTROL REGULATION

The days when the U.S. could afford to consider environmental protection without regard to its costs have ended. The U.S. Environmental Protection Agency (EPA) estimates we now spend over $100 billion annually to comply with federal environmental laws and regulations.[2] There is heightened concern over the impact of these regulations on the strength of our national economy and on our ability to compete in international markets. As a result, policymakers are eager to hold regulatory burdens to a minimum.

Federal, state, and local budget shortfalls make it harder than in previous decades to spend more money on public environmental-protection programs. There is new sensitivity to private costs as well. The failures in 1990 of the "Big Green" referendum in California and a major environmental bond issue in New York State are just two examples of environmental initiatives that were defeated, in part, because compliance costs were perceived as too high. While there is strong and increasing support among the public for environmental protection, citizens and policymakers are giving increased attention to making the most of scarce resources and maximizing returns on the resources we invest—business costs, regulatory effort, political capital, taxes—to improve the quality of our environment.

This increased sensitivity to compliance costs and burdens has focused, in large part, on the conventional command-and-control approach to environmental regulation in the U.S. Command-and-control regulations tend to force all firms to behave the same way when it comes to pollution, shouldering identical shares of the pollution-control burden regardless of their relative costs. Holding all firms to the same target can be expensive, because this approach typically forces some firms to use unduly expensive means of controlling pollution.[3] The reasons are simple: The costs of controlling emissions can vary greatly among and even within firms, and the right technology in one situation may be wrong in another. Indeed, the cost of controlling a given pollutant may vary by a factor of 100 or more among sources, depending upon the age and location of plants and the technologies available to them.[4]

This regulatory approach also tends to freeze the development of technologies that could provide greater levels of control. Command-and-control standards typically give firms little or no financial incentive to exceed their control targets and create a bias against experimentation with new technologies. A firm that tries a new technology subsequently may be held to a higher standard of performance, without significant opportunity to benefit financially from its investment. As a result, dollars that could be invested in technology development are diverted to legal battles over what are, or are not, acceptable technologies and standards of performance. For example, under Best Available Control Technology (BACT) standards for water-pollution control, a firm that adopted an improved control technology would likely face a stricter standard as a result. Thus, the unintended consequence of such policies is to reduce the demand for new and better pollution-control technologies, and hence to reduce the market for, and development of, those technologies.

Command-and-control policies seek to regulate the individual polluter, whereas market-based policies train their sights on what is, in most cases, our real target of concern: the overall amount of pollution for a given area. What we care about, after all, is not how many particulates the local factory emits, but the quality of the air we breathe while walking downtown or sitting in our backyards. Thus, under a market-based approach, government establishes financial incentives so that the costs imposed on firms drive an entire industry or region to reduce its aggregate output of pollution to a desired level; then, as in any regulatory system, the government monitors and enforces compliance. In policy terms, market-based policies achieve the same *aggregate* level of control as might be set under a command-and-control approach, but they permit the burden of pollution control to be shared more efficiently among firms.

Market-based incentive systems do not represent a laissez-faire, free-market approach. They recognize that market failures are typically at the core of environmental degradation. At the same time, an incentive-based policy rejects the notion that such market failures justify scrapping the market and dictating the behavior of firms or consumers. Instead, they provide freedom of choice to businesses and consumers in determining the best way to reduce pollution. By ensuring that society's environmental costs are factored into each firm's (or individual's) decision making, incentive-based policies harness rather than impede market forces and channel them to achieve environmental goals at the lowest possible cost to society at large.

Despite these benefits, which economists have highlighted for decades, several sources of resistance have slowed the adoption of market instruments for environmental protection.[5] The first is the adversarial attitude that characterized the beginning of the environmental movement.[6] Throughout much of the 1960s and 1970s, that movement typically characterized pollution more as a moral failing of corporate (and political) leaders than as a by-product of modern civilization that can be regulated and reduced, but not eliminated. While the former characterization may have been necessary and successful from a political standpoint, it resulted in widespread antagonism toward corporations and a suspicion that anything supported by business was bad for the environment. Thus, for many years, market-based incentives were characterized by environmentalists not only as impractical, but also as "licenses to pollute."

A second source of resistance to market-based approaches has been the self-interest of segments of the environmental bureaucracy whose work routines, organizational power, or even existence might be threatened by such market-based approaches. Within the EPA, resistance has come from staff whose expertise in setting technology-based standards would become obsolete if the rules of the game were changed. There has also been resistance to market-based approaches from players in the legislative system who, having learned to use their influence to fine-tune a command-and-control regulatory system, are understandably reluctant to allow any major changes in the rules of the game. Thus, lobbyists for both environmental organizations and the private sector, as well as some legislators, resist market-based approaches in part to protect the value of their own expertise. The resistance from some industry lobbyists to putting these ideas into practice is especially notable given that CEOs and other leaders of the business community have long endorsed the *theory* of cost-effective, market-oriented approaches to environmental protection.

There are other sources of resistance to market-based approaches. Many policymakers resist pollution charges, for example, because such charges can be characterized as taxes (even if all the revenues raised are returned, as will be discussed). And there is resistance, of course, from those who simply oppose all attempts at environmental protection.

Over the past several years, however, there has been a rapidly growing recognition among policymakers and activists that market forces, once characterized solely as the problem, are also a potential part of the solution. Part of the new interest in these ideas emerged from within the Executive Office of the President. Some in the environmental community, notably the Environmental Defense Fund, responded by participating actively in the development of such ideas.[7] Much of the academic and political interest in these new approaches coalesced around the release of a report from the bipartisan *Project 88*, an effort co-chaired by Senator Timothy Wirth of Colorado and the late Senator John Heinz of Pennsylvania, which proposed a range of market-based policies to prevent pollution and reduce the waste of natural resources.[8] And much of the business community continues to speak in support of cost-effective, market-oriented approaches to environmental protection.[9]

The new interest in market-based approaches has resulted in several important new policies. The best known of these is the creation of a tradable permit system to combat acid rain, as part of the 1990 amendments to the Clean Air Act. But there have been other market-based initiatives as well, including other tradable permit systems,[10] congressional efforts to reduce government subsidies that can distort markets and harm the environment,[11] and efforts to remove barriers to the negotiation of voluntary water transfers in the western U.S.[12]

The new President can avail himself of a range of market-based tools for protecting the environment. We focus on three in particular: pollution charges, deposit-refund systems, and tradable permits. Different ones will be better for tackling different problems. For some problems, such as regulating pesticides that cannot pass basic thresholds of safety, traditional command-and-control approaches may remain the best remedy. But the new administration can and should act to place more reliance on market-based strategies.

POLLUTION CHARGES AND SOLID WASTE

The first category of market-based policies is pollution charges, or green taxes.[13] Pollution poses real costs to society (for example, health consequences, property damages, and aesthetic degradation), but firms typically do not have to pay for these damages and hence face little or no incentive to take them into account in production decisions. Pollution charges force firms to pay for the external costs of pollution and to incorporate these added costs into their daily decision making. Despite the intuitive appeal of this approach, the U.S. has little experience with green charges at the federal level.[14] Charge mechanisms could be used to address a range of environmental challenges, from air and water pollution to various forms of solid and hazardous waste, and they can work at various levels of government. They work best when the central question is not *whether* but *how much* emission of a pollutant is acceptable, when emissions can be monitored reliably and at reasonable cost, and when the health hazards of moderate variations in emissions are not extreme.

The new administration should focus, in particular, on the use of charge mechanisms for reducing the volume of solid waste generated at the state and local level. The increasing volume of such waste has emerged as a pressing problem in many parts of the U.S. over the past decade. Many areas are running out of landfill space, and many communities have effectively blocked the construction of new facilities. While some communities have turned to incineration of these wastes, concerns exist that garbage burning contributes to air pollution and that the ash it generates poses its own disposal problems.

Faced with the difficulties of providing safe and adequate disposal, many communities have sought to reduce the amount of solid waste generated. Most waste reduction efforts to date have used conventional command-and-control regulations. In some cases, states and municipalities have enacted strict measures such as product bans or across-the-board recycled-content standards for packaging with little regard for costs or consumer preferences. These policies have raised costs, despite having little effect on the amount of solid waste generated. Indeed, a lack of markets for old newsprint caused many communities with mandatory separation requirements to store or even dump their collected newspapers into local landfills.

What is needed to reduce the volume of municipal solid wastes is not stricter regulation, for the most part, but a better means of pricing waste disposal. Most individuals and firms never directly "see" the costs of waste disposal. In many communities, these costs are simply imbedded in local property or income taxes. Some cities have made the costs of waste disposal more apparent to consumers by "unbundling" these costs from other municipal services; that is, citizens pay a separate charge for waste collection. Unfortunately, even these charges do not provide incentives for decreasing the amount of waste; they are typically fixed, *flat* monthly payments that *do not vary* with the quantity of waste generated.

With such pricing systems, it is not surprising that the throwaway ethic has thrived. The cost of throwing away an additional item of refuse is essentially zero; residents merely place their empty bottles, cans, lawn clippings, and other wastes in a trash chute or at the curbside and they magically disappear when the municipality or a contractor picks them up. Imagine what kinds of cars we would buy and how much we would drive if our total annual bill for gasoline were *independent* of the quantity of gasoline we used. This is essentially what is happening today with municipal solid-waste management in almost all communities in the U.S. Effective waste-management strategies must "get the prices right"—they must communicate to consumers the true, total social cost of throwing things away.

In many communities, the best market solution for reducing the volume of residential solid waste will be to charge citizens for the specific quantity of waste they put out at the curb—an approach known as "unit charges." These volume-based fees motivate households to reduce the quantities of waste they generate, whether through changes in their purchasing patterns, reuse of products and containers, or the composting of yard wastes. Furthermore, placing different unit charges on unseparated refuse and specified, separated recyclables can induce households to separate the recyclable components of their trash.

In Seattle, which has adopted a unit charge system, customers choose from four sizes of receptacles, ranging in price from about $11 per month for a 19-gallon container to almost $32 per month for a 90-gallon container. The program appears to be having its intended effect: in 1979, the average family was setting out approximately four 30-gallon containers per week; by 1989, 87 percent of households subscribed to one 32-gallon container or less.[15]

One potential problem with per-can pricing is that customers are charged for a full can even if it is not used or only partially filled in a particular week. "Bag and tag" systems avoid this problem. Under such systems, households dispose of unseparated refuse only in specially designated trash bags sold by the municipality. Another approach involves the sale of stickers that are placed on cans or bags of specified dimension. In Perkasie, Pennsylvania, where the bag-and-tag approach was adopted, the total amount of solid waste collected fell by 60 percent in the program's first year of operation, and total collection and disposal costs decreased by 40 percent.[16]

While experience with unit pricing to date indicates that it can significantly reduce waste generation, concern naturally arises about the policy's fairness to low-income households that, some argue, would pay greater shares of their income for pickup services than would higher-income households. Surprisingly, unit pricing tends to be *less* regressive than conventional payment systems, although there is substantial variation among communities.[17] The

Seattle system uses a tactic similar to the low "life-line rates" provided by electrical utilities for initial blocks of power usage—customers pay only the fixed cost of curbside pickup for their first 32-gallon container.[18]

In addition to unit charges for trash disposal, there are other market-based mechanisms to reduce the volume of solid waste generated. These include retail disposal charges, which add a surcharge to goods based on their disposal costs, and virgin material charges, which raise the cost of a product if it uses a high level of virgin (unrecycled) materials. Separately, and possibly in combination, these policies could help reduce solid-waste disposal costs and preserve natural resources while ensuring a high level of individual choice.[19]

Carbon and Gasoline Charges and the "Greening" of America's Taxes

One major by-product of charge systems is a flow of money from polluters to the government. These revenues, which would be considerable for some pollution charges, create the opportunity for a "double dividend": At the same time the pollution charge is providing an incentive to reduce pollution, the revenues raised make it possible to *lower other taxes*, such as payroll and income taxes.[20] By replacing taxes on socially desirable activities, such as labor and investment, with taxes on socially undesirable activities, such as environmental pollutant emissions, the new administration can use revenue-neutral pollution charges to make the overall tax code more supportive of economic growth.[21]

In particular, the new administration should consider two key examples of this potential double dividend: charges on greenhouse gases and gasoline. Concern over greenhouse gases, particularly carbon dioxide (CO_2), relates to global warming: Many scientists believe that if greenhouse-gas emissions continue to grow at current rates, global mean temperatures may rise by two to five degrees Fahrenheit over the next century. Such an increase could cause widespread changes in precipitation patterns, storm frequencies and intensities, and ocean levels. International negotiations have focused on how much to limit emissions and how to allocate the control burden among nations. If truly enforceable national targets are agreed upon, the U.S. will need to find ways to achieve its national emission-reduction goals.

There are currently a range of mechanisms in use or planned

that could help the U.S. achieve many greenhouse-gas reduction goals, such as reducing emissions to 1990 levels by the year 2000. But for longer-term goals, or if additional tools are eventually needed to meet short-term goals, one of the best alternatives is a properly designed CO_2 charge system. Such a system would tax carbon-based fuels in order to make CO_2 emissions more expensive. The charge would vary by type of fossil fuel—coal, oil, or natural gas—depending upon the CO_2 emissions associated with it. In particular, a tax based on the carbon content of fossil fuels could be imposed at the point of entry for imports and at the point of primary production for domestic sources. This would reduce direct demand for fossil fuels, encourage conservation, lead to a better mix of resources, and stimulate the development of new, less-carbon-intensive technologies.

The impact of a carbon charge on U.S. economic activity cannot be overlooked; if a phased-in $100/ton charge were adopted *unilaterally* by the U.S., it could lead to a 2 percent annual loss in GNP (from baseline projections) by the time it was fully implemented. But the impact would be substantially less if other nations acted in concert. And rebating the revenues from this CO_2 charge by reducing other taxes could offset any projected loss in GNP altogether.[22]

We also believe the new administration should endorse a revenue-neutral gasoline tax to address a broader set of environmental and economic concerns, from urban smog to highway congestion to excessive dependence on imported oil as an energy source.[23] Numerous studies suggest that even a modest increase in the gasoline tax would significantly reduce gasoline consumption, oil imports, and air pollution, and would generate significant new revenues.[24]

It is important that any change in gasoline taxes be revenue neutral. Revenues collected should be transferred to the Social Security Trust Fund and credited to current workers, as a way of reducing their payroll taxes. This use of the revenues should address the greatest concern about higher gas taxes—they can hit hardest on working families and particularly on workers who must drive to their jobs. If the revenues from a federal gas tax were paid into Social Security, the payroll tax—the employee contribution to Social Security—could be cut proportionately, and workers would take home (and retain) larger paychecks. Most important, the extra income would more than offset the cost of the gas tax, except for those who continued to drive the greatest distances in the least fuel-efficient cars. Such a tax could be phased in gradually, allowing individuals and firms to adjust their consuming and producing behavior.

These are just some of the many examples of how charges and fees can deal with environmental problems; many other potential applications exist. For instance, a charge could be placed on the sales of pesticides and other agricultural chemicals to encourage farmers to use these chemicals more efficiently and to provide incentives for manufacturers to find less environmentally harmful substitutes (although in some cases the use of such substances clearly must be tightly regulated or banned altogether). Similarly, the U.S. could follow the example of Germany and impose effluent charges on water pollution. Such charges could encourage firms to reduce emissions below levels currently allowed through discharge permits. Emission charges could also be used for some air pollutants, even where standards are already in place. One such example proposed by the EPA Economic Incentives Task Force is for imposing fees on major stationary sources of volatile organic compounds (VOCs), precursors of urban smog.[25] A set of related policies could help address environmental problems associated with automobile use in major cities. In particular, "congestion pricing" could be used to charge drivers a toll for rush-hour trips, based upon existing electronic-scanner technology.[26] Other mechanisms that could reduce the total miles traveled in automobiles and therefore air pollution include employee parking charges, increased charges for public parking, and smog taxes, as described above.

DEPOSIT-REFUND SYSTEMS

We noted earlier that improved price signals can reduce the volume of waste reaching landfills and incinerators. In some cases, however, the problem is the toxicity of the waste, not just its volume. Front-end taxes (virgin materials taxes and retail disposal charges) give firms and individuals incentives to find safer substitutes and to recover and recycle taxed material. But such charges, if levied on hazardous materials, may encourage some firms to circumvent the process through illegal emissions ("midnight dumping"). And such systems do not provide incentives to change disposal methods. There is a second category of market-based policies—deposit-refund systems—that potentially represents a cost-effective way to manage these and other categories of toxic wastes. Deposit-refund systems create incentives for firms and individuals to dispose of wastes properly and to search for more benign substitutes.

These systems combine a special front-end charge—the deposit—with a refund payable when quantities of the substance in question are turned in for recycling or proper disposal. This is the concept behind the bottle bills many states have adopted.

Although deposit-refund systems have been applied primarily at the state level, a federal approach is advisable for some substances and problems. This is true when firms face national markets with easily transportable products and when the consequences of improper disposal do not vary significantly from one location to another. Geographic homogeneity of charges also reduces the cost and complexity of control, both to firms and to administering agencies.

The new administration should adopt a federal deposit-refund policy for one problem in particular: the disposal of lead-acid batteries. The amount of lead that enters landfills and incinerators is a major hazard. Contamination of groundwater aquifers below landfill sites and emissions of lead oxides and particulates from incinerators can pose real threats to human health. The linkage between lead exposures and childhood learning disabilities is one well-documented example.[27] Most of the new lead entering the environment each year is from the improper disposal of storage batteries. Although a substantial amount of lead from motor-vehicle batteries is recycled each year, the share of batteries recycled has been decreasing during the last 30 years. At present, over 20 million unrecycled batteries enter the waste stream annually and this number may increase by more than 30 percent by the year 2000.[28]

Under a deposit-refund system, a deposit would be collected as a tax when manufacturers sold batteries to distributors, retailers, or original equipment manufacturers; retailers would collect their deposits by returning their used batteries to redemption centers; and these redemption centers, in turn, would redeem their deposits from the administering agency. A national program could be designed to accommodate existing deposit systems for batteries, such as those found in Maine and Rhode Island. The deposit must be large enough to encourage a substantial level of return but small enough to avoid a significant theft problem.

The federal government should also investigate a deposit-refund system for ensuring safe management and disposal of certain "containerizable" hazardous chemicals—for the most part, liquid chemicals stored in metal drums. About 30 percent of industrial wastes are types which may be generated in small enough quantities per unit to be containerized. One category of such chemicals is chlorinated solvents. While most chlorinated solvents are recycled to some degree by the thousands of firms using them, substantial amounts still reach the environment. Some of the solvents escape in the production process and are released into the atmosphere; more seriously, highly contaminated spent solvents are often not economical to recycle and may be illegally dumped to avoid disposal costs.[29]

Another potential application of the deposit-refund approach is to used lubricating oil. The improper disposal of lubricating oil, currently unaddressed by federal regulations, has both health and ecological consequences. When used oil is dumped into storm sewers or placed in unsecured landfills, it can contaminate groundwater and surface-water supplies; when it is burned as heating fuel, it produces air pollution. Enforcing proper disposal of lubricating oil through conventional regulations would be exceedingly costly, since hundreds of thousands of firms and millions of consumers would have to be monitored. A deposit-refund system promises to be much more cost-effective.[30]

TRADABLE PERMITS FOR RECYCLING AND OTHER CHALLENGES

A third market-based approach, tradable permits, allows the government to specify and efficiently achieve a given target of aggregate pollution control. The total quantity of allowable emissions, consistent with that target, is allotted in the form of permits distributed among polluters. Firms that keep their emission levels below the allotted level may sell or lease their surplus allotments to other firms, or use them to offset excess emissions in other parts of their own facilities. Such a system tends to minimize the total societal cost of achieving a given level of pollution control. It is important to note that both charges and permit systems can be used to improve environmental quality—that is, to achieve steadily lower pollution levels—not just to maintain the status quo.[31]

As noted, the 1990 Clean Air Act Amendments used a tradable permit system to combat acid rain. The new administration should apply this concept to promote corporate use of recycled materials, as a response to growing demands for recycling. Policymakers increasingly view recycling as an important element of viable waste-management strategies, but as more states and municipalities have adopted recycling programs, the increased supply of recovered materials has often outpaced demand for recycled, or "secondary" materials. In some instances, this glut has resulted in the subsequent landfilling of separated, recyclable materials. In order to bolster demand for recycled materials, several states have enacted legislation requiring manufacturers in certain industries to increase the use of secondary materials in their products.

Recycled-content regulations in isolation could lead to significant economic inefficiencies because such uniform standards ignore the great degree to which the costs of compliance will vary among firms. Some manufacturers, for example, may not have the capacity to use recycled materials effectively with their existing production technologies; for some of these firms, new capital investments would be prohibitive. Conversely, other firms with different technologies might be able to meet and even exceed minimum-content requirements at relatively low cost. Thus, recycled-content requirements could be made more cost-effective through the use of permits that are tradable among firms.

Under such a system, the federal government would set an industry-wide recycling rate (or recycled content standard) which individual firms could meet in one of two ways: They could use the required percentage of secondary materials *or* they could use fewer secondary materials and buy permits (credits) from other firms that exceeded their recycling requirements. To ease potential disruptions, standards could start low and increase gradually over time. The result of a tradable permit program would be that the same amount of total recycling would occur as under a uniform standard, but the total costs of compliance would be less, since those firms in the best position to recycle (or use recycled materials) would essentially be paid by other firms to undertake the bulk of the recycling burden. Recycling credit systems could conceivably be used for a variety of products, including newsprint and used lubricating oil.[32]

Local air pollution problems can also be addressed through the use of tradable permits. First, a logical extension of the EPA's initiatives with "emissions trading" would be a comprehensive system of marketable emissions permits, as is now being explored in the Los Angeles region. Since mobile sources, such as cars, play a major role in air pollution problems in most cities, offset and tradable permit programs ought to include motor vehicles wherever possible. "Cash-for-clunker" programs, in which major stationary sources, such as factories and electric utilities, can offset their own emissions by purchasing and retiring high-polluting, pre-1971 vehicles, are a promising route. Finally, the EPA's initial forays into permit-trading programs to control point-source and non-point-source water pollution need to be improved and expanded.

A related, international application of the tradable permit principle is the notion of preventing deforestation through "debt-for-nature" swaps. Concern in developed nations about tropical deforestation is associated both with the role of forests as reservoirs of carbon (and hence CO_2) and as the habitats of plant and animal species. The world's less developed countries are the main repositories of the planet's tropical forest resources. Many of these countries have found that they can no longer meet their massive debt obligations and invest adequately in growth at home. The developed and less developed nations thus share a common interest in the tropical forests. This common interest can and should be furthered by extending the concept of offsets through debt-for-nature swaps, several of which have already been arranged.

THE ROLE OF RISK ASSESSMENT: ESTABLISHING OUR PRIORITIES

So far, we have only discussed the *means* to achieving our environmental protection goals. But before society selects an instrument to achieve its environmental goals, it must first determine what those goals are. In this choice, too, there is an important opportunity to improve our policy making in ways that are more efficient and that transcend the old, adversarial relationships.

The staggering costs of controlling today's environmental threats make it abundantly clear that we must focus our attention on those problems which pose the greatest risk. At present, government attention and action on environmental threats is seriously out of alignment with scientific, let alone economic, estimates of relative risks.

In 1987, a major EPA study found that the federal government's spending on environmental problems was almost *inversely correlated* to the ranking of relative risk by scientists within the agency.[33] A recent EPA Science Advisory Board study has confirmed these findings; its primary recommendation was that the "EPA should target its environmental protection efforts on the basis of opportunities for the greatest risk reduction."[34] Going one step further, a 1991 report from the U.S. General Accounting

Office recommended that the "EPA work with the Congress to identify opportunities to shift resources from problems of less severe risk to problems whose risks are greater."[35]

Scientific rankings of risk, of course, are not the only relevant factors in establishing environmental-protection priorities. Many others deserve consideration, including the disproportionate impact of some risks on certain populations, such as minorities and the poor; public perceptions of risk; aesthetic and spiritual values; intergenerational considerations; and political and historical questions about who is responsible for environmental damage. Still, assessments of relative health and ecological risks should be a major consideration.

Some environmental advocates and legislators, however, have long been hostile to the idea of weighing relative risks, insisting instead that all environmental threats are of the highest order. This view was perhaps understandable during an era when the executive branch was repeatedly hostile to environmental protection. But this absolutism is scientifically wrong and may prove to be politically shortsighted because it will ultimately undermine the credibility of the nation's enviromental-protection efforts. Refusal to establish priorities among environmental problems has resulted in a misdirection of our efforts. Whether we are concerned with risks to human health or threats to ecological integrity, we can accomplish far more by targeting our efforts at those problems where we can achieve the greatest impact.

Calling for higher and higher levels of standards and spending on each and every environmental problem is not by itself a useful agenda for action. Indeed, it can be a cause of inaction. As some sectors of private industry argue that no environmental threat is serious, and as some environmental advocates refuse to set priorities, the environmental debate becomes polarized and paralyzed. The time has come to begin setting real environmental priorities for real action, drawing not simply upon political and popular perceptions of risk, but also upon the best scientific and economic evidence we can develop. Rather than opposing risk assessment as a threat, progressives and the new administration should support responsible risk assessment and the research on which it depends as a way to heighten public understanding, inform the debate, and improve the democratic process. In addition, it is time to make a major effort to bring scientists and citizens together in a national dialogue to improve mutual understanding and evaluation of environmental risks.

MARKET MECHANISMS IN THE POLITICAL ARENA

No single policy mechanism can be an environmental panacea, but market-based instruments can provide more cost-effective solutions for some pressing environmental problems, while spurring important technological advances. Ultimately, the greatest service that market mechanisms for environmental protection may render is to bring environmental policy formulation "out of the closet." Americans have always been shielded from many of the very real trade-offs involved in establishing our environmental goals, programs, and standards. Policy formulation has been shrouded in technical complexity, which frequently obscures the more basic question of whether we are getting our money's worth on our choice of environmental goals and the means for achieving them. Conventional regulatory approaches impose costs on industry that are not readily visible (but are partially passed on to consumers). Because neither policymakers nor citizens can see how much they are really paying for given levels of environmental protection, they have little basis for weighing relative risks or alternative policies that might yield more environmental quality for the same investment of public and private resources.

Pollution charges and other market-based instruments can bring these important questions into the open by making the incremental costs and advantages of environmental protection explicit. As a result, policy discussions can move away from a narrow focus on technical specifications to a broader consideration of goals and strategies. This shift should help get the American public involved in constructive debates regarding the desirable level and types of environmental protection. In this way, the public can recapture the critical decisions of environmental goal setting from bureaucrats, technicians, special interest groups, and politicians specializing in spreading fear rather than information.

But good ideas are not self-adopting. Even if the 1990 Clean Air Act provisions signaled the beginning of a new era of environmental policy, that does not mean that all resistance to market-based approaches has disappeared. In addition to opposition from those who simply oppose environmental protection, new market-based proposals will have to overcome the same combination of self-interest and suspicion from those *within* the environmental-protection process that has obstructed market-based approaches for decades.

Promoting the selective use of market-based mechanisms will

require political courage, but it is the right thing to do for a variety of environmental problems—for both environmental and economic reasons. Furthermore, market-based approaches offer potential political dividends: Most Americans will agree with the common sense that underlies these approaches—"the polluter ought to pay."

MANDATE FOR ACTION

1. **Create a tradable permit system to promote solid-waste recycling, and explore its application for water pollution and other environmental challenges.** A tradable permit system would induce firms to recycle, and to use recycled materials in their production processes. Generally, by using this policy instrument to allocate the pollution-control burden among firms, the total costs of control can be reduced dramatically.

2. **Create national deposit-refund systems for lead-acid batteries and some solvents.** By applying the approach already used by a number of state "bottle bills" to the health threat posed by illegal disposal of lead-acid batteries, we can reduce significantly, and cost-effectively, the number of batteries that wind up in landfills and incinerators.

3. **Promote "unit pricing" for trash pickup at the state and local level.** By charging households more if they produce more trash, municipalities can reduce solid-waste disposal costs, encourage recycling, and reduce the use of virgin materials, while preserving a high degree of individual choice.

4. **Enact carbon charges domestically, with revenues recycled to consumers by lowering other taxes, if needed to achieve internationally established and enforceable long-term goals for controlling greenhouse gases.** By reducing taxes that discourage desirable behavior such as labor and investment and relying more on taxes that discourage undesirable behavior such as pollution, we can protect the environment and increase the efficiency of the tax structure.

5. **Enact a moderate increase in the gasoline tax to reduce air pollution and traffic congestion, with revenues used to reduce Social Security payroll taxes.** By

dedicating the revenues from federal gas taxes to the Social Security Trust Fund, we can reduce workers' payroll taxes while providing important incentives for increased fuel efficiency.

6. **Expand scientific research on, and use of, risk assessment as part of a national effort to set environmental priorities**. In an era of constrained resources, we need to target our environmental-protection efforts (and limited dollars) at those problems that will yield the greatest reductions in risk, whether to human health or ecological conditions.

10

Replacing Welfare with Work

WILL MARSHALL AND ELAINE CIULLA KAMARCK

THE NEW SOCIAL DILEMMA

America has lost the initiative in the war on poverty. Despite rising social spending and moderate growth, the U.S. has made negligible progress against poverty since 1973. Our poverty rates are twice those of other advanced countries. And poverty in America increasingly wears a child's face: One out of every five of our children is poor. Most alarming of all is the emergence of an angry and demoralized "underclass" that is at once dependent on government yet isolated from society at large. The U.S. is in danger of developing a caste system in which scattered pockets of impoverished and mainly minority citizens are permanently barred from taking part in the nation's productive and civic life.

The nature of America's social dilemma has changed in important ways since Lyndon Johnson launched the Great Society in 1965. Far fewer elderly Americans and far more children are poor today. Teen pregnancy and family breakdown have reached staggering proportions. Suburban flight by a growing black middle class has left behind heavier concentrations of urban poverty and deprived many communities of role models and stabilizing institutions. Blue-collar jobs have been vanishing from our cities, so that black males without college educations face lower earnings and poorer job prospects than a decade ago. Some women's use of

217

crack cocaine has brought new tragedies: the birth of addicted "boarder babies" and the advent of "no-parent families."

The percentage of Americans living in poverty fell sharply in the 1960s, remained stable throughout the 1970s, and then rose in the 1980s. Between 1959 and 1973, the poverty rate fell from 22 percent to a record low of 11 percent; today over 14 percent (35.7 million Americans) are poor.[1]

All Americans pay dearly when social ills are allowed to fester. Our country is forfeiting the productive potential of millions of citizens who lack the education and skills to compete in an information-based, global economy. At the same time, our taxes rise to finance higher public spending for police, courts, prisons, remedial education, emergency medical care, drug treatment centers, and shelters for the homeless. And America's great cities continue to deteriorate as those who can afford to flee to the relative safety and better schools of the suburbs and job-creating enterprises steer clear of city centers ravaged by crime, drugs, and other symptoms of social disintegration.

Agreement is widespread across the political spectrum that the welfare system fails to address our most virulent social ills. At best, it offers palliatives rather than cures; at worst, it fosters dependence rather than self-sufficiency, seeking only to cushion the blow of poverty rather than helping people to escape it. Deeply unpopular at all levels of society, welfare is failing both the needy people it is supposed to help and the working people who pay for it.

The facts are grim, the case for action urgent. Yet for 12 years, Republican presidents have pursued a course of studied inaction and neglect. A growing gap between rich and poor, the spread of poverty among children, and a yawning racial chasm that threatens to divide America into separate, unequal societies—these are the most shameful legacies of the Reagan-Bush years.

The new President must do better. He must launch a new generation of social innovations intended to empower the poor and help them liberate themselves not only from poverty, but also from a debilitating dependence on welfare. This chapter proposes a plan for replacing welfare with a work-based social policy that reinforces mainstream values, rewards individual initiative, and demands responsible behavior from recipients of public assistance even as it expands opportunities to achieve self-sufficiency. Such a strategy would:

- Replace permanent welfare with a two-year transitional program.

- Shift public subsidies from welfare to work.
- Assure all Americans access to health care.
- Create social insurance for children through guaranteed child support.
- Offer people who cannot find private jobs work in community service.
- Expand welfare-to-work efforts by nonprofit groups and businesses.

THE WELFARE DEBATE

America's welfare system is beset by conflicting impulses. According to Harvard sociologist David Ellwood:

> Welfare brings some of our most precious values—involving autonomy, responsibility, work, family, community and compassion—into conflict. We want to help those who are not making it but in so doing, we seem to cheapen the efforts of those who are struggling hard just to get by. We want to offer financial support to those with low incomes, but if we do we reduce the pressure on them and their incentive to work. We want to help people who are not able to help themselves but then we worry that people will not bother to help themselves. We recognize the insecurity of single-parent families but, in helping them, we appear to be promoting or supporting their formation. We want to target our money to the most needy, but in doing so, we often isolate and stigmatize them.[2]

Republican leaders have exploited public hostility toward welfare, using it as a racially charged symbol for liberals' supposed profligacy and penchant for social engineering. At bottom, they say, the problem is cultural; no amount of social spending can compensate for a lack of individual responsibility and initiative among the poor. Nonetheless, they have not been honest or daring enough to call for welfare's abolition or to replace it with something better; even Ronald Reagan, nemesis of America's welfare queens, affirmed his support for a social "safety net." This stance merely serves to thwart fundamental reform, leaving us with the worst of all worlds: a stingy welfare system that offers poor citizens bare subsistence but little dignity or hope of advancement.

Many Democrats, however, have played into conservative hands by reflexively defending the welfare status quo. They argue that our social dilemmas are rooted not in culture but in economics—in society's failure to provide sufficient resources for the poor.

Yet to many working Americans, this stance seems to absolve poor citizens of the responsibility to do their part by working hard, playing by the rules, and avoiding self-destructive patterns of behavior: teenage pregnancy, the avoidance of marriage, crime, drug abuse, and the failure to stay in school or to work. While commendably compassionate, the liberal approach too often puts inordinate faith in bureaucratic mechanisms to do for others what only they can do for themselves.

The welfare debate thus remains deadlocked over an uninspiring choice between conservative prescriptions for "less of the same" and liberal demands for "more of the same." But shrinking or expanding the safety net is a false choice. The real challenge facing national leadership today is to combine equally valid insights about culture and economics, collective and individual responsibility, in a new strategy for building ladders out of poverty and dependence.

The new administration must marshal a sustained, national commitment to end dependency on welfare and break the walls that separate the underclass from the rest of society. It will require what America has lacked for 12 years: strong presidential leadership. The new President must rekindle a sense of moral urgency and reciprocal obligation, and spell out the harmful consequences for all Americans of continued inaction. And he must be willing to embrace radical changes in social policy. Just as we did in the 1960s, Americans need to launch a new era of social experimentation in the 1990s. But in the next round, we must do a better job of demanding results, both to restore public confidence in the efficacy of governmental action and to avoid immortalizing programs of dubious worth.

SOCIAL WELFARE: FOUR FAILURES

A sweeping overhaul of America's welfare system must begin with a candid assessment of its shortcomings. Social scientists fiercely dispute whether or not welfare itself breeds a self-destructive "culture of poverty."[3] But beyond this argument is broad agreement that the system suffers from four failures:

1. Welfare undercuts the incentive to work and isolates the poor from the economic and social mainstream. Nearly half of those who go on welfare stay for under two years. But for those who do not escape the system quickly, welfare can become a way of life:

Fully a quarter of those on the rolls remain there for more than 10 years.

Social supports inevitably reduce the pressure to work. But even for people determined to work, the low-skill, low-wage jobs they are most likely to get cannot compete with the welfare economy. Those jobs rarely pay enough to propel the typical welfare family out of poverty. They seldom offer health insurance, child care, or other benefits like food stamps or housing vouchers. "There's no question that lots of women on welfare can't earn their way out of poverty—probably more than half couldn't, and many can't earn as much as they are receiving in welfare," said Irwin Garfinkel, a professor at Columbia University School of Social Work.[4]

To close the gap in skills that typically frustrates welfare recipients' efforts to find good jobs, some welfare experts propose expanding education and training. Unfortunately, in recent years academic and anecdotal evidence has called this strategy into question. In 1980 *The Washington Post* tracked down approximately one-third of the original 1965 Job Corps members. The men claimed that only two in their group made any significant break from poverty as a result of training and education provided by the Job Corps.[5] More damning was the fact that the participants said their current lives are virtually indistinguishable from those of their peers who were not in the Job Corps in 1965. Two studies, one of a Seattle/Denver income maintenance experiment and another of a New Jersey/Maine training program, support the conclusion that adult education and training provide limited benefits for recipients.[6] And government-funded job training programs frequently have been criticized as elaborate boondoggles that train workers for minimum-wage jobs like flipping hamburgers.[7]

Moreover, even when training programs seem to work, the cost per person is so extravagant that it calls into question the cost-effectiveness of such programs. In the 1988 presidential campaign Michael Dukakis touted his E.T. Program (education and training) which had been very successful in getting welfare mothers off welfare and into jobs. The program was criticized however, because the cost per client was so great. The Job Training Partnership Act links trainees with private industry and labor unions at a much lower cost per person. But its training program is managed by private industry.[8]

The myriad of disincentives to work that are built into the current system create what Housing and Urban Development Secretary Jack Kemp has called two economies: an incentive-driven market economy and an inner-city "socialist" economy of bureau-cratic commands and controls. The first rewards work and taking risks, the second, passivity and dependence. Says Kemp, "Since at least the late 1960s, our ever-expanding web of welfare rules has gradually cut the ties between the poor and the rest of American society, creating a separate and unequal economy in the inner cities, segregating the poor from the rest of us and shattering the link between effort and reward."[9]

The result is that the poor are isolated from the rest of society, in every sense. To the tax-paying public, the welfare system appears to undermine rather than reinforce mainstream values. Means-tested programs represent a direct transfer from taxpayers to the poor, many of whom are not working and have other problems that keep them dependent on public largess. The recipients of targeted programs are seen as personally deficient, undermining public support for programs designed to help them. For this reason, William Julius Wilson and other analysts have called for replacing means-tested and race-specific programs with universal programs that, like Social Security, address the needs of working and middle-class people as well as the poor.

Physical isolation reinforces social isolation. The effects of physical isolation—for instance, the concentration of poor in public housing projects and in racially segregated neighborhoods—work to isolate poor blacks in particular from communities where they could find work and be referred to work. A study by Wilson, as reported in *The Los Angeles Times,* that compares the experiences of poor blacks to poor Mexican immigrants concludes that Mexican immigrants were better able to find jobs, "because they could plug into a tight subculture established by a chain of prior immigrants, some of whom came from the same villages."[10]

2. Welfare penalizes marriage and underwrites single parenthood. Welfare rules traditionally have imposed a stiff "marriage penalty": Women recipients who marry a man with a job usually exceed AFDC limits on household income and thus lose their benefits. Couples who choose to live together instead of marrying suffer no such loss of income. Moreover, some conservatives argue that welfare makes marriage less necessary by allowing women to secure a steady income and other benefits by, in effect, marrying the state.[11]

Because marriage is the means by which most women escape welfare, eliminating the marriage penalty must be a top priority of welfare reform. As chapter 7 details, children from single-parent families are more likely to be poor than children from two-parent families. Family structure—particularly the rise in out-of-wedlock births in the black community—is a powerful variable in explaining the rise in childhood poverty, especially among blacks. Family structure also explains the growing distance between the wealthiest and the poorest blacks: The proportion of black families earning $50,000 or more annually jumped from 7 to 15 percent between 1970 and 1989. At the same time, families earning $10,000 or less increased from 23 to 26 percent. Or, to put it another way, two-parent black families now earn 78 percent of that earned by two-parent white families, while female-headed single-parent black families earn only 30 percent of that earned by two-parent white families.[12]

According to Wilson, the disappearance of traditional manufacturing jobs that pay low-skill workers relatively high wages has contributed to higher poverty rates and to a dearth of "marriageable males" in poor communities.[13] In contrast, Lawrence Mead links rising urban poverty rates to non-work, which he regards as a by-product of a welfare system that induces recipient passivity.[14] Whatever the causes, non-work and non-marriage have both been on the rise: In 1969, the proportion of able-bodied poor who did not work all year was 12 percent; in 1987 it was nearly 22 percent. In 1960 the proportion of out-of-wedlock births to black women accounted for 21.6 percent of all births to black women but by 1989 this figure had risen to 64.5 percent.[15] While the disappearance of marriage among poor urban blacks may have been caused initially by the absence of work for the men, several decades of poverty and fatherless families has meant, as Wilson himself now acknowledges, that other, cultural factors could be at work as well.[16]

Over a period of time, all of these factors have made marriage a rarity in too many poor and inner-city communities.

3. The welfare system is inefficient and empowers bureaucrats rather than the poor. Washington spends roughly $150 billion a year at what the public thinks of as "welfare"—about 75 means-tested programs targeted on the poor. And welfare benefits are hardly generous: The median benefit (income support and food stamps combined) for a family of three in 1992 was $647 a month, 72 percent of the poverty level. In addition to providing cash income, these programs immunize children against disease, offer poor mothers prenatal care, give underprivileged youngsters a head start in education, and provide food, shelter, health care, and drug and alcohol abuse counseling to millions of poor Americans. It is important to understand from the outset that although welfare rolls are growing, welfare spending is *not* driving America's enormous federal deficit: All 75 of the government's targeted benefit programs account for 12.5 percent of the national budget, or 3.9 percent of gross national product.[17]

The problem is not that we are spending too much, but that too little of what we spend goes directly to the poor. Despite spending more than $3 trillion on antipoverty programs since 1965, conditions in poor communities have gotten worse rather than better.

The problem is twofold. First, much of the spending has been absorbed by an expanding bureaucracy for delivering social services that eats up a disproportionate amount of the funds available for fighting poverty. For instance, in 1984 a study found that two-thirds of every dollar spent by Cook County (which includes Chicago) went to social service providers rather than to the poor.[18] A housing project in Louisiana has a 32 percent vacancy rate, an 11 percent uncollected rent rate, and hundreds of stories like the one in which a woman spent ten years waiting for a broken window to be fixed. Yet the housing authority responsible spent $4.7 million operating the project.[19]

Second, through the creation of multiple categorical grants, each of which has its own rules for eligibility and its own bureaucratic systems, the government has created a crazy quilt of services—most of which are targeted toward the same population. The absence of integrated social services means that a 15-year-old welfare mother with a new baby faces an obstacle course of scattered programs that often defeats the efforts of even the most energetic. As often as not, the absence of home-based services means that government programs do not reach the intended audiences.[20]

4. Welfare fails to buttress American values. The welfare system does not encourage and reward the values most Americans live by: work, family, individual responsibility, and self-sufficiency. Many Americans, comfortably well-off and poor alike, believe it subsidizes dysfunctional behavior. In the words of Kimi Gray, a former welfare mother and leader of the nation's first experiment in tenant ownership of public housing, welfare rewards failure, not success.[21]

The perverse impact of the welfare system gained national attention in May 1992, when *The New York Times* ran the story of Sandra Rosado, a young girl who had saved $4,900 to go to college. This violated AFDC limits on personal savings, and Ms. Rosado's mother was fined for her daughter's industriousness.[22]

Not only does the current welfare system fail to reinforce mainstream values, it also fails to reflect the new realities of working men and women in America, particularly working mothers. For much of our history, women who were mothers were actively discouraged (if not actually prohibited) from going to work. Ironically, it was primarily black mothers who worked—because they had to. When the predecessor of AFDC was launched in 1935, however, most women were not expected to work outside the home—especially if they were mothers. This program grew out of the Mothers' Pension laws, a Progressive Era innovation that gave aid to the children of widows. A 1913 report on the mothers' movement asserts that, "No woman, save in exceptional circumstances, can be both the homemaker and the breadwinner of her family."[23]

Today these "exceptional circumstances" are the norm. Most women are both homemaker and breadwinner. The sources of this revolutionary change are both cultural and economic. The women's movement legitimized the idea that women could seek careers other than motherhood, and its agitation led to increased opportunities and wages for female workers. In addition, just as women were moving into the work force in large numbers, America's economy began to slow down. After decades of robust growth, median family income suddenly stopped growing in the early 1970s. To maintain a middle-class standard of living, families sent more women into the labor market, had fewer children, bought fewer homes, and borrowed more money.

These factors have led to an interesting and ironic phenomenon. Middle- and lower-middle-class women, many of whom would prefer to stay home with their children, are now forced for economic reasons into the workplace, where their taxes go to the support of, among other things, women who are on welfare. One black working mother put this changed reality in focus during a discussion of welfare: "I don't think it is fair when I am a hard-working average person and I have limited my family to two because I can't afford to have more children. I don't see why I as a working person should take care of your children."[24]

With most mothers now working outside the home, welfare programs predicated on the idea that mothers do not or should not take jobs are strikingly at odds with the reality faced by most American families. A November 1991 Gallup Poll found that 79 percent of those polled favored requiring "able-bodied people on welfare, including women with small children, to do work for their welfare checks." And with most American women having fewer children for economic reasons and most American families sending mothers out into the work force for economic reasons, it was inevitable that people would begin demanding similar restraint from welfare recipients.

STATE WELFARE REFORM

Passage of the Family Support Act of 1988 opened the door for state-by-state efforts to reform the welfare system. Not surprisingly (as the reforms flow from a common critique), they share a common theme—a growing public and expert consensus that antipoverty programs should tackle the behavioral roots of poverty as well as provide the poor with financial support. The engine behind the new state reforms is as much cultural as monetary, reflecting the widespread perception that the welfare system does not reinforce either family values or values of personal responsibility.[25] Advocates and critics alike dub this "the new paternalism"— an insistence that welfare and other social benefits be conditioned on changes in the recipients' behavior.

In the past few years, several states have taken the lead in efforts to reform the system. While the Family Support Act conditioned welfare benefits on participation in education and training programs, the states' efforts go much further in demanding what legislators deem to be responsible behavior from welfare recipients. New Jersey, for example, now denies payments for a second child born to mothers on welfare, but it does allow family members to increase their earnings and to keep more of what they earn when a second child comes along.

Wayne R. Bryant, the New Jersey Assemblyman who pushed for the change—and whose district is overwhelmingly black and poor—believes that poor people should not be immune to the same economic incentives and disincentives that working people face. While that means that welfare mothers should hesitate before deciding to have another child, it also means that government must make sure that work does not reduce their standard of living. Bryant's plan thus offers a substantial work incentive: It allows welfare recipients to collect their full benefits while earning an income equal to 50 percent of their grant in order to support another child.

A second prevalent theme of state welfare reforms is recognition of the importance of the two-parent family. While aware that family disintegration is a long-term and complex phenomenon (which does not easily lend itself to government intervention), reformers have become alarmed at the near disappearance of marriage and of two-parent families among the poor. The stark differences in well-being between the children of two-parent and one-parent families have led reformers to, at a minimum, get rid of the disincentives to marriage and, in some cases, to actively encourage it.

Wisconsin has proposed a "Wedfare" or "Bridefare" initiative that would encourage young couples to marry and work by allowing married welfare recipients to keep more of their earnings than single ones. The plan also seeks to make fathers more responsible for their children by ensuring the establishment of paternity for all AFDC applicants. Once paternity has been established and it has been determined that the father cannot pay child support, all unemployed, noncustodial parents (almost always fathers) will be required to participate for 40 hours per week in a combination of education, parenting, and work activities put on by the state. In addition, attendance of all parents (including spouses and noncustodial fathers) under 20 years of age in parenting classes is mandatory under the new plan.

Under the 1988 Family Support Act, states can require minor single parents to live with their parents in order to receive AFDC benefits. The Wisconsin plan will exercise this option statewide to remove any incentive that may exist for teens to get pregnant so they can move out of the house. Work incentives allow participants to keep more of their earnings each month and still be eligible for AFDC benefits, medical assistance, food stamps, and child-care expenses. Since 1988, Wisconsin has operated its "Learnfare" program that reduces welfare payments to teenage mothers or to families whose children fail to attend school regularly. Using a carrot-and-stick approach, Ohio gives a $62 bonus to teenage parents on welfare who go back to high school and another $62 per month if they attend class regularly—or a $62 penalty for each month they fail to do so.

Maryland requires welfare recipients to keep their children in school and obtain preventative health care for them or face an across-the-board 20 percent reduction of state welfare payments. California also is considering a welfare plan that would limit benefits for additional children and would give grants only to the parents or legal guardians of teenage mothers living with them. The plan proposes cutting welfare grants by 25 percent and limiting the first year of benefits for people who have recently moved into the state.

Many of the efforts to reform welfare now under way in the states are too recent to evaluate. In most other human social systems, some combination of rewards and punishments, carrots and sticks, operates to produce the desired behavior. But some social scientists, such as Douglas Besharov of the American Enterprise Institute, argue that the emphasis should be on rewarding positive behavior rather than on imposing penalties: "Benefits send the same signal as penalties, with fewer drawbacks. Tangible rewards for doing the right thing can uplift and encourage; penalties threaten to discourage recipients who may already feel psychologically beaten down. . . ."[26]

FROM WELFARE TO WORK: ENABLING STRATEGIES FOR WELFARE REFORM

While the new emphasis on individual and reciprocal responsibility is long overdue, it is doubtful that incremental changes in the existing welfare system can bring about dramatic behavioral changes or lasting improvements in the lives of the poor. To truly seize the initiative in the war on poverty, the new administration also must replace the welfare system with a new strategy for enabling America's poor. While the welfare state is organized around the goal of income maintenance, the enabling state should be organized around the goals of work and individual empowerment. Above all, it should help poor Americans develop the capacities they need to liberate themselves from poverty and dependence. And it should do so directly, bypassing whenever possible public bureaucracies and service providers and placing responsibility and resources directly into the hands of the people we are trying to help. An enabling strategy should see the poor as the prime agents of their own development rather than as passive clients of the welfare system.

Building on a generation's worth of experience with social welfare programs and a generation's worth of experience with the failures of welfare bureaucracies, the new administration should adopt a different strategy for the war on poverty guided by four principles.

1. Welfare reform should make work pay. It makes little sense to exhort welfare mothers to take low-productivity, low-wage jobs if the result is to lower their family's standard of living.[27] Instead of paying people to stay on welfare, it makes more sense to transfer public subsidies to work—to supplement wages so that welfare recipients will not be worse off if they take a job. This change alone, however, will only make the poor's financial plight more acute unless accompanied by other steps intended to make work pay, substitute parental for public support, ensure universal access to health care, and otherwise buttress their efforts to work while also caring for their children. Therefore, a comprehensive strategy for replacing welfare with work also must include the following components:

Eligibility for welfare should be limited to two years. After two years, able-bodied recipients would no longer be eligible for AFDC payments. Thus, welfare would be a way station on the road to work and productive citizenship, not a final destination. Placing a two-year limit on welfare, as President Clinton has advocated, while at the same time increasing the opportunities for poor people to become self-sufficient, is a first and critical step toward ending welfare as a way of life.

Those unable to find jobs in the private sector should be offered an opportunity to work in community service corps at the minimum wage. To this end, the new President should press for adoption of the national service program described in chapter 6. By mixing poor women with youths from low-income and middle-class families, we would avoid isolating poor people in a "make-work" public jobs program. Unlike existing requirements for workfare, community service volunteers would be earning their way rather than simply working off a welfare check. Yet they would not be earning enough to dissuade them from seeking a better job.

If we are serious about making work rather than income maintenance the foundation of our social policy, we must acknowledge that many jobs pay too little to lift a family out of poverty. *The new administration should adopt PPI's proposal for a "guaranteed working wage"—essentially an expanded earned income tax credit—which would ensure that no family with a full-time, year-round worker will live in poverty.* [28] To help working mothers pay for child care, we should also make the child care tax credit refundable.

Medicaid, the public health insurance program for the poor, is linked to AFDC. Leaving the welfare rolls means losing medical protection—a serious disincentive for welfare recipients hoping to find a job. *A work-based system can only work if everyone has access to health care.* The best solutions, as Jeremy Rosner proposed in chapter 5, are to use the power of consumer choice and competition rather than government price controls to discipline soaring health care costs, and to let the states experiment with different ways to extend basic medical protection to all.

The new administration should expand efforts by nonprofit organizations and even private businesses to place welfare recipients in private jobs. That approach is likely to have a higher payoff than obliging welfare recipients to enroll in costly adult education and job training programs. While underscoring their responsibility to strive toward self-sufficiency, such programs rarely lead many to permanent jobs. Studies show that education and training do raise the earnings of welfare recipients, but rarely by enough to lift them out of poverty.[29] "The end result is often a skilled worker, and potential employee, who still doesn't have a job and continues to collect a welfare check," says Peter Cove, founder of America Works and a pioneer in welfare-to-work experiments.[30]

An alternative to expanding public education and training programs is to let private entities—nonprofit and for-profit—bid for the chance to place welfare recipients in private jobs and keep part of the money a state saves when someone leaves the rolls. For example, America Works is a private company that makes a profit by placing welfare mothers in New York and Connecticut in jobs with decent wages and benefits. For every person it moves from welfare to work, it collects $5,000, or about a third of what it costs the state to support an average family on welfare for a year. The state, which pockets the rest, has saved over $20 million by contracting with America Works.

Cove attributes America Works' success to intensive, personalized support for welfare mothers after they take a job. America Works' staff works with mothers and their employers to cope with child care, transportation, housing, and other problems that typically lead poor people to lose jobs. Why don't welfare agencies do the same? Because, Cove says, they have no incentive to do so: Public employees are hard to fire and they are paid whether or not they succeed in helping welfare recipients find and keep jobs. To encourage both private nonprofit and for-profit job placement ventures, the new administration should change AFDC rules to allow money saved when people leave welfare to be reinvested in further efforts to move people onto payrolls. Doing so would shift federal money from training and education programs that perpetuate dependence to private efforts that get people off welfare.

Finally, an innovative welfare-to-work strategy should include expanded public support for small "microenterprise" loans that can enable enterprising poor people to become self-employed. In inner cities and impoverished rural areas, microenterprise programs can foster self-employment by providing small, uncollateralized loans and business advice to groups of poor people trying to start their own businesses. Many such projects are patterned on the Grameen Bank in Bangladesh, which has helped thousands of poor rural women start small enterprises and which uses peer support and pressure to achieve a 98 percent repayment record. Using similar methods, the Women's Self-Employment Project in Chicago makes loans of $10,000 or less to poor women, who have used them to open dress shops and catering businesses. The Southern Development Bancorporation likewise fosters economic activity among low-income residents of rural Arkansas.

The new administration should increase federal support for microenterprise experiments and reduce legal and regulatory barriers—such as limits on assets and prohibitions on work in the home—that prevent poor people from choosing self-employment rather than welfare. It should also use federal funds to leverage the spread of community development banks, which make larger loans to build housing and stimulate small business development in poor communities.

2. Welfare reform should strengthen families and assure child support. The breakdown of families, though not exclusively a problem of the poor, lies at the heart of the self-defeating patterns of behavior that help perpetuate the urban underclass. The poverty rate for families headed by single mothers is six times that of two-parent families. Social researchers have found strong correlations between single-parent families and high rates of crime, teenage pregnancy, gang membership, and welfare dependency.[31]

An enabling strategy should remove disincentives to marry and reinforce parental responsibility by toughening child support enforcement. Many poor mothers depend on welfare because they receive little or no financial help from the fathers of their children. *The new administration should adopt a national child-support system, as described in chapter 6, to ensure that absent parents pay a percentage of their incomes for child support through tax withholding.* While lowering welfare payments, ensured child support would pose no disincentive for work. And if absent parents are unable to pay, government would guarantee a minimum child-support payment. Ellwood calls such a system "Social Security for children." It would also give single parents—who have to juggle the roles of breadwinner and homemaker—the option of working part time.

3. Welfare reform should stress community initiative and empower the poor, not the social service providers. When citizens enter the world of public assistance, they surrender control of their lives to bureaucrats, social service providers, and other presumed experts—what Robert Woodson of the Center for Enterprise Development calls the "poverty pentagon." These providers are trained to tell poor people what they must do to receive standardized social services, not to consult with them about what they really need to solve their problems. Moreover, too little of the money we spend to fight poverty trickles down through these paternalistic bureaucracies. *An enabling state would use vouchers, bank-style debit cards, savings accounts, tenant management and other non-bureaucratic means to empower poor people to take charge of their own lives.*

Vouchers concentrate purchasing power in the hands of the poor, allowing them—rather than welfare professionals—to choose the services and providers that best suit their needs. Vouchers can improve the provision of social services that are essential to self-sufficiency and independence for the poor, the disabled, and others: child day care, home health care, employment training, care for the disabled, and counseling. Moreover, vouchers can help sustain and increase political support for social service programs, spur innovation in the delivery of such services, create new entrepreneurial opportunities for social service professionals, and help bring low-income and other service recipients into the mainstream of the nation's economy and society.[32]

While government can direct the war on poverty, it needs the "little platoons" of civil society to wage the battles on the ground. In addition to the vital work already done by religious and charitable organizations, the voluntary or independent sector plays an increasingly important role in fighting social ills in ways less coercive, more flexible, and more sensitive to local conditions than public bureaucracies. During the 1980s, as Washington cut aid to cities, nonprofit Community Development Organizations cropped up around the country to build low-income housing and encourage commercial development. Community development banks, like Chicago's Shorebank, are likewise trying to arrest the decay of urban neighborhoods by offering loans to local entrepreneurs and businesses. *An enabling strategy should use government to leverage such community institutions and encourage businesses to enter the market for social provision.*

Nothing better symbolizes the failure of antipoverty programs than the squalor in public housing. Created during the Depression to provide houses to people temporarily down on their luck, public housing has become a permanent repository for the most abjectly poor Americans and a breeding ground for the problems associated with the underclass: drugs, crime, broken families, and

dependency. *The new President should seek to restore public housing's transitional status and expand opportunities for tenants to
manage and even own their own housing units.* The experiences
with tenant management in Chicago, Washington, and St. Louis
confirm that when residents are given responsibility to regulate
their own affairs, rent collections improve, crime, unemployment
and welfare dependency rates fall, and people fight to preserve and
improve their communities. Another essential step—pioneered by
Chicago Housing Authority Chief Vince Lane—is to bring working families back into public housing, to provide role models and
to foster sound values.

*Whether the government or the private sector is delivering social
services those services should be integrated so that they work to the
maximum benefit and ease of the clients, not the bureaucrats.* This
initiative is especially important for those services directed toward
young mothers and their children for the reasons discussed in
chapter 7.

**4. An enabling strategy for welfare reform should buttress
America's basic values, especially reciprocal responsibility.** Only
a social policy grounded in the values and experiences of most
Americans—work, individual responsibility, family, and community—is likely to yield results and win sustained public support.
Social responsibility is a two-way street: Government can help
only those determined to help themselves. An enabling state
should condition social supports on recipients' willingness to work
and strive toward self-sufficiency.

It follows, therefore, that welfare should reward, rather than
punish, productive behavior. Welfare abounds with perverse disincentives: a $1,000 limit on assets for AFDC recipients penalizes
thrift and saving; in 26 states, AFDC parents who take a full-time
job at minimum wage lose their benefits almost immediately; a
federal rule pegging public housing tenants' rent at 30 percent of
their income means their rent goes up automatically if they get a
raise or a better job; many states do not allow mothers to receive
welfare benefits if they marry; and many cities discourage self-
employment by barring people from operating small businesses out
of their homes. *A comprehensive reform approach should abolish all
disincentives to productive behavior in the system.*

The current welfare system focuses too narrowly on income
transfers, offering low-income and poor Americans few incentives
to save and build personal assets. In fact, the welfare system's limit
on assets encourages welfare recipients to spend their money. Yet,
as social policy analyst Michael Sherraden notes, people rarely

spend their way out of poverty.[33] While income supports fuel consumption and foster a "live-for-today" mentality, building assets leads people to save, defer consumption, plan ahead, and work harder to parlay what they have into bigger assets, such as a home.

This is the classic formula for upward mobility in America—a formula that rewards work and deferred gratification. Yet social policy assumes it is not for the poor. Just as middle-class families build assets with public support—for example, tax breaks for buying homes and investing in private pensions—*the next administration should create "Individual Development Accounts" (IDAs) for low-income families.* Like Individual Retirement Accounts, IDAs would be tax-favored and restricted to specific uses: college, home ownership, retirement, and starting a small business. But government would also offer matching contributions to encourage the poorest families to save.

CONCLUSION

The enabling strategy is designed to reinforce work, family, individual responsibility, and community. It renegotiates the terms of America's social compact: Instead of no-strings-attached income supports, society's help will henceforth be based on reciprocity. While government's responsibility is to expand opportunities for the poor to enter the mainstream of American life, the poor have a reciprocal responsibility to work hard, exercise individual responsibility, and avoid behavior that has high social costs.

The elements of this enabling strategy are mutually reinforcing. A temporary welfare system will make work imperative while the guaranteed working wage will make it rewarding. A competitive welfare-to-work system will rely on community initiative and market incentives to prepare welfare recipients for work and place them in good jobs. Ensured child support will lessen dependence on public assistance, offset AFDC's marriage penalty (it would not count against income limits), and underscore the notion that both parents must take responsibility for their children before government steps in. National service will offer income and other supports in exchange for work that mainly will benefit needy people and communities. And universal health coverage will eliminate one of the most serious obstacles facing the vast majority of welfare recipients who want to work and be independent.

The purpose of this work-based approach is to liberate the poor from poverty and dependence, not to save public money. On the contrary, a true compact of mutual obligation requires that government make significant new social investments: wage subsidies, child-care support, universal health care, national service. The greatest challenge facing the next administration is to convince the public that higher spending today will yield lower social and economic costs over the long run as the poor become taxpayers rather than tax consumers and add rather than subtract from our nation's productivity. It must also shift resources from existing social programs that are not yielding demonstrable gains. The costs of community service will be partially offset by reductions in welfare spending: By one estimate, a two-year limit on AFDC would save $18 billion.[34] Finally, we can also do more for less by relying less on bureaucratic service delivery and more on the voluntary sector and market incentives to empower poor citizens.

MANDATE FOR ACTION

1. **Make welfare temporary.** The new President should propose that AFDC eligibility be limited to two years for all able-bodied recipients.
2. **Subsidize work, not dependence.** We should expand the Earned-Income Tax Credit in order to lift all families with a full-time worker out of poverty.
3. **Create a civilian GI bill.** The U.S. should offer young people a chance to earn federal college and job training benefits by volunteering to serve needy people in their communities. Community service also should offer minimum-wage jobs to welfare recipients unable to find a private job after their AFDC eligibility has expired.
4. **Establish a social insurance system for children.** A minimum child-support benefit guaranteed by government will reinforce parental responsibility and lessen single mothers' reliance on public assistance.
5. **Change AFDC eligibility so that married recipients can keep some portion of their benefits.** The system should foster marriage and offer a transitional stage.
6. **Ensure universal access to health care.** A work-based social policy requires that welfare recipients not lose medical protection when they take a job. The new administration should adopt the market-based approach presented in chapter 5.
7. **Stress job placement over education and training.** The

---

new administration should shift money from education and training programs to private efforts—by nonprofit groups and businesses—to place welfare recipients in jobs with decent pay and benefits.

8. **Promote microenterprise.** The new administration should permit states to use federal community and rural development and job training funds to make direct loans to nonprofit groups that lend to microbusinesses and poor entrepreneurs. Such groups could also raise money from business and foundations.

9. **Encourage saving money and building assets.** The new administration should spend $1 billion to leverage community-based efforts to encourage low-income Americans to save through Individual Development Accounts. Community development corporations and other nonprofit groups would compete for federal grants and raise money from other sources in order to match IDA deposits of up to $2,000 a year.

10. **Expand choice through vouchers.** The new administration should convert into vouchers the $4 billion now spent under Title XX of the Social Security Act, AFDC and transitional child care, and the child care and development block grant.

11. **Foster management and ownership by tenants.** The new administration should expand funding for tenant management and ownership projects. It should also encourage further experiments like Chicago's Mixed-Income New Communities Strategy, which sets aside a percentage of housing units for working families.

11

A New Federal Compact: Sorting Out Washington's Proper Role

DAVID OSBORNE

INTRODUCTION

The federal government is in crisis. The American people believe Washington doesn't work. The typical American believes nearly half of every federal tax dollar is wasted. Only 17 percent of the public approves of Congress. Only 13 percent of senior federal executives would recommend that young people start their careers in government. And 17 of every 20 Americans want radical change: In a late May poll, 51 percent said the federal government needed "fundamental changes," another 34 percent called for a "complete rebuilding."[1]

These problems have many sources. Beneath most of them, however, lies a very simple truth: The world has changed dramatically since the 1930s, while government has not. In most of its activities, the federal government is using an outmoded way of doing business—a bureaucratic, centralized, command-and-control methodology inherited from the industrial age. The federal government also suffers from historical overload: Too many programs have been piled up over too many years. Today, entire departments stagger under their weight, while state and local governments, which carry out many of these programs, strangle in red tape.

If we are to improve the performance of the federal government we must answer two sets of questions: First, what roles should the federal government play in American life, and what roles should it not play? What responsibilities should remain federal, what should be devolved to state or local governments, and what should be eliminated altogether? Second, once we have sorted out the federal government's proper role, how can we restructure and reinvent those functions that remain federal so that they work? This chapter focuses on the first question; chapter 12 takes on the second.

THE FEDERAL ROLE

The federal government is involved in virtually every aspect of American life today. The Department of Agriculture finances fish ponds, runs 4-H Clubs in Harlem, and has at least one field office in almost every county in America—rural, urban, or suburban. The Department of Education finances local libraries and awards grants to encourage the study of *The Federalist Papers*. The Department of Commerce promotes travel and tourism.

Much of this activity is obsolete. Yet federal programs, once begun, seldom die. As a result, the federal government continues to expand, despite promises from three presidents in a row to shrink it. In 1975, civilian federal employees numbered 2,896,944. By May of 1992, they numbered 3,115,056.[2] (None of this growth was in Defense.) The Department of Agriculture now employs 124,855 civilians. The Department of Health and Human Services employs 132,301; Transportation 70,400; Commerce 37,485.[3]

Many federal programs are actually grants to state and local governments. By 1991 there were 557 grant programs, encompassing everything from economic development to police protection.[4] Some were mammoth; others were tiny. Together they accounted for $158.6 billion in federal spending.[5] The Advisory Commission on Intergovernmental Relations (ACIR) described the situation well a decade ago:

> It is estimated that approximately 63,000 of the nation's 80,000 state and local governments receive one or more such grants. Many states and large local governments receive so many different grants that they have hired specialists simply to apply for them and keep required records. Grantsmanship has become a recognized profession. Many private consultants make a living at it.[6]

By the 1970s, in ACIR's view, we had reached "a condition of overload":

> Administratively, federal grants too often frustrate effective and efficient public service by state and local governments. Some are so narrowly drawn that what needs to be done is ineligible for funding. Most bear so much red tape as to waste time and resources which should be spent on program objectives. Many are spread so thinly and targeted so poorly that they do not meet their objectives, or meet them only marginally.[7]

Today ACIR's words remain accurate.[8] Mayors and governors still rage at federal rules and red tape. Mayor John Norquist of Milwaukee, a Democrat, believes Congress should simply eliminate grant programs for local governments, because they distort local priorities and cost more in staff time than they are worth.[9] Mayor Richard Daley of Chicago, when asked by fellow Democrat Bill Clinton what the federal government could do to help the city of Chicago, responded with four words: "Have no urban policy."

To solve these problems, the new administration must transform the federal government's entire approach to state and local grant programs. This chapter will recommend that President Clinton undertake three initiatives:

1. **An American Perestroika Act to Create a Commission for a New Federal Compact.** The President should appoint a commission to draft legislation eliminating roughly 100 categorical grant programs and consolidating more than 400 others into performance-based block grants, called "Challenge Grants."
2. **A State and Local Deregulation Initiative.** The commission should develop proposals to increase dramatically the number of waivers to federal regulations granted state and local governments.
3. **A Federalism Czar.** The President should appoint a cabinet-level czar to chair the commission, move its recommendations through Congress, and oversee their implementation.

This approach would devolve operational control over roughly $140 billion of current federal spending to state and local governments. Specifically, it would eliminate some $17 billion in grants, devolving most of the savings back to state and local governments. It would also fold another $140 billion in grants into Challenge

Grants, cutting administrative costs substantially. Of the money saved by these actions, perhaps $10 billion should be earmarked for federal deficit reduction. While the efficiencies gained through devolution justify reserving modest savings for deficit reduction, the primary objective is not to save money. It is to empower state and local government to use federal money in more *effective* ways. If the objective were to take money away, state and local officials would block any action. If the objective is to make their governments more *effective,* state and local officials will lead the charge.

THE HISTORY OF FEDERAL CENTRALIZATION

The first major wave of federal expansion crested in the 1930s, during the Great Depression. At that time, the technologies of the day required that many activities be administered centrally, if they were to have national impact. State and local governments had far less capacity than they have today. Public work forces were far smaller and far less educated. Information systems were rudimentary, and communication was difficult.

Today's technologies, in contrast, create an imperative to decentralize. In today's rapidly changing, information-rich, knowledge-based economy, centralized systems are too slow, too cumbersome, and too rigid. We no longer have time for information to flow up the chain of command, for those at the top to receive enough information and pressure to make a decision, and for orders to flow back down the chain of command. Fortunately, we now have alternatives, thanks to the information-sharing power of modern computers and telecommunications. Today, no modern corporation administers its operations directly from headquarters. Headquarters is for managing, for making the large decisions, for steering the corporation. Operations are delegated to decentralized offices all over the world—offices that are given a great deal of freedom to develop their own best methods to do the job at hand. This is how efficient, effective organizations operate in the 1990s.

The second major expansion of federal authority occurred during the 1960s, for reasons that were largely political. Our national leaders decided that we needed a major effort to fight poverty and racial discrimination—and that state and local governments often stood in the way. At the time, state and local governments were broadly unrepresentative of their populations. Racial minorities were disenfranchised in much of the nation, and state legislators and city councilors were rarely elected from districts of equal size. Many state legislatures had not been reapportioned for decades. Too often, state and local leaders fought federal efforts to promote integration by denying minorities their rights and preventing antipoverty programs from reaching their intended recipients.

This too has changed. A 1962 U.S. Supreme Court decision led to the reapportionment of state legislatures along one-person, one-vote lines. In the 1970s and '80s, many large cities shifted from at-large election of city councils to district election, thus giving poor and minority areas equal representation. Meanwhile the South reconciled itself to civil rights, and state and local governments began to modernize. Today, state and local legislatures are more representative than Congress—and often more progressive on racial and social issues as well.

A BIAS FOR STATE AND LOCAL ACTION

These shifts—political, technological, and social—have undermined the rationale for many federal initiatives. Today many programs work best if left to the discretion of state and local governments. Even the simplest federal efforts—education aid, low-income housing, job training—are deeply flawed, while state and local governments compete to find the most effective new solutions to the same problems. Thirty years ago, a bias for federal action made sense. Today, a bias for state and local action makes sense.

This is true for many reasons:

1. State and local governments have far more fiscal discipline than Washington because their constitutions and charters require balanced operating budgets. Hence, the more we push up to Washington, the deeper we sink into debt.
2. Congress has proven itself generally incapable of targeting programs to the needs of specific regions. Over time, the political process forces even the most targeted efforts to spread the wealth (or pork) fairly evenly, and even the broadest grant programs to impose identical solutions in states and cities with very different problems.[10]
3. Federal programs, by their nature, are vastly larger in scale than state or local efforts. This is not a problem for most entitlement programs, which do little more than mail Social

Security checks or hand out food stamps. But in more complex operations, large federal programs bring with them greater inefficiencies and more bureaucracy.

4. Centralized systems administered from afar undermine the commitment and initiative of those who deliver the actual services. Because they take most of the important decisions out of local organizations' hands, they frustrate and demoralize those who do the hands-on work.

5. Top-down, centralized approaches are never flexible enough to respond to rapidly changing environments in hundreds of different cities and states. When Congress passed the Job Training Partnership Act ten years ago, for instance, it tried to create a decentralized structure that would allow states to tailor their training programs to meet local needs. But federal rules and regulations have gradually negated the good intentions. Title III of the act, known as the Economic Dislocation and Worker Adjustment Assistance Act (EDWAA), is designed to help states respond immediately to plant closings and large layoffs. Yet even the most flexible money, the "national reserve fund," is so fraught with red tape that many states choose not to apply for it. As the Congressional Office of Technology Assessment found, "the process is simply too obstacle ridden. . . . Many state EDWAA managers cannot handle the complexities of the grant application, and those that do know how are too busy responding to clients' urgent needs to write demanding, detailed grant proposals."[11]

6. Political pressures push Congress to earmark so much of its funding for specific purposes—even in broad block grant programs—that administration at the state and local level becomes extremely complex. Consider the words of Delaware Governor Michael Castle about a relatively new grant program:

> The McKinney Act, recently enacted by Congress to address the growing homeless population across the country, became an administrative nightmare for state and local implementation. Some programs included in the act provided money to states, others directly to local agencies or nonprofit community organizations. Coordination of various funding streams has been almost impossible.[12]

7. Federal initiatives carried out by state and local governments dilute any sense of accountability to the local community. As

ACIR points out, "No one is sure exactly who should be held responsible when the aid program falters. In fact no single body or official can be tagged or expected to remedy the difficulty single-handedly."[13]

8. This diffusion of accountability empowers organized interest groups in Washington, which are often successful in pushing for ever more spending regardless of the success or failure of the program in local areas. Program beneficiaries are often well organized, while taxpayers footing the bill are far flung and unorganized. A dynamic in which beneficiaries concentrate their fire in Washington while taxpayers remain oblivious thousands of miles away often results in waste and inefficiency.

THE CRITERIA FOR FEDERAL ACTION

The question of what level of government should act to solve a particular problem is seldom decided by rational criteria. Such decisions have always been made by politicians, for largely political reasons. But a new administration that intends to improve federal performance and get control of the deficit has little choice but to weed out obsolete federal functions. In addition, it is clear to most observers that a rational sorting of state, local, and federal responsibilities is long overdue. Some influential liberals have even begun to suggest radical approaches in which the federal government devolves all responsibility for many areas, including elementary and secondary education, job training, economic and community development, housing, highways, and social services.[14]

Given this situation, the President needs a rigorous set of criteria he can use to decide which functions should be devolved to lower governments and which should remain federal responsibilities. Past efforts by ACIR and others suggest a number of criteria. The most basic is quite simple: To justify federal action, a problem must be of vital concern to the nation as a whole—not simply to one state or city. For example, because an educated work force is the key to our economic competitiveness today, and because our work force is so mobile, the quality of education in Tennessee or Oregon is of vital concern to those of us who live in other states. A state with an inferior education system affects our future. This is not true of public safety, however. High crime rates in Detroit do not affect people in Idaho. Arson in Lawrence, Massachusetts, has little impact on residents of Florida.

Some problems of vital national concern can be solved without federal action. To justify federal action, at least one of four other criteria should be satisfied:

1. **Interstate Issues.** Many of the problems we face transcend state boundaries and capacity; they cannot be solved state by state or locality by locality. Some problems—such as the savings and loan crisis—are inherently national in scope; state governments simply do not have the leverage or legal standing to address them successfully. In other areas, including national defense and international trade, solutions cannot be provided for one state without being provided for all. In still other areas, states and localities, if left to their own devices, would create "spillover effects" on other regions. If we allowed states to handle the problem of air pollution, for example, Ohio would be able to export the sulfur emissions from its power plants to states downwind. Finally, some activities, such as scientific research, create almost as many benefits for those in other states or nations as those in one's own state; this undermines the incentive of any state or locality to finance them.

2. **Uniform National Standards.** Some policies are most effective if they are uniform across the nation. We have chosen, for example, to have a uniform monetary system, uniform citizenship requirements, uniform civil rights policies, and uniform social insurance benefits. We could do otherwise. In fact, states once had their own currencies, their own civil rights practices, and their own old age pensions. But in each case there were compelling arguments, whether on grounds of efficiency, effectiveness, or equity, to establish national standards.

3. **Destructive Competition.** Some policies are so sensitive to competition between states or localities that such competition creates negative consequences that outweigh the benefits of decentralization. For example, if the states handled all environmental and consumer product regulation, corporations would have to juggle 50 different sets of rules for their products and processes. If the states handled all corporate taxation, large, mobile corporations could play off one state against another until there were virtually no corporate taxes.

4. **Fiscal Redistribution.** Some problems of vital national concern must be addressed at the federal level because many state and local governments simply do not have the fiscal

capacity to solve them. This is particularly true of problems related to poverty: The states that need to do the most are precisely those with the fewest financial resources. If a problem is of vital national concern (because it affects the skill level of the work force, for instance), federal funding or federally mandated redistribution of state funds is justified.

APPLYING THE CRITERIA

In 1981, ACIR examined 473 federal programs, looking for those that might be devolved to lower levels of government.[15] It found that the 19 largest programs—Medicaid; lower income housing assistance; highway research, planning, and construction; Aid to Families with Dependent Children; Food Stamps, etc.—accounted for 80 percent of the funding. The smallest 424 programs accounted for only 10 percent of the money. ACIR recommended that most of these small grant programs be phased out.

ACIR grouped the 473 programs in clusters: housing, highways, employment and training, community development, and so on. It then ranked each cluster according to a "fragmentation index," which reflected both the size of each program and the number of programs in the cluster. (High fragmentation meant a cluster had a great number of small grants.) The results are duplicated in tables 1 and 2.

The next administration should ask ACIR to update this exercise, using the most recent fiscal year for which data is available. It should then apply the criteria outlined above to each cluster. On first analysis, the clusters appear to fall into the three categories depicted in table 3.

This is not to provide final answers, but to suggest the kind of analysis the next administration should undertake. Clearly, major devolution of current federal grant programs is in order. Most grant programs in category III should be eliminated, while many in category II should be restructured and, in some cases, pared down. (Category I grants also beg for restructuring, as we will see below.)

In 1991, the most recent year for which data is available, the devolution of category III grants would have saved roughly $10 billion in spending on non-interstate highways. (Because of shifts in highway spending, this figure would have jumped to $13.4 billion in 1992.) Another $2 billion in savings would have come

Table 1
Federal Aid Program Clusters
Ranked by Average Funding per Program

Cluster Name	Number of Programs	Dollar Amount of Cluster (000)	Average Dollar Amount Per Program (000)	
			Mean	Median
General Revenue Sharing	1	$ 6,863,000	$ 6,863,000	$ 6,863,000
Housing	6	22,606,628	3,767,771	409,200
Highways	6	8,829,143	1,471,524	194,463
Food and Nutrition	14	11,386,968	813,355	224,800
Employment and Training	18	13,998,608	777,700	162,740
Community Development	9	4,359,964	484,440	53,000
Public Transit	5	2,344,850	468,970	55,000
Public Assistance	24	10,686,794	445,283	18,928
Water Pollution Control	17	4,850,013	285,295	8,220
Airports	2	560,100	280,050	—
Medical Assistance	57	15,069,424	264,376	19,000
ALL PROGRAMS	473	$ 116,227,388	$ 245,720	$ 13,000

Economic Opportunity	5	$ 554,354	$ 110,871	$ 52,854
Education	77	7,345,617	95,397	9,750
Vocational Rehabilitation	14	842,243	60,160	27,500
Medical Research	45	2,506,362	55,697	39,466
Occupational Safety and Health	4	201,320	50,330	9,400
Natural Resources Conservation and Development	21	945,980	45,047	9,215
Civil Preparedness	7	242,549	34,650	3,827
Criminal Justice	20	613,296	30,655	5,028
Volunteer Services	5	104,502	20,900	23,214
Miscellaneous	10	198,410	19,841	23,705
Environmental Protection (except water)	16	246,301	15,394	9,200
Economic Development	29	443,581	15,296	5,019
Libraries	6	88,012	14,669	9,975
Other Transportation	10	80,290	8,029	1,940
Arts and Humanities	30	217,355	7,245	5,700
Rural Development	3	16,440	5,480	5,000
Energy	9	24,709	2,745	800
Fire Protection	3	843	281	255

Source: U.S. Advisory Commission on Intergovernmental Relations, The Federal Role in the Federal System: The Dynamics of Growth; An Agenda for American Federalism (Washington, D.C.: 1981), 127.

Table 2
Federal Aid Program Clusters
Ranked by Fragmentation Index, FY 1980

Cluster Name	Percent of Programs in Cluster (A)	Percent of FY 1980 Estimated Obligations in Cluster (B)	Fragmentation Index *
General Revenue Sharing	0.21%	5.90%	0.04
Housing	1.26	19.45	0.06
Highways	1.26	7.60	0.17
Food and Nutrition	2.95	9.80	0.30
Employment and Training	3.80	12.04	0.32
Community Development	1.90	3.75	0.51
Public Transit	1.05	2.02	0.52
Public Assistance	5.06	9.19	0.55
Water Pollution Control	3.59	4.17	0.86
Airports	0.42	0.48	0.88
Medical Assistance	12.02	12.96	0.93
All Programs	**100.00%**	**100.00%**	**1.00**

← Less Fragmented

	More Fragmented →			
Economic Opportunity	1.05%	0.48%	2.19
Education	16.24	6.32	2.57
Vocational Rehabilitation	2.95	0.72	4.10
Medical Research	9.49	2.16	4.39
Occupational Safety and Health	0.84	0.17	4.94
Natural Resources Conservation and Development	4.43	0.81	5.47
Civil Preparedness	1.48	0.21	7.05
Criminal Justice	4.22	0.53	7.96
Volunteer Services	1.05	0.09	11.67
Miscellaneous	2.11	0.17	12.41
Libraries	1.26	0.08	15.75
Environmental Protection (except water)	3.38	0.21	16.10
Economic Development	6.12	0.38	16.11
Other Transportation	2.11	0.07	30.14
Arts and Humanities	6.33	0.19	33.32
Rural Development	0.63	0.01	63.00
Energy	1.90	0.02	95.00
Fire Protection	0.63	0.0007	86,858.81

* Column A divided by Column B.

Source: U.S. Advisory Commission on Intergovernmental Relations, *The Federal Role in the Federal System: The Dynamics of Growth; An Agenda for American Federalism* (Washington, D.C.: 1981), 128.

Table 3

Levels of Federal Action

I. Federal Action Is Strongly Justified

Program Types	Reason
Housing	Fiscal redistribution
Food and Nutrition	Fiscal redistribution
Employment and Training	Uniform standards, fiscal redistribution
Community Development	Fiscal redistribution
Public Assistance	Uniform standards, fiscal redistribution
Environmental, Water Pollution Control	Interstate issues, destructive competition
Medical Assistance	Destructive competition, fiscal redistribution
Economic Opportunity	Fiscal redistribution
Education (higher)	Interstate issues
Occupational Safety and Health	Uniform standards, destructive competition
Medical Research	Interstate issues
Vocational Rehabilitation	Uniform standards

II. Some Federal Role Is Justified, But Most Responsibility Should Be State/Local

Program Types	Reason
Airports	Uniform standards (safety regulation only)
Highways	Interstate issues (interstate highways)
Public Transit	Fiscal redistribution
Education (K-12)	Fiscal redistribution
Resource Conservation, Development	Interstate issues, destructive competition
Civil Preparedness (disaster relief only)	Uniform standards, fiscal redistribution
Energy	Interstate issues

Table 3 (continued)

III. No Federal Role Is Justified

Program Types

Highways (non-interstate)
Criminal Justice (state and local)
Volunteer Services
Libraries
Economic Development (state and local)
Other Transportation (state and local)
Arts and Humanities
Rural Development
Fire Protection

Key:

Interstate Issues: Problems cannot be solved without federal action, because state and local governments lack leverage, incentives, etc.

Uniform Standards: Solutions require uniform national standards (e.g., social security, environmental regulation, civil rights).

Destructive Competition: Policies are so sensitive to competition between states or localities that such competition creates negative consequences which outweigh the benefits of decentralization.

Fiscal Redistribution: Solutions require redistribution of national resources, because poor regions cannot generate the necessary resources.

from eliminating six other transportation grants ($82 million), 18 categorical grants for criminal justice ($677 million), six grants for libraries ($134 million), five arts and humanities grants ($343 million), and nine economic development grants ($725 million).[16] The economic development figure excludes grants for Appalachia, on the grounds that such funds target poor communities and should be preserved as community development spending.

Devolution of category III grants, in other words, would eliminate roughly $15 billion in federal spending. Elimination of category II grants that do not meet our criteria would save another $1–$2 billion, in areas such as natural resource conservation, energy, public transit, and civil preparedness. In total, this approach would eliminate perhaps 100 categorical grant programs, saving roughly $17 billion.

Most of the savings should be handed back to state and local governments. This could be done in any number of ways—perhaps by increasing category I and II spending, perhaps with revenue sharing, perhaps by handing certain federal taxes back to the states. Not all the savings should be returned, however; some should go toward deficit reduction. Eliminating 100 categorical programs would free state and local governments from many restrictive rules and allow them to eliminate functions they now fund only to get federal money or meet federal mandates; hence it would yield significant efficiency gains.

A NEW MODEL FOR FEDERAL ACTION

As table 3 points out, there is every reason to continue federal activities in many areas, from community development to employment and training. However, this does not mean the current approach is the best one. Categorical grants and centralized programs administered from Washington have severe disadvantages. The fact that the federal government chooses to set policy and provide funding for a particular area does not mean that it has to micromanage.

Consider the Department of Housing and Urban Development. Federal funding for community development in poor areas is fully justifiable, on grounds of fiscal redistribution. But with 14,000 employees and an annual budget of $25.1 billion, HUD is far too big. It has enormous overhead expenses: By its own admission, 28 percent of its employees—some 4,000 people—"provide indirect program support and management functions."[17] And much of what HUD employees spend their time on has no business being administered from Washington:

- HUD has 1,400 people working on public housing, a program enacted during the Depression to build apartment complexes for working people who had fallen on hard times.[18] There are now 1.3 million public housing units in the United States; we spend $4.7 billion a year on them.[19] Local public housing administrators complain bitterly about HUD's excessive regulation and centralization. Would any business administer an operation this large from headquarters, with rigid standardization all across the nation?
- Some 465 full-time HUD employees spend their time making direct 40-year loans to finance apartments for the elderly and handicapped. In 1989, these 465 people made $474 million in loans, to build or rehabilitate 9,164 housing units—a ratio of 20 units per employee.[20] Would any bank be satisfied with that ratio? And why is HUD making direct loans, rather than using mortgage insurance and the Government National Mortgage Association to create incentives for banks to make these loans, as it does with FHA-insured loans?
- In 1989, HUD had 498 full-time employees in its Office of Fair Housing and Equal Opportunity, which works to prevent racial discrimination by landlords and mortgage vendors. They received 6,442 housing discrimination complaints.[21] Why take complaints at headquarters? Why not let local governments and community organizations do the job, with partial HUD financing?
- HUD operates a tiny Minority Business Enterprise Program, which duplicates efforts at both the Small Business Administration and the Commerce Department. Why?

Much of this work could be done more effectively by using one of two methods: a broad federal grant for state and local governments, or a market incentive to encourage private lenders to invest in low- and moderate-income housing. HUD already uses both devices extensively. It administers a $3.4 billion Community Development Block Grant program, and it uses market devices such as tax credits, FHA insurance, loan guarantees, the Government National Mortgage Association, and the Federal Home Loan Mortgage Corporation to draw more capital into low- and moderate-income housing. It should move much further in this direction, transforming itself from a large "rowing" organization into a smaller "steering" body. Using government's power to shape the marketplace is far more effective than using government to provide services, delivered by a Washington bureaucracy.

In other federal agencies, the problem is not too much direct service delivery but the proliferation of dozens of tiny, narrowly targeted categorical grant programs, each with its own bureaucracy. In 1991, Congress funded almost 100 social service grant programs, more than 80 health care grant programs, and close to 30 grant programs that dealt with housing or development in poor communities. Many of these were for amounts of only $3 or $4 million. Of the Education Department's more than 90 separate grant programs, the majority were for less than $15 million.

When one department administers so many tiny grant programs, something is wrong. Thousands of public employees, in Washington and in state and local governments, spend countless hours writing regulations, publicizing grant programs, and writing and reviewing grant applications. Billions of dollars go to the professionals and bureaucrats who do this, rather than the intended recipients of federal largess: the students, the poor people, the urban residents.

For 20 years, the favored method of shifting program administration from Washington to state and local governments has been the block grant, which consolidates many categorical grant programs into one grant with—at least theoretically—little earmarking and few strings attached. But block grants have their own problems: They distribute money without regard to the quality of the resulting initiatives. Wasteful, ineffective programs get the same priority as the most innovative, cost-effective approaches.

We need a third way: a competitive block grant that is distributed based both on need and on the quality of a state or local program. This kind of model has already been developed at the state level. For example, Pennsylvania's Ben Franklin Partnership, perhaps the nation's most effective economic development initiative, uses what it calls "Challenge Grants" to fund local economic development centers.[22]

AN AMERICAN PERESTROIKA ACT TO CREATE A COMMISSION FOR A NEW FEDERAL COMPACT

The President should propose an American Perestroika Act, which would create a commission to plan a sweeping devolution of the federal government. The commission—composed of leaders from federal, state, and local government and representatives of business, labor, and community organizations—would draft plans for eliminating 100 categorical grant programs, consolidating more than 400 categorical and block grants into broad Challenge Grants, and devolving most of the savings to state and local governments.

To illustrate the use of Challenge Grants, consider the idea of a Community Development Challenge Grant, administered by HUD. Under this approach, the federal government would establish broad guidelines, objectives, and performance measures. State and/or local governments would then compete for Challenge Grants based on three major criteria:

1. *Need:* A community's unemployment rate; poverty rate; median income; etc.
2. *Quality of Strategy:* For example: Is the proposed strategy market-oriented? Does it empower communities to solve their own problems? Does it use competition and choice? Does it measure results?
3. *Results:* The number of jobs created; changes in the poverty rate and unemployment rate; job placement rates; private investment leveraged; changes in indicators of family health; incidence of graft or corruption; etc.

The higher a government ranked on these criteria, the more funding it would receive. State and local governments would be free to combine their funds from different Challenge Grants—or from other streams of federal money—to create more integrated strategies. For example, a local government might develop a homeless initiative that combined Community Development Challenge Grant money, Medicaid money, Job Training Challenge Grant money, and Education Challenge Grant money. Ideally, integrated strategies such as this would be encouraged by the quality criteria used in rating applications.

This approach would create powerful incentives for states and/or localities to act, but it would allow them to design their own strategies. The federal government could articulate the mission and goals of the grant without dictating the process lower governments used to fulfill them. By measuring outcomes and rewarding success, it could create powerful incentives for lower governments to achieve its goals. And by initially asking states and/or localities to compete based on design criteria, it could drive them toward entrepreneurial strategies, without dictating those strategies. Local entities could focus on their own areas of greatest need and hand-craft their own strategies, without micromanagement from above. They could not, however, continue to collect their full grants without producing results.

If this approach is to work, one other element is necessary: sharing of information between states and localities about new, successful policy and program innovations. If the federal government wants to spur innovation and heighten the effectiveness of state and local efforts, it must make sure that good ideas spread rapidly. Creating new federal institutions to do this would be a mistake, because state and local officials have little confidence in federal bureaucrats—particularly as purveyors of innovation. Many information-sharing networks already exist at the state and local level, from the National Governors Association or the International City and County Management Association to such private efforts as the Ford Foundation's and the Kennedy School's Innovation Awards program. The federal government should simply provide these networks with additional funding, so they can be more effective. As part of each Challenge Grant program, a small percentage should be set aside for competitive grants to such networks.

Challenge Grants would be the heart of a genuine New Federalism. As noted earlier, the elimination of 100 categorical grants would save roughly $17 billion, with most of the savings returned to state and local governments. The consolidation into Challenge Grants of more than 400 other categorical and block grants—totaling $140 billion—would vastly increase their impact, by em-powering state and local governments to find the best solutions to their problems, unencumbered by federal micromanagement. Most of the savings that stem from cutting administrative costs—perhaps $10 billion—should be set aside for federal deficit reduction.

Just three programs account for roughly half of the $140 billion in consolidated grants: Medicaid, Aid to Families with Dependent Children (AFDC), and Unemployment Insurance. Because these are entitlement programs, where benefits are fixed by law, states would have less discretion with these Challenge Grants than with others. But the fundamental principle—greater flexibility in return for accountability for results—would still apply.

THE STATE AND LOCAL DEREGULATION INITIATIVE

The Commission for a New Federal Compact should also develop a State and Local Deregulation Initiative to increase dramatically the number of waivers granted state and local governments. Such waivers would free these governments from specific federal rules and regulations, allowing them to operate more flexibly.

Waivers would give states and localities more latitude in complying with federal mandates and in operating non-grant programs such as public housing. They would also help recipients of Challenge Grants combat creeping overregulation on the part of Congress or federal agencies.

When President Bush focused on welfare reform in his 1992 State of the Union Address, he promised that his administration would encourage innovation by granting rapid approval to states that applied for waivers to regulations that stood in their way. By and large, the Bush administration kept its promise. But welfare is not the only program deserving of waivers. Medicaid waivers are still difficult to get. Congress still refuses to give the Department of Education *any* authority to grant waivers. Often states must apply to half a dozen different agencies for waivers. And federal decisions on most waivers remain slow. For example, Florida has a two-year waiver allowing it to provide hospice care to AIDS patients under Medicaid. Simply to *renew* the waiver takes 18 months, so Florida officials had to reapply after only six months of experience.

Several years ago Booth Gardner, governor of Washington, described the problems that arise when states go after waivers. His administration was trying to create a new approach to welfare, called the Family Independence Program (FIP).

> FIP required scores of waivers from the secretaries of the U.S. Departments of Health and Human Services and Agriculture. . . . As with everything, the Office of Management and Budget is involved. . . . Each of these agencies has divisions, bureaus, or offices with separate authority over waivers and evaluation. . . .
>
> For public assistance, the Department of Health and Human Services has one definition of a family. For Food Stamps, the Department of Agriculture has another. Our proposal to include the case value of Food Stamps in the benefit package found us between the agencies' definitions. . . .

The federal agency officials with whom the state negotiated were remarkably out of touch with the federal system. They were impatient in confronting the diversity of the states and in acknowledging the balances required to enact a welfare reform . . .

. . . without a new approach to waivers, the value of state reforms is compromised. We lost pieces of FIP to the waiver process and person-years of effort to negotiations. Our implementation schedule has been delayed. . . . The Congress should recognize that the federal agencies, which approve waivers, have a direct interest in the outcome of reform. Their control stands to be reduced for the first time in decades.[23]

The commission's Deregulation Initiative should request that Congress grant the President broad waiver authority. Meanwhile, the President should encourage state and local governments to apply for waivers and require all federal departments to expedite the process. He should ask every cabinet secretary and agency head to develop a list of regulations ripe for waiver. The President could also ask each cabinet member or agency head to designate an assistant, reporting directly to the secretary or commissioner, to be in charge of the waiver effort. The President should then create a Waiver Office in the Office of Management and Budget to coordinate the effort.

This strategy would be most effective, however, if federal offices outside Washington, in close touch with state and local governments, carried the ball. The ten Federal Regional Councils, which include the regional executives of major federal offices around the country, would be ideal hosts of such an effort. With small staffs, they could encourage their state and local counterparts to apply for waivers, push agencies in Washington to expedite their decisions, lobby for approvals, and ensure that the results were evaluated objectively. When necessary, they could call upon high-level support from the Waiver Office. The administration could also develop a "double-waiver" procedure, in which governments applying for waivers would be required to deregulate their local counterparts and/or service providers in similar fashion.

HOW THE COMMISSION WOULD WORK

Fifty-five years ago, President Franklin Roosevelt asked Louis Brownlow, then director of the Public Administration Clearing House and former president of the International City Management

Association, to chair a committee to examine the reorganization of the executive branch. The Brownlow Committee recommended that the 100 executive agencies be reorganized under 12 departments; that the civil service system be restructured; that the White House staff be expanded; that managerial agencies such as the Bureau of the Budget be strengthened and brought within the executive office; and that an auditor general be put in place to audit all federal fiscal transactions. In so doing, it created nothing less than the modern structure of the executive branch.

A decade later, President Truman asked former President Herbert Hoover to chair a Commission on the Organization of the Executive Branch of the Government, to recommend ways to limit spending, increase efficiency, eliminate duplication, and abolish unnecessary activities.

If we are to accomplish the sorting out of federal roles and the restructuring of federal, state, and local relationships suggested here, we will need another commission with the scope and power of the Brownlow and Hoover commissions.

Such decisions cannot be made through the traditional political process of submitting individual bills to Congress. Every federal grant and every federal program has an organized constituency, which will defend it to the bitter end. Many mayors, governors, and state and local legislators would support a New Federal Compact, but they will not have the time or organization to fight each battle. Proposals to change hundreds of programs, one by one, will be defeated and diluted, one by one. As Machiavelli wrote almost 500 years ago, "There is no more delicate matter to take in hand, nor more dangerous to conduct, nor more doubtful in its success, than to set up as a leader in the introduction of changes. For he who innovates will have for his enemies all those who are well off under the existing order of things, and only lukewarm supporters in those who might be better off under the new."[24]

If this commission is to succeed, it must develop one or two comprehensive, coherent proposals, which Congress must be required to vote up or down, without amendment. In a battle limited to one or two votes, the administration can organize a formidable coalition for change. This is the model that brought success to the Military Base Closing Commission.

If a commission proposal is approved by the President, Congress should have 30 days to vote it down before it automatically goes into effect. Once commission proposals have cleared Congress, the commission staff should work with federal agencies and OMB to implement them. The commission would remain intact, meeting to review Challenge Grant proposals and implementation of the waiver strategy. Its approval would be required before institution of all Challenge Grants. Once that has been accomplished, the commission should go out of existence.[25]

A FEDERALISM CZAR

The new President should appoint a cabinet-level Federalism Czar to chair the commission and bring the New Federal Compact to fruition. He or she would work with Congress and with organizations such as the National Governors Association, the National League of Cities, the National Association of Counties, and the International City and County Management Association, to solicit ideas and build a constituency for change. The czar would then take the lead in moving the commission's recommendations through Congress and overseeing their implementation.

CONCLUSION

This agenda is ambitious. Politically, it will not be an easy sell in Congress. But if enacted, it would have a tremendous impact upon government in America. By minimizing federal regulations and red tape, it would empower state and local governments to focus on results, rather than process. By stripping away hundreds of small categorical grants and combining most others into large Challenge Grants, it would allow the federal government to focus less on administration and regulation, more on setting goals and measuring results. It would save billions of dollars in administrative overhead, while dramatically increasing the effectiveness of federal efforts to fight poverty, improve education and training, and solve our most pressing social problems.

Some might argue that by minimizing the number of federal programs, we would be weakening the federal government. Nothing could be further from the truth. Federal bureaucracies preoccupied with the administration of hundreds of small categorical programs are a recipe for weak, ineffective government—not strong government. As Peter Drucker wrote long ago:

> We do not face a "withering away of the state." On the contrary, we need a vigorous, a strong, and a very active government. But we do face a choice between big but impotent government and a govern-

ment that is strong because it confines itself to decision and direction and leaves the "doing" to others. . . . [We need] a government that can and does govern. This is not a government that "does"; it is not a government that "administers"; it is a government that governs.[26]

MANDATE FOR ACTION

1. **Pass an American Perestroika Act to create a Commission for a New Federal Compact.** The President should appoint a high-level commission to plan a sweeping devolution of federal government grant programs—eliminating roughly 100 grant programs and transforming more than 400 others into Challenge Grants. Once the commission's recommendations are approved by the President, both houses of Congress would have to defeat them within 30 days or they would automatically go into effect. Amendments would not be permitted.

2. **Develop a State and Local Deregulation Initiative.** The commission should request broad waiver authority from Congress to cut through the overregulation and red tape strangling state and local implementation of federal programs.

3. **Appoint a Federalism Czar.** The President should appoint a cabinet-level czar to chair the commission, rally support for its recommendations, push them through Congress, and oversee their implementation.

12

Reinventing Government: Creating an Entrepreneurial Federal Establishment

DAVID OSBORNE

INTRODUCTION

Government is virtually the only sector of American society that has yet to confront the need to reinvent itself for the information age. Business leaders have spent the last decade decentralizing authority, flattening hierarchies, empowering their employees, focusing on quality, and getting closer to their customers. Voluntary, nonprofit organizations have launched a thousand new initiatives, often working in partnership with the public or for-profit sector. But government, by and large, has remained the same: sluggish, centralized, and bureaucratic. Even during the Reagan–Bush years, while officials gave speeches about cutting the bureaucracy, the federal government added 239,000 civilian employees.[1]

The model of government we inherited from the industrial age achieved great things in its day, but it is no longer effective. With its monopolies, its preoccupation with rules and regulations, and its hierarchical chains of command, it simply cannot keep up with the rapidly changing, highly competitive, information-rich society and economy within which we live.

The federal government is approaching paralysis. It faces much the same crisis American industry faced a decade ago. In the first 40 years after World War II, our largest corporations dominated the world economy, doing business each year just as they had the year before. Meanwhile, the Japanese and the Europeans were constantly improving their manufacturing processes, their exporting strategies, and their training systems. Suddenly, they caught up, and major American corporations such as Chrysler almost went under. Finally, a decade ago, American businesses began to restructure. Today, government must follow their example.

When public-sector leaders talk of restructuring, they normally mean reorganizing—moving the organizational boxes around. They also are fond of creating "efficiency commissions": blue-ribbon panels of business leaders who look over everything the government does and recommend functions to be eliminated, consolidated, or streamlined. (The Grace Commission offers a recent example.) Because few business people understand how government really works—how both the bureaucratic process and the political process work to protect even the most obsolete programs—they seldom develop the strategies necessary to implement their recommendations.

What we must do, instead, is restructure the *incentives* that drive public managers, public employees, and elected officials. Our federal bureaucracies grow so large and sluggish not because those who work for them want it that way, but because the basic incentives operating on those bureaucracies literally *demand* that it be that way. Most public programs are monopolies whose customers cannot go elsewhere for a better deal. Most are funded according to their *inputs*—how many children are eligible for a given program, how many families are poor enough to qualify for public assistance—rather than according to their *outcomes*, or results. Most are considered important not because they achieve tremendous results, but because they spend tremendous sums of money. Their managers earn greater stature and higher pay not because they have demonstrated superior performance, but because they have built up a larger bureaucracy. Their employees are hired, fired, and rewarded not because they have done their jobs well, but because they have held them for a long time.

With such perverse incentives embedded within our federal government, is it any wonder that we get bureaucratic rather than entrepreneurial behavior? Is it any wonder that federal managers spend so much of their time writing memos and covering their backsides? Is it any wonder that so much federal "work" consists of little more than sending memos up the chain of command, rewriting those memos, and sending them back down the chain of command?

To change behavior within the federal government, we must change the basic incentives that shape that behavior. We must create a new set of dynamics—through the use of competition, the measurement of results, the decentralization of authority, and the creation of real consequences for success and failure. These dynamics would give public organizations *no choice* but to strive for continual improvement, *no choice* but to rid themselves of the obsolete and invent the new. We must not redesign the organizational chart so much as redesign the basic systems—budget, personnel, pay, procurement, even accounting—that give our public organizations their unwritten marching orders. Our goal must be to have public organizations that constantly improve, redesign, and innovate; that constantly drive their costs down and their quality up. After all, a typical business strives to increase its productivity by 3 to 4 percent every year. Why shouldn't government do the same?

This chapter offers a set of principles around which entrepreneurial public organizations structure themselves. In applying these principles to the task of reinventing the federal government, it focuses on changing the basic incentive systems that drive federal employees and organizations.[2]

To create a mission-driven federal government—one that focuses on results rather than rules—the new administration should:

- Establish a performance-based budget system that offers flexibility in exchange for results
- Overhaul the Civil Service system
- Negotiate a "Grand Bargain" with federal employee unions and create a Labor-Management council
- Establish a Sunset Law and Commission to eliminate obsolete federal programs and regulations

To create an enterprising government—one that seeks opportunities to earn rather than spend—the new administration should:

- Propose a non-tax revenue act, creating incentives for federal agencies and employees to search for new revenues
- Create an innovation fund, so that federal agencies can borrow to invest in ways to increase revenues or cut costs

To create a catalytic government—one that focuses on steering (or policy management) rather than rowing (or service delivery)—the new administration should:

- Cut the budgets of designated federal agencies by 6 percent a year to force their transformation from rowing to steering
- Create a new national information agency to upgrade statistical capacity throughout the federal government

To create an anticipatory government—one that focuses on prevention—the new administration should:

- Propose a "Truth in Spending" bill, calling for new accounting standards, a capital budget and ten-year spending projections for all budget items, to force leaders to confront the long-term implications of all spending decisions

To create a competitive government—one that injects competition into federal service delivery—the new administration should:

- Force service delivery organizations such as the General Services Administration, the Postal Service, and Amtrak to compete with private ventures in the delivery of certain services

MISSION-DRIVEN GOVERNMENT: RESULTS, NOT RULES

"Never tell people how to do things," Gen. George S. Patton said in 1944. "Tell them what you want them to achieve and they will surprise you with their ingenuity." Too often, the federal government does just the opposite. Elected officials wrap each new program in a tight web of regulations—ordering certain activities, forbidding others, and dictating precisely how much can be spent on personnel and program expenses. Senior bureaucrats then tighten the noose, spelling out the exact process by which the program is to be administered and fracturing budgets into myriad line items. As a result, managers learn to follow every rule and spend every penny of every line item, whether it makes sense or not.

In short, bureaucratic governments focus on inputs—how much we spend, how many people are covered—but pay little attention to results. Schools are funded according to how many children enroll, not according to how well children do in one school versus another. Welfare is funded according to how many poor people are eligible, not according to how many poor people get off welfare into stable jobs. Lending programs are judged based on how many loans they make, not on what happens to the businesses that receive the loans.

An entrepreneurial government would change these incentives. It would minimize rules and line items. It would emphasize missions and outcomes. It would define agencies' missions and goals, measure how well they achieve those goals, and develop budget and pay systems that reward organizations for success. When institutions are funded according to inputs, they have little reason to strive for better performance. When they are funded according to outcomes, they become obsessive about performance.

Performance-based Budgeting

Few people outside government pay any attention to budget systems. But budgets control everything a federal agency does. Perhaps the most important step the new President can take to change the incentives driving federal agencies is to change the budget system. This cannot be done in a single stroke, but will require three separate steps, unfolding over a period of five to six years: First, liberate managers from microscopic line-item control and allow their agencies to keep part of any money unspent at the end of the year; second, develop performance measures for all federal programs; and, third, devise a budget that specifies performance targets and rewards agencies that exceed those targets. All three approaches have been used effectively by state and local governments and by the Defense Department.[3]

Federal managers cannot focus on broad missions when their budgets are divided into narrow line items. In one military branch, installation commanders have 26 different line items for housing repairs alone.[4] The proliferation of line items stems from congressional appropriations bills, from committee reports that accompany these bills, and from the departments themselves.

Whatever the source, the results are often perverse. When money is trapped within line items that made sense last year or the year before, but conditions have changed, federal managers cannot always shift their funds. Consider the military base that had no line item to purchase snowplow equipment, but had a maintenance account. When the snowplow died, it spent $100,000 a year to lease a snowplow it could have purchased for $100,000. This happens all the time in the federal bureaucracy. By corralling money in line items, we waste billions of dollars every year.

Even worse, managers who do not spend their entire budgets by the end of the fiscal year normally must return the excess. They are also likely to receive less in the next appropriation. Many managers know where they could trim 10 percent off their budgets, but they have no incentive to do so. Why bother, if they just have to return the savings, and they get less money in the future? As a result, smart public managers spend every penny of every line item, whether they need to or not. This explains why there is a rush to spend money at the end of every fiscal year—despite rules that forbid it. It also explains why federal bureaucracies continue to grow: The budget system actually encourages managers to waste money.

The solution, as developed by state and local governments, is a budget that has one line item for each program with a distinct mission and allows agencies to roll over half of what they do not spend in a year. To reduce further the tendency toward end-of-the-year spending, the President and Congress should also shift to a two-year budget cycle.

In return for these new flexibilities, the managers of all non-entitlement programs should be asked to increase their productivity by 3 percent per year—thus beginning to reduce federal spending. Unless the President or Congress makes a policy decision to expand or contract a program, the budget should automatically give these programs and agencies 3 percent less each year than the year before, after adjusting for inflation.

If the President or Congress wants significantly more work from an agency, or significantly less, they would of course adjust its budget up or down. But by adopting an automatic formula for most agencies and programs, Congress would protect them from retroactive raids on their savings. Typically, when an agency saves a significant amount, the legislature responds by cutting its budget in subsequent years. This quickly destroys any incentive to save. An automatic formula is necessary to protect against such raids.

By freeing agencies from most line items and some rules, Congress would be loosening its control over inputs. In return, it should be given increased control over *outcomes.* Agencies that are no longer accountable for so much process should become accountable for delivering results.

A few federal programs, such as those funded by the Job Training Partnership Act, already collect information about outcomes. But most examination of results at the federal level is done by inspectors general, whose focus is almost entirely on who broke the rules or overspent their budgets. The federal government desperately needs a new focus on effectiveness: What outcomes is it buying with its money?

Therefore, the new President should introduce legislation requiring the development of performance measures for all federal agencies and programs. A similar measure passed the Senate in October, 1992.[5]

The third step would be the creation of a budget that specified results expected of each program and tied rewards to the achievement of those results. Some of these outcomes might be levels of satisfaction reported on customer surveys; some might be quantifiable accomplishments (percentage of welfare recipients placed in jobs; wage rates; retention rates; etc.); some might be subjective ratings by expert evaluators. For most programs, some combination of these three approaches would yield a relatively good picture of performance.

To motivate managers and their agencies, financial rewards should be attached to achievement of the performance goals. In some programs, bonuses for managers might be most effective; in others, bonuses for all employees might be more powerful; or, alternatively, agencies might receive their money only for accomplishing specific goals (say, $5,000 for each welfare recipient placed in a private sector job). When an agency exceeds its goals, its new performance level should become its expected base for the next year. In this way, the budget would ratchet up performance, year after year. (This approach is already used by some local governments and by portions of the Defense Logistics Agency.)[6]

To pay for the shift to performance-based budgeting, the new act should require that one percent of the funds for every program be set aside to finance the development of performance measures: evaluation of performance measures and agency efforts to improve performance. This performance measure fund would also apply to state and local governments that received federal money, although the President could waive or reduce it for particular programs.

Part of this money would fund a Performance Review Office, which would help agencies develop performance measures, ensure that the measurement was honest, and make sure the results were made public. Independent auditors were created decades ago to ensure honest bookkeeping and accounting; today we need independent performance auditors. The office could be set up like our independent regulatory commissions, to ensure insulation from political pressure from a President or Congress. It would publish objective, readable information about agency outcomes—the equivalent of a *Consumer Reports* for the federal government.[7]

Overhauling the Civil Service

The personnel system we use to hire, promote, reward, and fire federal employees dates, in its basic outlines, from the early twentieth century. Known as Civil Service, it was invented in 1883, and its last significant redesign took place in 1949. It successfully accomplished its original mission—to control political patronage and manipulation of public employees. But today it is a straitjacket. Civil Service is a personnel system for a government of clerks, when we need a government of knowledge workers.

The horror stories are legion. It takes the average federal manager roughly a year to fire an employee, even when he or she can prove that employee's incompetence.[8] When layoffs occur, employees with seniority get to "bump" newer employees, regardless of their abilities or expertise or performance—so we end up with people in jobs they don't want and haven't been trained to perform. According to Paul Volcker's National Commission on the Public Service, "Even when the public sector finds outstanding candidates, the complexity of the hiring process often drives all but the most dedicated away."[9] We waste millions of dollars on personnel officers whose job it is to classify each employee within a system so complex that it has 459 job series, 15 grades, and 10 steps within each grade. (The Office of Personnel Management, which does the classifying, has 6,872 employees.)[10]

The National Academy of Public Administration recently concluded that the Civil Service job classification system should be scrapped. According to the Academy, it is expensive, cumbersome, time-consuming, and intensely frustrating to managers. It often takes months to get positions classified and filled. Classification standards are "too complex, inflexible, outdated, and inaccurate." They "create rigid job hierarchies that cannot change with organizational structure." They "weaken the link between pay and performance." They drive high performers out of their fields of expertise into supervisory positions, to get higher pay, and they make it difficult to recruit quality employees.[11]

President Carter's Civil Service Reform Act of 1978 authorized several demonstration projects that experimented with a different classification system. For example, the "China Lake Experiment," at two naval facilities in California, classified all jobs in just five career paths—professional, technical, specialist, administrative, and clerical—and folded all 18 General Schedule grades into no more than six pay ranges (called "bands") within each path. It allowed managers to pay market salaries to recruit people, to increase the pay of outstanding employees without having to re-classify them, and to give bonuses and salary increases based on performance. And it based layoffs primarily on performance rather than seniority.

This new set of rules solved many of the problems the two naval facilities had encountered. Turnover rates declined and managers were able to retain more of their skilled employees. More than 80 percent of the employees surveyed in 1987 preferred it to the old system.[12]

The Office of Personnel Management has proposed that other agencies be allowed to adopt the China Lake approach and to create their own performance pay and award systems. With OPM's proposals, NAPA's report, and the demonstration projects, a consensus has emerged. It is now time to act.

A bill to overhaul Civil Service would not abandon protections against political patronage and manipulation, nor expand the number of federal political appointees. It would simply change the rules by which Civil Service operates, to create more flexible, performance-driven federal organizations. The new approach should include:

- A broad-band pay and classification framework, drastically reducing the number of job classifications and grades and allowing more use of market salaries
- Widespread use of performance pay and gainsharing, with latitude for agencies to design their own systems
- Layoffs by a combination of performance and seniority, with greater weight given to performance
- Further decentralization of the hiring process, with OPM simply helping agencies advertise, recruit, and screen applicants
- Aggressive use of advertising, bonuses, and other recruitment devices
- A streamlined appeals process when employees are fired for failure to perform
- Increased investments in training
- Authority for a new round of demonstration projects, some of which would test alternatives to the current tenure system of Civil Service[13]

A Labor-Management Council and a " Grand Bargain"

Many of those who have campaigned to change the federal government have used federal employees as whipping boys. They have blamed wasteful *bureaucrats* for the problem, when in fact wasteful *systems* are the problem. Our employees did not create the dysfunctional programs and systems that hamstring the federal government—hence they should not be asked to pay for the solutions with their jobs. By and large, the federal government has good people struggling within bad systems. Our goal must be to change those systems, not to lay off people—to liberate and empower employees, not to punish them.

Many of the changes suggested in this chapter will require support from public employees and their unions. That support will not be forthcoming unless employees and their representatives feel that they will have input into key management decisions at the highest levels of government. Hence, one element of a reinventing government strategy must be cooperation with organizations that represent public employees.

To tap the creativity of federal employees and improve employee input into major management decisions, the President should create a Labor-Management Council. He should offer federal employee unions a "Grand Bargain," under which he would guarantee no layoffs and bring union representatives to the table in decision-making about structural reforms, if the unions would support his efforts to change the Civil Service and budget systems and to shrink the federal work force.

During the presidential campaign, Governor Bill Clinton proposed to reduce the federal bureaucracy by 100,000—roughly 3 percent. This is a laudable point of departure. But if the recommendations of this chapter are implemented, the first-term goal could easily be twice this amount.

This level of downsizing can be achieved without layoffs. According to the Office of Personnel Management, the annual attrition rate in the federal government is 10 percent. If managers had sufficient budget and personnel flexibility, they could use attrition to shrink their agencies—retraining employees and moving them around as their positions were eliminated. Those whose positions were eliminated would be offered generous severance or retirement packages; those who chose to stay on would be guaranteed new jobs, preferably in their old agencies.

A Sunset Law and Commission

Congress often creates new programs, commissions, and agencies, but it seldom eliminates them when they become obsolete. Consider the Commission on the Bicentennial of the U.S. Constitution and the National Board for the Promotion of Rifle Practice—both of which still exist.[14]

Or consider the Rural Electrification Administration (REA). Set up during the depression to give low-interest loans to rural cooperatives so they could bring electricity to rural areas, the REA was a tremendous success story. By 1953, 90.8 percent of farms had electricity. In 1949, Congress expanded the REA's mission to rural telephone service—and by 1975, 90 percent of farms had telephones. Today, 98.8 percent of farms have electricity and 96 percent have telephones—compared to 93 percent of households overall. The REA is an agency that long ago accomplished its mission.

Yet the REA lives on. By 1990, its Rural Telephone Bank, which loans money to telecommunications firms at five percent interest rates, cost the government $1 billion a year. A quarter of these subsidized loans went to five large holding companies, one of which owned three satellites and had annual revenues of $3 billion.[15] In 1990 Congress put the REA into the broader development business, in the name of rural development. This was a classic case of finding a new job for an obsolete institution—a job that is not only performed by numerous other federal agencies, but which belongs at the state and local levels.

The same problem exists with government regulations. For the past two decades, Republican administrations and Congressional Democrats have worked, with mixed success, to deregulate American industry. In many cases this was warranted; in some it was overdone. The irony is that while deregulating industry, both Congress and the past two administrations were vastly increasing the regulatory burden on *government.* Federal agencies are smothered in rules and regulations. Our largest agencies are much like Gulliver in the land of the Lilliputians—giants tied down by miles of red tape.

The Defense Department has 2000 pages of procurement regulations, including 12 pages on how to buy cream-filled cookies, and 14 pages on how to buy fruitcakes. Deputy Assistant Secretary of Defense Bob Stone estimates that "a third of the defense budget goes into the friction of following bad regulations—doing work that doesn't have to be done.[16]

It is time to cut through this thicket of overregulation. To eliminate programs and regulations that have outlived their usefulness, the new President should call for a Sunset Law and Commission. The law would stipulate that every federal program and regulation go out of existence after seven years if not reauthorized.

The Sunset Commission would review all programs and regulations to determine whether they should be reauthorized, then make recommendations to the President and Congress. In addition, the Sunset Law should require federal agencies to eliminate two administrative regulations for every new one they adopt.

ENTERPRISING GOVERNMENT: EARNING RATHER THAN SPENDING

Reinventing Government tells a story that illustrates one reason we have a $350 billion federal deficit:

> In 1990, Ace-Federal Reporters, Inc., offered to pay the Federal Energy Regulatory Commission (FERC) for the privilege of transcribing its hearings. Ace had discovered, over the previous eight years, that it could make whopping profits by selling transcripts to the thousands of law firms that argued before FERC every year. When FERC rebid the contract in 1990, three of Ace's competitors offered to perform the service for free. But Ace went them one better: it volunteered to pay $1.25 million.
>
> FERC turned down the offer. As FERC officials explained, they couldn't keep the money. They would have to turn it over to the U.S. Treasury, and they would have to hire a clerk to set up the account and monitor the contract. To FERC, in other words, it was an expense, not a source of revenue. Who needed it?
>
> Ace sued, of course. "I never thought I'd see the day that I'd have to sue the government to force them to take money," its lawyer mused.[17]

This story is repeated somewhere in the federal bureaucracy every day. The Customs Service lost $204 on every vehicle it seized from drug dealers, according to a 1989 GAO report—principally because it paid towing and storage and then junked many cars.[18] The Interior Department sells land at absurdly low prices. National parks bumble along with outdated fee schedules and concession charges that are practically giveaways.[19]

Why? Because federal agencies have no incentive to earn money. If they do, they just have to turn it over to the Treasury. When this incentive is altered, departmental behavior changes. In 1989, for instance, the GAO discovered that the Veterans Administration (VA) had failed to recover $223 million in health payments from third parties, such as insurance companies. Congress then allowed the VA to plow a portion of the third-party payments it recovered back into staff and equipment. Since 1989, it has recovered more than $500 million.[20]

Aggressive efforts to raise revenues such as this could add up to significant money—perhaps $10–20 billion a year. The task is to create incentives that impel agencies to go after such revenue.

A Non-Tax Revenue Act

The new President should send Congress legislation creating incentives for federal agencies and employees to find new revenues by allowing them to keep a portion of all new non-tax revenues they generate. Agencies should be allowed to keep half of any new non-tax revenues they generate, including revenues from fees. While only 50 percent of these revenues would go toward deficit reduction, 50 percent of a large number is better than 100 percent of a small number.

Individual employees should be allowed to keep 10 percent of any new revenues or savings their ideas generate during the first two years of their application, up to a maximum of $50,000. To get employees thinking about new revenues and major savings, we need to give them a real incentive. Typical suggestion programs, offering rewards of $50 or $100, have little impact. An amount like $50,000, in contrast, gets everyone's attention. Phoenix, which saves $2 million a year this way, even shares the savings when an employee volunteers that his or her job is obsolete. (It also moves the person to a new city job.) The federal government should do the same.

Some public agencies already rely on their own revenues for most or all of their income. These are often called "enterprise funds." The Postal Service and Amtrak are two examples. When such agencies rely primarily on their own revenues, they naturally have an incentive to increase them. Unfortunately, Congress weakens this incentive by making up any revenue shortfall they experience. The legislation proposed here should expand the number of enterprise funds and prohibit Congress from making up their shortfalls. If an enterprise fund falls short of its expected revenue target, it should be forced to make the cuts necessary to balance its books.

An Innovation Fund

In business, corporations routinely raise new capital to pursue attractive investments they believe will generate a positive return.

Most federal managers cannot do this when they see opportunities to generate new revenues. They must go to the Congress for an appropriation—a process far more dependent on political clout than on return-on-investment projections. We all know that enterprises must spend money to make money, but government seldom acts on that premise.

A performance-based budget would encourage agencies to accumulate savings, which they could then invest in new opportunities to generate revenue. The new President also should create an Innovation Fund, from which federal agencies could borrow to make investments that would increase their revenues or cut their costs. Such a fund would give officials yet another means of making investments to help their agencies earn money rather than spend it. Agencies might be allowed to borrow automatically up to a certain dollar limit; with the approval of the Office of Management and Budget up to a second limit; and with congressional approval beyond that.

Such a fund would not only encourage enterprising behavior, but would create the market discipline of required repayment. Because such loans would have clear, enforceable repayment schedules, managers would tend to borrow only if they had genuine prospects of generating a positive return. If the return failed to materialize, they would have to dip into their own budgets to repay the loan.

CATALYTIC GOVERNMENT: STEERING RATHER THAN ROWING

Traditional governments provide services, using administrative bureaucracies. Entrepreneurial governments provide *governance*, using dozens of different tools. Entrepreneurial leaders know that nations are healthy when their families, neighborhoods, businesses, schools, and voluntary organizations are healthy—and that government's most profound role is to steer these institutions to health. Hence, entrepreneurial governments act more as catalysts, brokers, and facilitators than do traditional governments, and less as service providers.

One of the principal methods entrepreneurial governments use to steer is the reshaping of private markets. They discourage pollution by raising its price, through effluent fees or green taxes. They catalyze the formation of new financial institutions. They induce companies to hire poor people by offering them tax credits. They change regulations. They jawbone the private sector. By changing what happens in the marketplace, a government can have 100 times the impact of the typical administrative program.

The federal government is primarily a steering organization. It is somewhat akin to an enormous holding company, which owns dozens of different businesses and operates around the globe. No private corporation of this kind would operate individual businesses out of headquarters. Top management would concentrate on steering the corporation, setting policy, and ensuring that individual businesses had the tools and incentives they needed to get their work done. In other words, top management would steer, but not row. This should be the primary role of the federal government: to steer American society to health, not to provide direct services.

Lester Salamon of Johns Hopkins University, who calls this approach "third party government," points out that it is already common in Washington. "This heavy reliance on third parties to carry out public objectives has, in fact, become virtually the standard pattern of federal operation in the domestic sphere," he says. This approach uses "government for what it does best—raising resources and setting societal priorities through a democratic political process—while utilizing the private sector for what it does best—organizing the production of goods and services. In the process it reconciles the traditional American hostility to government with recent American fondness for the services that modern society has increasingly required government to provide."[21]

Unfortunately, there remain too many exceptions to this norm. The Commerce Department promotes travel and tourism and prepares trade leads for businesses. The Department of Housing and Urban Development (HUD) operates public housing and gives direct loans to developers. The Department of Agriculture operates field offices in virtually every county in America.

Indeed, Agriculture is a good example of a federal department that does far too much rowing. It has five field services, most of which have changed little since the 1930s: the Agricultural Stabilization and Conservation Service, the Soil Conservation Service, the Farmers Home Administration, the Extension Service, and the Federal Crop Insurance Corporation (FCIC). Only one of these, the FCIC, is primarily a steering organization: It uses both public and private insurance agents to provide crop insurance to farmers. The other four operate elaborate field organizations.

The Agricultural Stabilization and Conservation Service and the Soil Conservation Service have offices in more than 85 percent of

America's 3,150 counties, the Farmers Home Administration in more than 60 percent.[22] Yet only 16 percent of all counties are still considered "farm counties." The Extension Service, which was designed in the 1930s to educate millions of small farmers about new developments in agricultural production, still has an agent in virtually *every* county in America.[23] It now sponsors initiatives as far afield from agricultural production as "urban gardening," "the plight of young children," and "youth at risk." In urban counties, extension agents work with community gardens, answer suburban gardener's questions, and sponsor 4-H clubs.

Even in rural counties, the old roles are largely obsolete. Most farming is now more accurately described as agribusiness. Many farms have computers, modems, and access to the latest weather and crop information from satellites. The notion that one extension agent can know enough to educate all the farmers in his county about all the things they need to know—or that such a method is the right one in a world of computers and databases—is quaint, to say the least.

In 1989, the five field services had 11,000 offices and more than 63,000 staff members, at an annual cost of $2.4 billion. If we use the USDA's definition of a farm as a place that sells $1,000 or more of agriculture products a year, this amounts to $1,100 in federal administrative costs per farm![24]

It is hard to believe that this is the most effective way to boost agricultural productivity. Surely the Extension Service could accomplish its core mission better with computers, modems, databases, and educational television. Surely the Farmers Home Administration could use market mechanisms, such as loan insurance or loan guarantees, to entice banks to handle its loans. Surely the Department of Agriculture should be focused on the broad policy issues of concern to American farmers, not on providing direct services to individual farmers.

Of course, some departments—Defense, Justice, the Census Bureau, the Coast Guard, and others—must do a lot of rowing. But if the new President is serious about reinventing government, he must move departments such as Agriculture, Commerce, and Housing and Urban Development from service delivery to policy setting—from rowing to steering.

This will not be easy. It cannot be done program by program, bill by bill, because every program has a constituency well organized to protect it in Congress. To overcome the interest groups that want to defend the status quo, the President will need one simple proposal that Congress can vote up or down. That proposal must give the agencies in question no *choice* but to embrace fundamental change. At the same time, it must give them the freedom to eliminate obsolete programs without a vote of Congress.

The new President should introduce a bill that would cut spending for designated agencies, such as Agriculture, HUD, and Commerce, by 6 percent a year (after inflation) for four years. In return, it would give these agencies the flexibility to transfer funds between programs, to shift personnel, and to eliminate obsolete programs.

No one in Washington is responsible for examining the design of federal programs. To help agencies and their congressional appropriating committees think through different redesign options, the President should create a new Program Design Office within OMB. It would hire experts, gather and sift the relevant literature, and begin to articulate design principles that underlie success. The President could require agencies facing the 6 percent cut to win the Office's approval for money-saving proposals. (The design office would work with all relevant departments and congressional committees to redesign programs as they come up for reauthorization.)

A National Information Agency

In addition to minimizing the amount of rowing done by the federal government, the new administration needs to maximize its capacity to steer—that is, to make informed policy decisions. One important step is to improve the federal government's capacity to collect, analyze, and disseminate data. We often operate today without reliable, accurate information. Indeed, the Federal Reserve Board misread the severity of the current recession in its early months because of faulty unemployment data.

Part of the problem stems from budget cuts imposed on our statistics agencies by the Reagan administration. But a more fundamental problem is simply the passage of time. As we move into a post-industrial, knowledge-based economy, we often collect the same data, organized in the same way, that we collected 40 years ago. This is true in part because no one is in charge of the federal information apparatus. It is spread between numerous organizations: the Census Bureau and the Bureau of Economic Statistics (in Commerce), the Bureau of Labor Statistics (at Labor), the National Agricultural Statistics Service and the Economic Research Service (in Agriculture), and perhaps a dozen other agencies.[25]

Overall, the federal government spends $2 billion a year on statistical programs.[26] But as the Congressional Office of Technology Assessment reported in 1989:

> The system suffers from the absence of any central organization able to develop a coherent strategy for adjusting to the challenges presented by today's economy. There is no national, systematic effort to articulate priorities in statistics and match budgets to these priorities, to anticipate future needs, to translate the complex and often conflicting objectives of data consumers into a practical set of tasks, or to ensure that the work of individual statistical agencies is adequately coordinated. . . . There is a pressing need for an organization where fundamental statistical priorities are periodically reexamined in light of the new needs of public and business analysts. . . . The computational systems available to BEA, BLS, and other major statistical services appear to lag far behind the systems available to many of the business service industries that rely heavily on government data.[27]

The new President should merge the Census Bureau and other appropriate statistical agencies into a new national information agency and charge this agency with upgrading statistical capacity throughout the federal government.

ANTICIPATORY GOVERNMENT: PREVENTION RATHER THAN CURE

The federal government spends little time or money on prevention. Typically, Washington waits until a problem becomes a crisis, then offers new services to those affected—the homeless on the street, communities victimized by violence, school dropouts, drug users. As a result, we spend enormous amounts of time and money treating symptoms—with more police, more jails, more welfare payments, and higher Medicaid outlays—while prevention strategies go begging. "Instead of anticipating the problems and opportunities of the future, we lurch from crisis to crisis," Alvin Toffler said 20 years ago, in *Future Shock*. "Our political system is 'Future-blind.' "[28]

As the pace of change accelerates, this lack of foresight becomes more and more dangerous. Hence, entrepreneurial organizations do everything they can to *anticipate* the future.

A Truth-in-Spending Bill

The new President should propose a "Truth-in-Spending" bill to force elected and appointed leaders to confront the long-term implications of all federal spending decisions. Such an act would mandate new accounting standards for all federal agencies, a capital budget, and ten-year spending projections for all budget items.

In any institution, people pay attention to what is counted. The budget is one method of counting; the accounting system is another. Unfortunately, the federal accounting system has serious problems. Different agencies use different methods of counting. Few officials have the capacity to track what an agency has spent in the current fiscal year. As many agencies prepared their fiscal year 1994 budget requests last summer, for example, their most recent information about actual spending came from fiscal year 1990. Consequently, feedback about spending patterns is so delayed that it has little impact on future budget decisions.

In addition, federal accounting systems fail to reflect future obligations. Businesses use "accrual accounting," in which any future obligation incurred, such as a commitment to pay a pension, is counted as an expense. The federal government uses "cash accounting," in which expenses are not counted until money is actually spent. When the federal government racks up enormous future obligations—far beyond its capacity to pay—no one is the wiser, because federal accounting is future blind.

Cash accounting also ignores the physical depreciation of assets, like highways, buildings, and weapons systems. These physical assets are investments: When a government builds a highway or dam, it is creating something of value, almost like a savings account. As that asset wears out, its value declines—because without expensive repair, it will ultimately be worthless. Consuming an asset is a form of spending; in business it is called depreciation. In government it is ignored. Most public accounting systems make it look cheaper to wear out assets than to keep them in good repair.

Our accounting systems reinforce politicians' natural preference for building large new structures that will impress the electorate rather than for spending money to maintain existing assets. They also allow politicians to cut maintenance budgets without appearing to incur any expense. In reality, such decisions create significant future expenses. Under accrual accounting, these would show up as current expenditures, in the form of depreciation. The new President should ask the Federal Accounting Standards Advisory Board to develop new accrual accounting standards.

State and local governments finance their long-term assets with capital budgets. They require balanced operating budgets, but they allow borrowing under their capital budgets to finance expenditures whose benefits will be long-term—just as families do when they buy houses and cars. Yet the federal government has no capital budget. It makes absolutely no distinction between spending on Social Security or Medicaid and investment in something that has continuing value, like a highway. Hence, the American people have no way of limiting their federal borrowing to genuine investments in their future. (See chapter 2 for a thorough discussion of this issue.)

Once accrual accounting systems and a capital budget are in place, the federal budget should project the cost of every spending item over ten years—within the appropriate department and across departmental lines. When Congress appropriates funds, its members rarely do so with information about the long-term impact of their decisions. OMB and the Congressional Budget Office publish five-year projections of spending and revenues, but only by major category. This information is not very useful when appropriations committees are debating specific spending measures. The President and Congress need projections every time they consider a specific appropriation.

The fiscal implications of simple decisions can be vast. Does anyone know, for instance, how much the decision to pour $480 million into the reconstruction of Homestead Air Force Base will cost over ten years? The initial $480 million may lead to billions of dollars in other commitments—to military equipment and personnel, to local taxing districts, to military pensions, and so on.

Local governments such as Sunnyvale, California, and state governments such as Minnesota have demonstrated that spending behavior changes when legislators are confronted with the long-term implications of their decisions. While future projections can never be made with scientific accuracy, they do give a rough estimate of the long-term implications of today's actions.

COMPETITIVE GOVERNMENT: INJECTING COMPETITION INTO SERVICE DELIVERY

Most Americans understand that monopoly in the private sector protects inefficiency and inhibits change. Yet we rarely apply this insight to government. It is one of the enduring paradoxes of

American government that we attack private monopolies fervently but embrace public monopolies warmly.

Entrepreneurial governments have learned to inject competition into service delivery, in order to foster innovation and excellence. They have discovered that when service providers are forced to compete, they keep their costs down, respond quickly to changing demands, and strive mightily to satisfy their customers.

The new administration should seek to inject further competition into the delivery of federal services, such as those provided by the General Services Administration, the Postal Service, Amtrak, the military, and the Coast Guard. Many of these organizations already use competition to one degree or another. The General Services Administration has dramatically expanded competition over the past four years by allowing federal departments to purchase many services from private vendors—with impressive results. Military organizations such as the Tactical Air Command have used competition between squadrons to drive their members toward greater performance.[29] Even the Postal Service regularly contracts out some functions, such as rural delivery and air transportation of mail, on a competitive basis.

The Postal Service provides a good example of how increased competition could improve delivery while avoiding the pitfalls of privatization. The traditional view holds that we have two alternatives: a continued public monopoly on first-and-third class mail or the privatization of mail delivery, by allowing private firms to compete for all classes of mail. If we do the latter, we will gradually destroy the Postal Service, and a market for mail delivery will emerge in which prices charged reflect the actual costs of delivery. Letters from New York to rural Montana will cost far more than letters from New York to Washington, and access to postal service will become unequal, just like access to any other service in the marketplace. This is not something the American people want.

There is a third way, however—an alternative that would preserve the Postal Service and its policy of equal access, but use competition to improve it. Some postal functions—management of post offices, sorting facilities, even local mail delivery—could be contracted out on a competitive basis. However, the Postal Service should be allowed to compete for contracts against any private organizations that choose to bid.

To protect postal employees, winning contractors could be required to hire those who lost their jobs at comparable wage and benefit levels. Those who preferred to stay with the Postal Service could be moved elsewhere, as spots opened up through attrition. This approach would spur major improvement in postal operations because current postal organizations would either improve or die.

OTHER PRINCIPLES

Like the principles of competition, several other principles of reinventing government apply primarily to service delivery. As we have stressed before, the federal government should not be heavily involved in service delivery. Hence, these principles would apply most directly to federal Challenge Grants.

One such principle is the notion of "community-owned government"—the idea of empowering rather than serving. In traditional public-service organizations, control is concentrated in the hands of professionals and bureaucrats. The people they serve—their "clients"—have little control; they are dependent upon the bureaucrats and professionals. This is true in most of our older public institutions: our schools, our social welfare agencies, our public housing authorities. It should come as no surprise when many of these clients learn dependent behavior—so many that welfare dependency, alcohol dependency, and drug dependency are among our most severe problems. Treat people as dependents, and they will eventually become dependent.

Entrepreneurial governments have begun to push ownership and control of public services out of the hands of bureaucrats and professionals and into the community. Consequently, the principle of community-owned government should be applied as a criteria in all Challenge Grant programs.

Another principle is that of "customer-driven government"— the idea of organizing public services to meet the needs of the customer, rather than the bureaucracy. The best way to do this is often to give resources directly to the customers and let them choose their own service providers. We use this approach with aid to students in higher education, through Pell Grants. We use it with low-income housing vouchers and food stamps. We even used it with the GI Bill, perhaps the most successful social program in the nation's history. But in most cases, we give money to programs, which assign recipients to service providers. Veterans are assigned to veterans' hospitals. Welfare recipients are assigned to job training and placement providers. Public housing applicants are assigned to apartments.

When we give customers a choice of service providers—and those customers have reliable information about the quality and cost of each provider—we accomplish three goals. We force service providers to meet the needs of their customers, to attract their business. We force service providers to compete, which encourages them to bring their quality up and their costs down. And we give customers a choice of services, rather than the traditional one-size-fits-all approach.

The final principle—which underpins many of the key recommendations in this and the previous chapter—is decentralized government. It recognizes that centralized, top-down institutions are not flexible enough to respond quickly to changing circumstances and customers' needs. Entrepreneurial governments empower their employees by flattening hierarchies, embracing participatory decision making, and pushing authority down through their organizations. The new administration should strengthen the federal commitment to employee empowerment, in part through a renewed emphasis on Total Quality Management.

IMPLEMENTATION STRATEGY

A president has three primary levers he can use to accomplish his goals. The first, and most important, is the bully pulpit—the ability to articulate a vision of where he wants the nation to go and an agenda that will get us there. The second is the personnel system, through which the President can, if he has enough leverage, swing three million federal employees behind his vision. The third is the budget, through which he can put some portion of the $1.5 trillion the federal government spends each year to work fulfilling his goals.

If a revolution in federal governance is to be one of the President's priorities, his first task is to communicate that vision to the American people. His second is to communicate it to federal employees, while creating the kind of personnel system that enables them to put that vision into action. His third task is to communicate his vision to Congress, while convincing its members to create the kind of budget system that will help bring it to life. Unless the President devotes some portion of his personal time and energy to these three tasks, his efforts to reinvent the federal government will fail.

As a first step, the President should create a high-level reinventing-government group within the White House Office. Its job would be to think through his strategy and begin to carry it out.

Second, on January 20, 1993, the President should issue Executive Order Number One, articulating in one page his vision of a reinvented government. As he swears in his cabinet members and agency heads, he should give them framed copies to hang above their desks and ask them to report monthly on their efforts to implement the order. He should also promise regular White House ceremonies to celebrate the success of their efforts and the achievements of their employees. By making this the subject of his first executive order, issued on inauguration day, the President can send a signal to the world: This administration intends to revolutionize the way business is done in Washington.

MANDATE FOR ACTION

1. **Create a performance-based federal budget.** Such a budget would minimize line items, encourage agencies to save money by allowing them to roll over 50 percent of any appropriated funds they do not spend in a budget cycle, and build performance measurement and accountability into the budget.

2. **Overhaul the Civil Service system.** The President must create a mission-driven, results-oriented personnel system. The new rules would create more managerial flexibility, encourage rewards for excellent performance, and convert from the overly cumbersome General Schedule classification system to a broad-band approach.

3. **Create a Labor-Management Council, negotiate a "Grand Bargain" with federal employee unions, and cut the federal bureaucracy through attrition by 200,000 jobs.** The President should offer a no-layoff guarantee and union representation in decision-making about structural reforms, in return for union support for reforming civil service and the budget and downsizing the work force.

4. **Enact a Sunset Law and Commission to eliminate federal programs and regulations.** A Sunset Law would require reapproval of all government regulations and reauthorization of all federal programs at least once every seven years. It would also require that agencies eliminate

two administrative regulations for every new one they put on the books.

5. **Pass a Non-Tax Revenue Act creating incentives for federal agencies and employees to raise new revenues.** This could raise $10–20 billion a year by allowing agencies and employees to keep some portion of all new non-tax revenues they generated.

6. **Create an Innovation Fund.** Federal agencies could borrow from the fund for investments that would increase their revenues or cut their costs.

7. **Cut spending for designated agencies such as Agriculture, HUD, and Commerce by 6 percent annually for four years to force their transformation from "rowing" to "steering" organizations.** In exchange for smaller budgets, these agencies would be granted greater flexibility to shift funds between programs, shift personnel, and eliminate obsolete programs. The new President would create a Program Design Office in OMB to help agencies redesign programs.

8. **Merge the Census Bureau and other appropriate statistical agencies into a new National Information Agency.** Charge this agency with upgrading statistical capacity throughout the federal government.

9. **Enact a Truth-in-Spending bill.** This would force elected and appointed leaders to confront the long-term implications of all federal spending decisions. The act would mandate new accounting standards for agencies, including a capital budget, and ten-year spending projections for all budget items.

10. **Inject further competition into the delivery of federal services.** Target services should include those provided by the General Services Administration, the Postal Service, Amtrak, the four military branches, and the Coast Guard.

13

U.S. Global Leadership for Democracy

WILL MARSHALL

THE DEMOCRATIC MOMENT

Americans in 1992 look out on a world moving in our direction. From a security standpoint, the U.S. faces more benign prospects abroad than at any time since 1918. No hostile power poses an immediate threat to us or our key allies; the terrifying specter of nuclear annihilation is mercifully receding; and no rival ideology is arising to challenge liberal democracy as the political and moral framework most conducive to human dignity, freedom, and prosperity.

For Americans, the sudden death of Soviet communism is a security windfall. But the Soviet Union's startling collapse also brings to full tide what Samuel Huntington has called the "third wave" of democracy to sweep the world since the American Revolution. Since 1974, more than 40 countries have moved from authoritarian to democratic political systems.[1]

Underlying this phenomenon are two related trends: the inability of centrally planned economies to succeed in the new global economy, and a communications revolution that undermines the state's power to monopolize ideas and information. People living under dictatorships in the satellite age increasingly are able to see through the delusional world created by official propaganda. They can compare their living standards and political conditions with those enjoyed by others. The inevitable result, from Latin America to Eastern Europe, and from China to South Africa, has been a phenomenal worldwide surge in popular demands for human rights, political pluralism, and free markets.

Yet, if this pivotal moment holds out the promise of a more civil world order, a *pax democratica*, it is also fraught with new dangers. Today's clamor for self-determination is bringing long-simmering ethnic, national, and religious conflicts to a boil. The rapid diffusion of technology throughout the world threatens to put nuclear arms and missiles in the hands of third-world tyrants— and perhaps terrorists as well. Stark disparities in wealth between North and South breed instability and new frictions over the exploitation of natural resources. And, should fledgling democracies on Europe's eastern flank, or in the developing South, fail to deliver economic growth, political stability and a perceptible degree of social progress, the idea of democracy could quickly lose its luster.

No nation has a greater stake than the U.S. in the outcome of today's democratic upheavals. Our hopes for abolishing nuclear weapons aimed at U.S. cities ride on the success of democracy in Russia and neighboring republics. Likewise, China's peaceable transition over time toward a democratic, market-oriented society would dramatically improve prospects for stability and expanded trade in the Pacific Basin. Closer to home, Mexico's determination to open its markets and political system to competition can yield big dividends for the U.S.: more exports, less illegal immigration, and better hemispheric relations.

But even where our security or economic interests are not directly affected, Americans still have more than a passing interest in the fate of other people's struggles for individual liberty, free enterprise, and democratic self-rule. Their cause, after all, is our cause. And if earlier generations of Americans were willing to fight and die to make the world "safe for democracy," surely ours can wield America's enormous power and influence in peacetime to build a new foundation for a more prosperous and democratic world.

America cannot lead if our own leaders lack clear vision and direction. It falls to President Clinton to complete the vital task his predecessor never really began: to articulate new organizing principles for U.S. global leadership after the Cold War. In the absence of an overriding external threat such as we faced from the Soviet Union, the American people need compelling reasons for supporting an active U.S. role in the world. Only a strategy that unites American interests and ideals is likely to meet that test.

This chapter proposes that support for democracy and free markets replace anti-communism as the conceptual basis for U.S. security policy in the 1990s and beyond. The pro-democracy doctrine has two corollaries: First, that America must reinvigorate its economy, not only to generate the resources we need to sustain our global leadership, but also to stimulate global growth, without which democracy will founder. Second, the U.S. must preserve strong, qualitatively superior military forces, even as we reduce our Cold War defense structures, in order to defend our interests and values.

To make support for democracy and free markets the animating principle of U.S. international policy as we approach the twenty-first century, this chapter recommends that President Clinton take the following steps:

- Put commercial diplomacy at the center of a new U.S. security strategy for the post–Cold War era.
- Lead a long-term, international campaign of economic, technical, and political aid intended to anchor Russia firmly in the democratic camp.
- Use U.S. trade policies and other leverage to encourage economic and political reform in China.
- Revamp U.S. foreign aid and end assistance to dictators and corrupt regimes.
- Expand U.S. support for building democratic institutions abroad.
- Replace America's Cold War military with a strong force that is more mobile, more flexible, and tailored to meet regional threats.
- Instruct the new secretary of defense to undertake a fundamental reassessment of military roles and missions.
- Reorganize U.S. intelligence agencies to eliminate redundancy and focus on new missions.
- Reform the War Powers Resolution to restore the balance of war-making power between the executive and legislative branches.
- Reinvigorate the United Nations and other institutions of collective security.

THE POST-COLD WAR WORLD

America's new security strategy must accommodate four key realities of the post–Cold War era:

1. The ascendancy of economics in international affairs. As old ideological and military rivalries wane, the competition for markets and technological supremacy is moving to the center of world politics. Nations that channel their most productive people and capital into an obsessive quest for armed power only disarm themselves in this commercial contest. As the currency of military power lately has been devalued, the new centers of influence are not East and West but the three most economically dynamic regions of the world: North America, Europe, and the booming Pacific Rim economy dominated by Japan.

Americans understand that the economic foundations of our strength need repair; indeed, polls show they believe that the most urgent threat to U.S. security today is economic weakness.[2] Restoring America's economic vitality is thus our top foreign and domestic priority. As our firms and workers compete increasingly on a global scale, U.S. diplomacy must be enlisted in a comprehensive national strategy for economic security. Just as we formerly aimed at military parity with the Soviet Union, our goal now must be to maintain living standards as high as those of our chief competitors.

As Bill Clinton said during the campaign, the traditional distinction between foreign and domestic policy is vanishing. In the global economy, U.S. fiscal policies influence interest rates in Germany and are influenced in turn by the propensity of the Japanese to save more than they consume. The crack epidemic in America's inner cities ripples outward, fueling corruption and narco-terrorism in the Caribbean and Latin America. Moreover, this interdependence is inescapable: Whatever temporary relief the U.S. might get by laying down the burdens of world leadership would surely be offset by the new problems this would create for our people. For example, by declining to defend open world trading, or to stem the spread of military technology, or to mobilize the world community to protect the earth's ecology, we could invite devastating job losses in our most competitive industries, a reversal in the downward trend of military spending, and new threats to public health.

America cannot play a commanding role on the world stage if we are weak at home; likewise, we cannot renew our domestic strength if we fail to exercise prudent leadership abroad. During the Cold War, economic and other concerns were often eclipsed by the exigencies of countering the Soviet threat. The absence of such a grand strategic imperative, coupled with our ailing economy and worsening social dilemmas, suggests a new and more prosaic test for America's international policy: Does it improve the daily lives of ordinary Americans? In addition to providing security against military threats, does it promote our competitive capacities and our quality of life? If no link can be shown between our actions abroad and economic and social progress at home, it's unlikely that those actions can win sustained public support.

2. The post–Cold War world remains a dangerous place. Anyone watching the tragedy of "ethnic cleansing" unfolding in the Balkans, the vicious endgame by rival rebel factions in Afghanistan, the agony of Somalia, the massacres in South Africa's townships, or Saddam Hussein's savage suppression of Kurds and Shiites will need little convincing on this score. While not directly threatened today, America needs to maintain a strong military as an insurance policy against local disorders that could spread and pose problems for us. And we must be especially vigilant toward the spread of nuclear, biological, and chemical weapons as well as toward the spread of advanced conventional arms.

To defend our far-flung national interests and reassure our democratic allies, the U.S. must maintain qualitatively superior military forces. To meet new kinds of threats and to free resources for economic reconstruction, we need to replace our costly and anachronistic Cold War structure with a smaller but more versatile and mobile force.

3. Ideas are a revolutionary source of power in the information age. The dramatic diffusion of information made possible by computers and other information technologies is transforming world politics as well as the nature of production and global economic competition. As former Czech president (and political dissident) Vaclav Havel has said, the human rights movement in Eastern Europe—midwifed by the Helsinki Final Act of 1975 and nourished by radio, television, cassettes, and the fax—led directly to the revolutions of 1989.

The information revolution confronts despotic regimes with a Hobson's choice between liberalization and decline: They must either dismantle the machinery of political repression and central planning or pay the price of economic isolation and technological backwardness. The totalitarian system built by Stalin rotted from within as its bureaucratic rigidities prevented the Soviet Union from embracing new ideas and technologies. In the end, the fatal gap facing the Soviets was not in missiles or tanks, but in microchips: When Gorbachev took power in 1985, there were only 50,000 personal computers in the Soviet Union, compared to 30 million in the U.S.[3]

Conversely, the new information technologies put a premium on economic and political freedom. Not only can open societies more readily absorb and use these technologies, but such societies are themselves an important source of ideas that influence and inspire people in other countries. The U.S. is particularly well-endowed with such "soft power,"[4] including the broad appeal of American ideas about individual liberty, democratic capitalism, and equal justice under a common law, as well as global demand for music, television, movies, and other products of America's media culture. An especially dramatic affirmation of the universal appeal of ideas came in December, 1989, when Chinese pro-democracy demonstrators erected a crude, papier-mâché Statue of Liberty in Beijing's Tiananmen Square.

4. Global problems are increasingly likely to threaten Americans' security and well-being. Such problems include damage to the earth's environment, with the attendant risks of skin cancer, respiratory diseases, and other health hazards; overcrowding and famine in developing nations; transnational disputes over oil or water or other natural resources; illegal immigration; and the flow of illicit drugs across national borders. Americans can neither solve these problems alone nor escape the consequences should the international community fail to fashion effective responses to them. Because of its enormous weight in world affairs, and because our own citizens' health and safety is at stake, the U.S. must take the lead in orchestrating global responses to global problems.

CHOICES FOR U.S. DIPLOMACY

The anti-communist consensus that sustained America's Cold War policy was unusually broad and deep. It united Republicans and Democrats, business and labor, conservative nationalists and liberal internationalists. In the absence of a unifying threat, however, that atypical consensus is breaking up. As Americans return to a more normal diversity of opinion about our country's role in the world, some traditional lines of cleavage are reemerging and new ones are appearing.

Inevitably, the Cold War's end has reawakened the recurring debate between isolationism and internationalism. Thus far, however, enthusiasm for neo-isolationism seems to be confined to the political fringes: Candidates who raised the banner of "America First" and sounded protectionist themes—such as Pat Buchanan and Jerry Brown—were soundly defeated in the 1992 presidential primaries.[5] In the first presidential election of the post–Cold War era, both major parties nominated staunch internationalists.

The real question facing Americans in the 1990s is not whether or not our country should remain engaged in the world, but on what terms and for what purposes? Although that debate is just beginning, it is possible to discern three main tendencies, or schools of thought, that are candidates for replacing containment as the central goal of U.S. international policy.

The first and most familiar is traditional balance of power diplomacy. As practiced by President Bush, but hard-boiled to perfection by his mentors, Richard Nixon and Henry Kissinger, this approach reflects the "realist" view that it is the relentless pursuit of power—not abstract and ephemeral notions like democracy or human rights or international law—that motivates leaders and determines the real character of relations among nations. It sees the distribution and balance of power as the preeminent concern of U.S. security policy.

The second option—economic nationalism—is just now coalescing. In this view, the victors of the Cold War are now pitted against each other in a fierce struggle to dominate world markets. It sees the old geopolitics as giving way to what Edward Luttwak has called "geo-economics": "Gorbachev's redirection of Soviet foreign policy had barely started when Japan began to be promoted to the role of the internally unifying Chief Enemy, judging by the evidence of opinion polls, media treatments, advertisements, and congressional pronouncements."[6]

Economic nationalists, who run the gamut from Ross Perot to many labor leaders and their Democratic allies, envision a stronger government role in protecting and promoting "strategic" U.S. industries through public subsidies, managed trade, and outright protectionism. They tend to oppose the North American Free Trade Agreement (NAFTA) and to favor a more confrontational approach on trade issues toward Japan and Europe.

The third choice—espoused during the presidential election by Bill Clinton and endorsed here—is U.S. global leadership for democracy. It stresses the connection between the internal character of regimes and their conduct in the world: Leaders constrained by popular institutions at home are less likely to be aggressive abroad. Its advocates believe that, in the coming era of world politics, the best way to ward off new threats to America's security and to international stability is to support the spread of free markets and democratic politics. This does not mean imposing American values or institutions on others; rather, it entails collective efforts by the world's leading democracies, led by the U.S., to encourage indigenous democratic forces that are struggling to establish individual rights, market economies, the rule of law, and popular sovereignty where they do not exist.

Unlike balance-of-power "realism," a pro-democracy doctrine would pursue America's interests without repeatedly compromising American values. During the Cold War, U.S. leaders often subordinated concerns about democracy and human rights to the larger geopolitical imperatives of the East–West struggle. We played the "China card" and forged strategic relationships with such "friendly despots" as the Shah of Iran and Philippine dictator Ferdinand Marcos. Yet such realpolitik too often aligned America with oppressive rulers rather than with their hapless subjects, to whom our rhetoric of freedom seemed merely to mask superpower arrogance.

The fall of the Soviet empire removes the strategic rationale for U.S. alliances with regional tyrants. In the new era, the demands of national security and support for democracy and human rights are far less likely to come into conflict.

To be sure, a pro-democracy stance is easily reconciled with concern for regional balances of power. The U.S. military presence in Europe and the Far East remains a vital linchpin of regional stability. But a purely realist view is the wrong guide to the U.S. today because it ignores the link between democracy and peace. Twentieth-century experience shows time and again that democracies generally don't attack each other and that nations that respect their citizens' rights are more likely to respect their neighbors' rights.[7]

Economic nationalism, a commercial version of realpolitik, plays to Americans' deep anxieties about our relative economic decline over the last generation. Its appeal, however, has been limited thus far by a sturdy public consensus that our economic problems are largely home-grown.[8] Eschewing protectionism, most Americans continue to see trade as mutually beneficial rather than as a zero-sum game between nations. They also hold fast to the internationalist tenet that the U.S. cannot go it alone in the world, economically or militarily. The public, therefore, is wary of policies that would embroil the nation in constant trade wars or otherwise put us at loggerheads with our democratic allies.

A pro-democracy strategy would acknowledge the need to revive America's competitive prowess through domestic economic reforms and, where necessary, through tougher trade policies. It would not, however, ignore the larger community of interests we share with democratic nations on security, trade, and other issues of common concern, such as environmental protection. Our security and commercial interests alike require us to work in partnership with Japan and Europe to open world markets and expand trade, as well as to support the cause of freedom and deter threats to peace.

THE DEMOCRACY DOCTRINE

With the Cold War over, the conceptual basis of U.S. international policy must shift from containment to support for democracy. Only by uniting our national interests with Americans' basic values can we mobilize and sustain solid, bipartisan support for U.S. global leadership in the new era. The pro-democracy doctrine aims at building a new concert of free nations in which America would be first among equals.

The new emphasis on promoting democracy explicitly rejects the realist premise that international peace is exclusively a product of the balance of power. Certainly, when faced with threats to our security, America must not only balance but exceed the power of potential adversaries. However, we recognize that, in the end, the spread of freedom rather than equilibrium or stability for its own sake is the best guarantee of peace.

The pro-democracy doctrine rests on a core premise: that nations with democratic institutions are less likely to menace their neighbors and more likely to meet the moral and material aspirations of their own people. However, it shuns the moralism that could lead either to U.S. withdrawal from a corrupt world or to indulgence in a messianic campaign to right all the world's wrongs. A democracy-centered security strategy should offer U.S. moral and diplomatic support to genuine democratic movements, while extending economic support and military aid in a more discriminate way, as prudence and the circumstances of each case warrant.

The financial costs of promoting democracy are dwarfed by the stupendous sums we have spent to contain communism over the last four decades. We can pay for promoting democracy by shifting a small fraction from defense spending without sacrificing our military strength and readiness.

The new President must do a better job than his predecessor of capitalizing on today's historic opportunity to reinforce and consolidate the spread of democracy. There are compelling security reasons to do so: The emergence of a democratic Russia—and eventually a democratic China—would radically diminish serious nuclear and conventional threats and would decisively tip the balance of world power in favor of freedom.

Moreover, democracies are less likely than dictatorships to pursue nuclear weapons. Germany and Japan obviously have the technical capacity to make such weapons, yet public opinion in both countries is overwhelmingly opposed to such a course. When they were governed by military dictators, Argentina and Brazil vigorously pursued nuclear technologies; under elected leaders, both countries have abandoned their nuclear ambitions. By contrast, the dictatorships in North Korea, Iran, Iraq, Libya, and Algeria continued to seek entry into the nuclear club.

Larry Diamond, coeditor of the *Journal for Democracy,* notes the practical advantages of a democracy-centered U.S. foreign policy:

> Democratic countries do not go to war with one another or sponsor terrorism against other democracies. They do not build weapons of mass destruction to threaten one another. Democratic countries are more reliable, open, and enduring trading partners, and offer more stable climates for investment. Because they must answer to their own citizens, democracies are more environmentally responsible. They are more likely to honor international treaties and value legal obligations since their openness makes it much more difficult to breach them in secret. Precisely because they respect civil liberties, rights of property, and the rule of law within their own borders, democracies are the only reliable foundation on which to build a new world order of security and prosperity.[9]

SOME CAVEATS

While promoting democracy should be the main theme of U.S. security policy in the 1990s, it cannot be the *sole* guide or rationale for our actions abroad. For instance, it offers few guidelines for resolving the trade and economic policy disputes that are moving to the fore of our relationships with fellow democracies. A pro-democracy strategy also must be tempered by prudence and patience. It must take into account real economic constraints on our ability to aid democratic movements abroad and not overreach. It must recognize the fragility of democratic gains in many countries and be prepared for the inevitable setbacks. It must be supple enough to craft different policies for countries in various stages of economic and political development. And, it must not preclude us from engaging in constructive diplomacy with nondemocratic countries. Between the extremes of moralizing and cynically ignoring concerns about democracy and human rights, we must strike pragmatic balances and push for steady, gradual progress rather than dramatic breakthroughs.

Moreover, the global clamor for democracy presents dangers as well as opportunities. Following the Yugoslav pattern, demands for ethnic self-determination could engulf other multiethnic nations in civil strife. Reconciling such demands with the need for stable borders and multicultural harmony will be one of the most difficult tasks of the new era. Democratic elections will not necessarily yield benign results: Gains by Islamic fundamentalists in Algeria, Jordan, and elsewhere raise the possibility that friendly regimes could be replaced by hostile ones.

In addition, we must bear in mind that not all countries have equal strategic weight. While the U.S. should certainly back democracy in Romania, it obviously has a far greater strategic stake in helping Russia build functioning markets and democratic institutions. A general policy of support for democracy does not rule out concentrating our efforts where the strategic rewards promise to be highest. At the same time, it may complicate U.S. relations with nondemocratic countries, especially where, as in the Persian Gulf, we have important strategic interests.

A PRO-DEMOCRACY STRATEGY

Although superior military forces will continue to be integral to U.S. security, Americans' well-being and security in the years ahead will not depend exclusively, or even primarily, on military power. They will depend on our ability to generate rising living standards at home and compete effectively with other technologically advanced countries. They will depend as well on our ability to prevent the emergence of new threats to our security by encouraging the development of democratic political systems and market economies in other countries.

These three strategic goals—growth, strength, and democracy—are closely linked. A robust economy will buttress our influence in the world and permit us to keep a strong military without sacrificing domestic goals. Success in promoting free political and economic institutions abroad will reduce security threats and obviate the need for a vast military, while creating new markets for U.S. trade and investment.

Hence, a comprehensive security policy organized around the theme of democracy rests on three main elements: restoring America's economic vitality and leadership, U.S. diplomacy for democracy, and military strength.

ECONOMIC RENEWAL

The gravest threat to U.S. security today comes not from the outside but from the chronic neglect of the economic and social foundations of American power. We cannot exercise world leadership or inspire others by our example with a weak, debt-ridden economy; an inferior school system; the highest rates of poverty and violent crime in the advanced world; decaying and dangerous cities; and a decrepit infrastructure.

Failures of leadership on the home front weaken America's hand abroad. Trying to compensate for an anemic economy with ad hoc subsidies and protections for agriculture and industry undermines our credibility in international negotiations on trade and investment. It is also difficult for the U.S. to urge other nations to change their economic policies when our own fiscal follies wreak havoc with world financial and exchange markets. The absence of a sound energy policy leaves the U.S.—the world's largest energy consumer—more vulnerable than it should be to turmoil in the Middle East. Our mounting public debts make us heavily dependent on foreign lenders and vulnerable to global financial markets that render daily judgments on the soundness of our economic policies. An enormous federal deficit constrains our ability to aid the nascent market economies of Eastern Europe and the former Soviet republics. The international drug trade spawns violence and misery here and abroad. And with poverty growing, especially among children, America continues to waste the productive potential of millions of poor citizens.

To maintain our position of global leadership, America must regain its economic vigor. The Clinton administration should adopt the strategies of Enterprise Economics: free our domestic markets and federal budget from layers of subsidies and protections that muffle market signals and constrain robust competition; shift the bias of economic policy from consumption to investments that empower our firms and workers to become more productive;

and exert continuous pressure for opening world markets to U.S. goods and services.

A growing world economy is the best answer to the zero-sum logic of protectionism, which sees one nation's gain as another nation's loss. It also offers the best hope to narrow the gap between the wealthy nations of the North and the impoverished nations of the developing South. By swiftly concluding the North America Free Trade Agreement and moving to break the impasse in the Uruguay Round of the GATT negotiations, the new President can reassert U.S. leadership for global growth.

In the new era, all American institutions must meet higher standards of performance. The measure of comparison is no longer with moribund communist countries, but with our most dynamic and successful economic competitors. The new President must lead a radical renovation of our public institutions, to lift the level of public education dramatically and expand access to job training and college; to contain runaway health costs while assuring the highest quality medical care for all citizens; to buttress American families struggling to provide for their children and give them sound values; to empower communities to defend themselves against criminals; and to transform social welfare into an opportunity-building system for poor Americans.

The new emphasis on economic security must be institutionalized in our national security apparatus. The new President should propose the creation of two deputies to the assistant to the President for national security: one for military affairs and one for economic security. The head of the new Department of Trade and Technology proposed in chapter 4 should also be made a member of the National Security Council. In addition, the State Department must upgrade pay and status for people involved in commercial diplomacy.

DIPLOMACY FOR DEMOCRACY

America cannot export democracy or remake the world in its image. But as the world's oldest and strongest democracy, we have the experience, resources, and moral authority to help others nurture seeds of economic and political freedom they have planted in their own soil. Since we cannot offer equal aid to all democratic reformers, we must focus our efforts where they will do the most good.

No challenge looms larger than aiding Russia's wrenching transition to democracy and markets. The stakes are high: an end to four decades of nuclear brinkmanship and a millennium of oppressive rule by czars and commissars. Russia's successful shift from central planning to market allocation of resources, and from a communist monopoly on power to political pluralism, also would be an enormous boost to the stability of the new democratic systems in the former Soviet republics and Eastern Europe.

Conversely, the failure of reforms in Russia could give rise to ultranationalist regimes, a resurgence of anti-Semitism and Great Russian imperialism, sharpened national and ethnic conflict, brutal oppression of minorities, renewed hostility to the West, an abrupt end to nuclear disarmament, and waves of immigrants pouring across the borders of Europe. The workings of electoral politics and open markets remain poorly understood in Russia, and there are disquieting signs that opposition to the Yeltsin reforms is by no means confined to communist apparatchiks.

Only the Russians themselves can bring about a historic transformation to democracy. But the world's democracies, led by the U.S., can help give markets and democratic politics a fighting chance in the former Soviet bloc. In addition to the loans already pledged, the new President should organize a long-term, international aid effort with our G-7 partners and such high-growth Pacific Rim nations as South Korea and Taiwan. It should rely principally upon world financial institutions: the World Bank, the International Monetary Fund, and the new European Bank for Reconstruction and Development. The Clinton administration should swiftly pay America's share of the IMF's operating costs.

Western loans can give Russia timely help in stabilizing the ruble and importing food, medicine, and the machinery and materials required to keep the economy functioning. Debt relief is also essential. However, the chief purpose of these loans should be to reinforce Russia's determination to build a market-oriented economy and to foster conditions conducive for more trade and private investment to begin flowing into the country.

The U.S. also has a compelling interest in continuing aid to Russia and other republics for dismantling and destroying nuclear warheads, and for helping to move defense scientists and technicians into the civilian economy. Just as the U.S. already is buying Russian uranium to prevent it from falling into the wrong hands, we and our allies should explore other means, such as exchanging debt relief for verified weapons destruction, for keeping the vast inventory of Soviet conventional arms off world markets. We should also press Russia to join us in eliminating chemical weapons.

Promoting democracy and markets abroad is not just a task for governments; private citizens also can be instrumental in helping post-communist countries build private enterprise and the institutions of civil society from the ground up. The new President should move quickly to establish the Democracy Corps, recently authorized by Congress. It would send thousands of volunteers with urgently needed professional skills to Eastern Europe and the Commonwealth of Independent States.

America also needs a more creative policy toward China. The new administration should throw in the "China card" and base its diplomacy on a fresh goal: fostering democracy in order to accelerate the demise of communist rule in China. It is likely that China will undergo a succession crisis during the next four years. The U.S. therefore should build relationships with the rising generation of Chinese leaders, especially those open to reform, as well as with the entrepreneurs who are feverishly building capitalism in southern China.

The Bush administration repeatedly blocked congressional attempts to make renewal of most-favored-nation trade status contingent on Chinese progress in respecting human rights and restraint in selling advanced weapons and military technology to other countries. The administration posed a false choice between "isolating" China and "keeping channels open," even if that meant ignoring China's human rights and trade abuses and weapons exports. There is an alternative: siding with the Chinese people rather than with their rulers, and targeting diplomatic sanctions on the central government rather than on the entrepreneurial sector. According to former foreign service officer Roger W. Sullivan, "Appropriate measures include restricting technology transfer, reducing China's textile quotas, selectively raising tariffs under Section 301 of the Trade Act on those Chinese exports manufactured in state enterprises, and actively opposing (not just abstaining from with a wink) any World Bank or Asian Development Bank loan that would strengthen state enterprises or the central planning system."[10]

The U.S. also should expand the Voice of America's Asian operations or create a Radio Free Asia to inform people in China, North Korea, Vietnam, and Burma (Myanmar) about events in their countries and encourage them to move toward democracy.

Aid for Democracy

The Clinton administration should strengthen the National Endowment for Democracy (NED) and other independent efforts to aid democracy abroad. America spends $273 *billion* a year to defend against potential military threats, but only $400 *million* to promote democracy.[11] Yet the latter may be a shrewder long-term investment in our security. President Clinton therefore should ask Congress to increase NED's budget of approximately $30 million to $100 million, and to expand public support for other nongovernmental organizations that openly aid democrats abroad, including Freedom House, the Asia Foundation, and the African-American Institute. Given the powerful global current toward democracy and markets, the U.S. can exercise enormous leverage from relatively small U.S. investments in helping others build the infrastructure of democracy.

Since its creation in 1983, the National Endowment for Democracy has helped pave the way for transitions to democracy in more than 20 countries, from Poland and Russia to South Africa and Central America. Where transitions have occurred, NED is helping to develop the civic infrastructure of democracy: democratic legislatures, local governments, political parties, trade unions, business associations, human rights organizations, legal assistance, voter education, and public interest groups. Though funded by government, it is a nongovernmental organization that operates with less red tape than most public bureaucracies. It works for the most part not with governments but with private and community groups, often at the local level. It offers small grants, seed money, to foster private initiatives. And today NED is supporting movements for democracy in China, Cuba, Iraq, and other dictatorships. Along with increased public support, the new administration should demand better oversight by NED of its many projects.

America's foreign aid program, an adjunct of our Cold War policy, no longer serves our changing strategic interests. In many cases, the rationale for security aid no longer exists, while development assistance to poor countries has largely been ineffective. Nonetheless, the U.S. should continue providing security aid to threatened democracies, such as Israel, as well as humanitarian and technical assistance to desperately poor nations struggling to raise their living, health, and environmental standards and curb their population growth.

To make U.S. foreign aid more cost-effective, the Clinton administration should end costly country-by-country aid programs and instead concentrate and target U.S. assistance on fragile democracies and countries moving in a democratic direction. This will require a thorough revamping of the U.S. Agency for International Development (AID), which is too ponderous, bureaucratic, and burdened by Congressional micromanagement to act with the requisite initiative, flexibility, and speed. The best solution is to replace AID with a new agency responsible for coordinating *all U.S. government assistance* to other countries. It should focus on the following key missions: fostering private sector growth, support for democratic institution-building, environmental protection, security assistance, and coordination of disaster relief and refugee resettlement with international organizations.

In the new era, there is no reason for America to give foreign aid to dictatorial regimes or "kleptocracies" such as Zaire under Seseseko Mobutu. However, the U.S. should make judicious use of all its diplomatic tools—trade, aid, debt relief, political and security assistance, and public diplomacy—to encourage progress toward democracy and apply what pressure it can on regimes that violate human rights. In short, we should attach conditions on nondemocratic countries seeking access to our markets, trade concessions, or economic assistance. There are ample precedents for a policy of strict conditionality. Many countries are liberalizing home markets under pressure from the IMF and World Bank and other international creditors. The European Community's requirement of democracy for membership is widely acknowledged as helping to speed the pace of democratic evolution in Spain, Portugal, Greece, and Turkey. Likewise, we should expand the North American Free Trade zone only to countries making measurable progress toward market and political reforms. And the Clinton administration should keep the pressure on South Africa to move toward full political and civil rights for its non-white majority.

Finally, the principle of burden-sharing should apply as much to promoting democracy and markets as it does to keeping the peace. Defending human rights and maintaining order, combating poverty in the southern hemisphere, controlling nuclear proliferation, and preserving our increasingly threatened global environment—such tasks can only be effectively pursued through international efforts. Strong U.S. leadership can help focus the institutions of collective security—the United Nations, the IMF and World Bank, and regional development banks and security organizations—on the task of bolstering emerging democracies and integrating them into an international system governed by common rules.

For example, the European Community should offer membership to Poland, Hungary, and the Baltic States. Conversely, multinational agencies should refuse support to regimes that chronically violate civil norms of international conduct. The IMF should refuse loans to China as long as it continues to export nuclear and other technologies to outlaw states such as Iran. Other multilateral initiatives worthy of more vigorous U.S. support include the Missile Technology Control Regime and the U.N. Conference on Environment and Development.

STRENGTH FOR DEMOCRACY

Along with a robust economy and adroit diplomacy guided by a clear, pro-democracy strategy, military strength will remain an indispensable pillar of U.S. global leadership. If our Cold War security goal was deterring Soviet aggression, our primary aim now must be the assurance that our nation will be prepared for a variety of more ambiguous, but still potent dangers. In a new era marked by the diffusion of military power, America must maintain a strong, technologically superior defense.

The Bush administration was slow to adapt U.S. military forces to changing security needs; President Clinton should accelerate that transformation. Defense planning was easier during the Cold War, when the potential adversary was known and the military threat clear. In a new era, we need new benchmarks for determining the right size and mix of military forces. Some experts, such as House Armed Services Committee chief Les Aspin, favor a "bottom up" approach based on an assessment of likely threats to global stability. Such potential threats include:

- **Nuclear blackmail by rogue states or terrorist groups.** Without more effective international action to curb the spread of advanced military technology, a U.S. president will inevitably have to confront hostile forces armed with weapons of mass destruction—nuclear, chemical, or biological—as well as the means for delivering them. A related challenge is to keep Russia's huge inventory of conventional arms off world markets.
- **Civil war within the former Soviet bloc, as political authority**

and economic conditions disintegrate. As Russia and its former satellites undergo a painful transition to markets, deprivation, hunger, and lawlessness threaten to engulf the region in chaos. Especially unsettling is the prospect that the four ex-Soviet republics with nuclear weapons could lose control of them. The worst scenario sees the emergence of a xenophobic regime in Moscow hostile to democratic values and determined to reassert Russian hegemony over the region.

- **New outbreaks of ethnic and sectarian violence as long-suppressed hatreds bubble to the surface, as we have seen lately in the Balkans, the Caucasus, and central Asia.**
- **The enduring risks of regional conflict.** The Middle East—the second most heavily armed region of the world—remains fundamentally unstable. And as we have seen repeatedly in the Persian Gulf, threats to peace may also arise from countries seeking regional hegemony: China, Iraq, Iran, North Korea.
- **Terrorist attacks on Americans traveling or working overseas, and the subversion of civil governments by drug cartels, such as we have seen in Colombia.**

In addition to gauging new threats, America's enduring interests and commitments abroad also provide points of reference for restructuring our defenses. It is likely the U.S. military presence will remain a force for stability in Europe, the Far East, and the Middle East throughout this decade, if not beyond. While new security arrangements are evolving in Europe, the U.S. should remain engaged in the North Atlantic Treaty Organization (NATO), perhaps the most effective political-military alliance in history. Likewise, U.S. power in the Pacific mitigates historic tensions between Japan, China, and the Koreas, not least by obviating the need for Japanese rearmament. President Clinton already has signaled the continuity of U.S. policy toward the Middle East, including support for Israel and for the peace process begun by President Bush. Other enduring missions for America's military include nuclear deterrence, even as superpower stockpiles shrink, and maintaining open sea lanes, as we did during the Persian Gulf reflagging operation.

Designing a Flexible Force

The previous administration failed to design a new security strategy or force structure for the post–Cold War world. Its "Base Force" plan—despite the abrupt disappearance of our Warsaw

Pact adversary—merely shrunk our existing Cold War military forces while leaving their essential structure intact. As a result, the U.S. continues to waste billions of dollars to support forces that no longer have a mission and do not fit our new security requirements. We face a basic tradeoff between quantity and quality: In order to maintain the current force structure more or less intact, we will have to forego capital investments in the next generation of military equipment.

This is a bad bargain. The adversaries we are likely to face in the new era will be regional powers, not superpowers. President Clinton's defense team should replace our 40-year-old Cold War doctrines and forces with a new defense blueprint geared for rapid response to flash points around the world. Barring a resurgence of the threat to Europe or the emergence of an expansionist power in East Asia, the U.S. will no longer need to maintain large ground forces abroad. Instead, we should trade military mass for modernization, building a smaller, rapidly deployable ground force that can be reconstituted through reserves if necessary.[12] Its hallmarks should be mobility, versatility, precision, and a clear qualitative edge in military technology and training.

As 1990 began, few Americans could have predicted that we would be embroiled in a war in the Persian Gulf within a year. Moreover, a unique set of circumstances permitted a more leisurely U.S. military buildup in the Gulf than we can expect in the future. With fewer bases and troops overseas, we will need ground forces that are lighter, more lethal, and more mobile, as well as more pre-positioning of equipment. And we will need a highly capable Navy and Marine Corps to project power around the world.

The flexible force must also be more versatile, because our military will be called upon to perform a greater variety of tasks: rescuing hostages, enforcing sanctions, providing humanitarian relief, operating with coalition partners, or fighting large-scale wars as we did in the Persian Gulf. The flexible force must be more precise, because our willingness to use force is often linked to our ability to limit casualties, both among our own troops and among civilians. The new force must also preserve our comparative advantage in "smart" weapons, sensors, space-based surveillance, communications and other military equipment, as well as in the highly skilled personnel necessary to use them.

To meet these goals, we must keep military recruiting and training standards high; maintain a robust program of research and development; develop a more mobile mix of light, mechanized, and armored ground forces; strike a better balance between weapons and combat support systems, such as aerial refueling and radar jamming planes; and invest more in additional sealift and airlift capacity, including the C-17 transport aircraft. The Clinton administration should also proceed with development of the V-22 Osprey, a versatile aircraft that can improve our amphibious, special operations and antiterrorist capabilities, and whose new, tilt-rotor technology could have important commercial uses.

Rather than shrinking the Cold War force symmetrically, as the previous administration proposed, we should reduce forces that were specifically designed to counter the Soviet threat. This means an asymmetrical builddown that will affect the Army most, followed by the Air Force, Navy, and Marine Corps. We should cut overall troop strength from 1.9 to approximately 1.4 million over the next five years; reduce U.S. troops stationed in Europe from 150,000 to between 75,000–100,000; continue closing bases at home and abroad; and reduce the number of carriers, air wings, and army divisions in our conventional force structure as circumstances abroad warrant. With the exception of the D-5 missile and the Minuteman III single warhead, U.S. strategic modernization programs already have come to a halt.

In designing a smaller and more flexible force, the administration should rely more on the National Guard and reserves to provide cost-effective combat support for our active-duty forces. An Army Guard ground unit costs 30–35 percent less than an active-duty unit and, with better training and higher personnel standards, could be quickly mobilized to add combat power to our regular forces in emergencies. In addition, the National Guard and reserves preserve a vital link between a professional army and citizens at large. According to a recent report by the House Armed Services Committee, " use of the Guard helps preserve the integral role of the citizen soldier in U.S. forces at a time when there is no conscription and a shrinking professional military."[13]

Missile Defenses

One of the most disturbing security trends today is the spread of missile technology, which means that more countries may soon be able to put U.S. cities at risk. Nations like Iraq, North Korea, and Libya are pursuing nuclear weapons and already have the capacity to equip missiles with chemical or biological as well as conventional warheads. Most potential aggressors undoubtedly would be deterred by the prospect of a heavy U.S. retaliatory blow.

But some might not, and there is the additional danger that nuclear warheads could fall into the hands of terrorists. And who can be confident that Saddam Hussein would not have launched missiles at U.S. cities, as he did at Israel's, had he been able to?

Since 1983 when Ronald Reagan unveiled his "Star Wars" proposal, the U.S. has spent $26 billion in pursuit of a space-based defense against a massive nuclear strike. The Bush administration modified the original conception, but its "Brilliant Pebbles" program likewise emphasized space-based missile interceptors. Even apart from questions about the staggering costs and technological challenges involved in space-based systems, the rationale for strategic defense is dwindling along with the vast Soviet arsenal of nuclear weapons.

President Clinton should therefore embrace a more relevant and attainable goal: defense against very limited (and perhaps accidental) launches of ballistic missiles. We should proceed with research and development on missile defense, and be prepared to seek revisions in the Anti-Ballistic Missile (ABM) Treaty, if necessary, to build the most effective system. The Russians, who are even more vulnerable to missile attacks from rogue states, have shown interest in this approach. Indeed, the global diffusion of military technology is making missile defense attractive to a growing number of countries around the world. In addition to countering anti-ballistic missiles, U.S. research on missile defense should focus on improving tactical or theater missiles (like the Aegis, Arrow, and THAAD high-altitude missiles) that embody newer technology than the Patriot missile.

The Defense Budget

Next January, the 1990 budget agreement's "walls" separating defense and domestic spending will come down. President Clinton must resist both conservative attempts to preserve the military status quo and liberal raids on the defense budget to fund domestic programs. He should also tailor the five-year defense plan he inherits from his predecessor to fit his priorities. With the collapse of the Warsaw Pact, the U.S. can and should reduce military spending—indeed, it is already at the lowest level in the postwar era—but only after we have determined what we need to spend in order to keep America strong and secure today.

The changes outlined here meet that test: They will modernize and adapt our armed forces and save money. They would reduce those forces by roughly a third and trim defense spending by about

$100 billion (in budget authority) by 1997. They would result in savings $50–60 billion greater by 1997 than envisioned in the current plan.

Restructuring the Military

In addition to reconfiguring the military for rapid response to regional contingencies, President Clinton has a rare opportunity to step back and take a fresh look at the basic organization of our armed forces. The current structure, based on four largely autonomous military services, is fraught with redundancy and waste. As Senate Armed Services Committee Chairman Sam Nunn has pointed out, for example, the U.S. has four separate air forces— one each for the four military branches, and similar redundancies in the Medical Corps, Chaplain Corps, Dental Corps, Legal Corps, and Nursing Corps. The Army and Marines both have light infantry divisions, while the Navy and Air Force have similar but separate fighter aircraft and tactical missiles. Each service also has its own training, logistics, and administrative facilities.[14]

Civilian leaders last tried to rationalize U.S. military forces in 1948, but deferred the task indefinitely as the nation shifted gears from demobilizing from World War II to rearming for the Cold War. Today we no longer face a threat so compelling as to justify costly duplication and redundancies in our armed forces, or to permit the military services to operate as distinct fiefdoms with separate plans and organizational cultures. Our economic and military goals alike require that President Clinton instruct his defense secretary to draw up plans for a thorough reorganization of our military forces. The new division of responsibilities should assign missions to specific services, rather than let each branch have a piece of the action. The likely result will be to minimize interservice rivalry and foster a new spirit of mutual dependence and cooperation.

America's intelligence agencies also need to be overhauled and dedicated to new missions. In addition to the military services' intelligence operations, the U.S. has three major intelligence agencies—the Central Intelligence Agency (CIA), the Defense Intelligence Agency (DIA), and the National Security Agency (NSA). These form a disjointed, loosely coordinated "intelligence community" whose main emphasis from birth has been monitoring the Soviet threat.

America has spent billions to keep track of other countries' military capabilities. We've had far less success—as the Bush administration's misreading of Saddam Hussein's intentions painfully reminds us—in understanding the motivations of potential adversaries. The intelligence community must do a better job of analyzing political and economic conditions in other countries that affect our military or economic security. Another crucial task in the new era will be to monitor the spread of military technology, so that defense planners can make informed decisions about which weapons systems to move from research to development and production. And, our intelligence agencies must assure U.S. "information dominance" of future battlefields, which means that our forces should know more, and know it faster, than their adversaries.

To foster closer cooperation and eliminate redundancy among our $30 billion intelligence community, the Clinton administration should back the National Security Act of 1992 proposed by U.S. Congressman Dave McCurdy, chairman of the House Intelligence Committee. It would create a new director of national intelligence (DNI), who would have the power to eliminate duplication of effort and excessive bureaucracy. The DNI, who would replace and supercede the director of central intelligence, would be responsible for preparing and submitting the budget for the entire intelligence community.

The Defense-Industrial Base

In his farewell address, President Eisenhower warned Americans about the growing power of the "military-industrial complex" engendered by the Cold War. Ironically, President Clinton may have to fight to save key parts of that complex as America demobilizes from the Cold War. One of the toughest challenges facing U.S. defense planners is shrinking our vast Cold War military establishment without losing the industrial and technological capacity to produce the sophisticated weapons our forces may need to prevail in some future conflict.

The Bush administration was willing to let production lines go cold on the unlikely assumption that firms later would be able to shift in and out of defense work as circumstances required. The Clinton administration should replace this policy of "military Darwinism" with an industrial base strategy that preserves the core skills and capacities essential to our military security. Such a strategy should include selective upgrading of existing weapons to keep key production lines open; limited development of new weapons capable of acting as "force multipliers"; and, robust research and development to prepare prototypes of next-generation weapons for production. The Pentagon also should explore new technologies with civilian as well as military uses and abolish useless military specifications that prevent it from buying commercial products off the shelf.

The special skills and capacities of workers in U.S. defense industries represent a strategic national asset in the global race for new technologies and markets. The Clinton administration should propose aid to help workers to relocate and retrain in civilian occupations. The Employment Insurance System proposed in chapter 3 would help laid-off defense workers to learn new skills. It is important to note, however, that all the retraining in the world will be wasted without a robust economy that creates jobs for people to move to. Defense transition policies can only work as part of a broader national strategy for investment in the productive capacities of America's firms and workers.

Highly skilled defense technicians and scientists would benefit from creation of a civilian version of the Pentagon's high-tech Defense Advanced Research and Projects Agency. This agency would identify emerging technologies with the potential to spawn new industries, and encourage their commercial development through grants and technical support. It also makes sense to permit U.S. businesses to join forces with the nation's defense laboratories, creating partnerships for developing new products and manufacturing processes.

For firms, converting from defense to civilian production is a far more difficult proposition. Military production often has little in common with commercial production, which is why past efforts at converting defense contractors to civilian work have rarely succeeded.[15] Even for the diversified companies that sell to the defense market, the real key to conversion is a growing, competitive national economy in which new markets emerge for their businesses.

America owes a special debt to the men and women of our all-volunteer force (AVF), who acquitted themselves with such outstanding skill and valor during the Persian Gulf War. For many of them, who volunteered in hopes of making a career of military service, the end of the Cold War means an involuntary and premature retirement to civilian life. However, Congress recently approved a series of inventive proposals by Senator Nunn for helping members of the AVF move smoothly into civilian life. These include offering bonuses for voluntary separation from the force; allowing military personnel to take educational leaves of absence to get civilian skills training; and, an early retirement option that allows people who leave the military to earn credit toward full retirement by taking jobs in areas of acute need, such as education, law enforcement, and health care. The Clinton administration should act quickly to implement these initiatives.

War Powers

If we are to promote democracy abroad we must invigorate it here at home. The new President should work with Congress to restore the constitutional balance of war-making power between the executive and legislative branches. During the Cold War, the power to commit America to war shifted perceptibly toward the executive branch, as the forward deployment of large ground forces in Europe and the advent of nuclear warhead and missile technology compressed the time for decision making in a crisis. Without impairing a president's ability to act in an emergency, we have a chance today to restore the normal peacetime process of democratic deliberation and decision-making in matters of war.

The 1973 War Powers Resolution was designed to redress the imbalance in war-making power. It has failed. We should reform the law by creating a permanent war powers delegation of congressional leaders to be consulted regularly by the President and his national security advisors. By institutionalizing collaboration between the President and congressional leaders on conflicts that may require the U.S. to resort to force, this step will foster wiser policy as well as wider legislative support for difficult operations.

Like all other governmental actions, America's conduct in the world must be subjected to the test of democratic legitimacy. A democratic republic cannot permit presidents to arrogate to themselves the power to commit the nation to war, simply for the sake of a more expedient foreign policy. Despite conservative claims of unfettered executive authority to commit U.S. forces to war, President Bush wisely chose to seek congressional authority for the use of force to free Kuwait. That authority—plainly required by the Constitution—gave Operation Desert Storm the legitimacy it otherwise would have lacked, and thereby helped to unify the country at a perilous moment.

Reviving Collective Security

With the end of the ideological rivalry between East and West, the world has a fresh chance to reinvigorate the idea and institutions of collective security. Now that there is wide agreement on first principles—the importance of democratic accountability in politics and market economies—the United Nations can play the leading role its creators envisioned for it a half-century ago. An expanded Security Council, no longer paralyzed by veto threats, can now become a more effective catalyst for U.N. action across a range of security and humanitarian needs. And the General Assembly, no longer a stage for anti-American posturing, can now become a key forum for North–South cooperation.

During the Persian Gulf crisis, the U.N. worked effectively to marshal an international coalition and campaign of pressure against Iraq. The Bush administration, however, failed to build on that hopeful precedent. The new President needs to fully exploit this opportunity to strengthen the efforts of the U.N. and other international bodies to enforce widely accepted norms of international conduct. From Cambodia to El Salvador, the U.N. is proving its ability to broker agreements aimed at quelling bloody civil wars. The next key challenge for collective security in the new era will be to empower the United Nations to engage in preventive diplomacy.

The U.S. should support the creation of a United Nations rapid-deployment force that could take on policing and relief duties that might otherwise fall into our lap by default. In addition to the U.N.'s traditional peace-keeping functions, such a force could be used, for example, to enforce sanctions against aggressors; to guard the borders of countries threatened by invasion; to provide humanitarian relief from the Kurdish regions of Iraq to the Horn of Africa; to combat terrorism; and even to intervene in countries to stop mass violence against civilians. This would not require the U.N. to maintain a large standing army, but rather a force that could be called up from units of national armed forces—including our own—and earmarked and trained in advance.

Of course, America must never abandon its prerogative to use force unilaterally when its vital interests are at stake. Still, we cannot allow every crisis to present us with a stark choice between the U.S. intervening or nothing happening. The alternative is for America vigorously to pursue its interests and those of the democratic community through the U.N. and other world bodies. As the Gulf War showed, U.S. leadership and armed might are essential catalysts for effective collective action against aggression. The U.S. should work with others whenever we can, while retaining the ability to act alone when we must.

In the post–Cold War world, burden-sharing thus takes on a

broader meaning. America must remain engaged in Europe and in the Pacific because we have vital interests there, and because our military presence contributes importantly to the regional balance of power. It makes sense, however, for the U.S. to begin gradually transferring responsibility to international and regional bodies not only for preserving the peace, but also for promoting democracy and market economies and for tackling environmental and other global problems.

The Balkan crisis offers a case in point: While most Americans are outraged by Serbian aggression and atrocities in Bosnia, few believe that our nation's vital interests are in jeopardy. Although military intervention may well be warranted on humanitarian grounds, the U.S. cannot afford to play the role of global gendarme or to "bear any burden" by itself. Instead, we may want to offer arms to the victims of aggression. In general, however, where our own strategic interests are not directly threatened, we should work in concert with the U.N., regional organizations such as NATO, Europe's Conference on Security and Cooperation, ASEAN, the Organization of American States, and other multilateral bodies.

CONCLUSION

In the late 1940s, when Harry Truman called on Americans to assume global responsibilities commensurate with our wealth and power, the nation responded with an unprecedented burst of creative diplomacy and institution building. With the formation of the North American Treaty Organization, we declared the defense of Western Europe as being integral to our own safety, thereby breaking a historic taboo against "entangling alliances" in peacetime. America confidently imposed democratic constitutions on Germany and Japan and generously offered the Marshall Plan to rebuild Europe. The U.S. became a charter member of the United Nations, successor to the moribund League of Nations. And we helped to establish the International Monetary Fund (IMF), the World Bank, and other multilateral institutions in order to foster international growth and cooperation.

As in Truman's time, the new President must invent a new security architecture for a transformed world. In the absence of a galvanizing and unifying threat, public support for energetic U.S. global leadership must be organized around a marriage of American interests and values. A pro-democracy strategy stands the best chance of winning broad, bipartisan support at home, without which U.S. foreign policy cannot command respect abroad. Such a strategy defends Americans' living standards, while offering protection to our democratic allies and consistently championing human rights in all countries. It stems from the conviction, confirmed again and again by twentieth-century experience, that the peaceful spread of liberal democracy is the best guarantee of U.S. security—the best hope for reversing the basic conditions that give rise to conflict and for building a more prosperous, just, and stable world.

MANDATE FOR ACTION

1. **Put commercial diplomacy at the center of America's new security strategy.** The Clinton administration must institutionalize the new emphasis on economic security at the highest levels of national decision-making. We should expand the National Security Council to include two new deputies to the national security advisor, one for military security and one for economic security. The President should also appoint a secretary of state who is committed to raising the status and career rewards of diplomats who specialize in helping advance U.S. economic interests abroad.

2. **Aid Russian democracy.** President Clinton should take the lead in orchestrating international loans, debt relief, and other support for Russia's painful transition to market economics and democratic politics. He should also expand U.S. aid for helping dismantle Soviet nuclear weapons and conversion from military to economic production. In addition, the administration should swiftly establish the Democracy Corps to send U.S. professionals with valuable expertise to the former Soviet bloc.

3. **Use trade policies and other leverage to encourage political and economic change in China.** The U.S. should be prepared to impose trade and diplomatic sanctions on China if its rulers fail to stop exporting military technology, curb human rights abuses in Tibet and elsewhere, and observe U.S. trade rules. Sanctions should be targeted as much as possible on state enterprises and the central government rather than on China's burgeoning entrepreneurial sector. To wage the war of ideas, the new administration should increase spending on VOA's Asian

operations or create a "Radio Free Asia" to give people in China, Korea, Vietnam, Burma (Myanmar) and other closed societies an alternative source of information.

4. **Expand U.S. support for building democratic institutions.** The Clinton administration should triple the National Endowment for Democracy's budget and increase support for other independent groups engaged in building democracy and free enterprise in other countries. For a relative pittance, the U.S. can give aid and encouragement to democratic forces struggling to hold honest elections, establish free labor unions and an independent media, create parliamentary and impartial judicial systems, and all the other civic institutions that underpin freedom.

5. **Revamp U.S. foreign aid.** The Clinton administration should replace the Agency for International Development with a new agency responsible for coordinating all U.S. government assistance to other countries. It should shift from country-by-country aid to a new focus on key missions: fostering private sector growth, support for democratic institution-building, environmental protection, security assistance, and coordination of disaster relief and refugee resettlement with international organizations. This approach will help to lessen congressional micromanagement of aid projects.

6. **Replace America's Cold War military establishment with a more mobile and flexible force that can respond rapidly to regional crises.** The Clinton administration should trade quantity for quality, reducing forces designed to fight the Cold War in order to invest in a new generation of military equipment. It should create a more mobile and versatile force capable of rapid deployment to trouble spots around the world. This flexible force should keep military recruiting and training standards high and maintain a robust program of research and development. It should include a larger role for the National Guard and reserves; develop missile defenses as a hedge against the failure of nonproliferation efforts; help uniformed personnel and defense workers move into the civilian economy; and ensure that America does not lose the productive and engineering capabilities necessary to build advanced weapons.

7. **Undertake a fundamental reassessment of military**

roles and missions. The President should instruct the secretary of defense to draw up plans for a sweeping reorganization of U.S. armed forces. The reorganization should aim at a new division of labor among the military branches that eliminates redundancy, shrinks bureaucracy, and fosters smoother interservice cooperation.

8. **Reorganize U.S. intelligence agencies.** America's various intelligence agencies should be consolidated and focused on new missions. These include monitoring the spread of military technology and weapons of mass destruction as well as better intelligence-gathering on political conditions in other countries that could affect U.S. interests. This will enable U.S. policymakers to anticipate problems and act before they swell into crises. To oversee the intelligence community and coordinate the flow of intelligence to the President and national security policymakers, a new position should be created: an independent director of national intelligence.

9. **Reform the War Powers Resolution.** With the Cold War over, the White House and congressional leaders should move to restore the constitutional balance of warmaking power between the executive and legislative branches. Reform should center on a permanent war powers delegation of congressional leaders who would be consulted regularly by the President and his national security advisors. This will ensure that the decision to commit U.S. forces abroad bears the stamp of democratic legitimacy.

10. **Reinvigorate the institutions of collective security.** Vigorous American leadership is essential to reviving the system of collective security envisioned by U.S. leaders in the aftermath of World War II. The Clinton administration should expand support for the International Atomic Energy Agency and other multilateral efforts to check proliferation and support preventive global diplomacy through a U.N. Rapid Deployment Force. It should also seek to bolster regional bodies such as ASEAN and the Organization of American States.

14

The Transition: Reasserting Presidential Leadership

WILLIAM A. GALSTON AND ELAINE CIULLA KAMARCK

> I must make the appointments now; a year hence I will know who I really want to appoint.
>
> —JFK to John Kenneth Galbraith, December 1960
>
> I can't afford to confine myself to one set of advisors. If I did that, I would be on their leading strings.
>
> —JFK to Richard Neustadt, explaining why he had commissioned multiple and overlapping transition memoranda

It has been 12 years since the Democrats last held the White House. In the American political system a party without a president speaks with many, often contradictory voices. Such has been the fate of Democrats during the Reagan–Bush years.

The principal challenge facing President Bill Clinton is to reassert presidential leadership over the Democratic Party. Unless the new President can bring the variegated factions of the Democratic coalition together behind *his* agenda, the urgent work at hand—reinvigorating the economy, rebuilding the social contract, and managing the transition to the post–Cold War world—will remain unfinished. The failure to unify the party on his own terms would all but ensure the resurgence of a fragmented, interest-group-based agenda and of the forces that undermined the presidency of Jimmy Carter.

There are two keys to reasserting leadership: The new President must act systematically to define his mandate, and he must place people loyal to his agenda in the key positions needed to carry out that mandate.

The American people vote for the winner of a presidential election for a wide variety of reasons, and the meaning of the majority they create through their millions of individual decisions is far from self-evident. The postelection statements of a President-elect should serve as the first step in defining his mandate. This is particularly true when the President-elect has defeated an incumbent, since the most obvious explanation for his success is the failure of the sitting President's administration. The fact that the people have rejected an incumbent makes it all the more important that the President-elect offer them an interpretation of what they have collectively affirmed. In so doing, he begins to shape both his administration and the public's understanding of it.

History suggests that a modest—even paper-thin—victory margin is no bar to claiming a mandate, as long as the substance of the claim is plausible. After defeating Richard Nixon by only one-tenth of 1 percent of the popular vote, John Kennedy unhesitatingly announced a mandate for change and encountered a minimum of disbelief. Nor is plurality rather than majority victory a bar—witness Nixon in 1968, Woodrow Wilson in 1912, and Margaret Thatcher throughout her 12 years in office. History also suggests that the clarity of initial presidential declarations is vital. Even though many voters disagreed with Ronald Reagan's specific policy proposals, he proclaimed a conservative mandate and made it stick. By contrast, Jimmy Carter's postelection statements were too general to convey a sense of direction that the people and the press could readily understand, and many of his immediate postelection pronouncements seemed to contradict the "soak-the-rich" populism of his campaign.[1]

President Clinton can claim a substantial mandate. As the first baby-boomer President, he is replacing the last of our presidents who will have served in the Second World War. His election embodies as well as symbolizes change. During the campaign, he spoke programmatically: of jump-starting the economy through accelerated public and private investment, guaranteeing access to health care while reining in soaring costs, ending the welfare system as a way of life, establishing a strict national system of child-support enforcement, and establishing a system of universal college aid and national service. But he also spoke thematically: of the need to make America competitive in the global economy, to repair the frayed fabric of our community through a renewed social contract or "New Covenant," to "revolutionize" government, and to promote democracy around the world. His postelection statements should meld the programmatic and the thematic elements of his campaign. Candidate Clinton won the pre-primary campaign in the fall of 1991 by laying out his agenda in a series of defining speeches; President Clinton may wish to seize the transition in the fall of 1992 by again systematically laying out his agenda for the American people.

The second crucial step in defining the mandate is the Inaugural Address. To be effective, it should be relatively short and thematic, establishing the principles, broad direction, and overall tone of the administration. Without seeming contrived, it should strive for heightened rhetorical effect to say something truly memorable. And it should convey a note of urgency—a call to arms for the administration and the American people. In this century, the inaugural addresses of FDR and JFK have come closest to meeting these standards.[2]

The final step in defining the mandate comes with the formulation of an early substantive strategy, often referred to as the "first 100 days." All administrations, especially Democratic ones, are influenced by the example set by Franklin Roosevelt in 1933, when the outlines of the New Deal were established within 100 days of his inauguration. The press is also influenced by this model: ever since FDR, the first important evaluations of how a new administration is doing have tended to occur at the 100-day mark.[3]

The incoming administration must therefore display focus in defining, and effectiveness in pursuing, its initial substantive agenda. This agenda (which may or may not be enacted during the first 100 days) represents a president's best chance to achieve fundamental change. There are severe penalties for being too cautious and incremental—opportunities squandered, momentum lost, cynicism reinforced. Reflecting on the challenge of pushing basic reforms through a fractious Congress, Lyndon Johnson once said, "You've got to give it all you can that first year. Doesn't matter what kind of majority you come in with. You've got just one year when they treat you right, and before they start worrying about themselves."[4]

The administration must establish a clear, limited agenda of new legislation as soon as the relevant players are in place. (History suggests that an elaborate policy planning apparatus operating in advance of key appointments is not likely to be very effective in shaping policy.) As the first year of the Carter administration demonstrated, the effort to get everything done at once is almost certainly self-defeating. (By contrast, both JFK and Reagan tried to do less during their first year but got credit for much more.) History also suggests that absent very special circumstances such as a large and malleable legislative majority or an urgent national crisis, no more than half a dozen pieces of major innovative legislation can be passed during the first 12 months. This is particularly likely to be the case if the short list includes proposals (such as health care reform) that cut across jurisdictional lines in Congress and mobilize powerful interest groups.

In crafting this early agenda, it is important to avoid legislative morasses that halt momentum and absorb disproportionate amounts of time and energy at both ends of Pennsylvania Avenue. In retrospect, for example, it seems clear that the Spring 1977 energy bill, which tied Congress up in knots for months, impeded the enactment of other, potentially more feasible, parts of the Carter administration's first-year program. It is also important to avoid the appearance of early policy reversals (such as the withdrawal of Carter's proposed $50 tax rebate) that can be interpreted by Congress and the press as calling into question the administration's consistency and commitment.

Even before the major policy proposals are ready for submission to Congress, however, the new administration may want to establish momentum by scoring a series of early successes. The President should choose some proposals that clearly differentiate the new administration from the old; accomplishing them early on would bolster his reputation as an effective leader. One component of a fast, effective early strategy is the selective use of the President's power to issue executive orders. (This is how JFK created the Peace Corps less than six weeks after taking office.) President Clinton could issue a call for states to submit innovative welfare reform plans. The promise of speedy grants of waivers to those states could serve as a first effective step toward welfare reform (as well as an important nod to the gubernatorial wing of the party), while the administration works out a larger, more comprehensive plan. A second element of a "fast start" strategy would be to ask for quick passage of a handful of the 35 pieces of legislation that George Bush successfully vetoed, such as the Family and Medical Leave Act.

But the real focus of the first 100 days should be on how President Clinton fulfills his mandate to tackle several large and difficult questions. Throughout his campaign he promised to be a "different kind of Democrat." Fulfilling this promise and avoiding a reversion to the discredited policies of the party's own past will challenge the new President's leadership on many different fronts.

Nowhere is this more important than in the appointment process, which the new President must use to continue his break with the past and to avoid being captured by the very forces he has undertaken to reform. His key appointees should display a genuine commitment to what the President has called the "third way" alternative to both Reaganism and tax and spend liberalism. For instance, his often repeated pledge to "revolutionize government" cannot be redeemed by a government that doesn't know what this means or that is too much a captive of the status quo to engage in change. Appointees should be open and hospitable to a fundamental government restructuring that may affect their own bureaucratic domain. They must be part of the solution, not an addition to the problem; their primary commitment should be to the new President's administration rather than to interest groups or personal agendas. For the Clinton administration, this may mean leavening the circle of Washington insiders with experienced state and local policy innovators, the kinds of people who will ask, not *why*, but *why not*?

This book has presented an agenda for action that transcends the stale options of the Left and the Right and that, if enacted, will help President Clinton break the policy gridlock and give definition to his administration. It has advocated management of macro- and micro-economic policy along the lines of Enterprise Economics; it has outlined a comprehensive market-based approach to national health care and the environment; a paradigm for welfare reform; and a new agenda for family policy. It has proposed a series of radical proposals for "reinventing" the federal government.

Should President Clinton attempt to implement his general mandate with the specific reforms advocated in his campaign and elaborated in this book, he may well encounter opposition from elements of his own electoral coalition. But if he is to keep the major promise of his campaign—the promise of fundamental change—he will have no other choice.

FORMING AN ADMINISTRATION: THE POLITICAL CONTEXT

In forming an administration, each incoming president operates within a context defined by the specific historical situation of his political party and by the nature of the broader coalition that elected him. The victorious coalition is often an untidy (frequently unruly) group encompassing a wide range of disparate interests and views. The management of fault lines within this coalition is crucial to the success of a presidency.

New presidents differ in the extent to which their successful campaigns are ideologically well defined. Some, like Ronald Reagan in 1980, who ran and won as a conservative, have the advantage of a relatively firm ideological stance through which to interpret their mandate. In contrast, candidates such as Jimmy Carter in 1976 and George Bush in 1988 ran campaigns that were less clearly defined.

New presidents also differ in the extent to which they have managed to impose their ideology on their party. In 1980, Ronald Reagan won his party's nomination as a conservative warrior. His victory signaled the triumph of movement conservatism over both Ford-style midwestern conservatism and the remnants of east coast liberalism within the Republican party. As a result, Reagan was able to conduct his general election campaign with an unusual degree of ideological coherence, and he was able to construct his first administration on the basis of a program to which the defeated factions within his party had been compelled to pledge their allegiance. Moderates like David Gergen and James Baker had little choice in the early going but to use their skills to advance the Reagan agenda.

In 1976, by contrast, Jimmy Carter ran as an effective manager. His campaign was designed to bring George McGovern doves and Scoop Jackson hawks, big government liberals and fiscal conservatives, black civil rights groups and white ethnic communities together under the broad tent. This strategy, which only barely succeeded, yielded two results crucial for the organization of Carter's administration. First, many different groups felt that they were holding promissory notes redeemable for appointments and influence. Second, the President's agenda had to be determined to a significant degree by the early power balance established among these contending forces.

These structural facts came to haunt the incoming presidency. In foreign policy, for example, Carter was seen during the campaign as reaching out to both liberals (e.g., Paul Warnke) and neoconservatives (e.g., Paul Nitze). But in the transition appointment process the neoconservatives were almost entirely shut out. That embittered them and reinforced a split that nearly defeated Warnke's nomination as chief arms control advisor, leading eventually to the stalemate over the SALT II treaty. The "neocons" were the first Democrats to lead the way out of the Democratic

Party four years later, as Jeane Kirkpatrick and others endorsed Ronald Reagan.

In domestic policy, although Carter immediately boosted spending for a wide range of programs, he could never heal, or even manage, the breach with northern liberals. Within his own administration, this showed up most dramatically in his repeated battles with HHS Secretary Joseph Califano over everything from smoking and tobacco subsidies to national health care. These tensions, which also soured White House/congressional relations, broke out for all to see at the party's 1978 Midterm Conference, at which the President pushed for a much tighter budget than the liberals advocated. This failure to work out a modus vivendi between southern fiscal moderates and traditional liberals was central to the difficulties encountered by Carter's administration.

President Clinton's situation combines key features of both 1980 and 1976. Like Reagan, he espoused a clear reform agenda. Throughout his campaign he captured the country's desire for change by calling for a "third way" alternative to Reaganism and traditional liberalism; he ran and won as a "different kind of Democrat." But unlike Reagan, who prevailed in the battle for his party's nomination by defeating its leading moderates and capturing its very soul (an effort 16 years in the making), Clinton did not have the opportunity to encounter and overcome the most forceful advocates of the traditional Democratic party.

The absence of a clear-cut, climactic ideological battle for the nomination leaves Bill Clinton with a coalition that may be less committed to his third way than he is himself. In assembling and orienting his administration, therefore, the new President must redeem the implicit promise of meaningful participation by all portions of his winning coalition. At the same time, he must unite these disparate forces behind his mandate for change in a manner that can sustain executive coherence, legislative momentum, and public support. To meet these challenges, President Clinton will have to adopt a third strategy, one for which he is uniquely qualified—neither Reagan-style warrior nor Carter-like manager, but rather Rooseveltian persuader.

These challenges are made even more difficult by a new cleavage that has developed within the Democratic party over the past two decades between its gubernatorial and congressional wings. Throughout the years of Republican presidential dominance, the gubernatorial wing has flourished. Not only have Democratic governors attained and maintained office in near-record numbers, they have also sparked a reinvigoration of state government based on principles of fiscal integrity, policy innovation, and direct responsiveness to the people.[5] They have often offered "a third way."

During this same period, by contrast, the congressional wing has been forced on the defensive. Its struggles to preserve historic liberal programs against attacks from a conservative-dominated executive branch have left little room for policy innovation. In the context of an unending federal fiscal crisis, these efforts have led to increased federal mandates on states and programmatic micromanagement that make governors' lives much more difficult. The new President, who comes to the White House with a wealth of state-based experience, will need all his skill to bridge the gap within the Democratic party between bottom-up and top-down approaches to governance, between micromanaging the federal government (as Democrats in Congress are wont to do) and reinventing it (as Democratic governors would like to see happen).

FORMING AN ADMINISTRATION: THE INSTITUTIONAL CONTEXT

It is tempting for the incoming President to think of himself as manager-in-chief of the federal government with its more than one thousand agencies and three million civilian federal employees, plus two million active military personnel. But this temptation must be resisted. There are more employees of the federal government than there are people in Arkansas (and in 18 other states). The sheer size of the executive establishment makes it unmanageable from any single central point. Even with the more than tenfold expansion of the White House staff since the New Deal and large number of presidential appointees, mid- and upper-level bureaucratic managers outnumber their political counterparts by a factor of 94 to 1.[6]

Furthermore, the constitutional status of the President's managerial claims is less than compelling. The vast majority of civil servants take direction not from the President of the United States, but from the laws that authorize their agencies and direct their tasks—not to mention the congressional oversight panels that monitor their performance. For many purposes it may make more sense to think of the bureaucracy as a fourth branch of government rather than as an errant part of the executive branch that must be brought to heel by the President and his appointees.

The President's effort to exert management control through political appointments typically comes to grief: the political appointee either engages in a frustrating battle with the professional bureaucracy or "goes native" by capitulating to its goals and perspectives. Even when the political appointee is serious about doing the President's bidding, the struggle is unequal. The average tenure of cabinet and subcabinet appointees is about two years; the average civil service professional stays ten times that long. Not surprisingly, even idealistic young civil servants quickly learn to prefer the enduring interests of their institution over the vagaries of the political appointments process.

For these and related reasons, as political scientist Richard Rose has said, the President can "no more manage the whole of the government than he could manage a herd of wild horses." Nor should he try. As a leading student of the presidency, Stephen Hess, puts it, "Rather than chief manager, the President is the chief political officer of the United States. His major responsibility . . . is each year to make a relatively small number of highly significant political decisions—among them setting national priorities, which he does through the budget and his legislative proposals, and devising policy to ensure the security of the country, with special attention to those situations that could involve the country in war."[7]

As chief political officer, the President's principal task is to lead the federal government, not to manage it. This proposition has profound implications for the transition process as a whole. Simply put: The new President should assess the bearing of personnel, process, and policy decisions on his capacity to exert effective political leadership—that is, to make and execute the handful of basic choices that will define his presidency.

APPOINTING PERSONNEL

Personnel appointments are the most visible, complex, and contentious aspect of presidential transitions. Although there is no way to make this process wholly smooth and conflict-free, history suggests some guidelines that can improve outcomes for the new President while signaling competence and leadership to the press and public. Typically, the President himself will select the most important members of his team—the cabinet and a handful of other senior people, all of whom will require congressional approval. The most visible and draining personnel decisions are those that get bogged down in debilitating confirmation battles (e.g., Carter with Sorensen and Warnke, Bush with Tower). These absorb the senior staff's time and energy. To the extent they can be avoided, they should be; to the extent that a controversial choice is important to the new President, the requisite time and attention should be set aside for the confirmation battle.

While the President himself usually selects the cabinet and other top positions, (Reagan was notable for the lack of interest he took in his cabinet appointments), a personnel search team is invaluable in conducting all the checks and clearances that are necessary to staff a modern government. To assist the President, a team should be announced as early as possible after election day. It should be balanced; it should contain individuals (such as Clark Clifford in JFK's transition) who are not seeking jobs for themselves; and it should enjoy, and be seen as enjoying, clear authority to do its job. To be avoided at all costs is the creation of competing power centers, such as the struggle between the Jack Watson and Hamilton Jordan groups during the Carter transition.[8]

In making appointments, a President tends to want political and policy compatibility, personal loyalty, and professional competence all in the same person—a rare combination. It may thus make sense to look at teams within each department or agency that collectively possess these desiderata. For instance, a President may pick a cabinet secretary who is politically compatible, an undersecretary with governmental expertise, and a former campaign worker as congressional liaison.

In those areas of government that have been identified during the campaign and again in the mandate as prime foci of change, it is especially important to blend policy competence with the ability to explain and sell policy innovations to the press and public. Here again, these skills may not always be found in the same person, and the personnel team should concentrate on forging teams that do have them.

Beyond these general observations, criteria for individual appointments are difficult to spell out in meaningful detail. Still, in the special context of the 1992 transition, a few points seem clear:

- Where the new President's legislative program is already clearly defined, the appointees should be loyal to the program. For example, it would make little sense to appoint as senior HHS officials individuals who reject the fundamental reform of the welfare system that the President has advocated. Arnie Miller, former director of presidential personnel in the Carter administration, advocates the creation of teams of subcabinet appointees compatible along policy lines as a means of breaking down bureaucratic and agency barriers. This is especially important in those areas where large-scale reform efforts are to take place. Take, for instance, the welfare reform agenda as laid out in chapter 10. In addition to the obvious HHS appointees, subcabinet officers from the Labor and Education Departments will be involved as well as appointees from the IRS.

- Where the new President's program is largely undefined, or the subject of continuing debate within his own camp, the appointment process should not be allowed to become a covert means of making important policy determinations to which the President has not explicitly assented. While a diversity of views can be an asset to a President in the formulation of complex policies, he must be prepared at some point to intervene and choose sides. Once the decision has been made he must be prepared to do what is necessary to bring bureaucratic conflict to an end.

  In the early years of his administration, Richard Nixon seems to have deliberately set out to institutionalize a debate on domestic policy by pitting Daniel Patrick Moynihan against Arthur Burns. Having watched this strategy as deputy to Moynihan, Stephen Hess concluded, "For a President to opt for a system of staff conflict, he must be prepared to assume a major role in mediation, assignments, and even hand-holding. This Nixon was unwilling to do."[9]

- Management experience is important but not always vital. For example, JFK's budget director, Harvard's David Bell, told the President-elect that he lacked experience running a large organization. Kennedy appointed him anyway, and Bell did a job that was widely recognized as superb. As we argued earlier, the prime function of senior political appointments is not to improve day-to-day management of the federal government, but rather to help the President make and execute the handful of decisions that will define his administration.

- In making senior appointments, many past Presidents have sought out good people from the opposition party. JFK went out of his way to select C. Douglas Dillon as treasury secretary; Nixon brought Pat Moynihan into his administration as senior domestic policy counselor and sought (but failed to win) Scoop Jackson's services as secretary of defense; Carter not only appointed Nixon–Ford veteran James Schlesinger as energy secretary but gave him authority to draft what turned out to be the most important legislation of the administration's first year.

  There is good reason to believe that in 1992 this bipartisan strategy is more relevant than ever. The electorate's partisan attachments are becoming ever more attenuated. Ross Perot's appeal reflects in part the electorate's impatience with traditional partisan disagreements and a desire for the best, most public-spirited people to serve in government regardless of party. Clinton may want to reach out to the group sometimes known as the "bleeding heart conservatives" (for their attention to such traditionally liberal issues as poverty), to experienced Republican moderates, or to the Republican entrepreneurs who supported his campaign as a means of adding diversity to his team.

- In making subcabinet appointments, recent transitions have presented stark alternatives. Jimmy Carter gave cabinet appointees the authority to make their own subcabinet choices. Many observers believe this strategy backfired by diminishing both the administration's coherence and the loyalty of many senior officials to the President. The Reagan transition, by contrast, retained tight centralized control over subcabinet appointments. This increased the overall coherence of the administration but may have discouraged some strong figures from accepting appointments to preside over departments whose senior deputies they could not control.

  Between these two extremes, some version of the Kennedy approach—shared power and negotiation—seems most balanced and workable. For example, JFK told Robert McNamara that he could select his own deputies, subject to presidential review and approval. This both allowed a strong leader with clear policy ideas to take charge of the Defense Department and ensured that the McNamara team would be loyal to the President and his basic policies.

- In foreign policy the President must face a dilemma that has confronted all modern presidents. Should he run foreign policy out of the White House, as Kennedy and Nixon did, or create a relatively strong secretary of state along the lines of the Eisenhower/Dulles or the Bush/Baker relationships? In view of President Clinton's background and programmatic focus during the campaign, the latter models may well be more appropriate this time. This is an example of the more general maxim that the President should put together strong teams, not just where he is already experienced and confident, but also—and especially—where he is less so.

  Second, and relatedly, the President must reach an early determination as to the relationship he wants between his secretary of state and his national security advisor. History presents two extremes: Tensions between the offices can be eliminated by uniting them in one person (Kissinger during the Nixon administration), or institutionalized by filling them with two individuals of radically differing views (Vance and Brzezinski during the Carter administration). In retrospect, each extreme generated serious difficulties. The Bush administration's Baker/Scowcroft duo—two experienced senior hands with compatible, but not wholly congruent views, and who enjoyed the President's confidence—seems about right and could be used as a structural model.

• Not all appointments are created equal; some must be made early in the transition. For example, the President will need to submit significant revisions to both the fiscal year 1993 and proposed fiscal year 1994 budgets within weeks of taking office. This timetable cannot possibly be met unless an OMB director is up and running quickly. Other key economic appointments such as treasury secretary and Council of Economic Advisors head must also be made promptly to send a message of reassurance and stability to the markets; the last thing an incoming president needs is a stock market crash or currency crisis. (Last September the international currency markets demonstrated their power to make mincemeat of national governments and their leaders.) Prior to Reagan's election, Ed Meese had identified 87 appointive positions in the economic policy arena that he targeted as top priorities to be filled; this was immensely helpful in getting Reagan's economic program in place.[10] Similarly, the President should appoint one or two key members of his foreign policy team to send the right signals to the world and to help him cope with unexpected foreign policy developments during the transition.

SETTLING ON A WHITE HOUSE STAFF STRUCTURE

A presidential transition must not only select, but also organize, key personnel. This is especially true for cabinet-level officials and the President's senior staff. The eventual White House organizational structure will reflect the President's distinctive personality and management style. Still, a few generalizations may prove useful.

Scholars and journalists have long been fascinated with Franklin Roosevelt's amorphous White House structure, which consisted of strong-willed and often warring aides with the President at the center. However, in the 1930s the federal government was significantly smaller than it is today, as was the range of activities that fell under the purview of the President and the executive branch.

Under contemporary circumstances, a strong chief of staff is likely to prove superior to the re-creation of the Rooseveltian ("hub and spokes") approach that Jimmy Carter employed early in his administration. As Carter discovered, the size of the White House staff and the number and complexity of the issues bearing down on the President made it very difficult for him to budget his time, avoid unnecessary details, and focus on the essentials without a vigorous chief of staff organizing the policy process. The chief of staff must be able to understand policy as well as politics and to keep minor issues off the President's desk while exposing him to a wide range of advice on the decisions that really matter. Ideally, the chief of staff should also be able to complement the incoming President's strengths—or, to put it more bluntly, compensate for his weaknesses.

The chief of staff must, of course, enjoy the President's full trust and confidence, but need not be the President's long-time friend or associate. One of the most effective staff heads, James Baker, had twice worked against Ronald Reagan (for Ford in 1976 and Bush early in 1980) before his selection by Reagan in the fall of 1980. In turn, Baker made appointments based on ability, experience, and compatibility, not on past relations with Reagan.[11]

Recent history suggests the importance of appointing the chief of staff early in the transition. Baker's prompt selection helped clarify lines of authority and accelerated the naming of other key White House aides.

Many presidents have come into office pledged to some form of "cabinet government," but none has made it work. The cabinet is simply too large and diverse to function well as a deliberative body. On the other hand, many key legislative issues cut across departmental lines. To reconcile these competing realities, the Reagan administration formed half a dozen "cabinet councils" consisting of cabinet-rank officials with overlapping interests. For example, the Council on Economic Affairs was chaired by the treasury secretary; its other members included the secretaries of state, commerce, labor, and transportation, the OMB director, the U.S. trade representative, and the chair of the Council of Economic Advisors. Each council was backstopped by a staff secretariat made up of subcabinet representatives of its member departments, and the White House Office of Policy Development provided an executive secretary to play the lead role in its staff activities. While the councils operated at varying levels of energy and relevance (the Economic Affairs Council met ten times as often as its Food and Agriculture counterpart) and the council system evolved significantly during the Reagan years, this structure worked better than the skeptics predicted and seems worthy of emulation.

Another key Reagan innovation was the Legislative Strategy Group which served as a coordinating mechanism for promoting the President's agenda. Chaired by Baker, its core members included the treasury secretary, OMB director, head of the White House legislative office, and policy/political strategists such as David Gergen. It met every morning to set priorities, resolve interagency conflicts, establish the daily message, and assign tactical responsibility for different parts of the legislative agenda. This group played a central role in guiding Reagan's first-year program through the Congress, and the incoming administration would be well advised to reconstitute it in some version with which the President and his chief of staff feel comfortable.

Many senior Democrats with extensive experience, wise counsel, and good press relations will be compelled by professional or family considerations to forego full-time participation in the new administration. Nonetheless, they have an important role to play. Staff members inside the administration typically find it difficult to tell the President things he doesn't want to hear; those who try are usually outmaneuvered and marginalized. Well-disposed outsiders are somewhat freer to be blunt. To receive their unvarnished advice in a timely and useful form, the incoming administration should constitute a Senior Advisory Group that meets regularly with the President or his chief of staff. Beyond serving as a policy sounding-board, such a group could give the President early indications of impending troubles with the press, Beltway establishment, and the electorate.

MANAGING RELATIONS WITH THE CONGRESS

It is difficult to overstate the importance of an effective congressional liaison operation in place early in the transition. This will allow the new President to cement key personal relationships, assess the potential pitfalls of his early agenda, and give members a sense that they are valued and involved and that their views will be taken into account. This should be one of the easier parts of the government to staff; for while the skills and background necessary to manage issues such as trade policy are not likely to be readily available among members of a political campaign, the skills that make for good congressional liaison staff are. A liaison staff that understands politics, respects local sensitivities in appointments and policy, and grasps the value of seemingly small things like giving members their due in inaugural activities can be invaluable in smoothing the way for congressional approval of top appointments and in alerting the President to the pitfalls in his early program as it is being developed.

While the end of divided government will increase public expectations for the prompt enactment of a coherent legislative program, congressional leaders will have agendas that don't precisely conform to the new President's. An effective liaison process (one that is substantive as well as political) will flag these problems and allow the new President to make substantive choices with adequate awareness of their political consequences. After all, members of congress know a great deal about public policy and should be made part of the process. The alternative (as Carter discovered) is unexpected and jarring resistance from within his own party that can undermine the fast start he wants—and the country needs.

CONCLUSION

The peaceful transfer of power from one President to the next is an enduring and gripping drama of American democracy. History suggests that courteous and respectful treatment of the outgoing President (Eisenhower by JFK, LBJ by Nixon) is a plus for the new President. It suggests strength of character and affirmation of our constitutional structure as something larger than partisanship. This course of action would seem especially desirable at a time when public disaffection with partisan wrangling is very high.

There are, as well, more immediate and practical reasons for showing respect. There is a perennial tendency for new appointees not to tap the experience of lame-duck officials. This temptation should be resisted. There is nothing to be lost, and something to be gained, from serious exchanges between these two groups—particularly because the 12-year hiatus since the last Democratic president means that many of the new President's appointees will not have had high-level federal experience. It be would wise to organize these contacts, as President-elect Kennedy did, by appointing a chief liaison to work with outgoing administration officials.

This brings us to our final point. The largest transition pitfall, put simply, is hubris, the naive conviction that "the problems of the past won't happen to me." The last three Democratic presidents have suffered from early self-inflicted wounds. For Kennedy it was the disastrous Bay of Pigs; for LBJ it was the decision to escalate in Vietnam; for Carter it was the promotion of his energy bill and the alienation of the Democratic Congress in his first year in office.

Hubris during the transition is hard to avoid. The new President goes from mere mortal to godlike stature as the entire apparatus of the presidency descends upon him. Campaign staffers go from hard working, often obscure grunts to the toast of the town. All in all, it is hard not to be taken in by the illusion of absolute power. But in a very short period of time the inevitable happens: the President becomes but one actor in a system of shared power designed by the Founding Fathers to make it very hard for any one person to exercise a mandate for change.

Afterword

This is our Mandate for Change.

For a great but frustrated nation entering a new global era, it offers a path toward growth, strength, and the promise of progress that has sustained the American dream across the generations. At a time of popular discontent with our government's ability to act, serve, or lead, this book aims to provide a new governing philosophy and a new set of ideas that can break the deadlock, move beyond the exhausted politics of Left and Right, and make a reinvented public sector once again into a catalyst for American greatness.

The day after the election, Bill Clinton told the American people that the coming years will be "a period of great challenge and extraordinary opportunity for our nation." We agree. It will be a time of intense and often disruptive global economic competition; yet it can also be a time when we build the foundations for a century of growing incomes and opportunities for America's workers—and for those who long to become workers. It will be a time when too many of our families lack the safe streets, skills, incomes, health care, and job prospects that are prerequisites to sharing fully in American life; yet it can also be a time when we embrace bold new efforts to empower the poor, revitalize our schools, make health-care coverage affordable and universal, and expand the ranks and horizons of America's broad middle class.

It will be a time when the bonds that sustain our families, neighborhoods, and civic institutions are tested by the economic and cultural strains of our day; yet it can also be a time when we cultivate a new ethic of reciprocity, responsibility, and community—an ethic that makes an increasingly diverse nation stronger and more unified in purpose.

We are unabashed believers in progressive governance. But we are unabashed critics of the failures of national government and leadership—from both parties—over the past two decades. We are determined to set national policy on a better course—a third way—which merges mainstream values with progressive objectives. This third way is not something we have invented. Rather, it is something we have witnessed. It is a new approach we have seen bubbling up from innovative public leaders in cities and states across the nation. It is a new kind of politics that the American people are creating—and demanding. They are the ones who have given this new and promising administration its mandate for change. Now we offer this book and its ideas in order to help make their hopeful mandate a reality for all Americans.

Notes

Chapter 1

1. The Congressional Budget Office (CBO) has recommended that the Treasury shift a modest portion of the national debt to shorter-term securities. CBO estimates that shifting $10 billion from 30-year bonds to shorter maturities would save $3 billion over ten years. The Internal Revenue Service estimates that unreported capital gains, dividends, interest, and rental income cost the Treasury more than $20 billion a year. Strict auditing and enforcement would raise at least $2 to $3 billion a year.

2. The globalization of capital and commerce creates conditions for U.S. competition with developing nations as well as other advanced economies. Today, low-wage countries are able to attract global capital to invest in labor-intensive industries. As these developing nations establish comparative advantages in these sectors, the U.S. should respond with measures to facilitate the reallocation of labor within our own economy, providing job training for displaced workers to build a more highly skilled labor force.

3. "OECD in Figures", Supplement to *OECD Observer*, 176 (June/July 1992): 24–25.

4. Ibid., 8–9, 24–25.

5. Ibid., 24–25, 60–61.

6. This conclusion follows from traditional economic analysis that most people's inclination to forgo consumption to invest is affected primarily by income and wealth, and only very weakly by modest changes in the marginal tax rate on the potential profits from a particular investment.

7. Substantial controversy exists over why these targeted incentives don't work; perhaps they raise the cost of capital for businesses that cannot take advantage of them, or the subsidy enables firms that use them to operate less productively. Whatever the reasons, the evidence is strong that they generate little or no general economic benefits.

8. Joint Committee on Taxation, "Explanation of Methodology," table 13.

9. Calculations from data reported in *Economic Report of the President*, Feb. 1991, Tables B-2, B-26, B-29, B-33, B-58, B-101.

10. These relationships depend upon the current system of floating exchange rates and would change if the U.S. and other advanced nations returned to fixed exchange rates.

11. Benjamin M. Friedman, "Reagan Lives!" *New York Review of Books*,

37 (Dec 20, 1990); for detailed analysis, see Benjamin M. Friedman, *Day of Reckoning: The Consequences of American Economic Policy Under Reagan and After* (New York: Random House, 1988).

12. Real GNP grew by 2.67% a year in the 1980s, compared to 3.98% a year in the 1950s, 4.05% a year in the 1960s, and 2.83% a year in the 1970s. See *Economic Report of the President,* Feb. 1990, table C-2.

13. Adjusted for inflation, the average weekly earnings of nonsupervisory workers, covering 75% of the U.S. work force, declined by 3.6% in the 1980s; in 1977 dollars, these earnings fell from $172.74 in 1980 to $166.52 in 1989. See *Economic Report of the President, 1990,* table C-44. For discussions of changes in income distribution, see Frank Levy, *Dollars and Dreams: The Changing American Income Distribution* (New York: Russell Sage, 1987); and Committee on Ways and Means U.S. House of Representatives, *Tax Progressivity and Income Distribution,* March 26, 1990.

14. The same dilution effect occurs when the Federal Reserve eases the money supply to encourage borrowing, investment, and consumption.

15. When the U.S. economy is stalled, the deficit is already large, and other advanced economies are expanding, additional deficit stimulus at home could push up U.S. and world interest rates by intensifying the global competition for funds. Large, fixed deficits also increase the likelihood that, during a recession, the government will print money to pay its bills. As a consequence, a persistent deficit raises inflationary expectations, increasing lenders' exchange-rate risks, the primary mechanisms by which the large, fixed U.S. deficit raises the cost of borrowing for U.S. businesses and reduces long-term investment and growth.

Chapter 2

1. The cost of foreign borrowing is likely to rise further if, as expected, the rebuilding in Eastern and Central European countries heightens global competition for funds.

2. This limit and the requirement that annual revenues finance the Present Budget would not apply in wartime, recessions, or other grave national emergencies.

3. This spending growth has been unaffected by waning or waxing support for specific kinds of spending. In the 1950s, spending pressure came largely from public works, succeeded in the 1960s by emphasis on spending for defense and discretionary domestic programs. In the 1970s, entitlement programs drove spending, followed in the 1980s by entitlements and defense, and then entitlements and interest payments. In the early 1990s health care programs and the savings and loan bailout have driven rapidly rising spending.

4. *Budget of the United States Government,* Fiscal Year 1991, "Historical Tables," tables 10.1, 10.2.

5. The share of federal spending going to investments in physical capital

fell from about 25% in the 1950s and early 1960s to not much more than 10% in the 1980s. See *Budget,* "Historical Tables," tables 9.1, 9.2, 9.3.

6. M. E. Sharpe, *America's Agenda: Rebuilding Economic Strength* (Armonk, N.Y.: Cuomo's Commission on Competitiveness, November 1992), chart 1.1.

7. Under most conditions, current revenues should finance the Past Budget as well as the Present Budget. Payments to acquit the government's obligations to savings and loan depositors, however, simply restore already existing balances and can also be financed by borrowing.

8. Stated another way, the distinction could be drawn between spending intended to promote common prosperity, often by means of providing a specific benefit, and spending designed to provide a specific benefit, often in ways that provide some common gain. The government should borrow to finance the first, but the bill for the second should be due on delivery. Military purchases are often (loosely) considered capital investments, because they *look* like other durable goods. Some military R&D has wealth-producing benefits; purchasing and maintaining most systems are forms of national consumption. These distinctions also provide a framework for resolving the debate over the budget treatment of payroll tax revenues. Current social security benefits would be part of the consumption or Present Budget, balanced by equivalent payroll tax revenues. Surplus revenues from the payroll tax should be applied to the capital or Future Budget as an investment in growth required to finance future benefits. No non-social security government operations would be financed by social security taxes. Surplus payroll tax receipts, like other government trust fund revenues, could be counted to reduce the burden of borrowing to finance public investments or to finance additional investment.

9. On a decade-by-decade basis, the average annual growth rate of federal spending exceeded the average annual growth rate of per capita incomes throughout the postwar period. Adjusting the data to exclude recessions and the year following a downturn, and the wartime buildups in the Korean and Vietnam conflicts, the 1980s are the only decade in which the average annual rate of spending growth exceeded the average annual rate of income gains in the year before. On an annual basis, the reform would have restrained growth in federal spending in 15 of the last 40 years: 1989, 1988, 1985, 1984, 1979, 1977, 1976, 1971, 1964, 1962, 1961, 1957, 1956, 1955, and 1951. These calculations are derived from data reported in *Economic Report of the President,* tables C-26 and C-27; and *Budget,* "Historical Tables," table 1.1.

10. A majority vote could be required before either house could consider legislation that would increase an appropriation or authorization faster than the rate of income growth the year before, or that with enacted legislation would breach the limit. At the end of the fiscal year, the amount of spending over the legal limit would be deducted from the spending ceiling for the following year.

11. Including interest payments, the average annual growth rate of spending

would have been 7.1% under the reform, as compared to the actual 8.8%.

12. See Robert J. Shapiro, *Paying for Progress: A Progressive Strategy for Fiscal Discipline* (Washington, D.C.: Progressive Policy Institute, Feb. 4, 1990).

13. For example, if national income increases from $5 trillion to $5.4 trillion and the population grows from 240 million to 245 million, the growth rate of national income would be 8% while per capita income would grow by 5.8%. Revenues would increase by 7 to 8% while spending increases would be limited to 5.8 percent. In addition, progressive tax rates also ensure that revenues normally increase faster than the growth rate of per capita income, as increases in income push some taxpayers into higher marginal tax brackets. Furthermore, some people's effective tax rate will rise with income even if their marginal tax bracket is unaffected, because the value of their deductions or credits does not increase. For example, a couple with a $20,000 combined income and $6,000 in deductions and exemptions would pay income tax of $2,100 (15% of $14,000), or an effective rate of 10.5%. If their income rose by 10% to $22,000, while the value of their deductions increased by 5%, they would pay income tax of $2,355 (15% of $15,700), raising their effective tax rate to 10.7%.

14. Congressional Budget Office, *Reducing the Deficit: Spending and Revenue Options,* Report to the Senate and House Committees on the Budget, (Washington, D.C., Feb. 1992).

15. Spending for health benefits in particular is projected to grow more than twice as fast as the economy. Spending on retirement programs is projected to increase at about the same rate as the economic growth, and other entitlement programs are likely to grow slowly or not at all.(See table, page 345.)

16. See table, page 345.

17. The connection between work and Medicare benefits is more tenuous. The program is financed through a tax on work income, but the receipt of Medicare benefits does not depend on having paid the tax, nor is the level of benefits related to how much work income was subject to the tax.

18. Task Force on Government Waste, *The Challenge of Sound Management,* Democratic Caucus, U.S. House of Representatives, June 1992.

19. Candidates for elimination include the American Battle Monument Commission, the Commission on the Bicentennial of the U.S. Constitution, the Franklin Delano Roosevelt Memorial Commission, the International Cultural and Trade Commission, the National Board for the Promotion of Rifle Practice, the National Critical Materials Council, the Commission for the Preservation of America's Heritage Abroad, the Technical Advisory Committee for Trade in Tobacco, the Office of Former Speakers, and the Federal Inspector of the Alaska Natural Gas Transportation System.

20. See Allen Schick, "Budgeting for Results: Recent Developments in Five

	Average Annual Rate of Increase	Rate of Increase as Share of Federal Budget	
	1993-97	**1993-97**	**Annual Average**
Health-Related	11.8%	36.6%	8.1%
Retirement	5.7	9.4	2.2
Poor Families	3.8	1.8	0.4
Middle-Class	−3.3	−23.5	−6.4
Total	7.1%	15.1%	3.6%

Key: *Health-related:* Medicaid, Medicare A, and Medicare B. *Retirement:* Social Security including disability, supplemental social insurance, railroad-workers' retirement, civil service pensions, military retirement, veterans' pensions, and veterans compensation. *Income supports for poor families:* Foster care and adoption assistance, supports for families with children (AFDC), housing assistance, food stamps, and nutrition assistance (WIC and school lunch program). *Middle-class benefits:* Farm supports, unemployment compensation, guaranteed student loans, vocational rehabilitation, and trade adjustment assistance.

Entitlement Payments as Share of Total Federal Spending

	1993	1994	1995	1996	1997
Health-Related	14.8%	16.3%	18.1%	19.5%	20.2%
Retirement	26.8	28.2	29.3	29.7	29.4
Poor Families	3.1	3.2	3.3	3.3	3.2
Middle-Class	3.1	2.9	2.7	2.3	2.4
Total	47.9%	50.6%	53.4%	54.9%	55.1%

Industrialized Countries," *Public Administration Review* (Jan/Feb 1990): 26–34; and Brian Usilaner, "Can We Expect Productivity Improvement in the Federal Government?", *Public Productivity Review* (Sept 1981): 237–46.

21. In some instances, additional, one-time expenditures will be required to upgrade software and purchase equipment.

22. See table, p. 346.

23. U.S. Office of Personnel Management, *Monthly Report of Federal Civilian Employment,* July 1992.

24. The data show that under current law, budding businesses do not attract the investment capital appropriate to their returns, because it costs investors and banks more to gather the information they need to make

	Total Workforce	Natl Gov. Workforce	Share of Workforce
United States	107,531,000	2,972,000	2.8%
United Kingdom	28,510,000	515,000	1.8%
Japan	64,050,000	893,000	1.4%
West Germany	27,560,000	311,000	1.1%

Sources: Interviews with the U.S. Dept. of Labor, Embassy of Japan, German Information Center, and U.K. Information Center.

a lending or investment decision about a new business, especially a small one, than it does for large, mature companies. In technical terms, an incentive to encourage investment in new businesses, far from distorting market decisions like most such incentives, could actually offset this market failure. See Robert Shapiro, *Bearing Fair Burdens: A Progressive Tax Agenda for Equity and Growth,* (Washington, D.C.: Progressive Policy Institute, December 1991).

25. Lawrence Goulder and Lawrence Summers, "Tax Policy, Asset Prices, and Growth: A General Equilibrium Analysis," *Journal of Public Economics,* 38:8 (April 1989).

26. Large, fixed deficits have coincided with the slowdown in the growth of personal incomes. It is reasonable to suppose that slow income growth intensified demands for income tax cuts while reinforcing the government's normal inclination to spend more.

27. Stated another way, the share of spending financed by payroll taxes grew faster than the share financed by borrowing.

28. The total federal income and payroll tax burden for a two-parent family at the national median income rose from 23.7% in 1980 to 24.1% in 1988, while the comparable tax burden for a family in the top 5% of taxpayers fell from 28.9% in 1980 to 25.7% in 1988. See Robert Shapiro, *The Tax Fairness Index,* Policy Report 6 (Washington, D.C.: Progressive Policy Institute, July 1990). The share of spending financed by direct taxes on individuals (federal income and payroll taxes), which had risen steadily from 53.5% in the 1950s to 67.5% in the 1970s, stabilized at 67.2% in the 1980s, when in the aggregate income-tax cuts offset payroll-tax increases.

29. The 36% tax bracket would apply to taxable income in excess of $120,000 for single filers, equivalent to Adjusted Gross Income of about $150,000.

30. Internal Revenue Service, *Income Tax Compliance Research: Gross Tax Gap Estimates and Projections for 1973–1992,* Pub. 7285 (Washington, D.C., March 1990), 7; and General Accounting Office, *Tax Administration: Profiles of Major Components of the Tax Gap,* Pub. GGD-90-53BR (Washington, D.C., April 1990), 19.

31. This reform should continue to protect 90% of all taxpayers—everyone

but very affluent people—by maintaining the current exemption for capital gains on assets willed to a spouse or donated to charity, and gains in a small business or farm. It also would provide general exemptions for the first $75,000 in capital gains and for up to $125,000 of the capital gains from sale of a principal residence, if this exclusion had not already been claimed.

Chapter 3

1. Economics and Statistics Administration, Bureau of Economics Analysis, Dept. of Commerce, *National Income and Product Accounts of the United States Vol. 2* (Washington, D.C., 1989), 1959–88; National Income and Wealth Division, Bureau of Economics Analysis, Dept. of Commerce, *Survey of Current Business, #7 Vol. 2* (Washington, D.C., July 1992); and Office of Productivity and Technology, Bureau of Labor Statistics, U.S. Dept. of Labor.
2. Lester Thurow, *Head to Head* (New York: William Morrow Co., 1992), 248.
3. National Science Board, Committee on Industrial Support for R&D, *The Competitive Strength of U.S. Industrial Science and Technology: Strategic Issues* (Washington, D.C., Aug. 1992), 17.
4. Thurow, *Head to Head,* 43.
5. Ibid., 165.
6. James Womack, Daniel Jones, and Daniel Roos, *The Machine That Changed the World* (New York: Harper Perennial, 1991), 262.
7. Doug Ross, "The New Work Place," *The New Democrat* (May 1992): 13.
8. David Hale, "For New Jobs, Help Small Business," *Wall Street Journal* (Aug. 10, 1992), A10.
9. Industrial Technology Institute, "The Michigan Foundation: A Study of the Modernization Process" (Ann Arbor, Mich., Nov. 1990), 9.
10. Erica Groshen and Colin Drozdowsky, "The Recent Rise in the Value of Education: Market Forces at Work," Economic Commentary Federal Reserve Bureau of Cleveland, August 15, 1992.
11. Employment and Training Administration, Department of Labor, internal report.
12. National Adult Education Professional Development Consortium (NAEPDC), *The Adult Education Program Annual Report, Program Year 1990* (Washington, D.C.: NAEPDC,1990: 30-1.
13. Office of Technology Assessment, U.S. Congress, *Worker Training: Competing in the New International Economy,* OTA-ITE-457 (Washington, D.C., September 1990), 15.
14. Lerman, "Why America Should Develop a Youth Apprenticeship System," 1.
15. Office of Technology Assessment, *Worker Training,* 236.
16. Thurow, *Head to Head,* 282.

17. National Science Board, *Competitive Strength of U.S. Industrial Science and Technology*, iii.
18. Ibid., ii.
19. Thurow, *Head to Head*, 157
20. Ibid., 45–6.
21. Leonhard Allgaier, "Focusing Technology to Create the 21st Century 'Agile' Manufacturing Enterprise," speech given at GM Tech Center, Warren, Michigan, Jan. 22, 1992.
22. National Science Board, *Competitive Strength of U.S. Industrial Science and Technology*, 3.
23. Robert B. Cohen, "The Impact of Broadband Communications on the U.S. Economy and on Competitiveness" (Economic Strategy Institute: Washington, 1992).
24. See Steven R. Rivkin and Jeremy D. Rosner, *Shortcut to the Information Superhighway: A Progressive Plan to Speed the Telecommunications Revolution* (Washington, D.C.: Progressive Policy Institute, 1992).

Chapter 4

1. See U.S. Council of Economic Advisers, *Economic Indicators, October 1992* (Washington, D.C.: U.S. Government Printing Office, 1992), 2. (Putting the figure at 22.8 percent of GDP in 1991.)
2. U.S. merchandise exports alone accounted for 25 percent of the growth in U.S. civilian jobs between 1986 and 1990. Lester A. Davis, "U.S. Jobs Supported by Merchandise Exports to Mexico," Research Series OMA-1-92 (Washington, D.C.: Office of the Chief Economist, Department of Commerce, 1992).
3. Bureau of Labor Statistics, Department of Labor, *Employment Hours and Earnings, United States 1909–1990* (Washington, D.C.: U.S. Government Printing Office, 1991); Bureau of Labor Statistics, Department of Labor, *Employment and Earnings, August 1992* (Washington, D.C.: Government Printing Office, 1992).
4. AFL-CIO Task Force on Trade, "North American Free Trade Negotiations: Prosperity for Whom?" No. 1, 1992.
5. Tools to help workers and firms adjust to competition are essential. But such tools must be employed as part of a strategy to enable Americans to regain competitiveness. For example, in order to build a more highly skilled labor force, the U.S. must provide displaced workers with job training, in addition to other transitional assistance. One reason this is especially important for U.S. workers today is that low-wage countries are able to attract global capital to invest in labor-intensive industries. As developing nations establish comparative advantages in these sectors, the U.S. must respond with measures to facilitate the reallocation of labor within our own economy. In addition, temporary trade assistance for industries will also be needed in certain instances. But protection must be explicitly transitional and linked to industry agreement to adopt

pro-competitive adjustment policies and practices. For the most part, this concept is not now incorporated in U.S. trade protection and import relief measures. One law that provides an illustration of how to begin to incorporate pro-competitive incentives is Section 201 of the Trade Act of 1974 (Section 201). Before granting trade protection under Section 201, the President needs to take into account the probable effectiveness of the assistance in promoting adjustment and the efforts being made by the industry to meet import competition without government support. Section 201 thus offers the administration some ability to foster corporate responsibility and a return to competitiveness.

6. Each of these points is discussed more fully in other chapters.

7. Free trade only expands economic growth for all parties when all parties practice it. When one country protects its industries, this action harms not only the protected nation's economy but also the interests of foreign firms and industries barred from competing freely. It is critical for governments to work together to offer real alternatives to maximize opportunities in open and expanding markets.

8. In the case of semiconductors, the Japanese began targeting the industry in the early 1970s, but no effective action was taken to address their actions until years later—and only after heavy pressure from Congress and industry. By the mid-1980s, when the Arrangement between the Government of Japan and the Government of the United States of America Concerning Trade in Semiconductor Products (Semiconductor Agreement) was reached, the U.S. market share had declined significantly. In the case of automobiles, a Voluntary Restraint Agreement (VRA) was agreed to by Japan after U.S. automakers realized that they were not cost-competitive. The VRAs, however, did not lead to meaningful U.S. industry adjustment—indeed it was the Japanese, not the American, automakers that flourished in the 1980s.

The particular situations of semiconductors and autos are quite different. Still, in both cases we should have been monitoring any changes in the competitive position of the industries, including any foreign targeting and its impact, from the beginning. Rather than waiting or relying on protection after an industry had declined, the government should have been both able and prepared, early on, to work with those affected, including producers and consumers, to advance a comprehensive competitiveness plan combining both incentives to make the industry more productive and aggressive market-opening measures, where appropriate.

9. By contrast, other advanced nations spend more than the U.S. on export financing both as a percentage of GDP and as a percentage of federal spending. Most nations also do more (sometimes far more) to support their firms abroad. See U.S. Department of Commerce, "Export Promotion Activities of Major Competitor Nations," (Washington, D.C., July 1988), p.6.

10. Americans strongly believe the U.S. should engage in the world both to compete and to advance our deeply held values. See generally, Daniel

Yankelovich, "Foreign Policy After the Election," *Foreign Affairs,* Fall 1992, 1–12.

11. An International Trade Commission study of U.S. steel quotas found that the protection preserved 17,000 jobs in the steel industry, at a cost to consumers of $22,000 per-job, while destroying 52,000 jobs on steel-using industries. Cited in "An American Trade Strategy, Options for the 1990s," Robert Z. Lawrence and Charles L. Schultze, eds. (Washington, D.C.: The Brookings Institution, 1990), 44.

12. It is true that special benefits flow from high-tech industries and that a healthy manufacturing base is essential to a nation's economic security. But the response that makes the most economic sense is to promote the productivity of critical sectors by supporting advanced education and training, research and development, and incentives for the commercialization of vital technologies, and by designing strategic policies to open up foreign as well as domestic high-technology markets.

13. The administration should not in all cases reject managed-trade or market-share agreements. But such agreements should be viewed with caution. At a minimum, any such strategy must be analyzed before it is implemented in order to judge whether it will have a net liberalizing or trade expanding effect. Often we believe a managed trade approach will not meet this test. However, in some cases, (as in dealing with the web of Japanese cultural and antitrust market-access barriers), the equivalent of an antitrust consent decree, such as we finally achieved in the semiconductor case, may be the only effective near-term solution.

14. The full range of U.S. economic leverage must be marshaled in a systematic fashion to ensure that American firms and workers succeed in all world markets, including our own. For example, our antitrust and investment policies must reflect global, not just domestic, market realities and the corresponding policies of our trading partners to ensure that we are not disadvantaging U.S. firms. Investment should be encouraged, but we should take steps to ensure that vital U.S. technology is not lost as a result. See generally, Subcouncil on Trade Policy of the Competitiveness Policy Council, "Summary of September 28, 1992 Meeting," (Washington, D.C.). We also must ensure adequate tax payments by foreign firms' subsidiaries in the U.S.

15. Anti-dumping cases provide at most second-best relief, since the alleged harm has already occurred by the time suit is brought. Moreover, anti-dumping relief is itself often anti-competitive. For both reasons, the explosion of anti-dumping cases must be controlled. The preferable alternative, as advocated in this chapter, is to root out the causes of predatory dumping—including systematic action to make markets more open, and multilateral collaboration on such matters as anti-trust policy. In the meantime, the U.S. should not unilaterally "disarm" itself of this or other trade tools.

16. "High Information Content Flat Panel Displays and Display Glass Thereof from Japan" (56 Fed Reg 43741), a 1991 case involving imports from Japan of certain display screens used in laptop computers.

17. The government should have assembled all key players early on (including the computer industry, the aviation industry, and the semiconductor industry), and devised an appropriate strategy to reinvigorate the U.S. industry (in the event it was determined that our foreign dependence was far too high for our economic security), or otherwise helped the industry to adjust.

18. The U.S. should not, however, perceive itself to be at war. As discussed above, an open, expanding global economy can benefit competitive workers and firms from all nations. Thorough preparation by all nations to meet the challenge of open markets can, in fact, help to prevent the type of protectionist backlash that causes trade wars.

19. Section 301 of the Trade Act of 1974, as amended, offers a framework for enforcing U.S. rights under bilateral and multilateral trade agreements, as well as for responding to "unreasonable," "unjustifiable," or "discriminatory" foreign government policies and practices that burden or restrict U.S. commerce. Section 301 may be used, for example, as a basis for negotiations (and sanctions) to address barriers to U.S. services, investment, or intellectual property exports not currently covered by international free-trade rules. Section 301 investigations may be initiated in response to a petition from industry, or may be self-initiated by the U.S. trade representative, who reports to the President.

20. In pursuing strategies to advance our competitive position, we believe that corporate nationality continues to matter. In general, companies tend to create more jobs, invest more, perform more R&D, concentrate top management and decision-making, and generally add more value in their own countries. But it makes no sense to ignore foreign-based companies in our commercial diplomacy—and certainly we must not consider them "the enemy." All other things being equal, if a Honda manufactured in Ohio is being kept out of the E.C. market, the U.S. should respond as it would if Ford encountered the same market barrier.

21. Critics frequently refer to the GATT as the "General Agreement to Talk and Talk."

22. Once Congress votes to give an administration "fast-track" authority, the President is able to submit a resulting international agreement for congressional approval subject only to a yes or no vote on the entire package, with no amendments to the text of the agreement permitted. Congress created the fast-track process as part of the Trade Act of 1974. Fast track was reauthorized in 1988 and 1991 (for two years).

23. As discussed in part in footnotes 24 to 27, there is a minimal "baseline" liberalization that must be secured by the new rules in key areas.

24. Participating countries are close to a fairly solid framework on service industries' liberalization, but there has been inadequate progress on the commercially essential "market-access" issues—specific commitments by each country to liberalize specific service sectors, such as telecommunications, transportation, financial services, and professional services. In addition, any deal should provide a framework for further liberalization

of services-market access, and should not preclude bilateral negotiations and action to liberalize beyond the GATT's multilateral rules.

25. The long phase-in time currently contemplated for protecting intellectual property rights should not be accepted unless the U.S. can take other action in the interim to protect rights and open markets.

26. We should achieve some immediate reductions in textile supports, as well as a framework for future contraction in this industry. It is likely that the U.S. and the E.C. will need to make commitments on these issues in order to attract acceptable market-access commitments from developing countries in other areas that are most important to developed nations, such as services and intellectual property.

27. Agriculture has received disproportionate time and attention in the Uruguay Round. At this writing, the offer by the E.C. is inadequate, and asks us to pay for crop subsidy and other domestic support reductions that the E.C. will be forced to make on its own to remain globally competitive. We should be willing to accept an agreement that lowers allowable E.C. and U.S. subsidies to comparable levels—without further concessions from the U.S. in any sector in connection with that agreement. We should specifically provide for further progress towards free markets in the future.

28. In fact, a strategic approach would call for even earlier and more aggressive diplomatic steps to put an end to French intransigence.

29. For example, as discussed below, poor labor or environmental standards can be thought of as a subsidy to industries. Industries can operate in countries with lower standards at an artificial cost advantage.

30. The United States, Japan, Canada, Great Britain, Germany, France, and Italy.

31. Linkage between trade and the promotion of noneconomic goals will be discussed below. In the case of the environment, we soon need to adopt new multilateral rules to protect legitimate environmental measures from reversal by trade tribunals. For example, an environmental standard or restriction should be upheld if it substantially advances environmental goals and is applied on a nondiscriminatory basis. Common environmental standards and GATT law changes are needed to address the types of issues raised, for example, in the tuna-dolphin case where the GATT would not allow the U.S. to restrict imports of tuna—a product—because of the way it was killed—a process—by nationals of another country. (The GATT has held that a country can't use trade measures to protect the environment beyond its borders. Moreover, the GATT requires equal treatment of products regardless of how they were produced.) The GATT should be amended to allow for action to prevent harmful "processes" instead of just products, and the broadest possible common environmental rules and standards must be developed so that as many nations as possible share a common notion of environmental harm. Both a GATT working party and the OECD have been examining trade and environment linkages. But there are no comprehensive proposals on the table in the Round to further incorporate environmen-

tal considerations into the GATT. The Round must at least provide a framework for incorporating necessary amendments on an accelerated timetable.

32. U.S. firms are currently placed at a disadvantage in many markets where corruption is widespread because other countries do not impose legal obligations on the operations of their firms abroad, whereas U.S. firms operate under the restrictions of the Foreign Corrupt Practices Act of 1977. We should seek common standards that would be enforced not only by each nation's own laws, but also by multilateral lending institutions. More uniform laws will not only be fairer to U.S. firms, but will have greater impact in changing corrupt regimes abroad.

33. The U.S., the E.C., and Japan together are responsible for almost two-thirds of the world's output. See International Monetary Fund, *World Economic Outlook, October 1992* (Washington, D.C.: International Monetary Fund, 1992), 86. Their leadership is necessary to the success of initiatives to develop a more stable monetary system and avoid huge trade imbalances.

34. Here as elsewhere, the U.S. should reject action that does not have a net liberalizing effect, and we should make it clear that we are willing to forego aggressive unilateral or bilateral action in exchange for rapid and substantial liberalization through the GATT process.

35. The administration should not seek to convince other countries to set up trade and economic systems that are identical to ours. But at a minimum, policies with regard to competition, investment, and the subsidization of new technologies need to be better aligned. As Alan Wm. Wolff has written, Japan needs to become "a better consumer of the world's goods," and the U.S. and the E.C. need to become "world-class producers of more classes of goods." "Improving United States Trade Policy," *Conflict Among Nations: Trade Policies in the 1990s,* Thomas R. Howell, Alan Wm. Wolff, Brent L. Bartlett, and R. Michael Gadbaw, eds. (Boulder, Colorado: Westview Press, 1992), 596.

36. We must work, in fact, with all trading partners in this context. It is not possible in this chapter specifically to discuss policies toward all key trading partners. But action to promote growth and expand opportunities, using the tools of the new commercial diplomacy in a range of markets, will be important. For example, we need to aggressively engage the newly industrialized countries and the less-developed countries in support of strong multilateral and bilateral rules in services, such as telecommunications, and in intellectual property. We must make it clear that the U.S. will insist on market openness in these areas that is comparable to what the U.S. offers, and that the consequences of failure to achieve this will be offsetting retaliation.

37. The E.C. procurement directive (the "Utilities directive") imposes new local content requirements on third-country suppliers that are harmful to both telecommunications and power-generation suppliers from the U.S. The restrictions are enforced by a 50 percent price preference and embargo authority.

38. The E.C. "broadcast directive" imposes local content requirements on films broadcast in E.C. countries, thereby undercutting the growth potential of one of our most competitive industries.

39. If implemented appropriately, this harmonization process, known as the Single European Market Program, should be good for U.S. commerce on balance, and should generally be pro-competitive, with ambitious deregulatory reforms in such sectors as energy and financial services.

40. See, for example, "Dissecting Airbus," in *The Economist,* Feb. 16, 1991, p. 51.

41. The civilian aircraft industry in the U.S. is a very strong one. The U.S. continues to run a large trade surplus and to employ many Americans in this sector. But E.C. subsidies had—and may still—put at risk high-wage, high-skill U.S. jobs in this important manufacturing sector. Both the E.C. and Japan are committed to being big players in this sector worldwide.

42. We should allow several years, both because we have made good-faith progress, and because any sanctions should be taken with enough lead time that the U.S. industry can adjust to any likely fallout. Moreover, U.S. industry is not anxious to have the government take steps that would unnecessarily provoke trade friction. Hasty action or unwillingness to see how the current agreement can help is not called for. However, to say the least, it must not be taken off our high-priority agenda.

43. The trade deficit was $43 billion in 1991. U.S. Council of Economic Advisers, *Economic Report of the President, 1992* (Washington, D.C., 1992), 415. Note that both the size and the composition of this deficit matter.

44. Alan Wolff and Thomas Howell have stressed the reluctance of Japanese leaders in the past to "set an agenda for Japan's participation in the world trading system commensurate with the country's economic size and strength, or even to control the domestic forces that increasingly spill over into the international arena," in "Japan," *Conflict Among Nations: Trade Policy in the 1990s,"* 47. In their July 1992 Aspen Institute Paper, "America and Japan: The Key Differences and What to Do About Them," Fred Bergsten and Paula Stern describe Japan as the classic free rider, "defended by someone else and benefiting enormously from an economic order created and nurtured by someone else." This tradition must be overcome.

45. Dumping involves selling products abroad at less than their "fair value," e.g., their cost at home. The Japanese have extensively engaged in long-term efforts—using a combination of economic tools—to preserve market share at home across many sectors and sell products abroad at less than their cost at home. The fact that Japan has enjoyed the advantages of far more open access to the U.S. market, while restricting its own market, has helped it to accumulate surplus revenue and economies of scale for cost reduction, and to engage in adversarial trade tactics such as predatory pricing over long periods.

46. U.S. high technology and other firms are generally disadvantaged in

both Japan and the U.S. because of Japan's relatively weaker antitrust measures, and its failure to implement completely or properly measures aimed at collusive business practices. Access for U.S. firms to the Japanese market continues to be impeded by cartels and cartel-like practices. For this and other structural reasons, even most of our companies that are relatively successful in the Japanese market have limited themselves to growing with that market, and finding partners and clients among less high-powered Japanese firms.

47. The U.S. should urge Japan to develop a procurement system that is more open and comprehensible to outsiders, and that features an improved dispute settlement system. In short, U.S. companies seek a binding bid-protest system, more open tendering, and increased transparency.

48. Japanese laws and practices, including the elaborate stock cross-holdings of Japanese corporate groups, make it difficult for U.S. firms to acquire Japanese companies. See Robert Z. Lawrence, "Why Is Foreign Direct Investment in Japan So Low?" (unpublished).

49. See, for example, Yoichi Funabashi, "Japan and America: Global Partners," in *Foreign Policy,* (Spring 1992): 24–39. Funabashi writes that "Japan and the U.S. must work together to consistently facilitate political and economic reform." In fact, he argues that the U.S. and Japan must go beyond economic cooperation to coordinate such matters as employment policy, education- and occupational-training policy, and policies on overseas assistance. Moreover, the President of the keidanren was recently quoted as saying "the time has come to reduce or eliminate factions between the different capitalisms." An advisory group to Prime Minister Miyazawa sounded a similar theme in reporting that Japan must adjust to the international standard by changing the keidanren system, the cross-ownership of corporate shares and the practice of grabbing global market shares at all costs. "Japan Gets a Hard Look from Within," *The Washington Post,* Oct. 18, 1992, H8.

50. Another means to get results is to link Japan's removal of structural trade barriers to our own efforts to reduce the budget deficit—a matter that is of concern to the Japanese as part of mutual efforts toward economic convergence. Both are likely long-term challenges. There is precedent for such linkage: The U.S. undertook to address certain of our own economic problems in the Strategic Impediments Initiative (such as the high cost of capital, problems with tax and capital structures, and low American savings rates), although the Bush administration did not consider itself under a real obligation to act as a result.

51. A regional approach to trade liberalization is appropriate where it creates more trade than it diverts and where it leads to global free trade faster than the multilateral process. Where trade flows between parties are relatively large, where tariffs are high before a deal is cut, and where tariff and other walls to keep out third parties are minimized, trade can be expanded. The NAFTA does fairly well on these points. Trade flows are very substantial between the parties (for example, more than 80

percent of Mexico's exports go the U.S.), Mexican tariffs are high, and protectionist rules have in many (although not all) cases been minimized. Regional trade arrangements such as the E.C.'s common agricultural policy must be avoided, however. The types of subsidies and degree of protection involved are trade diversionary and highly restrictive. They violate even current GATT rules and guidelines.

52. Not on all points, however, as our trading partners are quick to argue. In certain sectors, such as autos and textiles, fairly strict local content rules are objectionable to non-parties because they seek to, and do, limit access to the NAFTA market. The U.S. frequently opposes local content rules when they arise, for example, in E.C. '92 directives.

53. For example, the NAFTA requires that international obligations concerning endangered species, hazardous waste, and ozone be respected. This is the first major international trade agreement to include such provisions. To the extent the agreement raises living standards in Mexico and the border area, it is also likely that environmental protection will improve, especially if plans for improved joint enforcement efforts are carried out in the U.S.–Mexican border area.

54. Improved enforcement of Mexican environmental laws would have positive trade effects as well. U.S. environmental technology and services firms have encountered barriers over the years as they try to bring their services to Mexico. For example, major U.S. waste management firms have had a limited Mexican market for hazardous waste treatment and disposal services because both federal and state officials in Mexico often have not enforced existing laws. Rather than hiring these U.S. firms, Mexican consumers have a cheaper—and in many cases, "free"—alternative: disposing of their wastes in unregulated open dumps.

55. In return for a more activist government role in opening foreign markets and promoting U.S. exports, corporate America must be asked to undertake increased responsibility for its behavior in foreign markets. Some U.S. programs are already beginning to move in this direction, albeit inconsistently and often unilaterally. The Overseas Private Investment Corporation (OPIC), for example, only operates in countries that have taken or are taking steps to adopt and implement laws that are consistent with internationally recognized workers' rights. Moreover, OPIC contract language—developed in consultation with Congress and U.S. labor organizations—conditions assistance on a U.S. firm's observance of certain worker rights and host country labor laws. OPIC also does not support investment in projects that would pose "unreasonable" or "major" environmental, health, or safety hazards, or result in "significant" environmental degradation of natural resources. These standards should be strengthened, applied to other trade programs, and coordinated with our trading partners and with multilateral lending institutions.

56. See, for example, Jessica Tuchman Mathews, "It's Not 'Jobs vs. the Earth,'" *The Washington Post* (April 26, 1992), C7.

57. See, for example, discussion by Jeffrey C. Smith in "Clean Air Regulatory Delay Hurts Economy," *Technology News* (Summer 1992): 2.

58. Companies involved complain that we have created a broader range of restrictions on these types of items than were eliminated in the widely supported process of streamlining traditional export controls.

59. See generally, National Academy of Sciences, *Finding Common Ground: U.S. Export Controls in a Changed Global Environment* (Washington, D.C.: National Academy Press, 1991).

60. It can of course be said that the long-term opportunities in Eastern Europe are actually quite significant. Moreover, in Latin America, arguments for expanded trade are buttressed by the economic reality that consumers in these countries buy disproportionately from the U.S. Indeed our fastest growing export markets are now in the developing world. But the importance of these markets for the U.S. is small in the near term compared with many in Asia and Western Europe.

61. At present, there are at least ten federal agencies involved in export promotion, and agricultural exports get the majority of moneys. In 1991, 74 percent of the outlays for export promotion and 45 percent of the outlays for loans and guarantees went to the Department of Agriculture, although only about 10 percent of our exports are agricultural goods. See Allan I. Mendelowitz, testimony before the subcommittee on foreign affairs, House of Representatives, "Export Promotion: Federal Approach Is Fragmented," Aug. 10, 1992.

62. The establishment of a new department will require statutory changes. Pending formal reorganization, we recommend that one person be named to head USTR and Commerce. See parallel suggestion by the Trade Policy Subcouncil of the Competitiveness Policy Council, in their October 26, 1992 memorandum, "Specific Recommendations of the Trade Policy Subcouncil (TPS) from Discussion at the June 10 and September 25 Meetings."

63. Many overlapping trade functions of other departments and agencies should also be subsumed in the new department.

64. Following-up on agreements that we negotiate to ensure that their terms are complied with and that they lead to market success for competitive U.S. firms is absolutely critical. Too often in the past, the government has considered its work done once the ink is dry and the cameras stop flashing on the deal.

65. The importance of export promotion must not be underestimated by the new administration. Only 12 percent of small firms (less than 500 employees) export. U.S. Census Bureau, Department of Commerce, *Company Summary: 1987 Enterprise Statistics ES87-3* (Washington, D.C.: Dept. of Commerce, 1987).

66. The establishment of the Trade Policy Coordinating Committee (TPCC) is a good first step towards better coordination. See H.R. 5739, "Export Enhancement Act of 1992," Oct. 1992.

67. Assistance should be focused on firms that will help themselves—those that can demonstrate management maturity and that have resources to

make a financial commitment. Financing for U.S. firms will also be needed in certain cases to offset foreign subsidies. However, the administration should seek to negotiate such support down on a multilateral basis.

68. For the most part, firms' needs are too varied for large-scale national programs alone to be effective. See generally, William Nothdurft, *Going Global: How Europe Helps Small Firms Export,* (Washington, D.C.: Brookings Institution, 1992). We endorse programs to improve the regional delivery of export financing services in the U.S., as well as efforts to increase the involvement of commercial banks in financing assistance to first-time exporters. States, in fact, are already heavily involved in export promotion: Forty-four states have offices abroad (in a total of 22 countries), and 27 states have export-financing programs. Coordination between federal and state efforts has been inadequate, however, and should be improved in the new department.

69. As part of this effort, the staff at U.S. embassies must give far greater attention to the needs of U.S. firms in their representative countries. The ambassador and his or her staff must understand that the new commercial diplomacy has gained equal status with traditional diplomacy. To this end, the Secretary of State must undertake immediate institutional reforms to ensure that economic concerns are given equal weight with geopolitical concerns at the State Department, at home and on the ground.

70. Some progress has been made recently in this direction. For example, organized labor is now represented on OPIC's Board of Directors. The trade agencies also have some private sector advisory boards (although they have been criticized by some as window dressing). Much more can be done, however, to forge a partnership with business, labor, and environmental groups.

Chapter 5

1. U.S. Dept. of Commerce, *U.S. Industrial Outlook 1992* (Washington, D.C., 1992), 43-1; Executive Office of the President, *Budget of the U.S. Government FY 1993* (Washington, D.C., 1992); U.S. Dept. of Education, National Center for Education Statistics, *Digest of Education Statistics* (Washington, D.C., 1992); and U.S. Department of Justice, "Justice Expenditures and Employment, 1990," *Bureau of Justice Statistics Bulletin* (Washington, D.C., 1992).

2. *Budget of the U.S. Government, FY 1993,* 17; U.S. Dept. of Health and Human Services, Public Health Service, *Health United States 1991* (Washington, D.C., 1992), 271.

3. U.S. Dept. of Commerce, *U.S. Industrial Outlook 1992,* 43–53.

4. Robert J. Blendon et al., "Satisfaction with Health Systems in Ten Nations," *Health Affairs* (Summer 1990).

5. U.S. House of Representatives, Committee on Ways and Means, *Over-*

view of Entitlement Programs: Background Materials and Data on Programs within the Jurisdiction of the Committee on Ways and Means (1992 "Green Book") (Washington, D.C., 1992), 323; and U.S. Bureau of the Census, "Money Income of Households, Families, and Persons in the United States: 1991," P-60, No. 180.

6. The administration's proposal included tax credits and deductions to help low- and middle-income households pay for insurance, state development of insurance packages affordable to those using such credits and deductions, insurance reforms to make coverage more affordable and available to small firms with protections to ensure issuance and renewability, and emphasis on "coordinated" (i.e., managed) care, malpractice reform, and some changes in Medicare and Medicaid. Executive Office of the President, "The President's Comprehensive Health Reform Program" (Feb. 6, 1992).

7. Alain C. Enthoven, "Commentary: Measuring the Candidates on Health Care," *New England Journal of Medicine* (Sept. 10, 1992): 808.

8. Examples of proposals that envision public price setting at the federal and/or state level include H.R. 5502, "The Health Care Cost Containment and Reform Act of 1992," sponsored by Rep. Pete Stark (D-CA); H.R.3205, "The Health Insurance Coverage and Cost Containment Act of 1991," introduced by Rep. Dan Rostenkowski (D-IL); and S. 1227, "HealthAmerica: Affordable Health Care for All Americans Act," co-sponsored by Sen. George Mitchell (D-ME). See also National Leadership Coalition for Health Care Reform, "Excellent Health Care for All Americans at a Reasonable Cost" (Washington, D.C., 1991).

9. They include disparities of information (for example, between doctors and patients, which can result in physician-induced demand), adverse risk selection (the tendency of sicker people to buy more insurance), moral hazard (the tendency of insured persons to neglect prevention), the paucity of providers in rural and certain other areas, and the difficulty for individuals to collect and analyze information about competing health care options.

10. Managed competition and managed care, though often confused, are different ideas. Managed care refers to health care delivery systems that take steps to coordinate and oversee patients' use of care. Managed competition, in contrast, refers to the process of establishing a well-constructed market in which consumers can choose among competing health plans. While many proponents of managed competition believe that managed care systems would do well under such a system, the competition also could be open to other delivery systems, such as unmanaged fee-for-service systems.

11. The Progressive Plan owes an intellectual debt to several other proposals that cover a broad ideological spectrum. In particular, it draws on many of the managed competition ideas developed by Alain Enthoven, Paul Ellwood, and other members of their "Jackson Hole Group"; see: Paul Ellwood, Alain C. Enthoven, and Lynn Etheredge, "The 21st Century American Health System: A Proposal for Reform," 1991. It also draws

on proposals by California Insurance Commissioner John Garamendi, Sen. Bob Kerrey, and the Heritage Foundation. The Garamendi plan combines a single-payer system of state financing with managed competition among private health plans. While the plan places some controls on premiums, it primarily relies on market signals rather than public price setting. See California Dept. of Insurance, "California Health Care in the 21st Century: A Vision for Reform" (Feb., 1992). Senator Kerrey's "Health USA Act of 1991" also proposes a single-payer structure with competing health plans (although it calls for public price setting) and emphasizes state administration and innovation. The Heritage Foundation plan replaces the current tax exclusion for health benefits with a tax credit and relies on individuals to purchase insurance directly from insurers. While it lacks many of the structures necessary to create well-managed competition, it focuses attention on the importance of choice for consumers and the regressive nature of the current tax treatment of health benefits. See Stuart Butler, "A Tax Reform Strategy to Deal with the Uninsured," *New England Journal of Medicine* (May 15, 1991).

The Progressive Plan differs from these proposals in key ways. First, unlike all of them, it specifically envisions varying reforms and financing mechanisms among the states. Second, unlike the Jackson Hole Group and Garamendi plans, it calls for full taxation of all employer contributions toward health benefits and creation of a new federal tax credit. Third, unlike the Heritage Foundation's proposal, the Plan calls for purchase of most health insurance through group purchasing cooperatives, definition and encouragement of accountable health plans, a fixed-amount tax credit, and substantial regulation of insurance toward community rating.

12. Justification of universal coverage on grounds of efficiency also avoids the excessive political assertion that health care should be "a right and not a privilege." This phrase makes for good campaign rhetoric but bad policy. The implication that individuals have a positive right to some level of health care dilutes the traditional liberal notion of rights as relatively absolute protections *against* government power. This new right, if accepted on its face, would also remove many of the key questions about health care policy from the political arena, where they belong, and entrust them to the judiciary. For example, would the new right enable individuals to sue the government to establish clinics in underserved regions? Would it give groups standing to block Congress from changing the nationally standardized benefits package? Questions about how to balance social equities and structure efficient markets are both properly matters for political, not judicial, resolution.

13. The standardized package would define both the medical procedures covered and the financial parameters, such as deductibles, co-payments, and annual caps on out-of-pocket costs, and would preempt all state laws. Any plan competing for consumers' tax-advantaged dollars would have to offer this package. A standardized benefits package is necessary

to facilitate comparison shopping by consumers and to stop insurers from "cherry picking" less costly customers. See Alain C. Enthoven, "Multiple Choice Health Insurance: The Lessons and Challenges to Employers," *Inquiry* (Winter 1990): 372. Consumers would be able to purchase additional health services and benefits through supplemental insurance or direct purchase, but these purchases would not be tax favored.

14. Large firms might still be permitted to offer their employees health benefits without compromising the system's overall effectiveness (although, in order to preserve the deductibility of their health benefit costs, such firms would have to offer a choice between accountable plans). Apart from this exception, consumers could not obtain their basic coverage outside of HIPCs and still receive the new health tax credit. States would be permitted to adopt somewhat different models of HIPCs, within federal guidelines. Differences might relate to: HIPCs' governance rules; their use of "risk adjusters" and reinsurance among accountable plans; and the scope of each HIPC's coverage. For example, a small or rural state might have one HIPC for the entire state; a more populous state might create several HIPCs, each with exclusive coverage of a region; another state might create multiple HIPCs within each region, with each HIPC covering different segments of the population.

15. This preemption operates through the federal Employee Retirement Income Security Act (ERISA).

16. Individuals who wish to purchase their basic insurance from nonaccountable plans could do so, but they would receive no tax credit against the purchase and they would still be subject to whatever funding provisions their states had enacted to finance their new systems. They would thus pay substantially more for the privilege. Firms providing such coverage, as well as supplemental coverage, could directly contact individuals as part of their marketing.

17. The exact amount of the credit would depend on the amount of federal revenue made available by ending the current excludability of health benefits, but the principle would be to return that full amount through the new federal tax credit. The structure of the credit is a political question, but it should be higher for bigger households and should increase substantially for those in and near poverty.

18. This provision is essential to achieve universal coverage and to ensure that people who expect few health costs do not "free ride" by going without health insurance. Additional measures could be used to achieve universal coverage, such as requiring employers to verify that new employees have coverage. Even with such steps, some people still might not obtain insurance. Arrangements for such individuals could be handled in various ways. They could be randomly assigned to local health plans when they presented themselves for treatment (such as at emergency rooms). Or the state could competitively bid a contract with a fallback insurer—a plan that would take all such persons for a given year; this idea is proposed in Mark V. Pauly et al., *Responsible National Health*

Insurance (Washington, D.C.: AEI Press, 1992), 14. To the extent they were not poor, individuals assigned under such provisions would be assessed for the cost of their coverage.

19. The exact extent to which premiums could be pegged to actuarial factors, such as household size, age, and sex, is largely a political decision and need not be addressed here.

20. Under any of these approaches, employees would be taxed on any contributions their employer makes toward their health benefits, whether to a specific HIPC, as under the Jackson Hole Group model, or to a statewide financing pool, as under the Garamendi proposal. In states that pursue a tax-credit approach, as under the Heritage Foundation's proposal, there would be a one-year period during which businesses would be required to convert their previous spending on health benefits into wages on an equitable, "maintenance of effort" manner. These wages would become taxable income, but in return most employees would get the new federal health care tax credit. All states would be required in various ways to rationalize funding burdens among employers.

   Several provisions of this Progressive Plan, such as the standardized benefits plan, should prevent this state-based approach from being onerous for multistate employers. Those multistate employers who believe they would prefer the consistency of one national system should weigh the disadvantages of centralization and uniformity and should recognize that for many other policy areas, from taxation to worker safety and health rules, multistate employers face different obligations from state to state.

21. In many rural states, whose population is too small to support competing health plans, the reform could be quite different from the general model described here; for example, it might involve competitive bidding of contracts for the entire population of a state or region for a single health plan. A variety of other adaptations will be needed for rural, inner-city, and certain other areas.

22. The relative lack of such data today is further evidence of U.S. cost unconsciousness when it comes to health care. Each year, the U.S. Dept. of Health and Human Services publishes a massive volume of statistical tables entitled *Health United States,* which purports to present "statistics concerning recent trends in the health care sector." Yet the official data on state-by-state expenditures for personal health care and hospital care are available only for scattered years—and stop at 1982. As a result, the U.S. government has reliable current figures on per capita health spending in New Zealand, for example, but not New Mexico. More recent state-by-state figures have had to be estimated by private consultants, for example, by Lewin/ICF in *Health Spending: The Growing Threat to the Family Budget* (Washington, D.C. Families USA, 1991).

23. Congressional Research Service, *The Federal Employee Health Benefits Program* (Washington, D.C., 1989), 255.

24. In 1985, the state changed the formula for its contribution to each

premium. Before that year, its contribution for an employee was equal to 100% of a large fee-for-service plan; it was then changed to 100% of the *lowest-priced plan*. This latter approach, which enables enrollees to benefit from choosing a cheaper plan and gives plans more incentive to lower prices, is basically the same approach used in the Progressive Plan, the Jackson Hole Group's approach, and the Garamendi plan. These changes and other aspects of the Minnesota experience are described in the appendix to Bryan Dowd et al., "Issues Regarding Health Plan Payments Under Medicare and Recommendations for Reform," *Milbank Quarterly* 70 (1992). "Average premiums" in this context equals total premiums paid (both the state's and the employee's portion) per contract (the state counts one contract for each employee and one contract for each of the employee's dependents, regardless of number). The 1993 figure is based on premiums negotiated for the coming year but the contract count for 1992. All figures exclude employees of the University of Minnesota, which accounts for less than a quarter of the total. Figures are from unpublished data, courtesy of John Klein, Minnesota Dept. of Employee Relations, Employee Insurance Division, October, 1992.

25. CALPERS's contribution to an employee's plan previously equaled 100% of the average of the four largest plans in the system, a formula that diminished incentives for enrollees to choose cheaper plans or for plans to offer lower rates. This formula was eliminated in 1991 and subsequently has been frozen at a fixed dollar amount for three years— an amount that is approaching the lowest cost plan in the system. The fact that this change would tend to make consumers more price sensitive was actively used in CALPERS's most recent negotiations with plans over rates (phone interview with Tom Fisher, chief, CALPERS Health Plan Administration Division, Oct. 13, 1992) and is seen as one reason for the dramatic fall in premium increases. Data on premium increases apply to basic coverage and exclude premiums for supplemental coverage, and are from California Public Employees' Retirement System, "Subject: Contract Renewal Summary for 1992/93 Contract Year," unpublished memorandum (February 10, 1992), courtesy of Alain Enthoven.

26. Certain aspects of these plans limit their ability to spur price-conscious consumption or reward high-value plans. First, none of them has an optimal system for providing participants with information on the financial and clinical performance of their plans. Second, all of them suffer from the skewed incentives created by the federal tax code's exemption for employer-provided health benefits. Third, each has faced problems with the way the competition has been managed. For example, benefit plans are not standardized. FEHBP, in particular, has suffered from risk segmentation among its plans because some insurers were allowed to offer "high-option" and "low-option" benefit plans. See Congressional Research Service, *The Federal Employees Health Benefits Program: Possible Strategies for Reform"* (Washington, D.C., 1989).

27. This choice was previewed in this year's efforts by the House leadership to craft a health care reform bill that would attract a majority of members. That effort foundered on disagreements between members who support a system of national price controls and those who support managed competition.

28. Price controls are notoriously subject to the law of unintended consequences, and one of the most telling examples involves health care policy. The wage and price controls enacted during World War II barred firms from increasing wages but not from increasing health benefits. Many firms thus met employee demands for higher compensation by expanding their health benefits, and this expansion is one reason for our employer-based system of health insurance. See Paul Starr, *The Social Transformation of American Medicine* (New York: Basic Books, 1982), 311. Price controls in health care are especially susceptible to the law of unintended consequences because, to be effective, they must address both the price and volume of services rendered, and prevent efforts to shift diagnosis, treatment, or billing from one loosely defined category to another.

29. Indeed, other nations with public price setting and national health budgets, such as Great Britain and the Netherlands, now find themselves trying to build more competition into their systems, in part to make their systems more responsive to considerations of value.

30. Of the six major states with mandatory hospital rate-setting programs during the 1980s, only Maryland and Massachusetts experienced growth rates in per capita hospital revenues below the national average. Per capita revenues from 1979 to 1989 grew by 237% in Maryland, 244% in Massachusetts, 257% in New York, 272% in Washington, 283% in Connecticut, and 284% in New Jersey, compared to a national average of 255% for this period. This information is based on data generated by Lewin/ICF for the Federation of American Hospital Systems, "Analysis of Hospital Expenditures and Revenues, 1979–1989," (April 1991, with calculations courtesy of Richard Smith, Washington Business Group on Health.) Similarly, state efforts to control capital expenditures (for example, through certificate-of-need programs) have not generally been viewed as successful. Finally, no evidence exists that states could succeed at regulating the full range of health costs—both physician and hospital costs, both public and private spending—as no state has ever attempted such an undertaking.

31. An analysis by Lewin/ICF estimates total cost shifting onto firms (including cost shifting caused by Medicare, Medicaid, and uncompensated care) to equal $17.2 billion in 1991. See Donald Moran and John Shiels, *Report on Employer Cost-Shifting Expenditures* (Washington, D.C.: National Association of Manufacturers, 1991).

32. For example, potential savings from the freeze on Medicare physician fees from 1984 to 1986 were offset substantially in part because physicians might well have compensated for the freeze by increasing the number of visits and procedures performed. See Janet B. Mitchell et al.,

"The Medicare Physician Freeze: What Really Happened?" *Health Affairs* (Spring 1989): 22. This relationship between price and volume was the reason for the creation of "volume performance standards," which essentially compensate for any increases in the volume of Medicare services delivered by further reducing Medicare physician rates.

33. The problem here is that efficient health care—good results at the least long-term cost—may result from services that cost more per unit in the short term. Honeywell, Inc., performed an experiment with Mayo Clinic and found that it would have saved 30% on its health bill if all its Minneapolis employees had been treated there—even though the price per procedure at the clinic is higher than at most of the region's hospitals and clinics. See Jack Meyer, Sean Sullivan, and Sharon Silow-Carroll, *Private Sector Initiatives: Controlling Health Care Costs* (Washington, D.C.: Healthcare Leadership Council, 1991).

34. Address by HCFA Administrator Gail Wilensky before the American Group Practice Association, April 6, 1990, 13, as cited in Robert E. Moffit, "Comparable Worth for Doctors: A Severe Case of Government Malpractice" (Washington, D.C., The Heritage Foundation, 1991), 15.

35. Thomas Rice and Jill Bernstein, "Volume Performance Standards: Can They Control Growth in Medicare Services?" *Milbank Quarterly* 68 (1990): 299.

36. Based on 8,743,367 covered lives for FEHBP in FY 1991 and 33,036,000 covered lives for Medicare for FY 1991. Unless otherwise specified, figures on Medicare are from 1992 Green Book, those on FEHBP from unpublished data, U.S. Office of Personnel Management, Oct. 1992.

37. HCFA employs 2,944 federal "full time equivalent" (FTE) workers to administer Medicare. One hundred forty-four FTEs at the U.S. Office of Personnel Management administer the FEHBP. These figures do not include the public employees in each system who enroll new recipients and provide them with literature on the program. For example, the Social Security Administration devotes an additional 3,074 FTEs to enrollment and other functions related to Medicare and some number of federal personnel management employees in the various federal agencies whose work includes enrolling new participants in FEHBP. Data on Medicare from an unpublished letter from U.S. Dept. of Health and Human Services, Division of Budget (Oct. 23, 1992); data on FEHBP from unpublished data, Office of Personnel Management (Oct. 1992).

38. These figures refer specifically to pages on each program in the U.S. Code of Federal Regulations and a variety of regulatory issuances for each program. There are 1,050 pages in the U.S. Code on Medicare, compared to 26 pages on the FEHBP. There are 1,156 pages on Medicare in the Code of Federal Regulations, and 83 pages on the FEHBP. With regard to other regulatory issuances, the figure in the bar graph refers only to the 19,150 pages of "HCFA Manuals" and approximately 1,000 pages of "HCFA Rulings." It excludes additional regulatory materials that pertain to Medicare, including "Provider Reimbursement Review Board Hearing Decisions" and "HCFA Administrator Deci-

sions" (approximately 2,000 pages). For the FEHBP, the additional regulatory issuance consists of 93 pages in the Federal Personnel Manual. Figures on pages of regulatory materials governing Medicare are from a search by Information Handling Systems, Englewood, Colorado, Oct. 1992. Figures on pages of materials governing FEHBP are from unpublished data compiled by the U.S. Office of Personnel Management, Oct. 1992.

39. Paul B. Ginsburg and Kenneth E. Thorpe, "Can All-Payer Rate Setting and the Competitive Strategy Coexist?" *Health Affairs* (Summer 1992): 73.

40. For example, "Universal Insurance for American Health Care: A Proposal of the American College of Physicians" (Washington, D.C., 1992).

41. Even at that future point, a concern for efficiency should dictate that budgets be imposed only at the most aggregated level. For example, a nationwide limit on annual increases in premiums for all health plans would be preferable to publicly set prices and rates on specific services and procedures. While regulating increases in premiums would compromise the effectiveness of the market in some ways, it would still enable markets to set relative prices and allocate resources. This approach is essentially the logic of the Garamendi approach, which creates a statewide budget for the cost of providing at least the cheapest plan to every resident (while leaving individuals free to pay more out of pocket for more expensive plans).

42. Lewin/ICF estimates, cited in Stuart M. Butler, "A Policy Maker's Guide to the Health Care Crisis, Part II: The Heritage Consumer Choice Health Plan," *Heritage Talking Points* (Washington, D.C.: The Heritage Foundation, 1992), 16.

43. Butler, "A Policy Maker's Guide," 20. Similarly, Urban Institute analyst C. Eugene Steuerle estimates that the average value per recipient household of federal tax subsidies for employer health insurance (including both income and FICA taxes) in FY 1992 was more than five times greater for those in the top quintile of household income than for those in the lowest quintile. See "Finance-Based Reform: The Search for Adaptable Health Policy," paper presented at American Health Policy: Critical Issues for Reform, Washington, D.C. (October, 1991).

44. A notable exception is Marilyn Moon and John Holahan, "Can States Take the Lead in Health Care Reform?" *Journal of the American Medical Association* (Sept. 23, 1992): 1588.

45. For example, Deborah A. Stone, "Why the States Can't Solve the Health Care Crisis," *American Prospect* (Spring 1992): 51–60.

46. See, for example, Alice M. Rivlin, *Reviving the American Dream: The Economy, the States, and the Federal Government* (Washington, D.C.: Brookings Institute, 1992).

47. Rice and Bernstein, "Volume Performance Standards," 310.

48. Estimates by Lewin/ICF in "Health Spending: The Growing Threat to the Family Budget" (Washington, D.C.: Families USA, 1991), table 1; and *Health United States 1991*.

49. Theodore R. Marmor and William Plowden, "Rhetoric and Reality in the Intellectual Jet Stream: The Export to Britain from America of Questionable Ideas," *Journal of Health Politics, Policy, and Law* (Winter 1991) 812.

Chapter 6

1. U.S. Department of Education, National Center for Education Statistics, *Youth Indicators 1991* (Washington, D.C., 1991), 50.
2. U.S. Department of Education, National Center for Education Statistics, *Digest of Education Statistics, 1991* (Washington, D.C., 1991), 155.
3. U.S. Department of Education, National Center for Education Statistics, *Youth Indicators 1991*, op. cit., 78.
4. Ibid., 5.
5. U.S. Department of Education, National Center for Education Statistics, *Digest of Education Statistics, 1991,* op. cit., 395, 398–400.
6. U.S. Department of Education, National Center for Education Statistics, *Youth Indicators 1991*, op. cit., 80–81.
7. For arguments for the need to increase funding for public schools see, for example, Jonathan Kozol, *Savage Inequalities* (New York: Crown, 1991).
8. Seymour Fliegel, "Public School Choice Works—Look at East Harlem," *Wall Street Journal,* October 29, 1992, A15.
9. Albert Shanker, informal remarks to the Itasca Seminar, an annual retreat sponsored by the Minneapolis Foundation, October 3, 1988.
10. Howard Fuller, "Strategy for Change," report to the Board of School Directors, August 6, 1991.
11. Theodore Sizer, *Horace's Compromise, The Dilemma of the American High School* (Boston: Houghton Mifflin Company, 1984), 209.
12. Gallup Organization, "Trends in Support for Parental Choice," *The Kappan* (September, 1990): 43–44.
13. See Marvin H. Kosters, "Wages and Demographics," in *Workers and Their Wages,* Marvin H. Kosters, ed. (American Enterprise Institute, 1991), 1–38.
14. David M. Cutler and Lawrence F. Katz, "Macroeconomic Performances and the Disadvantaged," in *Brookings Papers on Economic Activity, 1991;* vol. 2, 1–74.
15. See William J. Wilson, *The Truly Disadvantaged* (Chicago: University of Chicago Press, 1987).
16. Robert A. Moffitt, "Earnings and the Welfare State," in *A Future of Lousy Jobs?,* Gary Burtless, ed. (Washington, D.C.: The Brookings Institution, 1990), 224.
17. John Bishop, "The Motivation Problem in American High Schools," presented at Tenth Annual Research Conference of the Association for Public Policy Analysis and Management, October 1988, Seattle, Washington.

18. John G. Wirt, et al, *National Assessment of Vocational Education: Summary of Findings and Recommendations. Final Report, Volume 1,* (Washington, D.C.: U.S. Department of Education, 1989).
19. Signithia Fordham and John Ogbu, "Black Students' School Success: Coping with the Burden of 'Acting White'," *The Urban Review;* 18, 3; 176–206.
20. Harry J. Holzer finds that informal methods of job search account for 87–90 percent of the black-white differentials in youth employment probabilities. See his "Informal Job Search and Black Youth Unemployment," in *American Economics Review* (June 1987): 446–52.
21. Howard S. Bloom, et al, *The National JTPA Study: Title II-A Impacts on Earnings and Employment at 18 Months* (Bethesda, Maryland: Abt Associates, May, 1992), 25.
22. See the remarks of Timothy McKee and Brian Sheets in Janet Novak, "Earning and Learning," *Forbes* (May 11, 1992): 150–154.
23. Charles Clark, "Youth Apprenticeships," *CQ Researcher, 2, 39,* (October 23, 1992): 908.
24. For a more complete description of the "Citizens Corps" see *Citizenship and National Service* (Washington, D.C.: The Democratic Leadership Council, 1988), which was the basis for the Nunn-McCurdy bill.
25. Charles Moskos, *A Call To Civic Service* (New York: Free Press, 1988), 178. See also, Donald J. Eberly, *National Service: A Promise to Keep* (Rochester, N.Y.: John Alden, 1988).
26. *Business Week* (October 12, 1992): 60.
27. Richard Danzig and Peter Szanton, *National Service: What Would It Mean?* (Lexington, Mass.: Lexington Books, 1986), 17–40.
28. Joel Berg, "Boston City Year: National Service Prototype?" (Washington, D.C.: Center for Civic Enterprise, 1990).
29. Tom Woanin, House Subcommittee on Post-Secondary Education in interview, November, 1992.
30. *Business Week* (October 12, 1992): 60.
31. William T. Grant Foundation, *The Forgotten Half: Non-College Youth in America* (Washington, D.C: W.T. Grant Foundation Commission on Work, Family and Citizenship, 1988).
32. Juergen Kuhlman and Ekkerhard Lippert, "The Federal Republic of Germany" in Charles Moskos and John Chambers, eds., The New Conscientious Objection (New York: Oxford University Press, 1993), 123.
33. *Citizenship and National Service* (Washington, D.C.: The Democratic Leadership Council, 1988), 47.
34. U.S. Bureau of the Census, "Population Characteristics," *Current Population Reports, series P-20,* 1988, no. 429.
35. William James, "The Moral Equivalent of War," in *Essays on Faith and Morals* (New York: Longmans, Green, 1910).

Chapter 7

1. Frank Levy, *The Economic Future of American Families: Income and Wealth Trends* (Washingon, D.C.: The Urban Institite, 1991), chapter 3.
2. Infant mortality and child death rates have fallen by more than 50% since 1960; the rate of high-school completion and the overall average of years of education have increased and some types of drug use among teens have plummeted. Source: Isabel V. Sawhill, "Young Children and Families Setting Domestic Priorities: What Can Government Do?" eds. Henry J. Aaron and Charles L. Schultze (Washington, D.C.: Brookings Institution, 1992), 148–149.
3. Katherine McFate, *Poverty, Inequality and the Crisis of Social Policy* (Washington, D.C.: Joint Center for Political and Economic Studies, 1991), 2.
4. U.S. Bureau of the Census, Current Population Reports, Series P-60, No. 181, *Poverty in the United States: 1991* (Washington, D.C., 1992), 4.
5. David T. Ellwood, *Poor Support: Poverty in the American Family* (New York: Basic Books, 1988), 46.
6. Ibid., 129.
7. Eugene Smolensky, Sheldon Danziger, and Peter Gottschalk, "The Declining Significance of Age in the United States: Trends in the Well-Being of Children and the Elderly since 1939" (Univ. of Wisconsin, Madison: Institute for Research on Poverty, July 1987).
8. David J. Eggebeen and Daniel T. Lichter, "Race, Family Structure and Changing Poverty Among American Children," *American Sociological Review* 56 (December 1991): 801–17. In a similar vein, Victor R. Fuchs and Diane M. Reklis note that the percentage of children living in households without an adult male has nearly tripled since 1960. In 1960 only 7% of children lived in households without an adult male; in 1988, 19%. The median income per child in 1988 for households with an adult male present was $7640; for households without an adult male, only $2397. See Victor R. Fuchs and Diane M. Reklis, "America's Children: Economic Perspectives and Policy Options," *Science* 255 (Jan. 3, 1992): 41–45.
9. U.S. Bureau of the Census, *Poverty in the United States: 1991,* 71.
10. Frank R. Furstenberg and Andrew Cherlin, *Divided Families: What Happens to Children When Parents Part* (Cambridge, Mass.: Harvard Univ. Press, 1991), 127.
11. William Julius Wilson, *The Truly Disadvantaged: The Inner City, the Underclass, and Public Policy* (Chicago: Univ. of Chicago Press, 1987), 95.
12. Robert Mare and Christopher Winship, "Socioeconomic Change and the Decline of Marriage for Blacks and Whites," in *The Urban Underclass, eds. Christopher Jencks and Paul E. Peterson* (Washington, D.C.: Brookings Institution, 1991).

13. Ibid., William Julius Wilson, "Public Policy Research and *The Truly Disadvantaged,*" Jencks and Peterson, 468.

14. Quoted in Jason Deparle, "Child Poverty Twice as Likely after Family Split," *The New York Times,* March 2, 1991. See also Lenore Weitzman, *The Divorce Revolution: The Unexpected Social and Economic Consequences for Women and Children in America* (New York: Free Press, 1985); and Martha Albertson Fineman, *The Illusion of Equality: The Rhetoric and Reality of Divorce Reform* (Chicago: Univ. of Chicago Press, 1991). For a review of the most recent empirical studies, see Marsha Garrison, "The Economics of Divorce: Changing Rules, Changing Results," in *Divorce Reform at the Crossroads,* eds. Stephen D. Sugerman and Herma Hill Kay (New Haven: Yale Univ. Press, 1990).

15. See, for instance, Frank L. Mott, "The Impact of Father's Absence from the Home on Subsequent Cognitive Development of Younger Children: Linkages between Socio-Emotional and Cognitive Well-Being," presented to the 1992 meeting of the American Sociological Association, Aug. 1992, 13.

16. On youth suicide, see K.D. Breault, "Suicide in America: A Test of Durkheims's Theory of Religious and Family Integration, 1933–1980," *American Journal of Sociology* 92 (1986): 651–52; and John S. Wodarski and Pamela Harris, "Adolescent Suicide: A Review of Influences and the Means for Prevention," *Social Work* 32 (1987): 477–84. On low intellectual and educational attainment, see Sheila Fitzgerald Krein and Andrea H. Beller, "Educational Attainment of Children From Single-Parent Families: Differences by Exposure, Gender and Race," *Demography* 25 (May 1988): 221–34; Robert W. Blanchard and Henry B. Biller, "Father Availability and Academic Performance among Third Grade Boys," *Developmental Psychology* 4 (1971): 301–5; Donald E. Carter and James A. Walsh, "Father Absence and the Black Child: A Multivariate Analysis," *Journal of Negro Education 49* (1980): 134–43; and Marybeth Shinn, "Father Absence and Children's Cognitive Development," *Psychological Bulletin* 85 (1978): 295–324. On drug use, see Ted L Napier, Timothy J. Carter, and M. Christine Pratt, "Correlates of Alcohol and Marijuana Use among Rural High School Students," *Rural Sociology* 46 (Summer 1981): 319–32.

17. Henry J. Aaron and Charles L. Schultze, eds., *Setting Domestic Priorities: What Can Government Do?* (Washington, D.C.: Brookings Institution, 1992), 175.

18. Marcia Slacum Greene, "Mothers, Sons Going It Alone," *The Washington Post,* July 19, 1992.

19. Douglas A. Smith and G. Roger Jarjoura, "Social Structure and Criminal Victimization," *Journal of Research in Crime and Delinquency* 25 (Feb. 1988): 27–52.

20. John Guidubaldi, H.K. Cleminshaw, J.D. Perry, B.K. Nastasi and J. Lightel, "The Role of Selected Family Environment Factors in Children's Post-Divorce Adjustment," *Family Relations* 35 (1986): 141–51.

21. See Judith Wallerstein and Sandra Blakeslee, *Second Chances: Men, Women and Children a Decade after Divorce* (New York: Ticknor & Fields, 1989), pp. 297–99. Similar conclusions are reached in two newer books: Edward Beal, *Adult Children of Divorce: Breaking the Cycle and Finding Fulfillment in Love, Marriage and Family,* (New York, Delacorte Press, 1991); and Claire Berman, *Adult Children of Divorce Speak Out: About Growing Up With and Moving Beyond Parental Divorce* (New York: Simon & Schuster, 1991.)

22. Furstenberg and Cherlin, *Divided Families,* 66–67.

23. Furstenberg and Cherlin, *Divided Families,* 35.

24. See, Peter Brimelow, "American Perestroika," *Forbes* (May 14, 1990): 82–86.

25. "Children in One-Parent Homes: The School Factor" *Principal* (Sept. 1980): 40. There is nothing new about this conclusion. Ever since James S. Coleman and his co-authors published their seminal study on this topic nearly a quarter century ago, research has consistently reinforced the importance of family for student achievement. See James S. Coleman et al., *Equality of Educational Opportunity* (Washington, D.C.: Department of Health, Education and Welfare, 1966). In addition, there is an overwhelming body of evidence suggesting that the "hidden curriculum of the home," which is critical to the development of language skills, is directly related to children's later success in school. See Dr. Samuel G. Sava, "Rescuing a Generation: Second Thoughts on 'Having It All' "—a speech given to the National Association of Elementary School Principals, April 9, 1990, San Antonio, Texas.

26. Sally Banks Zakariya, "Another Look at the Children of Divorce," *Principal Magazine* Sept. 1982): 35. See also R.B. Zajonc, "Family Configuration and Intelligence," *Science* 192 (April 16, 1976): 227–36; and Ann M. Milne, David E. Myers, Alvin S. Rosenthal and Alan Ginsburg, "Single Parents, Working Mothers and the Educational Achievement of School Children," *Sociology of Education,* 59 (July 1986): 132.

27. Before we lay out the elements of a new family agenda we want to emphasize that there is also a deferred agenda, embraced by most Democrats, of adequate funding for existing programs whose effectiveness has been clearly demonstrated. Given the extent of knowledge and agreement concerning these matters we will not spend time in this chapter further discussing Head Start, WIC, child immunization, or other valuable programs that promote the health and welfare of women and children. Instead we will turn our attention to some emerging, less well understood areas of policy that we believe should become the core of a comprehensive family agenda. See, for instance, the work of the Children's Defense Fund.

28. Daniel Patrick Moynihan, "Family and Nation Revisited," *Social Thought* 16 (1990): 52.

29. Western European countries recognize that nurturing has great societal value. From 18-month maternity leaves in Sweden to children's allow-

ances in France, these societies have acknowledged that there are some things that only families can do and that if families are placed under so much stress that they cannot raise children effectively, the rest of society cannot make up the difference in later years. See Harold L. Wilensky, "Common Problems, Divergent Policies: An 18-Nation Study of Family Policy," *Public Affairs Report* (May 1990): 1–3.

30. See, Eugene Steuerle, "The Tax Treatment of Households of Different Size," in *Taxing the Family,* ed. Rudolph G. Penner, (Washington, D.C.: American Enterprise Institute, 1984), 76.

31. Ibid. and Robert J. Shapiro, "The Tax Fairness Index: Who Pays for the National Government," Policy Report No. 6 (Washington, D.C.: Progressive Policy Institute, July 1990), 4.

32. Steuerle, "Tax Treatment of Households," 78.

33. How should we arrive at the value of this "children's tax credit"? Simply adjusting for inflation would put the 1948 personal exemption near $3,000. But the best way to decide on the appropriate level is to use not only a measure of inflation but a measure that takes into account both the rising costs of raising a child (in its first year at least) and the growth in real incomes. In 1990, *American Demographics* put the cost of a baby in its first year in 1990 at $5,774. In 1958, that same publication put the cost of a baby in its first year at $800. Whether coincidental or not, the personal exemption in 1958 was very close to the actual cost of raising a new baby in that year. When economists try to match the value of the 1948 personal exemption for today's families, they come up with estimates between $6,000 and $7,500 per dependent—numbers that are, coincidentally, close to the actual first year cost of raising a child in 1990.

34. Letter from Ronald A. Pearlman, Joint Committee on Taxation, June 12, 1990.

35. Lawrence Lindsey, *The Growth Experiment: How the New Tax Policy Is Transforming the U.S. Economy* (New York: Basic Books, 1990), 223.

36. Melinda Beck, "Trading Places," *Newsweek,* (July 16, 1990): 48–54.

37. The authors are indebted to Dr. Robert J. Shapiro of the Progressive Policy Institute for the analysis summarized here, which originally appeared in "An American Working Wage: Ending Poverty in Working Families," Policy Report No.3 (Washington, D.C.: Progressive Policy Institute, Feb. 1990).

38. Ellwood, *Poor Support,* 159.

39. In the course of developing these proposals, we have come to believe that establishment of a system of child support assurance depends on the establishment of an adequate enforcement mechanism.

40. Ellwood, *Poor Support,* 163–65. States are experimenting with a variety of child support enforcement innovations. Arizona, like Massachusetts, is moving to tie the award of state professional licenses to punctual child support payments. Minnesota is beginning to accept other states' enforcement orders as is, without the traditional extra in-state hearings. Other jurisdictions are offering amnesty periods for overdue payments, followed by police roundups of tardy fathers.

41. Weitzman, *Divorce Revolution,* 342.
42. Mary Ann Glendon, *Abortion and Divorce in Western Law* (Cambridge, Mass: Harvard Univ. Press, 1987), 93–95.
43. Marilyn Garner, "Putting Children First: The New English Precedent," *Christian Science Monitor* (March 30, 1990): 14.
44. Carol Lawson, "Requiring Classes in Divorce," *The New York Times,* Jan. 23, 1992.
45. *Revised Code of Washington Annotated,* Title 26–26.09.184 Permanent Parenting Plan, 42–46.
46. Act 70 and Act 474 of the Third Extraordinary Session of the 1989 Arkansas legislature.
47. Susan Diesenhouse, "Drug Treatment is Scarcer Than Ever for Women," *The New York Times,* July 7, 1990.
48. For a review of these studies, see U.S. Dept. of Labor *Employers and Child Care:* Benefiting Work and Family (Washington, D.C., 1989), 7.
49. If the U.S. is to become truly competitive in the world, we must establish an information infrastructure for the 21st century that will link the country in an information superhighway in much the same way that the interstate highway system of the 1950s linked America.
50. Aetna Life and Casualty found, for instance, that, in 1987, 21% of the women who left technical positions did so because of family obligations. At American Bankers Insurance Group, the absentee rate for employees who use the company's on-site daycare center is 7% versus the company wide figure of 17%. See *Challenges* (Washington, D.C.: Council on Competitiveness, May 1990).
51. "Parental Leave: Revised Cost Estimate Reflecting the Impact of Spousal Leave" (Washington, D.C.: Government Printing Office, April 1989), 2.
52. Credit for some of these ideas should go to Dr. Margaret Beyer, "Families under Intolerable Stress," in *Putting Children First: A Progressive Family Policy for the 1990s,* (Washington D.C.: Progressive Policy Institute, Sept. 27, 1990), 34.
53. Foster care figures are from American Public Welfare Association.
54. Children psychiatric hospital admittance figures are from National Institute of Mental Health.
55. U.S. General Accounting Office *Home Visiting: A Promising Early Intervention Strategy for At-Risk Families* (Washington, D.C., July 11, 1990), 3.
56. J.C. Barden, "Counseling to Keep Families Together," *The New York Times,* Sept. 21, 1990.
57. Mellman and Lazarus, Mass Mutual American Family Values, "1991 American Family Values Study: A Return to Family Values," Table 7.
58. The Family in an Unfriendly Culture," *Family Affairs,* 3:1-2 (Spring/ Summer 1990).
59. Isabel Sawhill, "Young Children and Families," in *Setting Domestic Priorities,* (Washington, D.C., Brookings Institution, 1992), p. 163.
60. An alternative to regulation, but with the same, if not better effects, may

come if and when we get rid of the regulatory blocks to the creation of a broadband television network with thousands of channels and programmers. Then, according to George Gilder, author of *Life After Television,* the economic imperative of appealing to the lowest common denominator would be broken.

Chapter 8

1. U.S. Department of Justice, *Crime in the United States 1991*, USGPO (Washington, D.C.) 5.
2. "The Police Corps and Community Policing: A Progressive Response to Crime," Policy Report No.4 (Washington, D.C.: Progressive Policy Institute, March 1990), Graph 1.
3. Ibid, 3.
4. Bureau of Justice Statistics, "Criminal Victimization in the United States, 1990" (Washington) 100.
5. Bureau of Justice Statistics, U.S. Deparment of Justice, "Lifetime Likelihood of Victimization," technical report, March 1987.
6. See *Crime in the United States*, 388-389, for comparison of reported crime rates and the National Crime Victimization Study, an estimate which excludes several violent crimes.
7. Bureau of Justice Statistics, U.S. Department of Justice, "International Crime Rates," special report, May 1988.
8. Bureau of Justice Statistics, *Justice Expenditure and Employment, 1990* (Washington) 3.
9. U.S. Senate Democratic Policy Committee, *Accomplishments of the 102nd Congress*, 1992 (Washington, D.C.) 15.
10. Marc Mauer, *Americans Behind Bars: One Year Later*, 1992, The Sentencing Project (Washington, D.C.), 4.
11. U.S. Senate Democratic Policy Committee, op. cit.
12. Ann Devroy, "Bush Rhetoric Subdued On Arkansas Crime; Gore Slams President on Cable TV Bill," *The Washinton Post*, September 29, 1992, A6.
13. "Uniform Crime Reports, 1988," op. cit. National Center for Health Statistics, Division of Vital Statistics, unpublished table.
14. Quoted in Chester, L., Hodgson, G., and Page, B., *An American Melodrama*, (New York: Viking 1969).
15. U.S. Senator Arlen Specter, statement, July 12, 1989.
16. Ibid.
17. Bureau of Justice Statistics, op. cit., 4.
18. Jonathan Rubinstein, "The Police Corps: A Plan for Augmenting Law Enforcement Resources—A Feasibility Study," study conducted under grant from National Institute of Justice, January 1985.
19. Data on pay levels collected by International City Managers Association, May 1989.
20. Gerald R. Lynch, "Cops and College," *America*, April 4, 1987.

21. Laurie Goodstein, "New York Police Fail to Reflect City's Diversity," *The Washington Post,* October 22, 1992, A3.
22. U.S. Senator Jim Sasser, statement, July 12, 1989.
23. Ibid.
24. Unofficial preliminary cost estimate by Cathy Ellman of the Congressional Budget Office, May 15, 1989.
25. Rubinstein, "The Police Corps."
26. Personal Communication, staff of Senate Permanent Subcommittee on Investigations, September 22, 1992.
27. Moore, M., Trojanowicz, R., and Kelling, G., "Crime and Policing," *Perspectives on Policing,* No.2, U.S. Department of Justice, June 1988.
28. James Q. Wilson and George Kelling, "Making Neighborhoods Safe," *Atlantic Monthly,* February 1989.
29. George Kelling, "Police and Communities: The Quiet Revolution," Perspectives on Policing, No.1, U.S. Department of Justice, June 1988.
30. Ibid.
31. Moore, Trojanowicz, and Kelling, op. cit.
32. Kelling, "Police and Communites."
33. Kelling, "Police and Communities."
34. Testimony by Lee Brown to the 1992 Democratic Platform Committee.
35. Ibid.
36. Terry Eastland, "Weed and Seed: Root Out Crime, Nurture Poor," *The Wall Street Journal,* May 14, 1992, A12.
37. Kelling, "Police and Communites."
38. George L. Kelling, "Reclaiming the Subway," *NY The City Journal,* 1:2, (Winter 1991): 18.
39. Ibid, 26-27
40. Andrew Cooper, Enabling the Underclass: Vince Lane's Campaign to Restore Rights and Responsibilities in Chicago's Public Housing (Washington, D.C.: Progressive Policy Institute, 1990), 7-9.
41. Ibid.
42. Michael Abramowitz, "Daley Plans Crackdown On Violence," *The Washington Post,* October 20, 1992, A3.
43. Personal Communication, staff of Senate Permanent Subcommittee on Investigations, September 22, 1992.
44. PRIDE, Inc., *PRIDE Questionnaire Report: 1991-92 National Summary Grades 6-12,* 1992 (Atlanta).
45. Personal Communication, staff of Senate Permanent Subcommittee on Investigations, September 22, 1992.
46. Ibid.
47. John. J. Dilulio, Jr., "A Limited War on Crime That We Can Win," *Brookings Review,* Fall 1992 (Washington) 5.
48. Ibid.

Chapter 9

1. One example is the high priority the administration has given to its Green Lights program to promote certain kinds of voluntary energy conservation measures within private industry. Although we certainly have no objection to voluntary approaches per se, it is important to recognize the severe limitation that is imposed by failing to take advantage of the awesome power of the market to achieve environmental goals through appropriately designed incentive-based policies. Private industry will inevitably respond most aggressively (and most efficiently) when environmental requirements show up in the proverbial bottom line.

2. See U.S. Environmental Protection Agency *Environmental Investments: The Costs of a Clean Environment,* Report of the Administrator to the Congress of the United States (Washington, D.C., Dec. 1990). This estimate excludes environmental activities not directly associated with pollution control or cleanup, such as wildlife conservation and land management. The $100 billion estimate covers spending by private business (63.0%), local governments (22.5%), the federal government (11.0%), and state governments (3.5%).

3. In eight empirical studies of air pollution control, the ratio of actual, aggregate costs of the conventional command and control approach to the aggregate costs of least-cost benchmarks ranged from 1.07 for sulfate emissions in the Los Angeles area to 22.0 for hydrocarbon emissions at all domestic DuPont plants. See T.H. Tietenberg, *Emissions Trading: An Exercise in Reforming Pollution Policy* (Washington, D.C.: Resources for the Future, 1985). ,

4. Numerical examples of the variance of incremental costs of air pollution control are provided by Robert W. Crandall, "The Political Economy of Clean Air: Practical Constraints on White House Review," in *Environmental Policy under Reagan's Executive Order: The Role of Benefit-Cost Analysis*, ed. V. Kerry Smith (Chapel Hill: Univ. of North Carolina Press, 1984), 205-25.

5. For example, President Lyndon Johnson's proposal for effluent fees and President Richard Nixon's recommendations for a tax on lead in gasoline and a sulfur dioxide emission fee were dismissed with little consideration.

6. For an analysis of past sources of resistance to market-based approaches to environmental protection and an assessment of why changes have occurred over recent years, see Robert W. Hahn and Robert N. Stavins, "Incentive-Based Environmental Regulation: A New Era From An Old Idea?" *Ecology Law Quarterly* 18(1991): 1-42.

7. A number of other prominent environmental organizations—including the Wilderness Society, National Wildlife Federation, National Audubon Society, Sierra Club, and Natural Resources Defense Council—now support at least selective use of market-based instruments.

8. See Robert N. Stavins, ed., *Project 88: Harnessing Market Forces to Protect Our Environment—Initiatives for the New President* (Washing-

ton, D.C., Dec. 1988), a public policy study sponsored by Senators Timothy E. Wirth (D-CO) and John Heinz (R-PA), December 1988. Two years later, Senators Wirth and Heinz sponsored a follow-up effort, Project 88/Round II, focusing on the design and implementation of effective and practical market-based environmental policy mechanisms. See Robert N. Stavins, ed., *Project 88/Round II: Incentives for Action: Designing Market-based Environmental Strategies* (Washington, D.C., May 1991), a public policy study also sponsored by Senators Wirth and Heinz.

9. See, for example, Stephan Schmidheiny, *Changing Course: A Global Business Perspective on Development and the Environment* (Cambridge, Mass.: MIT Press, 1992). Similarly, General Motors has endorsed the adoption of a broad-based carbon fee to limit emissions of greenhouse gases. See George C. Eads, comments prepared for a workshop on "Economics of Sustainable Development" sponsored by the United Nations Economic Commission for Europe and the U.S. Environmental Protection Agency, Washington, D.C., January 25, 1990.

10. Two other federal examples of tradable permit systems are EPA's Emissions Trading Program for local air quality and the nationwide phase-down of leaded gasoline. While state impediments and uncertainty about the future course of the Emissions Trading Program have sharply limited trading by firms, the limited trading that has occurred has saved more than $4 billion with no adverse effect on air quality. According to EPA, the lead program, with much higher trading among firms, reduced overall compliance costs by approximately 20% (about $200 million annually). See U.S. Environmental Protection Agency, "Costs and Benefits of Reducing Lead in Gasoline," Final Regulatory Impact Analysis VIII-31 (Washington, D.C., 1985).

11. For example, Congress has moved to reduce the federal subsidy given to U.S. Army Corps of Engineers flood-control projects (which provide incentives for individual landowners to convert forested wetlands to agricultural cropland), and there have been discussions in Congress regarding the U.S. Forest Service's "below-cost timber sales," which recover less than the cost of making timber available. See Robert N. Stavins and Adam B. Jaffe, "Unintended Impacts of Public Investments on Private Decisions: The Depletion of Forested Wetlands," *American Economic Review* 80 (1990): 337-52; and Michael D. Bowes and John V. Krutilla, *Multiple-Use Management: The Economics of Public Forestlands* (Washington, D.C.: Resources for the Future, 1989).

12. The most notable transfer plan to date has been the $223 million agreement between the Imperial Irrigation District of California and the Metropolitan Water District of Los Angeles. See Robert N. Stavins, *Trading Conservation Investments for Water* (Berkeley, Calif.: Environmental Defense Fund, March 1983).

13. This and the following two parts of this chapter draw upon Robert N. Stavins and Bradley W. Whitehead, *The Greening of America's Taxes:*

Pollution Charges and Environmental Protection (Washington, D.C.: Progressive Policy Institute, Feb. 1992).

14. A few federal policies have embraced some pollution charge characteristics, but they have aimed primarily at generating revenue rather than discouraging pollution. In 1989, Congress enacted an excise tax on chlorofluorocarbons (CFCs), which deplete stratospheric ozone and are potent greenhouse gases. The tax does *not* materially affect either the level or rate of the CFC phasedown. It simply ensures that any windfall profits associated with constrained supply flow to the government rather than to private industry. Likewise, the chemical and petroleum feedstock taxes that finance the cleanup of abandoned hazardous waste sites under the Superfund law (the Comprehensive Environmental Response, Compensation, and Liability Act, or CERCLA) are also not pollution charges; Superfund levies taxes on production (i.e., it is revenue based), not emissions. As a result, no direct link exsists between environmental controls undertaken and taxes paid and therefore no direct incentive for pollution control.

15. See Seattle Solid Waste Utility, Public Information Dept., *Municipal Solid Waste Management Program Description* (Seattle, 1991).

16. Bill Paul, "Pollution Solution: Pennsylvania Town Finds a Way to Get Locals to Recycle Trash," *Wall Street Journal,* June 21, 1989, A1.

17. See Roger Bolton, "Equity in Financing Local Services: The Case of Residential Refuse," *Resources and Conservation* 11 (1984): 45-62. Furthermore, the deductibility of local property tax payments from federal income tax liability is significant in this regard. Given the progressive nature of federal income taxes, a change from the status quo financing approach (through property taxes) to increased reliance on unit charges will tend to reduce the regressive nature of the overall system.

18. Unit charges could also lead to increased illegal dumping. The experiences of Seattle, Perkasie, and other communities suggest, however, that properly designed systems can prevent this problem. New programs can be introduced incrementally, with charges rising gradually until they equal the true costs of disposal. Municipalities can remove much of the incentive for illegal dumping by providing free or very low-cost disposal at transfer stations.

19. Retail charges can act as a *substitute* for unit curbside charges when the latter are impractical (for example, in a community with many large, multi-unit residences). Retail charges can also serve as a *supplement* to curbside charges for specific products whose cost of disposal are well in excess of the costs associated with their volume. They might include household products whose ingredients have significant environmental consequences when they find their way into landfills or incinerators. Examples include electrical-appliance batteries, inks, paints and paint solvents, and household pesticides. See Peter Menell, "Beyond the Throw-Away Society: An Incentive Approach to Regulating Municipal Solid Waste," *Ecology Law Quarterly* 17 (1990): 655-739. Virgin-material taxes ought to be viewed as potential substitutes for unit curbside

charges or retail disposal charges; a system that added one on top of the other could create double taxation.

20. See, for example, Dale W. Jorgenson, Daniel T. Slesnick, and Peter J. Wilcoxen, "Carbon Taxes and Economic Welfare," *Brookings Papers on Economic Activity*, Microeconomics 1992 (Washington, D.C.), 393-454. Studies indicate that, on average, U.S. personal and corporate income taxes generate distortions or pure losses of 20 to 50 cents for every new dollar of tax revenue collected. See, for example, Charles Ballard, John Shoven, and John Whalley, "General Equilibrium Computations of the Marginal Welfare Costs of Taxes in the United States," *American Economic Review* 75 (1985): 128-38.

21. Of course, the revenues from green charges could be used in other ways. First, they could be used to reduce the federal budget deficit. This alternative has obvious appeal in an era of unprecedented levels of government borrowing. For example, Paul O'Neill, of the Aluminum Company of America (Alcoa), suggested in the summer of 1990 that energy taxes could accomplish most effectively the dual goals of reducing pollution and reducing the budget deficit. See *Environmental Policy Alert* (June 27, 1990): 33. A second option would be to use the tax revenue to finance other programs related to environmental protection. Such programs might entail further cleanup or mitigation of pollution. They might also be directed to assisting those who are economically hurt by the change to a system of green charges. However, in order to overcome the natural political aversion to taxes, and to ensure pollution charges are progressive *and* pro-growth, we advocate using the revenue from these charges to lower other taxes, such as regressive payroll taxes.

22. For a summary of studies carried out as part of the Stanford Energy Modeling Forum analysis of greenhouse gas mitigation (EMF 13) and the related research sponsored by the U.S. Environmental Protection Agency, see Neil A. Leary and Joel D. Scheraga, "Lessons for the Implementation of Policies to Mitigate Carbon Dioxide Emissions," in *Reducing Carbon Dioxide Emissions from the Energy Sector: Cost and Policy Options*, ed. Darius Gaskins and John Weyant (Cambridge, Mass.: MIT Press, forthcoming 1993).

23. Other, more direct ways can be used to internalize the "national security externality" associated with imported oil, for example, import levies.

24. See, for example, Daniel J. Khazzoom, "The Impact of a Gasoline Tax on Auto Exhaust Emissions," *Journal of Policy Analysis and Management* 10 (1991): 434-54.

25. See U.S. Environmental Protection Agency, Office of Policy, Planning, and Evaluation, *Economic Incentives: Options for Environmental Protection*. Report 21P-2001 (Washington, D.C., 1991).

26. This and the following mechanisms, intended to increase the overall efficiency of urban transportation systems, are described in detail in Michael Cameron, "Transportation Efficiency: Tackling Southern California's Air Pollution and Congestion," (Oakland, Environmental De-

fense Fund and Regional Institute of Southern California, March 1991).

27. See U.S. Environmental Protection Agency Science Advisory Board, *Reducing Risk: The Report of the Human Health Subcommittee, Relative Risk Reduction Project*, Appendix B. EPA SAB-EC-90—021B (Washington, D.C., September 1990).

28. U.S. Environmental Protection Agency, *Characterization of Products Containing Lead and Cadmium in Municipal Solid Waste in the United States, 1970-2000* (Washington, D.C., January 1989).

29. The administrative complications associated with such a program should not be underestimated. Verification would be an important issue, as a deposit-refund system could encourage users to dilute solvents.

30. For an examination of deposit-refund systems and other incentive-based policy mechanisms for used lubricating oil, see Robert C. Anderson, Lisa A. Hofmann, and Michael Rusin, *The Use of Economic Incentive Mechanisms in Environmental Management*, Research Paper #051 (Washington, D.C.: American Petroleum Institute, June 1990).

31. Many important administrative choices pertain to tradable permit systems. If the number of regulated sources of emissions is great, the administrative (transaction) costs of these systems can be very high. On the other hand, if very few sources are involved, problems of concentration in the permit and product markets could arise, with consequent inefficiencies introduced by noncompetitive behavior. Finally, regulators must decide how to allocate permits among sources: Should they be given away as an endowment, or should they be sold through an auction? If they are distributed free of charge, what criteria should be used in the allocation?

32. For detailed discussions of tradable permit systems for these three products, see Stavins, ed., *Project 88/Round II*.

33. Among the higher-risk problems EPA cited were indoor air pollution (including radon gas), exposure to chemicals in consumer products, and surface water pollution; government spending in these areas is at relatively low levels. Among the lower-risk problems EPA cited were hazardous waste sites and underground storage tanks, both of which receive very high levels of federal funding. See U.S. Environmental Protection Agency, Office of Policy Analysis, *Unfinished Business: A Comparative Assessment of Environmental Problems*, Overview Report (Washington, D.C., Feb. 1987). Trace amounts of dioxin in surface waters is another example of a lower-risk problem that receives a relatively high level of regulatory attention, John Graham Harvard School of Public Health, personal communication, Oct. 15, 1992.

34. U.S. Environmental Protection Agency, Science Advisory Board, *Reducing Risk: Setting Priorities and Strategies for Environmental Protection* (Washington, D.C., Sept. 1990).

35. See U.S. General Accounting Office, *Environmental Protection: Meeting Public Expectations with Limited Resources*, Report to the Congress, GAO/RCED-91-97 (Washington, D.C., June 1991).

Chapter 10

1. A report by the Joint Center for Political and Economic Studies reached this conclusion: "Among industrialized countries, the United States has the highest incidence of poverty among the nonelderly and the highest distribution of poverty across all age and family groups. It is also the country in which the poor experienced the longest spells of poverty." Joint Center for Political and Economic Studies, *Poverty, Inequality, and the Crisis of Social Policy* (Washington, D.C.).

2. David Ellwood, *Poor Support: Poverty in the American Family* (New York: Basic Books, 1988), 6.

3. Conservatives like Charles Murray say that the welfare economy causes the underclass. Critics of Murray's thesis note that welfare payments have actually been falling, when inflation is factored in, since the early 1970s, and so cannot be blamed for fostering single-parent families and dependency. According to Robert Greenstein's article "Relieving Poverty," in *The Brookings Review* (Summer 1991), AFDC benefits for families with no other income are now 40% lower in purchasing power in the median state than they were in 1970. But if cash welfare doesn't create the underclass, it nevertheless sustains it: urban welfare mothers derive 57% of their income from welfare.

4. Julie Kosterlitz, "The Marriage Penalty," *National Journal* (June 20, 1992): 1454.

5. Dale Russakoff, "Tales from America's War on Poverty: The Kids Government Tried to Save," *The Washington Post*, Dec. 7, 1980.

6. Judith M. Gueron and Edward Pauly, *From Welfare to Work* (New York: Russell Sage Foundation, 1991).

7. Katherine Boo, "Beyond Beauty Schools," *The Washington Monthly* (March 1991): 26-31.

8. Susan Kellam, "Agreement on Everything, Almost," *Congressional Quarterly* (August 1, 1992): 2280.

9. Jack Kemp, remarks before the U.S. Conference of Mayors, Houston, Tex., Jan. 22, 1992.

10. Bob Baker, "Buzzword With Bite: Work Ethic," *The Los Angeles Times*, Sept. 17, 1992.

11. Robert Rector, "How to Strengthen America's Crumbling Families," *Heritage Foundation Report* (Washington, D.C., Apr. 1992).

12. U.S. Bureau of the Census, *Statistical Abstract of the United States*, (Washington, D.C., 1991).

13. William Julius Wilson, *The Truly Disadvantaged* (Chicago: Univ. of Chicago Press, 1987).

14. Lawrence Mead, *The New Politics of Poverty: The Nonworking Poor in America* (New York: Basic Books, 1992).

15. It should be noted that while this trend is cause for concern, the numbers are somewhat exaggerated because of the large drop in births to married black women that has occurred over this same period of time. Stephanie J. Ventura, *Trends and Differentials in Births to Unmarried Women:*

United States 1970-76 (Washington, D.C.: National Center for Health Statistics, 1980); National Center for Health Statistics, Monthly Vital Statistics Report, vol. 40, *Advance Report of Final Natality Statistics 1989* (Washington, D.C., 1991).

16. See discussion in chapter on family policy.

17. Congressional Research Service, Report 91-741 EPW (Washington, D.C., Sept. 30, 1991).

18. Diane Kallenback and Arthur Lyons, "Government Spending for the Poor in Cook County, Illinois: Can We Do Better?" (Evanston: Center for Urban Affairs and Policy Research, Northwestern University, April 1989).

19. See the series by Jon Eig, "Decaying Homes, Blighted Hopes," June 18, 1990, and "Desire Pays Price for Short Cuts," June 19, 1990, in *The New Orleans Times-Picayune.*

20. For further explanation, see chapters 11 and 12 on Challenge Grants and the discussion of home-based social services in chapter 7.

21. Kimi Gray at the Democratic Leadership Council 1989 Fall Conference, Washington, D.C., Nov. 13, 1989: "If [welfare] would only stop rewarding failures and begin to reward success, then you'll find there'll be a change. . . ."

22. Constance L. Hays, "Girl's Plan to Save for College Runs Afoul of Welfare Rules," *The New York Times,* May 15, 1992.

23. See Irwin Garfinkel and Sara S. McLanahan, *Single Mothers and Their Children* (Washington, D.C.: The Urban Institute, 1986), 98.

24. Daniel Yankelovich, "American Values and Public Policy: How Reciprocity and Other Beliefs Are Reshaping American Politics," (Washington, D.C.: Democratic Leadership Council, Fall 1991), 30.

25. While welfare costs have been rising, they are not a large enough portion of state budgets (only 3.4% on average) to be a significant source of savings.

26. Testimony of Douglas Besharov before the House Select Committee on Hunger, May 21, 1992.

27. For example, a single mother with two children who works full-time at the minimum wage today still winds up $2,800 below the poverty line and loses her health insurance and possibly other benefits to boot.

28. Robert Shapiro, "An American Working Wage: Ending Poverty in Working Families," Progressive Policy Institute Policy Report (Feb. 1990).

29. Gary Burtless, "When Work Doesn't Work," *The Brookings Review* (Spring 1992): 26–29.

30. Peter Cove, Statement of Democratic Leadership Council 1992 Conference.

31. Karl Zinsmeister, "Left and Right Conference," (Washington, D.C.: Progressive Foundation and Heritage Foundation, Oct. 30, 1991).

32. David Stoesz, "Social Service Vouchers: Bringing Choice and Competition to Social Services," (Washington, D.C.: Progressive Policy Institute, 1992).

33. Michael Sherraden, "Stakeholding: A New Direction in Social Policy" (Washington, D.C.: Progressive Policy Institute Policy Report, Jan. 1990).

34. Christopher Jencks, "Can We Put a Time Limit on Welfare?" *American Prospect* (Fall 1992), 38–39.

Chapter 11

1. Poll data: "The typical American . . . ": Sen. William Roth, *Congressional Record*, 138, 51 (April 7 1992), Senate, 1; "Only 17% . . . ": CBS/*New York Times* poll released April 1, 1992, cited in ibid.; "Only 13% . . . ": National Commission on the Public Service, *Leadership for America: Rebuilding the Public Service* (Washington, D.C., 1989), 3; "And 17 of every 20 . . . ": CBS News Poll, May 27-30, 1992.

2. The figure for 1975 is from U.S. Bureau of the Census, *Statistical Abstract of the United States: 1990*, 110th ed., (Washington, D.C., 1990), table 527. The figure for May 1992 is from U.S. Office of Personnel Management, *Federal Civilian Workforce Statistics: Employment and Trends as of May 1992* (Washington, D.C., 1992), table 1.

3. U.S. Office of Personnel Management, ibid., table 9.

4. U.S. Advisory Commission on Intergovernmental Relations, *Characteristics of Federal Grant-in-Aid Programs to State and Local Governments: Grants Funded FY 1991* (Washington, D.C., March 1992), 1.

5. Ibid., table 2.

6. U.S. Advisory Commission on Intergovernmental Relations, *The Federal Role in the Federal System: The Dynamics of Growth; An Agenda for American Federalism: Restoring Confidence and Competence* (Washington, D.C.: 1981), 112.

7. Ibid.

8. See U.S. Advisory Commission on Intergovernmental Relations, *Characteristics of Federal Grant-in-Aid Programs to State and Local Governments,* 92.

9. Interview with author.

10. In 1973, for example, Congress brought 17 small job-training programs together into the Comprehensive Employment and Training Act. In 1982 this structure was again revamped, under the Job Training Partnership Act. The idea was to have a broad block grant, but today JTPA includes seven or eight programs, targeted at different categories of people. The Alcohol Drug Abuse and Mental Health Block Grant, another supposedly broad program, requires states to spend 50 percent of their money on intravenous drug users, even if, like Arkansas, Wyoming, or Montana, they have few. See, for instance, Cheryl Arvidson, "As the Reagan Era Fades, It's Discretion vs. Earmarking in the Struggle over Funds," *Governing* (March 1990): 21-27.

11. Office of Technology Assessment, U.S. Congress, *After the Cold War: Living With Lower Defense Spending,* OTA-ITE-524, (Washington, D.C., Feb. 1992), 81.

12. Michael N. Castle, "To Provide Efficient Service Delivery," in *Restoring the Balance: State Leadership for America's Future* (Washington, D.C.: National Governors Association, 1988), 40.
13. U.S. Advisory Commission on Intergovernmental Relations, *Devolving Federal Program Responsibilities and Revenue Sources to State and Local Governments* (Washington, D.C., March 1986), 112.
14. See Alice M. Rivlin, *Reviving the American Dream: The Economy, the States and the Federal Government* (Washington, D.C.: Brookings Institution, 1992), 118.
15. U.S. Advisory Commission on Intergovernmental Relations, *The Federal Role in the Federal System.*
16. These numbers rely on data from Office of Management and Budget, *1992 Catalog of Federal Domestic Assistance* (Washington, D.C., 1992); and U.S. Advisory Commission on Intergovernmental Relations, *Characteristics of Federal Grant-in-Aid Programs.*
17. U.S. Dept. of Housing and Urban Development, *Profile of HUD*, (Washington, D.C., Sept. 1990), 11.
18. U.S. Dept. of Housing and Urban Development, "FY 1991 Full-Time Equivalents and Salaries and Expenses," provided by HUD.
19. U.S. Office of Management and Budget, Budget of the U.S. Government FY 93, (Washington, D.C., 1992), 179–80.
20. Dept. of Housing and Urban Development, *Profile of HUD*, 4.
21. Ibid., 7.
22. See David Osborne, *Laboratories of Democracy* (Boston: Harvard Business School Press, 1988), chap. 2.
23. Booth Gardner, "To Provide for Income Security," in *Restoring the Balance*, 86-89.
24. Niccolo Machiavelli, *The Prince*, 1532, (New York: Dover Publications, Inc., 1992), 13.
25. Sen. William Roth (R-DE) has proposed a similar idea in his "New American Revolution Act." With some refinements, the President could make this bill the starting point for devolution.
26. Peter Drucker, *The Age of Discontinuity* (New York: Harper Torchbooks, 1978), 241-42.

Chapter 12

1. The 1980 figure is from U.S. Bureau of the Census, *Statistical Abstract of the United States: 1990*, 110th ed., (Washington D.C., 1990), table 527.
2. See David Osborne and Ted Gaebler, *Reinventing Government* (Reading, Mass.: Addison-Wesley, 1992), for a more complete discussion of these principles.
3. Ibid., chap. 5.
4. Deputy Secretary of Defense for Installations, *The Unified Budget Test* (Washington, D.C., March 1988), 6.

5. Called the Government Performance and Results Act, it was introduced by Sen. William Roth (R-DE) and co-sponsored by Senator John Glenn (D-OH).

6. For a more detailed explanation, see Osborne and Gaebler, *Reinventing Government*, chapter 5.

7. To help federal, state, and local agencies develop effective measures and improve their performance, the act should fund a series of Performance Institutes. Set up in partnership with think tanks like the Urban Institute and public policy schools like the Kennedy School of Government at Harvard and the Humphrey Institute at the University of Minnesota, they would provide technical assistance, consulting, and the like. They could raise some of their own money by charging fees for their services.

8. James Q. Wilson, *Bureaucracy: What Government Agencies Do and Why They Do It* (New York: Basic Books, 1989), 145–46.

9. National Commission on the Public Service, *Leadership for America: Rebuilding the Public Service* (Washington, D.C., 1989), 28.

10. U.S. Office of Personnel Management, *Federal Civilian Workforce Statistics*, table 9.

11. National Academy of Public Administration, *Modernizing Federal Classification: An Opportunity for Excellence* (Washington, D.C., July 1991), xxv, 1, 2, 17–18, 19, E-1-2.

12. See Wilson, *Bureaucracy*, 146–48. The three other demonstration projects have also been successful. One included "gainsharing"—allowing employees to pocket some of the savings achieved through cooperative labor-management efforts to cut costs. It achieved $5 million in productivity savings, improved performance, cut down on grievances, complaints, sick leave, and absenteeism, and improved labor-management relations. For more information on the demonstration projects, see National Academy of Public Administration, *Modernizing Federal Classification*, appendix E; and Public Employee Dept., *Reinvigorating the Public Service: Union Innovations to Improve Government* (Washington, D.C.: AFL-CIO, March 1992), 34–46.

13. One demonstration project might test an approach under which new employees would work for three to five years before they are eligible for the job security protections of Civil Service. Agencies would choose to promote to Civil Service status only those who demonstrated excellent performance. Another might test the elimination of tenure for new employees in non-policy positions, coupled with continued use of objective hiring and firing criteria, such as examinations and interviews by neutral personnel experts, to protect against patronage. The uncoupling of life-time tenure from objective, nonpolitical hiring and firing is one area that has not yet been adequately explored.

14. Task Force on Government Waste, *The Challenge of Sound Management* (Washington, D.C.: U.S. House of Representatives, Democratic Caucus, June 1992), 17.

15. The facts on REA are from James Bennett, "Power Failure," *Washington Monthly* (July-August 1990): 12–21.

16. Osborne and Gaebler, *Reinventing Government,* 9.
17. Originally reported in Dale Russakoff, "The Government's Not Like You or Me," *Washington Post,* Weekly Edition, (Feb. 15, 1990).
18. Task Force on Government Waste, *Challenge of Sound Management,* 18.
19. Ibid., 34–35.
20. Ibid., 30.
21. Lester M. Salamon, "The Changing Tools of Government Action: An Overview," in *Beyond Privatization: The Tools of Government Action,* ed. Lester M. Salamon (Washington, D.C.: Urban Institute Press, 1989), 10–11.
22. *U.S. Department of Agriculture: Farm Agencies' Field Structure Needs Major Overhaul RCED-91-09* (Washington, D.C.: General Accounting Office, January 1991), 10–11.
23. Ibid.
24. Ibid.
25. Office of Technology Assessment, U.S. Congress, *Statistical Needs for a Changing U.S. Economy*, Background Paper OTA-BP-E-58 (Washington, D.C., Sept. 1989), table 1, 2.
26. Ibid., 1.
27. Ibid., 2–4.
28. Alvin Toffler, *Future Shock* (New York: Bantam Books, 1970), 471.
29. See Osborne and Gaebler, *Reinventing Government*, 255–59.

Chapter 13

1. Samuel P. Huntington "Democracy's Third Wave," *Journal of Democracy* (Spring 1991), 12–34.
2. According to Daniel Yankelovich, "What frightens them is the prospect of fewer good jobs, college tuition climbing out of reach, skyrocketing health-care costs, pensions and retirement benefits at risk and a humiliating rise in homelessness, poverty and urban decay—a shameful America unable to take care of its own." Yankelovich, "Foreign Policy after the Election," *Foreign Affairs* (Fall 1992), 1–12.
3. Joseph S. Nye, Jr., "The Power of Information," *The Wall Street Journal,* September 10, 1992.
4. Joseph S. Nye, Jr., "Soft Power," *Foreign Policy* (Fall 1990), 153–78.
5. Yankelovich, "Foreign Policy after the Election," 5–6.
6. Edward N. Luttwak, "From Geopolitics to Geo-Economics: Logic of Conflict, Grammar of Commerce," *The National Interest* (Summer 1990), 20.
7. Americans traditionally have been loath to embrace the cold calculus of realpolitik. While noting that the "traditional moralism" of U.S. foreign policy can be hypocritical and counterproductive, former State Department official Francis Fukuyama nonetheless acknowledges that ". . . a democratic majority of voters cannot be brought to support a

strong internationalist role for America except on the basis of a 'vision' higher than that of power politics." Fukuyama, "The Beginning of Foreign Policy," *The New Republic* (Aug. 17 & 24, 1992), 28.

8. Yankelovich, "Foreign Policy after the Election," 8.

9. Larry Diamond, "Promoting Democracy," *Foreign Policy* (Summer 1992), 30–31.

10. Roger W. Sullivan, "Discarding the China Card," *Foreign Policy* (Spring 1992), 22–23.

11. Diamond, "Promoting Democracy," 46.

12. Theodore H. Moran, Peter A. Wilson, and Gordon Adams, "The Influence of Alternative National Security Strategies on the Defense Industrial Base," Center for Strategic and International Studies (Washington, D.C.: Georgetown University, forthcoming 1992).

13. House Armed Services Committee, FY 93 Defense Authorization Bill, Summary of Major Actions, Committee Markup, May 13, 1992.

14. Floor speech by Senator Sam Nunn (D-GA), July 2, 1992.

15. See Kenneth L. Adelman and Norman R. Augustine, "Defense Conversions: Bulldozing The Management," *Foreign Affairs* (Spring 1992), 26–47.

Chapter 14

1. See Peter Goldman, "Now It Begins," *Newsweek* (January 24, 1977), 16–21.

2. There are also important symbolic aspects of inaugural day activities that can prove significant. The mother of all symbolic inaugurals was Andrew Jackson's populist decision to open the White House to the "muddy-booted rabble," thus signalling the end of the aristocratic founding generation. John Kennedy's inclusion of Robert Frost at the swearing-in ceremony signified his determination to raise the tone of our public life; Jimmy Carter's walk down Pennsylvania Avenue symbolized a deimperialized presidency brought closer to the people. On a more subtle note his use of solar heating units to warm the main reviewing stand at the inaugural signalled his commitment to the environment. Dramatic inaugural day innovations can convey the appropriate tone and sense of direction and the inaugural itself is an important part of the transition. But in this chapter we set these and many other matters aside to focus on a handful of core issues.

3. For example, a summary of the evaluations of Reagan's first 100 days is in Dom Bonafede, "From a 'Revolution' to a 'Stumble'—The Press Assesses the First 100 Days," *National Journal,* May 16, 1981; one evaluation of Bush's first 100 days is in David Hoffman, "Bush Credits Himself with 'Good Start' on Job, Relations with Congress," *The Washington Post,* May 25, 1989.

4. Stephen Hess, *Organizing the Presidency* (Washington, D.C.: Brookings Institution, 1988), 17.

5. The story of the gubernatorial party is told by David Osborne, *Laboratories of Democracy* (Boston: Harvard Business School Press, 1988).
6. There are 253,000 competitive managers in the federal Civil Service, versus approximately 2,700 presidential appointees.
7. Hess, *Organizing the Presidency*, 6.
8. See Carl M. Brauer, *Presidential Transitions* (New York: Oxford Univ. Press, 1986), chap. 4. We wish to acknowledge a debt of gratitude to the excellent work of Dr. Brauer, whose history informs much of our conclusions.
9. Brauer, *Presidential Transitions,* 140.
10. Ibid, 233.
11. For example, as transition scholar Carl Brauer notes, of the 27 original members of the legislative affairs office, only two had worked for the Reagan campaign. See Brauer, *Presidential Transitions,* 233.